American Sports History Series

edited by
David B. Biesel

1. *Effa Manley and the Newark Eagles* by James Overmyer, 1993.
2. *The United States and World Cup Competition: An Encyclopedic History of the United States in International Competition* by Colin Jose, 1994.
3. *Slide, Kelly, Slide: The Wild Life and Times of Mike "King" Kelly, Baseball's First Superstar* by Marty Appel, 1996.
4. *Baseball by the Numbers* by Mark Stang and Linda Harkness, 1997.
5. *Roller Skating for Gold* by David H. Lewis, 1997.
6. *Baseball's Biggest Blunder: The Bonus Rule of 1953–1957* by Brent Kelley, 1997.
7. *Lights On! The Wild Century-Long Saga of Night Baseball* by David Pietrusza, 1997.
8. *Windy City Wars: Labor, Leisure, and Sport in the Making of Chicago* by Gerald R. Gems, 1997.
9. *The American Soccer League 1921–1931: The Golden Years of American Soccer* by Colin Jose, 1998.
10. *The League That Failed* by David Quentin Voigt, 1998.
11. *Jimmie Foxx: The Pride of Sudlersville* by Mark R. Millikin, 1998.
12. *Baseball's Radical for All Seasons: A Biography of John Montgomery Ward* by David Stevens, 1998.
13. *College Basketball's National Championships: The Complete Record of Every Tournament Ever Played* by Morgan G. Brenner, 1998.
14. *Chris Von der Ahe and the St. Louis Browns* by J. Thomas Hetrick, 1999.
15. *Before the Glory: The Best Players in the Pre-NBA Days of Pro Basketball* by William F. Himmelman and Karel de Veer, 1999.
16. *For Pride, Profit, and Patriarchy: Football and the Incorporation of American Cultural Values* by Gerald R. Gems, 2000.
17. *Sunday at the Ballpark: Billy Sunday's Professional Baseball Career, 1883–1890* by Wendy Knickerbocker, 2000.
18. *Major Leagues* by Thomas W. Brucato, 2001.
19. *Whose Baseball? The National Pastime and Cultural Diversity in California, 1859–1941* by Joel S. Franks, 2001.

20. *The Encyclopedia of American Soccer History* by Roger Allaway, Colin Jose, David Litterer, 2001.
21. *Football's Stars of Summer: A History of the College All-Star Football Game Series of 1934–1976* by Raymond Schmidt, 2001.
22. *Major League Champions 1871-2001* by Thomas W. Brucato, 2002.
23. *Biographical Directory of Professional Basketball Coaches* by Jeff Marcus, 2003.
24. *Mel Ott: The Gentle Giant* by Alfred M. Martin, 2003.
25. *The Fierce Fun of Ducky Medwick* by Thomas Barthel, 2003.

A related title by the series editor:

Can You Name That Team? A Guide to Professional Baseball, Football, Soccer, Hockey, and Basketball Teams and Leagues by David B. Biesel, 1991.

The Fierce Fun
of Ducky Medwick

Thomas Barthel

American Sports History Series, No. 25

The Scarecrow Press, Inc.
Lanham, Maryland, and Oxford
2003

SCARECROW PRESS, INC.

Published in the United States of America
by Scarecrow Press, Inc.
A Member of the Rowman & Littlefield Publishing Group
4501 Forbes Boulevard, Suite 200
Lanham, Maryland 20706
www.scarecrowpress.com

PO Box 317
Oxford
OX2 9RU, UK

British Library Cataloging in Publication Information Available

Library of Congress Cataloging-in-Publication Data

Barthel, Thomas 1941–
  The fierce fun of Ducky Medwick / Thomas Barthel.
    p. cm. — (American sports history series ; 25)
  Includes bibliographical references.
  ISBN 0-8108-4668-3 (alk. paper)
  1. Medwick, Joe, 1911–1975. 2. Baseball players—United
States—Biography. I. Title. II. Series.
GV865.M397 B37 2003
796.357'092—dc21
        2002152308

∞™ The paper used in this publication meets the minimum requirements
of American National Standard for Information Sciences—Permanence of
Paper for Printed Library Materials, ANSI/NISO Z39.48-1992.
Manufactured in the United States of America.

For Florence Hanley Barthel, my mother, and not just because
she knew when Campy was about to hit a home run.
For Henry John Barthel, my father, and not just for buying
me a Pee Wee Reese model in Davega.

Contents

Prefatory Note   ix

Acknowledgments   xi

Prologue   xiii

1   Down Chrome   1

2   The Playing Fields of New Jersey   4

3   Scottdale, 1930   14

4   A Ducky Buffalo, Houston, 1931   22

5   Waiting for the Call, Houston, 1932   31

6   With the Big Club, St. Louis, September 1932   38

7   Playing Left Field for the Cardinals, 1933   49

8   The Gashouse Year, 1934   63

9   Ten in the Top Three, 1935   89

10   Sixty-Four Doubles, 1936   105

11   A Triple-Crown Year, 1937   116

12   Three RBI Crowns in a Row, 1938   134

13 In the League's Top Five in Five, 1939   145

14 Traded, 1940   158

15 The Bums Go to the World Series, 1941   179

16 The Best Clutch Hitter in the League, 1942   199

17 Rickey Again, 1943   219

18 The Best Right-Handed Hitter in Baseball, 1944   236

19 New York and Boston, 1945   256

20 The First Play-Offs, 1946   263

21 Yogi in the Spring and Sportsman's Again, 1947   272

22 Up and Down, 1948   284

23 Miami Manager Medwick, 1949   290

24 Insurance Man, 1950   296

25 Raleigh, 1951   298

26 Tampa and Out, 1952   305

27 Amadee and the Billikins Until . . . , 1953–1967   308

28 A Godlet, 1968   329

29 Batting Teacher, 1969–1974   336

30 Muscles, 1975   340

31 Since Medwick   342

32 Medwick's Legacy   343

Bibliography   346

Index   355

About the Author   369

Prefatory Note

This is a book written almost entirely from primary sources. I read one newspaper for every day Medwick was in the minors and two newspapers for every day he played in the major leagues. The majority of quotations, then, are from contemporary sources.

Acknowledgments

In New Jersey: Rick Malwitz, newspaperman; Frank Siekierka (thanks, Pinkie); Frank Tomczuk, a fine local historian; Bill Beisel (what a guy!); David Roth (thanks, Doc).

In Scottdale: Matt Miller, engineer, writer, and superb host.

In St. Louis: Margaret Lee, for her stories; Bob Broeg, for three hours of his time; Carl Gentile, for the St. Louis University stories; Bill Lee, batboy and Frontier League president.

Players and team men: Bob Kennedy; Harry Danning, in a letter to S.A.B.R. (Society for American Baseball Research) member Ace Parker; Don Gutteridge; Bobby Bragan; Barney Shultz; Max Lanier; Bing Devine; Red Shoendienst; Pete Coscarart; Tot Pressnell; Ted Kubiak; Terry Moore.

Writers: Norman Macht, Gene Carney, Jack Lang, and Eliot Asinof.

Helpers: Jon Birnbaum, Dave Wilson, Col. John F. Feltham, Davis O. Barker, and Amadee Wohlschlaeger. Walt Eckhardt, my pal at the Utica Blue Sox games who gave me a Branch Rickey Book. My Blue Sox pals, Linda and Bob and Jill Kostura; Scott Brown. Dave Kelly at the Library of Congress. The staff of the Kirkland Town Library in Clinton, New York. The Libraries at Colgate, Hamilton, and one nearby; the state libraries at Albany and Austin. To all the kind and smart men and women at the Hall of Fame Research Center, especially Jim Gates, Scott Mondore, and Bruce Markusen. Edward Marcou, for one of the first offers of help; Evelyn Begley, for the encouragement. E. G. Fischer, for the thousands of e-mail words. My brother Jack for taking me to so many games down Bedford Avenue. Tim Wiles, for being serious when he had to be. Valerie Prescott, a librarian who not only knows how to look, but how to keep looking.

Finally, for the two: Judy Lewis Barthel, my wife, for her keen understanding. And Michael Lewis Barthel, my son, who flabbergasts me.

Prologue

No game was ever won . . . until Medwick was out in the ninth.

—Mungo

Well, maybe it's all over now, he thought. Maybe it's all golf from now on. Sitting at the first tee in suburban Sappington, Missouri, his hands opening and closing on a one-wood, Joe Medwick looked down and did not want to think that these hands would never again be around a baseball bat. These hands had taken him from New Jersey to Pennsylvania to Texas to St. Louis, and then to Havana and Ponce and Caracas. And to Naples wearing a soldier's helmet, and to Rome to visit the Pope. These hands had brought him into two World Series. These hands had put him on a Wheaties box.

The phone rang at the starter's desk and Medwick looked up to see the starter motioning the 35-year-old ex-ballplayer to the phone. "Who'd be calling me at the golf course?" Joe wondered, walking to the phone. He was told that Sam Breadon was on the phone for him. "Some old-timers' game," Joe thought.

"Joe?"

"Yes, Mr. Breadon."

"You want to come and play for us? Part-time, of course."

"Yes, sir, I sure do." Joe knew he was smiling into the phone.

"Well, come on then."

"I'll just get my shoes and my glove. I'll be there in an hour."

"See you then."

After telling his golfing partners good-bye, Joe drove home and picked up his spikes and his well-worn glove. The New York Yankees, his sixth big-league team, had released him at April's end. The newspapers had talked about his being at the end of his career. But manager Eddie Dyer needed a right-handed pinch hitter. Joe was just such a hitter.

In Sam Breadon's familiar office at Sportsman's Park, the contract was quickly signed. Medwick told the owner that he had not held a bat in his hands in three weeks. He was told not to worry.

Downstairs in the clubhouse, good old Butch Yatkeman shook his hand, gave him a smile, and handed him number 21 to wear. Joe joined his new Cardinal teammates out on the familiar grounds of Sportsman's Park, grounds he had first walked on fifteen years before. Fans and writers wondering who number 21 was could find no entry in their scorecards.

In the second game of the doubleheader against the Pirates, Dyer told Joe, "You're the hitter."

As he walked onto the on-deck circle, he swung three bats in a wide circle over his head. When it was his time to hit, the public address announcer said, "Now batting for Hearn, number 21—Joe Medwick."

The crowd greeted him with a happy roar and Joe was surprised. They had booed him here many times. He had been traded away almost exactly seven years before—the fans angry with him, blaming him.

Joe saw a pitch he could hit and the ball rose to left center and hit the top of the fence. The hit brought in a run and Joe stood on second base watching the umpire throw out a new ball for Fritz Ostermueller to pitch. Then manager Eddie Dyer sent out a pinch runner for Medwick, and as the fans watched Medwick's familiar trot, they roared warmly again. As he ran, his head down, Joe noticed the Cardinal above his heart on his uniform shirt, then looked up. As he looked to the owner's box, he saw Mr. Breadon applauding.

As he crossed the first-base line heading for the dugout, fans with tears in their eyes might have seen tears in Joe's eyes.

Tears? *Joe?*

1

Down Chrome

Joe Medwick's family was Hungarian. His father, John, and his mother, Lizzie (Erzebiet, in Hungarian) Schultz Medwick, came to Carteret, New Jersey, from the Austro-Hungarian Empire before the turn of the century. One came from Buda and the other from Pest; they settled in what came to be called Carteret, then called Roosevelt, in New Jersey, just across the Arthur Kill from Staten Island. Soon they were citizens of the United States.

Medwick's brother, John, was born in 1901; then came sisters Helen in 1903 and Anna, called Bennie, in 1906. Joseph Michael Medwick, the last child, was born on November 24, 1911, with Medwick's mother, age thirty-three, attended by a midwife, Meir Roknek. The Medwick residence—55 Union Street—had a store underneath, with stairs on the side, front, and in the back. The neighborhood was called "down Chrome," an area southeast of the main street of Carteret and named after a factory, the Chrome Steel Works, and the whole Arthur Kill waterfront industrial area.

At Creosote, nicknamed the "tie yards," Medwick's father worked with raw wood, wood that was carried on overhead carriages and then dipped into creosote to become ties for the Port Reading Railroad. Townspeople remember his father as a small, quiet man who was uneasy with English; during Medwick's boyhood, he used the room under the family's living space as a poolroom. The room had two tables in it, which brought in a little extra money for the family. Medwick's mother, who friends called Liz and who Medwick called "Moms," was a delightful, plump woman—able, loving, and strong. Medwick's friends still talk about her excellent cooking, particularly her Csirke Paprikas, Kolbas, toltott Kaposzta, and apple pies. The entire family spoke Hungarian, Joe being fluent all his life.

Children played games that cost nothing or came from discarded material. David Roth, one of Joe's friends, told of sitting with Medwick by the roadway down Chrome playing license-plate poker. Another game, which Frank Siekierka played with Medwick, was called "Caddy." First cutting off five inches from an old broomstick, you sharpened both ends and lay that piece down in a two-foot square box drawn in the dirt. The broomstick bat was used to strike one end of the pointed piece, making it rise into the air, at which time you struck it like a baseball and sent it flying. The distance would be marked and the winner was the person who made the longest hit.

Everyone in Chrome worked at jobs demanding caution, strength, and adroitness, and most seemed to have pride in doing those jobs well. When it came time for relaxation, people down Chrome used their bodies with dexterity to shoot pool, dance, slap handball, and roll bocce.

In this atmosphere of sport and competition, Joe Medwick was unlike any athlete the town had ever seen. Partly because he did not smoke or drink as young boys might, he was always in shape for games. He seemed to run everywhere. He played football, basketball, and baseball around the neighborhood. While attending St. Joseph's, a Catholic school, Medwick became an altar boy, serving without absence, and he was taught basketball by the pastor, Father O'Connor.

When he shifted to Columbus Elementary School in the fall of 1925, Joe, already well known to the five hundred other students, was given a lesson in how to use golf clubs by the principal. After two swings, young Medwick hit the golf ball further than the principal had ever seen anyone hit one. Joe was unbeatable when he played handball against Benny Zussman, using the wall at Jake Brown's candy store. No one could best Joe at ping-pong. He was also the best diver (off the Central Railroad of New Jersey trestle into the Rahway River in West Carteret).

Always on the move, Medwick shot straight pool at the Red Star Billiard Academy run by the Casaleggi brothers, Peanuts and Beaner. He could hang out at Joe Solomon's drugstore where a boy could get ice cream and sodas. Plus running—always running.

He worked, too. At his father's small poolroom, Joe ran the cash register, swept the floor, and racked balls. Sometimes, when he had chores to do, like chopping wood, he would trade friends pool games for the wood chopping.

Since there were no baseball fields down Chrome, Medwick had to leave the neighborhood to play at the town's fields. And soon there was a team and a name—the Young Yanks. The boys had no uniforms, but the team was strong and young. "I liked to catch," Medwick remembered. "I wanted to be where the action was—base runners to throw out, fouls to chase, balls to catch. I had a strong arm. I loved to throw to the bases, and when runners slid home trying to score, I liked to block them off at the plate." The Young Yanks were an ethnic mix that shadowed the mix down Chrome: Hungarians, Irish, Poles, Jews, Ukrainians, and Slovaks.

One day a pitcher bounced a ball into the dirt in front of the plate. Medwick dove for the ball, forgetting about the batter. "That was unfortunate," he said years later, "because the batter swung at the ball—why I'll never know—and he hit me on the back of the head. When I woke up, I had a long cut on my scalp and a splitting headache. You know what they say in the big leagues—the farther away from the plate you can get, the better off you were. Well, I finished up as far away as I could get—left field."

2

The Playing Fields
of New Jersey

Within two years, the Young Yanks had become the unofficial town team for Carteret, replacing a group of older players known as the Carteret Field Club. In 1926, their third year together, the team bought a floor lamp, organized a raffle, and collected enough money to pay for the floor lamp and for uniforms, too. Because there was no local sports supply store, local hardware store-owner Max Brown offered to measure the players and order the uniforms. Pinkie Siekierka, who worked for a bakery, delivered bread at 5 A.M., and sometimes stole flour that he could use to draw the foul lines.

By that summer of 1926, Medwick had a clear idea of what a capable athlete he was, and he knew how much pride he felt for his skills. He welcomed the hellos from the people down Chrome who looked at him admiringly. The "Hi ya, Meddi" call was heard throughout Carteret. But as one aspect of his life developed, other aspects—in Joe's case, non-kinetic aspects—did not. Though muscles may be taught and tactics of the games may be learned, and while Joe was being rewarded for his skill at games, he was not learning social skills. In the narrowness of youth, he could only see games. Few people can be skilled at many things. Joe didn't think he needed many social skills because he was the object of admiration, the one for whom people wanted to do things because he could play a game. His celebrity was his charm. Yet he was not without pals.

By now his friendship with Benny Zussman, who lived above Solomon's, was very strong ("Bennie was like a brother," said Bill Beisel), and almost as strong were his friendships with Beaner Casaleggi and John Szelag. The four would often go to games at Yankee Stadium together, where $1.10 admitted them to the grandstand and they could chase foul balls to bring home.

By now, John, Joe's oldest brother, ten years his senior, was twenty-five. His nearest sister, Bennie, was nineteen. Joe's father was still not, to Joe, really an American, and almost more than anything, Medwick wanted to be an American boy. As a last-born child, Joe was pampered by his mother, yet he felt really alone in the family. But in various ways, Joe's separation from his family led him to becoming a man who made his own fun by himself. And his talent on the athletic field separated him even further from everyone else.

In 1926, the first class of fifty-one children, twenty of them boys, began classes in the new high school and the man who coached every sport was Frank McCarthy, a man who would ride around town checking on his athletes. If he found one smoking, that boy was off the team. In addition, an athlete's school record was checked every Friday to see if he was doing his work at an acceptable level.

Medwick was an immediate star athlete, earning four letters his first year. On the baseball diamond, he frequently was called on to pitch against the stronger opponents.

The next year, 1927, feeling that he was not contributing enough to the family, Medwick dropped out of school and was hired at the Copper Works, a factory that took in scrap batteries and cables, and by stripping or melting, would recover the copper, which was then formed into ingots of one hundred pounds. It was a large, noisy, and dangerous place to work. Overhead cranes swung their loads. Luckily for Medwick, Coach McCarthy convinced Joe and his parents that the boy's future could best be found elsewhere, and Medwick returned to school.

Also in the summer after his sophomore year, Medwick's semipro team decided to become the Young Cardinals, and bought new uniforms when a dance they sponsored produced the cash for them. At all of these Young Cardinal games, a hat was passed to pay for bats and balls, for the upkeep of the field, and for the umpire. When the team needed to travel to games, dimes were collected from the players to pay a peddler with a pickup truck for a round-trip ride to the ball grounds. The players all sat behind the cab, their equipment bouncing around as they drove to play the Rahway A.A. or the Polish American Club of Jersey City.

At that time, Medwick was also playing American Legion baseball in both the outfield and at third base. In the morning, he practiced with Perth Amboy, a ten-mile bus trip away. If he missed the one bus to get him there on time, he knew he could hitchhike or ride his bike. Often in the afternoon he would be playing somewhere else. He played for the American Cyanamid factory team. "After riding two buses and a streetcar, when I came home," Medwick said later, "I was even." Joe always knew the cost. Medwick also played on older pickup teams against barnstormers, like the barnstorming teams starring Babe Ruth and Lou Gehrig that came to Perth Amboy in 1928.

Joe's ability—he was running on the school's relay team now as well—was so well known at this point that scouts for the big leagues started appearing. The first of these was Ira Thomas, a catcher who had played from 1906 to 1915, mostly for Connie Mack; he was evaluating Medwick for Mack. But the 47-year-old scout and former coach did not turn in a favorable report. Still, Medwick knew he was being inspected. Medwick knew what that had to mean. Someone would pay him to play baseball. Some of the salaries Joe had read about in the newspaper—the salaries paid to major league players—were indeed fabulous. But even for lesser stars, salaries averaged about $150 a week. Minor league players could average $75 a week. His father, dipping railroad ties, was paid about $25 each week. But more than anything, Joe would be playing American baseball.

In 1929, according to a story written in 1940,

Dave Driscoll was handed a letter from a New Jersey pal [Bob Murphy president of the Lackawanna League] extolling a kid semi-prospect named Joe Medwick. The letter said in part "We have a boy playing the outfield on our Summit Lackawanna League who I am sure one day will be a big league star. . . . I would like you to come out any Saturday and go to the game with me where you can look Medwick over. If he suits you, I am sure he will be tickled to death to sign up on the spot. . . . Take it from me, Dave, he was a coming fence buster that any of you fellows will be willing to pay good money for some day." He . . . galloped right over to New Jersey and put the peep on the youngster. The kid's name was Joe all right and he wanted dough. To be exact he wanted $500 to sign a Dodger contract. Mr. Driscoll told the late Frank

York [president of the Dodgers from 1930 to 1932] that Joe was worth every penny of it. Well York said no. Joe didn't get the dough.

Medwick had never known much failure as an athlete; he had never been hurt badly—he had never been anything but confident. Nothing but approbation had ever come his way. He could wait. He could see his future success, and he knew how to measure it.

His friend—jokingly called his "manager," as if Medwick were a prizefighter—Benjamin Zussman, took him to Newark in September 1929 to try out with the Newark Bears, a farm team of the New York Yankees. The two boys traveled by trolley to the tryout, Medwick carrying his high school uniform rolled up under his arm, along with a bat, spikes, and his glove. When Joe arrived at the Bears' park, Tris Speaker said to him, "I've been looking for you, my boy," and told Medwick to put on his uniform quickly. Speaker, who had played so many years with the Boston Red Sox, was the manager of the Newark team, and although "he didn't fancy messing in midseason with a rookie who had no professional experience," G. A. Falzer wrote in the *Paterson Sunday Call* in 1934, "grudgingly he agreed to let Medwick work out with the team."

Jocko Conlan, soon to be an umpire, was the center fielder then and Wally Pipp was the first baseman. A pitcher named Carl Fischer was throwing batting practice. Robert E. Hood's book, *The Gashouse Gang* (1976), relates, "Medwick's voice rose and his eyes flashed as he remembered the incident. 'I got angry and hit a few balls out of the park. Then Fischer really got angry. He wanted to show me up, because I was a good hitter. He knocked me down,' Medwick said. 'And Wally Pipp hollered at him: "Give the kid a chance."' 'He knocked me down in batting practice. Deliberately.'" Medwick would remember Fischer very well.

When Medwick was finished with his tryout, Speaker told Medwick he was too young. "I would advise you to finish your education before you enter professional baseball." He then gave Medwick a bat signed by John J. McGraw. Zussman overheard Speaker talking while Medwick changed out of his uniform and spikes for the trolley ride home. Speaker believed that Medwick was a bad-ball hitter and would consequently never make the majors. A sportswriter later said of the tryout, "The Yanks had passed up a clouter that Carl Hubbell once said was more dangerous than Joe DiMaggio."

Getting turned down by Speaker motivated Joe in a very powerful way. "I was heartbroken when the Bears did not sign me," Joe admitted. Medwick could see himself in the Yankees' outfield with
Ruth. From then on, Medwick told everyone he knew that he would
be a major league player very soon.

Medwick's last year in high school began in the fall of 1929, and
he made sure he was remembered. He played fullback and then
quarterback. He could drop-kick a football fifty-five or sixty yards,
and pass an equal distance with ease. He was the team's punter,
passer, and key runner. The Carteret football field at Washington Avenue had few bleachers, but those who followed Medwick's season
saw the quarterback and captain score 145 points in nine games by
passing, receiving passes from the wing back, running as a fullback,
and kicking off and drop-kicking field goals and extra points. He
played defense as well, as was the rule at the time. He scored all of
the team's points in three of the games. "I was a triple-threat man,"
he said. "You played every minute, too. My parents wanted me to
play baseball. But my mother didn't want for me to play football, because she thought I might get injured and not play baseball." Joe
Medwick was named by the New Jersey Interscholastic Athletic Association to the honor football team, the all-state recognition of all
classes (sizes) of schools.

Being an athlete meant many things to young Medwick. For one
thing, it separated him from everyone else. It meant, too, that Joe's
role models were likely to come from sports rather than his family.
The demanding and strict Coach McCarthy was one. The baseball
men he knew about were others. There was the ferocious John Mc-
Graw, manager of the Giants, and McGraw's equally ferocious and
skillful second baseman, Frankie Frisch, who was a football player
like Joe. Another second baseman and a right-handed batter like Joe,
was Rogers Hornsby. Hornsby was not the slugger that Ruth was,
but his excellence in the field, and even more at bat, fixed him in
Joe's mind as a great player. Then there was the fact that Hornsby
was known as a "brusque, blunt, hypercritical, dictatorial, moody,
and argumentative [man who] alienated almost everyone sooner or
later." All of the times he was traded proved that, but did those traits
make him a good hitter or detract from his skill? Did having those
traits really make any difference to the mind of a young man like
Medwick? Many of the players, after all, lived in a world, for example, where they expected to be thrown at when the count went to

0-2. A man, a major league baseball player, must not be intimidated. There were many bullies in sports, and Joe had seen them by now. Medwick's ability and power had blunted their effect and he could use that power in his life.

But Medwick's life began to change, as did the lives of all Americans who felt the shock of the stock market crash of October 1929. Medwick began spending time at the house of his sister Anna and her husband, Bill Beisel, who seemed to function as a big brother to him. Bill was closer in age to Joe than Joe's own brother, John. Joe's father's poolroom was gone; his classmate Paul Roth's father also had business setbacks. It was during that time that Jack Law, a graduate of the University of Notre Dame, along with other alumni from South Bend, had come to Carteret to talk to Medwick, saying that they "thought Joe, being a good Hungarian, would fit in very well with the 'Irish' [football players] such as Savoldi, Schwartz and Carideo." The grads told Medwick that Rockne himself was interested. Other coaches as well would like to bring Joe's skills to their institutions, and scholarship offers began to appear in the Medwick mailbox—twenty-seven of them, from nationally known schools such as Princeton, North Carolina, and Duke. American Catholic families, particularly families new to the country, tended to hold up Notre Dame as an ideal, a place for the Catholic elite. During that era it probably would have been unusual for some of the other schools to recruit a Catholic and a Hungarian. Medwick decided that what happened to him after he graduated from high school would have to depend on what else came his way.

Later in the fall, as he had for the previous three years, Medwick played basketball forward for Carteret High School, along with his baseball teammates, against, among others, the Hungarian Catholic Club Juniors of Perth Amboy and the Rahway Phantoms. Once, Medwick scored all of the points in the 48-12 victory over Perth Amboy, and against Metuchen on January 30, 1930, in a game that ended up 84-9, he scored forty-seven points. He also played for teams in Elizabeth and Perth Amboy. The New Jersey Interscholastic Athletic Association unanimously named him to the all-state basketball team. By the time he accepted the award, it was almost baseball season again.

When talking to Robert E. Hood in 1974, Joe said, "[The Depression] didn't hurt me. I had nothin' anyway." In 1930, Medwick was just an 18-year-old high-school student who knew it was time to begin to consider his future. He knew he had already been seriously considered by the New York Yankees and Philadelphia Athletics as a future major league player. In addition to Medwick's playing for his high school, for an American Legion team, and for the Young Cardinals, there was plenty of baseball around for Joe to play, and that he did, playing for the Summit of the Lackawanna League as before; the semi-pro Interborough League, which played only on Sundays; the Perth Amboy City League, which played twice a week; the Carteret City League, and the Middlesex County Industrial League, which played on Saturday. With teams of fifteen to twenty players, with some juggling, Medwick could play in all of these leagues and sharpen his skills in about one hundred games from May to September.

Medwick was mad for baseball and followed the major league games closely. During this spring of 1930, Medwick knew that many major league baseball teams were evaluating him. The assessment report written by the Cardinal scout said that he had "all of the requisites to a high degree—arm, speed, punch, ambition, a great athlete." The two faults listed were "youth and hitting bad balls."

Medwick knew, too, that the Cardinal left fielder Chick

Hafey . . . who had everything you could ask for in a ballplayer except good health. Hafey . . . [had such] weak eyes [that] have been handicapping him this season, [that he] had been forced to leave the team and will return to St. Louis for treatment. A new pair of glasses had failed to improve his eyesight. He was unable to distinguish objects with one eye and the other was below normal. [His manager Gabby] Street had been depending on Hafey to supply a large part of the team's punch. George Watkins probably will replace him.

Or Joe Medwick could.

Still, the colleges urged him to play football for them. Graduates and coaches came to see him or wrote to him. But colleges could not pay him. What did he know about college life? And who was he to go to college anyway? He had not grown up in a place where people went to college or even talked about it, except for the very best students, and for most of them, it was a dream far beyond their reach. How could he be sure that some of these colleges would even survive? If banks were closing, why not colleges? True, Notre Dame was appealing to him and to his parents, but the Holy Cross fathers and Knute Rockne could wait.

After the 1929–1930 school year, Joe was not graduated because he lacked one credit for graduation. The University of Notre Dame wanted Joe to go to LaSalle Prep in Chicago. That summer, Medwick was playing the outfield in a game at Island Heights, New Jersey, for yet another team, Boonton, against a team from Toms River. Watching him that day was C. S. "Pop" Kelchner. On a warm Sunday afternoon, probably June 16, 1930, Medwick hit four doubles in five times at bat. As Joe walked off the dusty field, a man stepped up to him, saying, "I'm Pop Kelchner, scout for the Cards, and if you got a minute, kid, we might be able to work something out you'd like." Medwick knew then that the Cardinals were interested in him enough to have him sign a contract. Here was a team for which he did not need a tryout. Here was a team that knew how good he was.

What Kelchner thought Medwick might like was a professional contract. The scout had seen the powerful, almost numbing effect that the offer had on young men. After all, hadn't they all spent a good part of their lives getting ready for just such a day as this? Medwick was being offered not only a chance to work at something he loved for a salary, and a very good salary in uncertain times; he was also being given the chance to do something that thousands of American boys would love to do. It was what Medwick was trained to do. The offer certainly had more attractiveness to it than a job offer to work at the tinning works or almost any other job Medwick could imagine.

But Medwick knew the finality of signing a contract with a major league team. The contract with its reserve clause simply meant that you played for the team you signed with for as long as it wished. If it desired, the team had the power to sell your contract to any other team. Or you would not work at all in professional baseball.

Medwick wanted to get what he thought he was worth, an idea that was to cause him trouble for most of his professional baseball career. Medwick would find out that many of the men who administered baseball teams were not interested in fairness or a player's worth; they had the same mind-set as many of the men who lived in the houses on the brick road down Chrome.

The Cardinal team had a system of player development that by now was coming to be called the "chain store" or "the chain gang." It was a new method in baseball that entailed training your own players rather than buying them from independent minor league teams. Branch Rickey, who had been in baseball at the major league level since 1904, was the managing partner of the St. Louis Cardinals and he had not only fostered this approach but also had talked owner Sam Breadon and his board into financing it. It was the Cardinal plan to sign many players to a contract and take the best of them up through the organization, having them play at stops along the way to test their abilities. The Cardinals would buy their own minor league teams and all of the players on that team belonged to them. Soon they would have six hundred players under contract. Medwick knew about the competition, but he was a confident young man and that did not worry him.

Medwick knew that the world of baseball could be an uncertain world; he knew that the Cardinals as a company dismissed employees whenever it wanted to. Fewer than four years ago, Rogers Hornsby was in charge of the team as field manager, and his acuity and .317 batting average took the team to the 1926 World Series, which the Cardinals won against the New York Yankees. He was traded seventy days later. The new manager, Bill McKechnie, won the 1928 pennant but was fired after the Yankees swept the Cards in the 1928 World Series.

It took three days of thinking, and talking to his parents, to Benny and Beaner, to Coach McCarthy, and to Bill. Three days to consider his chances of making the Cardinal major league team some day. Branch Rickey even came to town, and he concentrated on telling Joe of his place in the organization. It took three days for the Cardinals to agree to the $500 bonus Medwick insisted on for signing the contract. Medwick also insisted that he be called Mickey (probably from Michael, his middle name) King, a name that would help preserve the amateur status of a possible Notre Dame football player named Joe Medwick. Owner Sam Breadon and managing partner Branch Rickey approved, and at a lunch with Pop Kelchner, Medwick signed a Cardinal contract, was handed a Cardinal check for $500, and was given a train ticket to Scottdale, Pennsylvania. The date was probably June 20, 1930.

On June 23, 1930, Elmer M. Daily, president of the Middle Atlantic League, received a letter from the Scottdale Baseball Club, whose nickname, The Young Cardinals, was printed in red letters, above the signature of H. E. Cramer, the president and treasurer. (Branch Rickey's name also was on the letterhead stationery as vice president.) "Attached hereto, contract of player Joseph Medwick, alias Mickey King for promulgation. His salary was $200.00 and he was classed as an absolute rookie." The letter shows a roster of fourteen other players, five of whom were being paid more than Medwick. Edwin H. Dyer was the manager.

One week later, President Daily received another letter concerning Medwick from H. E. Cramer ("Special Delivery, Copy to B. R."):

> Upon advice that this player was a minor, I asked him to sign another contract over the signatures of his parents, John Medwick and Lizzie Medwick, Father and Mother . . . replacing the original contract.
>
> Now Mr. Daily, this young man appears to be a wonderful prospect and seems to have all the natural ability to become a great ballplayer, with proper coaching. I do not want to slip up on anything that would make our title to his services doubtful; also I do not care to hamper him in his proposed future college career.

Medwick had his way.

3

Scottdale, 1930

Joe Medwick waited with his mother, father, brother, and sister and brother-in-law, Bill Beisel, at the Chrome train station to travel to Carteret, to Philadelphia, and then on to southwestern Pennsylvania to his first professional team.

Then he boarded the Central New Jersey train, his $9 ticket to Scottdale at the ready, and rode the 80 miles to Philadelphia eager and excited. There was no sign that he doubted his abilities. In Philadelphia he changed to the Pennsylvania Rail Road to travel the remaining 273 miles to Scottdale. Scottdale townspeople read on June 20, "Mickey King, an outfielder whose home was in Carteret, New Jersey, was expected to report here any day," and "Mickey King, the kid wonder . . . was reputed for his terrific hitting."

As the train moved through the miles and the thirteen tunnels, Medwick was about to become part of one of the twenty-three minor leagues in 1930. Scottdale, near Pittsburgh, was part of the Middle Atlantic League, founded in 1925. A class C league of eight teams in Maryland, Pennsylvania, and West Virginia, Scottdale was the smallest city, with 6,695 residents, and the ball yard, Scottdale Athletic Park, had the fewest seats, at 1,700. With so few seats in the ballpark, the team had to be underwritten by the townspeople each year. It was also the only park in the league without lights. Scottdale paid the Cardinals $7,500 and maintained the park.

14

When Joe got off the train, he lifted his new bag and walked a short distance down Broadway to the Candy Land store (which offered homemade candies and Rieck's ice cream) at Pittsburgh Street, the town's main street, and then continued up one block to Spring to a big stone building. Up three stone steps, through doors, and up six more steps, and then he was in the lobby of the YMCA. To the left of the lobby was a brick-wall basketball gym. He was directed up to the third floor dormitory where some of the other players stayed.

Later that Saturday, he met Eddie Dyer, who told him that there was a doubleheader the next day. As players began to troop in, chances were Dyer left Medwick in the hands of Mike Ryba, a friendly player eight years older than Joe. Ryba talked to Medwick about the team's routine.

After dinner, a communal meal on the YMCA's second floor, Joe may have walked around town, trying to walk off some nervous energy. New to the team, determined to succeed, he wanted tomorrow to be here.

After lunch that June 22, with many other players at the second-floor cafeteria, Mike and Joe walked down into the basement. Next to the indoor pool, a locker room was set aside for the use of all the players, even those who lived in the Central Hotel or boarded in a private home. With most of the eighteen players dressing, the room got crowded quickly and Joe got out of the room to leave space for others. When he asked Mike, "Now what?" Mike said "Come with me," and they went up to the lobby and down the stairs out onto Spring Street. In the sun, the red word "Cardinals" on the shirt's chest shone brightly, as did the two Cardinals perched on each end of the bat. Each hat had an "S" for Scottdale on it, the bills red, the crowns with the familiar red lines radiating evenly out from the button. Like players today, no doubt Medwick was thrilled to be a professional baseball player.

Boys waited in the street for some of their favorites. Some players carried bats over their shoulders, their spikes hanging from the bat. Most players had their gloves folded into their back uniform pockets. As Mike hoisted the catcher's equipment, the team, strolling in a group with children following and talking, moved first up Spring Street, a brick street, past slate sidewalks. When this procession passed a park on the left, more kids joined the parade to the ballpark. Down the hill at the end of Spring Street to Broadway, they all crossed five sets of Pennsylvania Rail Road tracks, some trolley tracks, and a creek. Then, as they approached the third-base ticket booth, giving entrance to the ballpark, a player might decide to take one of the parading kids into the ballpark with him—for free. These were children who could not afford the $1.50 for a membership card in the Knothole Club that was, in effect, a season's ticket.

The park was a no-frill ball yard: bare wood for the roofed grandstand and bleachers, very little grass on the field, and only outhouses for patrons and players. There was a 10-foot-high wooden fence all around, probably 320 to left, 470 to center, and 420 to right—an odd sort of rectangle.

Then it was almost 2 P.M. and time for batting practice. The two ripped-shirt kids working at the ball yard were Buck Kaczmarek, the batboy, and his assistant, Happy Zemanski. Working there did not necessarily mean the boys were paid; to them it was an honor. They showed Joe the dugout—it was wooden with lots of knotholes. Joe put on his spikes and went out to throw in front of the dugout. The grass was sparse on the field because there were no water pipes to irrigate it—water and pipes cost money—and since they were playing in a mill town, the combination of mill smoke and dust often made the air pretty thick and dirty. The manager of the Scottdale team, who was also the secretary of the company, Eddie Dyer, had pitched with the Cardinals from 1922 to 1927. Not yet thirty, Dyer was about the same size as Medwick; his Louisiana accent contrasted sharply with Medwick's Jersey urban speech. Medwick knew that one reason he could have been sent to Scottdale was because a player named Harry Potter was under suspension. This young New Jerseyian had 75 games remaining on the 130-game schedule to show his ability.

After Joe had his spikes on for practice, Dyer looked over his new player. His batting stance used what baseball players describe as a "foot in the bucket." The lead foot, the left foot for right-handed batters like Medwick, rather than ending up parallel to his back foot as the swing was completed, would end up further down the left field line. The idea was that you somehow lost power as your stride toward the pitch moved away from where the ball was centered, and so the force was deflected. (There have been many bucket-foot hitters in baseball; two of them are in the Hall of Fame, both known for their power: Al Simmons and Roy Campanella.) But batting stances were highly individualistic. This muscular young man, foot in the bucket, foot lifted off the ground as he strode like Mel Ott, like Babe

Ruth, hit everything thrown to him. Pitches in the dirt or over his head, he hit all of them. Pitches inside or outside, change-ups or fast-balls—he hit all of them for distance and to all fields. Curveballs, the finish of many professional careers, were his favorite pitch. Balls whacked against the thin wooden fences. The best bad-ball hitter who ever played the game had begun his professional career.

And Medwick's love of hitting was evident as the season progressed. He worked very hard at his craft, both in the outfield and at the plate, as he did for his whole professional career. Joe came from a place where hard work was a primary virtue. Medwick hit when anyone would pitch to him. He understood that he was being paid to hit; the better he made himself as a hitter, the better he would be paid.

Each hitter must teach his muscles what to do (Ted Williams advised one hundred swings each day) and must develop precisely those muscles that are used in hitting. Today, hitters stretch and then lift weights to train for that discipline. Medwick, seventy years ago, used the force of the bat meeting the ball to be stronger, to have more power, to hit better.

Dyer soon found that Medwick was a quiet young man. At 5 feet and 10 inches, carrying 180 pounds, he was in fine condition, and he neither smoked nor drank alcohol. And he was baseball crazy. Dyer saw that Medwick was temperate in other ways too, spending his money very carefully, sending most of it home for his mother to manage.

Soon Dyer was setting the batting order; fans began to trickle in. The 25¢ admission equaled about 1 percent of the workers' take-home pay for a week. Because this was a Sunday doubleheader against the Charleroi Governors and the school year was finished, the crowd grew quickly. Kids waited outside the park for foul balls, because bringing a foul ball to the gate earned a ticket into the park. Baseballs cost more than a quarter.

After batting practice, Joe could read on the taped-up-batting order that Dyer had put him in right field and in the third batting spot. The park announcer verified this through his megaphone just before game time. Then Joe ran out on the field for his first game. The newspaper the next day said, "His fielding was a big factor in these contests." It failed to mention that Joe went 3-6 with six RBIs. The paper at least repeated that "Mickey King, the kid wonder, was reputed for his terrific hitting."

After a big communal dinner on the second floor at the "Y" that night, Joe could see the coke fires, hundreds of them, burning in a circle all around him. Frick, the King of Coke, had put the coke ovens right next to the coal mines of Pennsylvania. Medwick could hear the trolleys running past, the trains on the Pennsylvania tracks. At 9:05 he heard a whistle blow, which meant, Mike told him later, that all the children in town ought to be home.

Tuesday the twenty-fourth was a day off and Joe was introduced to some of the pleasures a place like Scottdale had to offer. The small town resembled his industrial home in New Jersey and Mike might take Medwick to Briercheck's pool, which was popular with the team; a round pool, players would take kids on their laps and go down the slide with them. At night, Joe could go see "Greta Garbo in her first all-talking picture, Anna Christie with Clark and McCullogh all-talking comedy, Paramount novelty and Fox Movietonews" at the Strand, seats 10¢ and a quarter. Or the players might haved checked the *Sporting News*. Joe Dematteo, the paperboy, was often paid $1 for the 10¢ weekly. Some minor league players read to find out how players playing their position on other Cardinals farm teams were doing.

Years later Casey Douglas, playing for Charleroi, told the following story: "The first time Medwick played against us . . . we had been warned how this kid could hit. So, I called for a curve ball in the dirt. The pitcher followed orders and couldn't have been more accurate following orders. And what did Joe do? He didn't jump or cringe, that's for sure. He just banged the ball right out of the dirt, leaving a cloud of dust at the plate."

The next day was another promotion, an annual event in Scottdale, called "Boys' Day." On that day an admission to the park cost 10¢. Before the game, boys gathered and then marched in a group from the "Y," led by "a drum and bugle corps of two troops of Boy Scouts. Tickets on sale at Brooks Drug Store, The YMCA, Broadway Drug Store and the Rutherford's Book Store. Boys will sit in bleacher[s] reserved near third base." Again Medwick/King overpowered the competition. "Mickey King, one of the most promising young players to come into the Middle Atlantic League for some time, joined the Scottdale club last Sunday and gave a good account of himself." The newspaper in Connellsville agreed: "Those fans who have not seen Mickey King play right field and sock the old apple have missed seeing the greatest young ballplayer in the Middle Atlantic League in many a moon."

The first half of the season ended on July 3 and the second half began with an unusual Fourth of July doubleheader. The night of July 3, Eddie Dyer went to O'Hara's to order the meals for the players for the next day. Dyer had to walk into the store because people in town believed it was impolite to use the phone for ordering meals. Next he saw to it that the two seven-passenger Studebaker touring cars with "Scottdale Baseball Club" painted on the back were gassed, and that the away-uniforms—those with "Scottdale" written on them—were ready. Then the team had to be assembled at 8 A.M. for the twenty-two-mile trip to Jeannette to play the first game of the Independence Day doubleheader at 10:30 A.M.

Joe made two hits, one yet another homer, in that game. Then the players, still in uniform, climbed back into the cars and, eating as they traveled, they were driven back to Scottdale where the Jeannette team would play them at Athletic Park at 3 P.M. The team would have to change out of their road uniforms first. But that way, both towns could have a Fourth of July baseball game with a home game for each.

It was also around this time that Joe met some animosity from a teammate. Some on the team were "absolute rookies" like Medwick, making $200 each month of the season. Others had been in the minors for some time, and some were ending their careers by working their way down from higher minors, or even from the majors, but still playing baseball for a living. Some men, for different reasons, did not like Joe. It's easy to imagine the fierce competition between players—easy to imagine aging players' anger at seeing a young prospect. One, a Southerner who disliked Joe's thick New Jersey accent, called Medwick "hunkie" one day when the pitcher thought Joe did not get to a fly ball fast enough. "Hunkie," or "bohunk," were slang insults for Hungarians, who were certainly not a majority group, and certainly not a group that a Southerner would be likely to be familiar with. Joe, though still eighteen and new to the team, challenged his attacker, and that was the end of it. Joe did not back down—people in Scottdale remember even now, more than seventy years later. Joe was going to succeed—he always had. He would not be intimidated. He belonged in this game.

Joe went 8-18 in the next four games, warming up for the visit of Branch Rickey and all the Cardinal scouts. It may be that he pressed during this time, for he went hitless in three games against Jeannette playing second, right field, and left field. Rickey, of course, had been getting frequent, if not daily, reports from Dyer on Medwick, so that even his continual weak hitting in the next four games, 4-19, didn't seem to trouble Rickey. He knew what a great player Joe would be. While Rickey was there, "Mickey King [Medwick playing second] made one of the nicest plays of the season [on July 15]. Pasquella hit a hard grounder out toward second and Mickey made a back handed stop of the ball on a dead run . . . leaped into the air throwing the ball to first while in the air to retire Pasquella and also the side."

On August 7, Rickey was back, something more than his usual two visits per team per year. Joe was in right and batting third. He made two hits, scored twice, and drove in one; the team won 11-0, which put the team in third at 19-15 for the second half, one back of Fairmont, and a half-game back of Clarksburg. It also put Joe at .386. From that game on, the seventh of August to the twentieth, he made thirty-eight hits for a .623 average in fifteen games, pushing his season's mark to .428.

Medwick later remembered an incident that made up for a lot of disappointment he felt after the tryout with Newark just one year before. "While I was hitting .400 for Scottdale, under the name of King, Newark rushed Jack Onslow over to look at me. He looked hard, and hid his head in shame. Then he tried to buy me for the New York Yankees. So did the Detroit Tigers. But Rickey would not sell." To Medwick this meant that even if Rickey grew tired of him, he still had a very prosperous career ahead of him with any of the major league teams.

The Scottdale team finished its season with fifty-nine wins and fifty-five losses, which was close to the top of the league in wins, yet it finished behind the league champion team by three and a half games. In the seventy-five games Medwick played in the Middle Atlantic League, he had a season's performance that matched the very best anyone had ever had, producing a .419 average with 22 home runs and 100 Runs Batted In. No one in the league had ever hit, or would ever hit, for a higher average. His hitting also produced a slugging percentage of .750, a combined total of 249 bases. He had 26 assists from the outfield.

Medwick had had an extraordinary year. He had performed even better in professional baseball than he had anywhere else against easier pitching. If he had any doubts of his worth as a player, they were gone now.

Joe returned home to Carteret, New Jersey, but not for long. Medwick found out what he might mean to the Scottdale team. Medwick's contract was sold by Scottdale president H. E. Cramer to the team in Danville, Illinois. Someone had offered "a huge pile of sheckels," and on September 8 Medwick's contract was bought for $3,000 by Robert R. Bookwalter. The president of the Danville Veterans wanted Joe to play for him in what the Danville *Commercial-News* was calling the "Little World Series," probably against left-handers since the Veterans had had trouble all season with left-handed pitching.

The Evansville, Indiana Hubs won the last-half championship of the Three I League after the Veterans had won the first-half championship, and a seven-game series was about to start. So on September 16, 1930, Joe left Carteret to join the team in a town about two hundred miles south of Chicago on the Indiana border. He reported to Soldiers Home Field in Danville, and though it was very likely that Joe was being considered as an investment—that is, the worth of his contract might go up and Bookwalter could turn a profit selling Joe to his next team, the *Commercial-News* noted Joe's arrival and guessed that "Medwick may break into the Danville lineup before the last of the series."

Game two on Saturday belonged to Danville and the write-up for Joe was not good: "Medwick . . . struck out on his first trip, singled the next time and fouled to Hackney the next two times at bat. In the field he didn't look so hot, making an error on Hamby's fly in the second at an inopportune time, and on other plays he didn't seem so sure of himself."

Back in Danville for game six, Medwick started in left but he did not finish. He scored a run by getting on base on a fielder's choice, his run was the second of three in the inning, while "Medwick's error in left field enabl[ed] Evansville to count the first of its two runs in the third." Cotelle, without an at bat in the game, finished in left as Danville won the series.

4

A Ducky Buffalo, Houston, 1931

O f course, back home in Carteret he was still "Meddi" to his pals, "Joey" to his Mom. Medwick's pay stopped on the last day of the season. But his $50 per week was equal to about twice the pay of the men who carried their lunches down Union and Chrome Streets and now his pay was about to be three or four times their take-home money. By January 1931, his contract belonged to the Houston Buffaloes, so yet another team—Danville—and perhaps Branch Rickey as well, made money from Medwick's abilities. Yet Medwick had jumped from class C over class B right up to Houston, a team not in the highest level of the minor leagues (being in class "A") but there was only one step above it. (There was no triple A baseball until 1946.)

By the end of spring training, two events made Joe Medwick even more certain about choosing baseball. First was Knute Rockne's death in a plane crash. The death of that famous Notre Dame coach made Medwick feel somehow that he had made the right decision about baseball. Then, too, being sent to Houston to play where the next step might very well be the big team—the majors—was another sign. The assignment to Houston with a salary that had risen from $200 a month at Scottdale to $450 a month made Medwick even more certain. More money meant that he could send more home to his mother, more money for his family—and a man was bound to look out for family.

The season of the eight-team league was 161 games in Texas and Louisiana from April 15 to September 13, the teams limited to eighteen players each. The home park in Houston, Buffalo Stadium, was three years old and had fourteen thousand seats.The Texas League was well known for its heat and notorious for its rule that stated that whenever a fight started on the field, the two involved would keep fighting until it was over. No one broke up the fight; "let the two men settle it," the saying went—the best man would win.

Texas was new to Medwick. His New Jersey accent seemed even thicker in the midst of the Texas twang. Joe was now among older men in this league, and he was just nineteen, so he was cautious and tentative. His frugality also became increasingly important. He knew how to save some of his meal money to use as spending money, and the local lore was that Medwick slept on the sand dunes of Houston to save rent. He was learning the tricks that people in those times learned. Wait for a newspaper to be read and discarded in a hotel lobby rather than paying for it yourself. Don't eat in the expensive places; instead, find the ones where the owners liked ballplayers.

Joe began to meet people working for the team and heard some talk about the league. The team's batboy was Joe Schultz, Jr., the twelfth son of the manager, Joe Schultz, Sr., 38. Reporter John Lloyd Gregory wrote on March 1, 1931, in the *Houston Post-Dispatch* that "Homer Peel, one of the greatest hitters in the league's history, and George Puccinelli, labeled as a future major league star, ought to take care of two of the outfield berths. There was a disposition to believe Joe Medwick from Scottdale or Jimmy Sanders from Greensboro can take care of the other job."

On March 2, the training season began with thirty-three players for a roster that would be cut to eighteen men. The group now included "Joe Medwick, well set-up youngster who played great ball last season for Eddie Dyer's Scottdale club."

On April 13, a Monday, "the Buffs were issued snappy new uniforms" and then practiced during an afternoon workout and a nighttime one. The uniforms had a picture of a buffalo inside a circle over the left breast.

For the first two games of the 1931 season, the team traveled by train for an hour to the home park of Galveston, a Tigers farm team. With Chick Hafey, the St. Louis left fielder, still unsigned, someone in the Houston outfield—Medwick, Peel, Puccinelli, or Jimmie Sanders—might be in the Cardinal outfield very soon.

Medwick, who was 1-5 in game one while playing center, and 2-6 in the second game, produced five of the team's twelve runs. Before the Friday night home opener, the team members attended the annual baseball luncheon at the Houston Kiwanis club hall. The meeting featured the song "Take Me Out to the Ball Game" and the question Who are the three ugliest men on the squad?—a hale-fellow-well-met sort of question that was asked many times throughout the season. Sometimes it was the opposite question—the kind of humor that calls tall men "Tiny."

Medwick started off slowly in the league. Not yet twenty, he was eager for the major leagues, somewhere he would never be if he hit .236 in Houston.

After the May 1 game, which Tex Carleton won 4-2, Joe's single raised him up to .260, and Dizzy Dean was sent back to Houston from the Cardinals. To differentiate him from P. Dean, the box score read "J. Dean, p," and this Dean threw a 6-0 three-hitter. Paul Dean was needed in double A Columbus to pitch in the American Association.

Joe was paired with Dizzy the next day as they left for a four-day series with Shreveport. Dizzy sized up Joe and decided that they must take just about the same fit in clothing. Dizzy weighed about the same as Joe but was four inches taller.

Almost two years older than Medwick, Jay Hanna was the classic braggart who demanded attention, whereas Joe's classic laconic personality let his actions speak for him. When Dizzy, using all of his charm, more than suggested that Joe give him free rein with Medwick's New Jersey attire, Joe refused him. Medwick knew he did not have Dean's verbal ability or his charm. Not having such attributes, Joe judged them to be of little value to a man. So he asked Joe Schultz to let him be roomed with Tom Carey, a shortstop five years older than Joe, who was from Hoboken, New Jersey. Outfielder Pooch Puccinelli had been sent to the Three I League. It was possible that Pooch was sent down to get the roster down to the allowable league level of eighteen It was also possible that he was sent down as punishment for holding out. Puccinelli may have blamed Medwick for supplanting him on the team.

Joe still had his problems. As Joe was in his slump, a cartoon and text appeared featuring the batting stance of Wally Berger and some words from Hack Wilson, who had 190 RBIs in 1930. The column concerned stepping in the bucket, which was Joe's batting method.

Yet Wilson warned, "You must get your body in your swing for long hits. When a batter steps to one side instead of toward the pitcher, he pulls his body away also, and only hits with his arms." Joe hit .419 at Scottdale doing what Hack Wilson warned against. Was Medwick wrong?

Almost thirty years later, Andy Anderson would write for the *Houston Press*, "Pitchers began throwing wide, high, into the dirt, and once in a while they tried to dust him off. No matter where they threw the ball, Mickey would swing at it. And he was hitting the ball, but old Joe Schultz was peeved. 'The kid was going into a batting slump as sure as anything. . . . He was swinging at anything they throw [sic] just because he was going good. But wait until he isn't hitting and he'll still be swinging at those bad pitches.'"

Trying hard, Joe dropped to .255 with a 0-3 day. George Payne now advised Medwick, telling him to play percentage ball and not to take chances. (Payne called Medwick "Mickey," as many people in Houston did by now.)

As Joe was coming to his 200th at bat for the 1931 season, three of the four games were won by his team, though Medwick could only make four hits in fourteen times up, and he drove in no runs.

But then Medwick's hitting picked up and his average rose to .284. "Joe Medwick, the 19-year-old major league prospect, carried the big stick for Joe Schultz's boys," Gregory wrote after the June 11th game. In left field, Medwick knocked down a line drive and was able to throw out Urban on a force on the same play, and in the seventh, "Medwick made a spectacular catch of Higgins' drive." Being a good hitter also meant that he had to learn to protect himself. Andy Anderson wrote that "Some of the pitchers were not averse to chunking a high hard one at a good hitter's head. They didn't do that that often with Medwick because Mickey knew how to allow that bat to slip from his hands and go flying towards a pitcher's shins."

Medwick continued "his vicious hitting" and the team was able to build a one-and-a-half-game lead over Beaumont. He was 7-19 to finish out the first half of June, batting .338 and driving in fourteen runs in June. The newspapers—the *Press*, the *Chronicle*, and the *Post-Dispatch*—began to see what Joe might be capable of.

When Branch Rickey arrived on June 25 to watch the team, Joe was placed back in right field and the Buffaloes took two from Wichita Falls, though their third baseman, Debs Garms, battled hard in the games. Joe knocked in RBI number fifty on June 26, Tex Carleton won his second in two days, and Medwick "made a great catch of Scharein's fly to short right to end the game. Manager Schultz and his men held a rousing celebration in front of their dugout."

Joe's two more RBIs at Fort Worth on June 27 again tied the Buffs with Beaumont. Dizzy Dean won both games of the doubleheader on the 28th but the next 2-1 loss—Joe supplied the run with an RBI fly—put the team one back on the 29th with one to go. The game at Fort Worth was "one of the most dramatic and most desperately fought in Texas League history." With Joe scoring three times and driving in one, the game featured a 10-9 score and a triple play in the tenth, combined with a Beaumont loss to Wichita Falls, which caused the first half of the Texas League season to end in a tie. The first-half championship would be decided when Beaumont and Houston played against each other in the regular season's second half. Meanwhile, though not yet hitting .300, Joe was close to the league lead in both doubles and RBIs.

While in Galveston, as everywhere in the league when there were night games about to be played, players woke at about 11 A.M. having had a big meal after the game, perhaps twelve hours before. Lunch at noon was followed by a movie show or a walk around town. At 4 P.M., it was time for a late lunch and then off to the ballpark.

Back home, against the San Antonio Indians, Joe raised his average to .296 and then made his 100th hit and RBI number sixty-two as Tex Carleton won his twelfth game. By July 17, Medwick, climbing steadily, raised his average to .297 while playing center.

As they packed for a three-city trip on the morning of July 24, the team members read a letter in the column of the *Houston Post-Dispatch*'s sports editor, Lloyd Gregory, a column called "Looking 'em Over." The second item began, "Here's a letter from a feminine admirer of Joe Medwick, clouting Buff outfielder. 'Please tell me about Medwick. I have heard he was an Italian and can hardly speak English. Was this true? Joe Medwick was my favorite player, and I have nicknamed him "Duckie" because he walks just like a duck. I understand he lives here with Eddie Hock. Was it true Joe was so young he had to have sheriff Hock look out after him?'" Gregory's answer included the information that Joe called his home state "Noo Joisy" and the columnist offered the opinion that "come to think of it, Joe does walk with a sort of duck-like waddle. But can't he massage that onion? We do believe Joe does need someone to look out for him, inasmuch as he was only 19." The section of the column was titled "About 'Duckie' Medwick."

There had been "Duckies" before in the big leagues and in the negro leagues, and there would be later ones as well: Ducky Dettweiler, Ducky Hale, Ducky Jones, Ducky Davenport. But Medwick's name had catchy sound repetition in it when put next to Ducky. The rest of the Buffaloes immediately gave Medwick the name as a clubhouse name—a nickname. It was not long before the name became "Ducky-Wucky." This did not at all please Joe, but he had gone through so many names by now: "Meddi" to his friends in Carteret, "Mickey," "Joey" to his "Moms." He would have many, many labels before he was through. But before very long, only Joe Medwick would be forever "Ducky."

The other players seized upon the nickname to tease their teammate. Although the newspapers loved it, Medwick loathed it, but there was not much he could do about it. It seemed to add color to the game, he was told. It was, he supposed, good for business—certainly for the newspaper business, but not necessarily for Medwick's business. The newspaper boys seemed to love tacking nicknames onto players. Soon his teammates made the name even more ridiculous by adding "Wucky" to the "Ducky." "Ducky-Wucky" Medwick it was, then. The more vivid the name—and in Medwick's mind the more childish and less dignified—the better the newspaper men liked the label and the more often they used it. The players had their own names for each other—it was a matter of being accepted that a player received a sort of clubhouse name—and those names were hardly ever the same as the newspaper ones. The clubhouse name was frequently "Mickey" for Medwick in Houston. Frequently, the clubhouse names were unprintable. But if the newspapers wanted color, then color would pay somehow for Joe Medwick. He would have his way yet.

The three regularly scheduled games in Beaumont were also going to count as three play-off games to determine the winner of the first half of the 1931 season, which ended twenty-four days before with Beaumont tied with the Buffaloes.

On July 25, Joe supplied the game-winning hit in front of seven thousand spectators at Stuart Stadium—five hundred fans came from Houston by train—to take the first play-off game. The next day, the scheduled play-off game two was a fifteen-inning tie, during which Joe walked and homered in the sixth and in the eighth. "Medwick's great throw cut off what would have been the winning rally," because "with the bases loaded and one out, Schuble flied to center. Medwick's peg caught Hamlin at the plate on a very close play to retire the side. Had umpire Lee Ballafant called Hamlin safe, Beaumont would have won the game 3-2 in nine innings." The game on Monday, July 27, was in Houston, during which three, instead of the usual two, umpires were used and the 14-11 win for the Buffaloes saw Joe drive in three runs and score one.

Lloyd Gregory wrote, "Joe Medwick, the slugging Buff outfielder who walks like a duck, continued to figure prominently in the inquiries from the lady fans. 'Please tell me . . . Mickey Medwick's height, weight and the color of his hair and eyes. . . .' Medwick was 5 feet 9 inches tall and weighs 175 pounds. The eyes of this husky, handsome Hungarian were brown. The color of his hair was rather indefinite; but we'd say it was brown."

Carey Selph said to Kerrn Tips, sports editor of the *Chronicle* in Houston: "Medwick is a great natural athlete. He's got the attributes of a Pepper Martin, combined with a Chick Hafey. He can run, hit, catch and throw. I wouldn't be surprised if he turned out to be a great major leaguer. Not just a good one—a great one."

On August 1, Joe made hit 125 of 1931, a home run to center field in the fourth, but the team lost to Wichita Falls 4-2. The doubleheader on Sunday had two stars: Tex Carleton won both games, his fifteenth and sixteenth, though Debs Garms, the Spudders' left fielder, drove in three runs. "Joe Medwick had a grand and glorious day with the bat." In the two games, he collected a homer, two doubles, and three singles out of eight times at bat. Batting fifth, Medwick also accounted for three RBIs and scored one of the nine runs in the doubleheader. The Buffaloes were now in the Texas League lead by six games.

After a North Texas trip, a home stand was preceded by another letter to Lloyd Gregory: "A large number of Houston soprano baseball fans were excited over the momentous question of whether Joe Medwick, slugging Buff outfielder, should be nicknamed 'Duckie' or 'Mickey.'" One letter said, "'He may be Mickey Medwick to you but he'll always be Duckie to me and the rest of the "goils" in this office.' Very well, girls," Gregory concluded, "we'll refer to Joe as 'Duckie' Medwick, because he waddles like a duck. And then too, 'Mickey' was not a fit name for a Hungarian."

The Hungarian Medwick made his 100th RBI on August 19 and the next day the team got its eighth day off since April 15. That rest was followed by a tie game due to more rain.

The Wichita Falls team split with Houston on August 23 and on the 24th, Dizzy won his twenty-fifth game by 1-0, thanks to Joe's game-winning RBI. The win was followed by "Mr. and Mrs. Fred Ankenman entertain[ing] the ballplayers and their families with a San Jacinto Inn dinner. The Houston president's party . . . [was] a jubilant one, with 'on to Birmingham for the Dixie Series' the dominant note." (The Dixie Series was a season-end series played between the winners of the Texas League and of the Southern Association.) Another jubilant note was that "Ankenman announced that the Houston Baseball association would add $1,000 to the players' pool for the Dixie series . . . the players had stated that they did not expect a pennant fund this year and that they felt the fans should not be asked to contribute to such a fund. . . . The added money will mean an additional $50 to each player on the Buff team."

The doubleheader on September 13 ended the championship season and the team finished with a .734 winning percentage, placing second in the league in team batting average. Joe's runs and RBIs equaled 28 percent of his team's runs, and 17 percent in RBIs alone. Medwick was second in doubles with forty-seven, and first in home runs and RBIs. He was one of the few batters in the league with six hundred at bats.

Medwick played in all 161 games, to tie for most games played in the league, led the league in home runs with 19, in RBIs with 126, in total bases with 308, in extra-base hits with 120, and he finished with a batting average of .305. For his performance that year, he was chosen as a member of the Texas League All-Star team along with teammates Dizzy Dean and Tex Carleton.

On Tuesday, after a Monday marked by an 11 A.M. workout, the team, with fans and a few wives, boarded a special train to Birmingham at 9 A.M. The first game of the best of seven was to be played Wednesday, September 16.

The home field for the Birmingham Baron, as well as the Negro National League Birmingham Black Barons, was Rickwood Field. The first game of the Dixie Series had more fans who wanted to attend than there were seats available. So, as often happened at every level of professional baseball, fans were allowed on the field itself, in this case, in front of the left and right field fences.

After splitting the two games at Rickwood, the team returned to Houston on the Louisville & Nashville Missouri Pacific Special. Aboard were sixty fans who paid the $26.15 round-trip fares, and the forty-five-member Birmingham Police Band (called "The Musical Coppers").

The Buffaloes won two games in Houston but the Barons then won two back at their home field to bring the series to 3-3.

Now Birmingham needed only one more win, the home crowd in Houston bringing the series total to 81,025. The Barons were again outhit, this game by 13-10, but scored the tie-breaking third run in the eighth inning on a Medwick error in center. But "Medwick showed he was a fighter when he came to bat in the last of the eighth. After fouling off a number of pitches, Medwick slammed a vicious drive to left. Many of the fans thought that the ball had cleared the left field fence, and so did Medwick; but the umpire ruled the ball had landed in the temporary left field bleachers and therefore good for only two bases." He was now the tying run but no one could bring Medwick in. Birmingham scored four runs in the ninth and the final score was 6-3. Joe had two hits but Houston left eleven on base as Dean took the loss. The Southern Association was now 3-9 in all of the Dixie Series.

With record admissions and gate receipts for the Dixie Series, and with the $1,000 contributed by the Houston Baseball Association, Joe and his teammates added about $600 to their wallets from the series play. That money alone was about 70 percent of what men back in Carteret brought home in a year.

5

Waiting for the Call,
Houston, 1932

By the time the 1931 World Series was over, everyone could see how the country was being affected by the Great Depression. Those salaries in Carteret factories that had not been cut in half, were cut by 20 percent; other jobs just disappeared. Men were being paid about $850 per year, but Medwick had just made $2,250 for five months in Houston.

The 1931 World Series, with Pepper Martin as the hero, was won by the Cardinals against a great team, the Philadelphia Athletics. Chick Hafey had been the Cardinals' left fielder for six years, and at age twenty-nine, was approaching his prime.

To his hometown, Medwick was in his prime. He was famous, at least in his area, if not in the state. He was the best athlete during an era and in a town that loved and praised athletes. He had spent his first two seasons in professional baseball and he had starred—not just played acceptably well. And he wasn't yet twenty years old.

Medwick spent the winter at the Red Star and at the dances at St. Elias. He continued to stay in top physical condition, consuming the "groceries" that his mother prepared for him. He visited with Bennie and Bill.

On April 1, a pre-season article on Joe appeared in the Houston newspaper, stating, "Joe (Duckie-Wuckie, Mickey) Medwick, the slugging outfielder, had an idea he can sing. As he dressed, Joe made the day hideous with what he chose to call his singing. He'll be crooning for the radio next . . . although his batting average last year was only .305, Medwick probably was the circuit's outstanding batsman. . . . While Medwick led the league, we expect Joe to be a much improved player this season. No reason why he shouldn't increase his batting percentage about 20 points."

April 3rd found scouts from the Giants and the Cubs in the stands in Houston; in St. Louis, Chick Hafey, the league's best hitter, was traded by Branch Rickey on April 11 to last-place Cincinnati for two players and $45,000. Why trade? Hafey had asked for a raise to $17,000. With Hafey not there, the outfield was penciled in as George Watkins in right and Pepper Martin (replacing Taylor Douthit) in center. For a left fielder, Rickey chose first baseman Ripper Collins.

Opening Day was April 13, and began with a parade at noon; both teams rode in automobiles through Houston to Buffalo Park. That first game, a 3-2 Houston win over visiting Galveston, took one hour and fifteen minutes. In the second inning, after Cox of Galveston singled and after a fly out to Sanders in center, "Medwick brought the crowd to their feet by making a sensational catch of McGhee's liner and his perfect throw doubled Cox off first." In the bottom half, Medwick "doubled down the third-base line. Medwick scored on [Homer] Peel's line single to center, and thereby won a pair of Florsheim shoes for the first run of the season." Medwick also drove in a run. And he stopped a run this way: in the ninth inning, with runners on second and third, Bud Hungling singled. "Ordinarily," *Post-Dispatch* sports editor Lloyd Gregory wrote, "a man would be expected to score from second on such a single and at such a stage in the game [tied 2-2]. But the Buccaneers had so much respect for the rifle that Joe Medwick, Buff right fielder, carries concealed in his right arm that McGhee was pulled up at third. Medwick shot in a perfect peg," which was cut off, led to a rundown, and then caused McGhee to be thrown out trying to score, ending the game.

The first road trip of 1932 was three hundred miles west to San Antonio, where Joe had a game to remember in League Park. The 20-5 win featured his 5-6 hitting with thirteen total bases and eight RBIs. Though hit in the ribs in the fifth inning on April 16, Joe homered in the eighth in the win, and homered again to support Ed Heusser's first win in the Texas League.

With a 2-4 game in Beaumont, Joe was hitting .391. Henry Greenberg, now the Explorers' first baseman, homered the next day to help his team to a 4-3 win. That April 21 game was on the anniversary of the battle of San Jacinto, and was also the first day that "a special candy bar to be known as the 'Duckie-Wuckie Bar' would be distributed—for a price—at each ball game." The candy bar may have been produced by the St. Regis Candies store. A newspaper cartoon showed Joe and a caption: "Speaking of candy, the popular Buff was already on par with Babe Ruth and Lindy." Early in the season, Medwick figured out how to make the nickname he so disliked—"Ducky"—work for him. "President Fred Ankenman had cashed in on this nickname for his popular player by having a special candy bar made called 'Duckie-Wuckie.' It was the best seller at Buffalo Stadium. And little children cried for it when their mothers took them into the stores." Medwick insisted that he receive a percentage from all the candy bars sold. How could he insist? Wasn't he owned by the Houston team? Yet Medwick sensed that the candy-bar scheme would not work without his cooperation and endorsement. Once he was sure he could insist, he did exactly that; the owner had to agree.

Sportswriter Lloyd Gregory's comments calling Joe "sweet" and "cute" spurred this letter: "I have seen Joe play ball a great many times and can never refer to him as sweet and cute because it takes a real, honest-to-goodness man to slap that old ball over the fence as often as Old Joe does and I never fail to be thrilled when I see him in action." After Gregory explained that he was only kidding, he pointed out that he knew that Joe "certainly can pickle that old 'termater.' Somehow, most of the fans get a kick out of that 'Duckie-Wuckie' nickname, plastered on the great young ball player by a young lady. . . . Did you ever notice how he waddles like a duck?"

At the end of the month as well, the newspaper featured another in the series of drawings and text by former player Al Demaree, this one about Athletics' left fielder Al Simmons, who was often called "bucketfoot," a style of hitting Joe also used. Simmons said, "Many people claim I step away from the plate when I hit. Perhaps I do but I do not pull away with my body. It does not make much difference what you do with your front foot, provided you get all of the power of your back, hips and back foot in your swing." Joe also lifted his leg, like Ruth and Mel Ott, but his idiosyncratic style suited him— and had done well by him. "There's plenty of power," Gregory wrote, "in Medwick's whip-like swing." By this, Gregory may have meant what is today called "bat speed."

After a month of the season had been played, Medwick received his first national attention in Lloyd Gregory's column in the May 19,

1932, issue of *The Sporting News*. The article was titled "Joe Medwick's Bat Real Spark Plug of Houston Buffs' Powerful Attack":

> The first month of the Texas League campaign had demonstrated that Manager Joe Schultz'[s] Houston Buffs will need all their resources. . . . Houston had a well-balanced outfit that had been getting sensational hitting from Joe ("Duckie Wuckie") Medwick, stalwart youngster who next season should be playing left field for the Cardinals. Medwick, a right-hand batsman with tremendous power, was hitting around .400 and driving in many runs. Before the first month of the season was ended, he had slashed out ten homers, whereas last year his 19 homers were enough to lead the league in round-trip wallops. Medwick's fielding was improving every day, and he throws a la Chick Hafey, the base runners never daring to attempt liberties.

Rain at Fort Worth forced two straight doubleheaders. With just a double and a single in the June 9 doubleheader, a split, Joe helped out with a "great throw in the seventh [that] cut off the tying run at the plate." In game two, Medwick drove in five with three.

On June 27 it was clear that the Buffaloes could not catch Beaumont, a better team in the first half, and a better team in the three games that ended June and began July. After hitting 3-12, Joe now had 121 hits in 321 at bats for a .377 average.

"Sisler Likes Joe Medwick," the *Post-Dispatch* reported. "I like the attitude of Joe Medwick. . . . Here's a boy who can do everything. He knows he's headed toward a regular job with the Cardinals. He's smart and he'll hit any sort of pitching. I like him very much." From 1915–1930, Mr. Sisler, then a Texas League manager, hit under .300 once, and over .400 twice.

Andy Anderson wrote in 1948: "Medwick would fight. In fact, he was a very belligerent kid and wanted his share of the base lines. I think that is one reason why he became a major league star."

By mid season, the July 7, 1932, issue of the *Sporting News* asked how making Joe a regular in the Cardinal lineup would be worked out:

> Houston fans have found another favorite in Joe Medwick, 20-year-old outfielder who had been hitting close to .400 all season. Medwick had none of the attractive, if eccentric, qualities of Dizzy Dean. Yet he had color that comes from the force of his activities with the bat and in the field. He is a hustling, aggressive young man with Tarzan-like shoul-

ders, whose admitted business just now [is] getting to the Cardinals as fast as he knows how. The 180-pound Medwick is a right-handed hitter and thrower. His stance at the plate is somewhat remindful of the earlier days of Al Simmons and his "foot in the bucket." So pronounced is the latter that many expert observers said early in the season that he "would never do"; that he would be a "sucker" for a curve ball on the outside corner. But he got there just the same and was the current sensation of the Texas League. Young Medwick had so much power in his swing [that] he drove the ball a long distance, even though he got "only a piece" of the horsehide.

"The Buffs of '32 were not such a hot ball club. They had no business being in the first division," Andy Anderson wrote years later, "I think it was Mickey's big black bat that kept them there. I used to love to see those outfielders back up when Mickey came up. And the infielders too. And some pitchers just threw 'em and ducked."

While the Buffaloes were winning and trying to catch Beaumont, Joe's 4-15 hitting allowed George Washington of the Tyler club to pass Joe in batting averages. But Joe's three hits the next day gave him back the lead, followed by a rare day off, his fifth day off since April 13.

Another rare day off in the Houston season was ended at 10 P.M. by a tremendous hurricane with "the greatest damage . . . in the oil fields" as well as at the airfield. Seven streetcar lines were out of service, including the Port Houston line, stopped by water in the Preston Avenue tunnel. The stadium's damage was "estimated at $4,000. The hurricane stripped the asphalt roofing from the grandstand, blew down the center field fence and knocked out of line the right field fence. 'We carried no tornado insurance,' President Ankenman said. 'However, there was some consolation in the fact [that] the repair of the damages will give a considerable number of men work.'"

Joe himself was like a hurricane in Tyler, making 3 hits to move him to 181; he scored 3 times to get him to 99; he drove in 8 to push his total to 104 in 125 games. With his third home run in two days, with 2 hits and a steal, with 3 RBIs, and 2 runs, Houston won again. When Medwick was hitless the next day, he still drove in a run with what is now scored as a sacrifice fly.

The announcement that Joe would go to the major leagues was made on August 27. Lloyd Gregory guessed $50,000 was paid to Houston to buy Joe. Against Tyler on August 28, Joe was 3-4 with two RBIs and two runs, pushing his average up to .354.

"Big Outfielder Bids Fans Goodbye with Long Homer in Second Game," a *Houston Post-Dispatch* headline read. Medwick, with the bases loaded in game one, "made a running catch of Chambers' drive to stop at least three runs." In game two,

> The crowd sensed Medwick was at bat for the last time for dear old Houston. With several thousand women and children and two thousand male cash customers screaming encouragement, Joe tipped his hat, thanking the fans. Medwick really was anxious to crack the old nugget on the nose. Medwick swung and missed a low pitch and the crowd groaned. The next pitch was about shoulder high and on the inside. Medwick tied into the ball with all the power in his stocky body and the ball sailed over the left field fence. When the game was ended, Medwick was surrounded by several hundred kids, all anxious to shake hands with him.

Medwick was then hitting .354 for Houston and had amassed fifty-two assists.

Robert E. Hood reported in *The Gashouse Gang* (1976), "But Medwick felt cheated even then. 'I was so damn angry,' he said. 'They used to give you a traveling bag or some damn thing when you leave the city. They didn't give me nothing.'"

After the game, the man who was in charge of handling the candy bars (the "Duckie-Wuckie" bars) approached Medwick, asking if he would let the sale of the candy bars continue even though he had moved to St. Louis. Medwick asked how many were left unsold, and the man took Joe underneath the stands and showed him cases of candy bars. "I want all the wrappers. You're not going to sell this candy without me getting my share," Medwick said. The man looked astonished. "You know the agreement," Medwick said. "When I leave Houston, you can't sell my candy bars. So give me all the wrappings now." Medwick stood by while the distributor did just that. Medwick shoved all the paper into a bag, leaving the candy man with all that chocolate and no wrappers; he would not be exploited. He resented the fact that someone would try to take advantage of him. Medwick had his way.

On April 1, Lloyd Gregory wrote, "While Medwick led the league, we expect Joe to be a much improved player this season. No reason why he shouldn't increase his batting percentage [of .305] about 20 points." Medwick had played in every game for Houston, hit .354, drove in 111 runs, and made 82 extra-base hits. He had 13 more putouts than in 1931, while playing in 22 fewer games. His slugging average was .610 and he had hit for 342 total bases. He had succeeded and starred for the third straight year—as he had always succeeded and starred.

6

With the Big Club, St. Louis, September 1932

Arriving at Houston's Union Station well before the train arrived on Tuesday, August 30, 1932, Medwick made sure he had the train ticket to Chicago, and a berth, since the 1,200-mile trek from Houston to Chicago lasted thirty hours. As he settled in, carefully stowing his glove, spikes, and bats, he may have read the *St. Louis Post-Dispatch* column called "Sports Salad," which announced "another Texas wonder" in its first headline. "Joe Medwick . . . bats like Al Simmons, throws like Hafey and runs like Ty Cobb. . . . If 'Duckie Wuckie' can live up to his reputation, it won't take him long to live down his name."

It seems clear that Medwick thought about his future. "When I first entered baseball, I figured about fifteen years for my top earning power in the game and planned accordingly," he said years later.

The young man had plenty of time to think of what he had accomplished and what yet remained for him to do. He had been told he was too young and that swinging at bad balls would not reward him, but he had proven his detractors wrong. Being a bad-ball hitter meant that pitchers would have trouble trying to find a weakness that they could take advantage of.

How much time would Medwick get to play? Dizzy Dean and Tex Carleton, two of his 1931 Houston teammates, had pitched all of 1932 with the Cardinals, becoming starters their first full year with the team. Many players came up at this time of year (after September 1) for "a cup of coffee," as the players called it—a brief time with the parent team so it could gauge how well a player might perform against big-league pitching or big-league hitting. Medwick believed very strongly that once he came to St. Louis to play, he would be at the big-league level for a long time, and that he would play well for a long time, and make a lot of money.

Medwick had no doubt that he was playing for money; he had no trouble understanding that as long as he played professional baseball, he would be paid well. He knew what a good a player he was; he hoped he was a major league player. He knew he was a worker for the team, and the better his work, the more money he would make. He knew that the Cardinals thought so, too. Back home in Carteret there was little work to be found. The few jobs available were awful work—dipping ties in creosote or melting batteries. Medwick had worked hard at baseball to get where he was in his career now; he would work even harder now that he was in the major leagues, and he had the confidence that he would get even better. All he needed was the chance to prove it. Medwick wanted what was his due. He wanted recognition for his talent—the kind of recognition he had gotten all his life.

But Medwick wondered, "What good did newspapermen do me? They would not increase my skills. They may know very little about baseball. Their skills were merely writing skills—time and energy spent on reporters might better be spent hitting or taking outfield practice." Medwick believed the only skills he needed were baseball skills. And yet he had seen Dizzy Dean in Houston surrounded after a game by the press. He saw how much Tex Carleton was slighted simply because the newspaper boys liked Dean more, and Carleton was a Texan playing in his home state.

So, on the other hand, maybe the photographers and writers could do Medwick some good. And since he was on his way to being a star, he decided he'd better get used to dealing with them, at least until he was a star—then *they* would need *him*.

But knowing how things were was not the same as being able to handle all those things well. Joe had little experience dealing with the different conditions at the major league level. Up until now, Medwick had been rewarded for batting in runs and for extra-base hits. Those things were why he was hired—he had concentrated on those things for a good part of his life. He had been rewarded because he had gone about doing things his own way. If Medwick had listened to others—those who said bad-ball hitters were not wanted—he might not have been as successful as he had been. He had gone his own way, trusting his own instincts, and he had succeeded. That was why the Cardinals had summoned him to St. Louis.

No one got to the major league level without being a talented player. Joe was just such a player. He now belonged to a group of four hundred major league players belonging to sixteen teams. He would be one of sixteen major league left fielders. He would settle for no less—he deserved no less. Anyone who tried to cheat him would have to be dealt with; he would keep his job. The candy-bar man found that out.

Medwick was a professional baseball player and he was very happy to be one. His manager, Gabby Street, or the coaches, could give him advice on his hitting. After all, that's what they were paid for. But Medwick didn't want anyone else giving him advice; he didn't want anyone to make him look bad.

Medwick was aware that this team was in tough shape. They had won the championship in 1931, but now in 1932, they were stuck near the bottom of the National League. There had been no suitable left fielder for the Cardinals since Hafey was traded. Joe was young. He played a position they needed to fill for a long time. That was okay with him.

He was here to hit, and he would; he was here to make money, and he would. Joe was here to stay.

That Wednesday night of August 30th, arriving at the Dearborn station at 6 P.M., Joe followed the signs to "Cabs," and told the driver to take him to the Del Prado Hotel. The Cardinals had not yet arrived from Keokuk, where they had played an exhibition game against one of the farm teams. Medwick found a room reserved for him.

Medwick was just about to go to sleep when his roommate, Cuban-born catcher Mike Gonzales, came into the room. Joe knew that Gonzales expected to be treated with respect; he was a sharp baseball man, although he did have trouble with English. A veteran of more than one thousand National League games with Boston, St. Louis, New York, Cincinnati, and Chicago, Gonzales turned out to be a good friend to Joe, as well as someone Joe could consult with on how to play hitters in the field. Four months later, Medwick "calls this the luckiest break he ever got. 'Gonzales was one of those chaps who live, eat and sleep with baseball uppermost in his mind. . . . He used to get the box score every day and go over National League players, tell me how they hit and where to play for them. Then he'd discuss pitchers and their peculiarities and our own team. It was a break the like[s] of which few young players get.'"

At Street's locker before the game, Medwick was told that he'd be hitting second, at least until things sorted themselves out. Next they went over the signs for "steal," "bunt," "take," and "hit and run."

Who did his new teammates see coming to join them before the game on September 1? A muscular kid, long-waisted and short-legged for his height, with thick arms and thick brown hair. A Hungarian kid with a thick New York accent whose eyes had a certain fire in them. When some players tried out the "Ducky-Wucky" label on him, Medwick didn't smile—he glowered. Then he dressed in the gray Cardinal road uniform—"St. Louis" written on the chest, across which a bat appeared, red cardinals perching on both ends. The sleeves had a red line around the end and the stockings were red on the top third, the rest, white. The shirt had four buttons and stopped buttoning three quarters of the way down. The cap had a red bill; red lines radiated from the button on top across a grayish-white cap.

It felt good to Medwick to have a bat in his hands again. Wrigley was a big park, which was an advantage for a hitter like Medwick, who was a line-drive hitter, as opposed to one who lofted the ball into the stands. During his turn at batting practice, Medwick hit long drives that cracked against the brick walls all over the park. He was pleased with himself, but he knew that batting-practice hitting was not the same as hitting against major league pitching. This was especially true that particular day because the pitcher, Burleigh Grimes, had a mean reputation. Making his way out to the outfield, Medwick could see a piece of plywood screwed into the left field wall that read "364," and when he drifted over, he saw that center field was marked "436" feet from home, with right field being the shortest distance at 321.

At three o'clock, the umpire yelled "Play!" and the game began. Medwick took his place in the on-deck area. When Joe came to bat, Wilson, the shortstop, was on first, but Medwick, concentrating as hard as he could, only hit into a force play at second. Medwick was determined to show them something; when Frisch doubled, Medwick ran hard past second, and as he approached third, he saw the windmilling arms of Street, who sent him on home. Joe's dusty slide marked the first score of the game.

In the third inning, Medwick drove in Wilson with a long fly to center. He did not get a hit in that first game, but he contributed. Although the team lost by 8-5, Medwick had both scored a run and driven one in; he was proud to have produced two runs in his first game.

That night J. Roy Stockton's report in the Sports Final pages of the *St. Louis Post-Dispatch* said,

> Medwick . . . made the big impression. Medwick just looks like money . . . showing brilliant speed and making a big league slide over the plate to beat the throw from the outfield. . . . [N]ewspapermen, accustomed to see[ing] young players break into the big leagues, were inclined to reach for superlatives in commenting on the young man's prospects. . . . Medwick [is] a right-handed hitter who steps in the bucket, much after the fashion of Al Simmons [who would hit thirty-five home runs in 1932] . . . and few batters are successful when they swing while stepping backward from the plate. However, Simmons is an exception and Medwick seems to be another. He steps backward with his left foot as he swings but he has so much power that he hits left and right field fences, despite what is generally considered a handicap to a batter. Medwick is only 20 years old, but he looks much older, and when you see him on the field, you would never classify him as a juvenile. He has the physique, the poise, the speed and skill of a much older athlete.

The next day was a Saturday and there was a doubleheader due to start at two o'clock. Medwick, like most players during that era, walked to the park. He arrived at noon; batting practice would start in another hour, and the Cubs were hitting when he got out on the field.

On Sunday, the team was reminded to bring their luggage to the ballpark since that day was a get-away day, that is, a day when the team would leave by train after they had showered in the clubhouse. When it was time to leave for the park, Medwick felt a little foolish getting on a trolley with luggage, but taxis were expensive, so he rode the trolley anyway, enjoying the breeze along the way.

After showering and dressing, the players made their way to the Dearborn station for the train to Pittsburgh, a ten-hour trip. After they were assigned their sleeper by the traveling secretary, most players headed for the dining car once the "first call for din-

ner" announcement was heard. They arrived in Pittsburgh at 4
A.M. with a game due to start at 10 A.M., part of a Labor Day doubleheader. They checked into the Schenley Hotel and tried napping for a few hours.

When they arrived at Forbes Field at 8 A.M., there were a few fans
lined up outside the park not far from a trolley stop. In that morning game, Joe hit his third double; in the afternoon game he hit both
a single and a double. "Medwick made his first spectacular play yesterday, making a diving catch of Paul Waner's line drive in the afternoon contest. He gets the jump on a ball and covers plenty of
ground. He looks like the best young player the Cardinals have
brought up in years," St. Louis fans read.

The train trip after the doubleheader got the team into Philadelphia at midnight after the three hundred miles from Pittsburgh, but
there was no game on Tuesday. On Wednesday, Medwick, with Ace
Wilson on first, hit a hard grounder to the Pirate first baseman, Don
Hurst, which Hurst had difficulty with. Medwick ran hard to first
and got there safely, but Wilson overran second and was put out.
Medwick growled "Wake up!" at Wilson in the dugout as Wilson
was putting on his catcher's gear.

After the game, some of the players who were friendly to Wilson,
a ten-year player, said loudly, so that Medwick could hear, "Cocky
bastard." "Well, if they don't like me," Medwick thought, "that's
fine. I'm not much of a talker anyway; I'm a doer. I'm here to hit, not
to win a popularity contest. And Wilson should not have been off
that base."

The next day Medwick likely found his locker stuffed with
newspapers. He knew the gag. Some of the players were mocking
him for being so cheap that he would pick up used newspapers in
the lobby rather than buy them new at a stand. Yet they were
afraid of facing Medwick. "You cowardly—," Medwick said quietly, looking at some of his teammates' faces as he opened the
locker. But Manager Street came over to him. "Get your monkey
suit on, Joe. Let's get the Phillies, not the jokesters." Medwick
noisily pulled the papers out of his locker and began to dress. In
front of one thousand spectators, Medwick singled to center, but
the Cardinals lost again by 3-0.

Friday was payday for Medwick—his first big-league check. He
gave it to the clubhouse man to put in the safe for him. Later, Medwick mailed his check home to his mother.

The headline for Stockton's column in the *Post-Dispatch* read "Play of Joe Medwick Dissipates Gloom of Cards Losing Streak," and the article used the "Ducky-Wucky" nickname:

> Medwick had made a hit on this disastrous trip of the Cardinals, and . . . he flashes into the favor of old and learned baseball men. "That kid sure had the power," Charley Grimm volunteered after a couple of games at Wrigley Field. "It looks like you have uncovered a real star in this young Medwick," was the declaration of the astute and gentlemanly Pie Traynor, after the double-header at Pittsburgh. "It looks like the chain-store system finally had developed a real star," was the consensus of the Philadelphia players and . . . Being only 20 years old and lacking the experience of veterans, Medwick will throw to the wrong base occasionally and make other mistakes but he looks like a real ball player. And listen, if you wouldn't call Jack Dempsey "Clarice," and if you wouldn't call Burleigh Grimes "Mehitabel," then please don't call Joe Medwick "Ducky Wucky." If you do, you're a big sissy yourself.

On Saturday, September 10, Medwick played at the Polo Grounds, the park he and his pals had traveled to so many times to watch the Yankees play, and to watch the Giants—the Giants with Frankie Frisch, who was now his teammate. But in the first inning, Medwick, running from second with his head down instead of up, caused Ace Wilson to leave third base so that Wilson had to try to run home, where he was tagged out. When Medwick got back to the dugout, Wilson said, "Well, kid?" Wilson was looking for Medwick to admit his base-running error. Medwick probably thought, "I'll let my playing do the talking for me." During the game, Medwick walked, hit an RBI double, and a two-run homer—his first—in the ninth inning. He also made an excellent running leaping catch in the fourth of Fitzsimmons's drives. But with this loss, the Cardinals found themselves eighteen games behind with sixteen to play. All they could hope for now, great as the odds might be, was to finish in the first division, among the first four in the league, to make bonus money out of the post-season proceeds.

On September 15, the crowd of one thousand at Ebbets Field in Brooklyn saw Medwick, now hitting fifth, double to left field, double to left center, get an infield hit to shortstop, and steal third base. This was against Dazzy Vance, the Dodger veteran who had won over 180 games in his career. For Joe, it was the beginning of many wonderful performances in Ebbets.

The *Sporting News* reported on September 22, "Duckie-Wuckie will do. Medwick continued to look like a real find. He hit two doubles and a single in the game that [Ray "Iron Man"] Starr won from the Dodgers and his two-baggers were tremendous wallops. . . . Medwick also had been steady in the field."

And above Medwick's picture, another article's headline read, "Brighten Cards' Gloom." The article read "he had all the necessary attributes for development into a star."

On the train to Boston that Thursday evening, Medwick may have read the report from the Texas League in the *Sporting News.* Houston had finished at 88-66, and though he had missed two weeks of the season, he led the league in runs batted in with 126, in total bases, and in extra-base hits, while losing the batting title by only 3 points, hitting .354. The All-Star team for the league listed, in addition to Medwick, three players who would soon be teammates in Detroit: Hank Greenberg, Luke Hamlin, and Schoolboy Rowe.

After two games in Boston, a tired group of Cardinals got on the train for the twenty-eight-hour trip over 1,180 miles back to St. Louis. In the ballparks that he had only read about—in Chicago, Pittsburgh, and Boston—Medwick hit nine doubles, one triple, two homers, and made a batting average of .325.

But even with that, as he tried to sleep on the rocking train in his upper berth among snoring teammates, Medwick hoped that those who were against him would stop. Otherwise, he must make them stop.

Some players—Medwick didn't know who—talked behind his back. They loved to call him "rookie," and when he got angry, they told him to "take it easy." How could he win their game? Would they take his job from him? Joe was determined that they would not.

Sometimes a man was measured, Medwick thought, by how much he could tolerate: how much annoyance, how many practical jokes, how many times he would allow himself to be mocked. "Do they want to find out how much of a man I am?" Joe thought. "Fine. I'll have to find a way to show them."

Frisch and Haines may have told him that others considered him unintelligent because his speech was slow and measured. Some wanted him to think that he was not easy to like. But Medwick wasn't at this job to be liked. Some of the team didn't like his confidence—he had heard sportswriters saying the words "brash" and "cocky"; some people thought that he considered himself "hot stuff." "Maybe that's because they don't have my talent," Joe likely thought. He had, of course, not yet shown them enough about his abilities. If they wanted to push, he would push back; he would not back down.

"Some teammates don't like me," Medwick may have thought. "Well, let's see how long they're up here, and how long *I'm* up here. Some teammates, Will Bill Hallahan is one, and Tex Carleton is another, do like me. As for the noisy ones—if they don't like me—tough. I'm here."

And Medwick was producing—producing against superior pitching. Could other players say the same? "The talkers will disappear; I won't," Joe probably thought.

Arriving in St. Louis, Medwick probably found a room, as Don Gutteridge recalled, "in the Forest Park Hotel, where players would stay with or without wives in St. Louis. The place was furnished and you could cook there, saving a lot of money." Historian Erv Fischer at the St. Louis Cardinal Hall of Fame said that Medwick may have rented a room at the Fairground Hotel, just two blocks down Spring Avenue from the ballpark.

Medwick first stepped out on his home field at 1:30 P.M. on September 20, 1932. The home uniform hanging in his locker was the same as the road uniform, except it was white, not gray. Sportsman's Park was one of the larger parks in the majors, with a right field fence at 310 feet, a medium-length left field at 360 feet, and a deep center field at 445 feet. Beyond the center field wall, there was a bar, the Club Boulevard, which was actually part of the ballpark. The outfield walls themselves were concrete and eleven and a half feet high until right center, where wire extended up another twenty-one and a half feet, all the way to the right field foul line. The wire was hung from the right center to the right field bleachers; those bleachers were called the pavilion. The left field stands were also bleachers—uncovered seating—with Sullivan Avenue directly behind left field. The flagpole was in center and in play. The two upper decks of stands wrapped around from one foul pole to the other. Thirty-four thousand spectators could be seated in the park. There was no scoreboard.

Against Cincinnati pitcher Bennie Frey, Medwick went hitless on September 20, but not so the next day. He singled in the second inning, and then stole second. Next, he hit a double to right field and scored in the fourth. In the field he was given an assist in the sixth, putting out Gink Hendrick, who overran second base.

Someone was tormenting Joe now, or trying to. It was, for now, someone Joe knew from Houston. Medwick had replaced George

Puccinelli, known as Pooch, while he was in Houston. Puccinelli had been sent to a lower league, the Three I League, while Medwick stayed in Houston. Puccinelli had played eleven games in the big leagues in 1930 and now he was on the team when Joe was called up. Pooch must have known that Joe was his competition yet again. Puccinelli was almost five years older than Joe, and he would have to make a major league team soon or it would be too late for him. Yet here was this brash kid, twenty years old, out to take his job again. Much Italian and Hungarian cursing probably went on between the two, with each refusing to back down. Other teammates may have been mad because Joe took the place of a former teammate, Chick Hafey. Medwick probably expected this hostility, but he seemed to be unprepared for the vehemence of it.

Thursday was a long day for the Cardinals, as the team owners put some money in their account by having the players play two games. In the day game, the Cardinals ended their sweep of the Reds with an 8-5 win, which moved them into sixth place. In the first inning, Medwick singled to right, advanced to third, and then scored on a double steal when Ray Blades was run down between first and second. In the fourth inning, he singled to center field and then went on to second when Taylor Douthit fumbled the ball. Medwick lined a single off the pitcher's glove in the seventh, moving a run across for a score. Joe typically aimed to take the extra base, which he had done twice in this game.

The second game of the date was previewed in a story with a photograph of ballplayers with beards:

> [T]he Cardinals meet the House of David club in the first night baseball game in the history of Sportsman's Park. . . . The illumination will be provided by the House of David portable lighting system. . . . The game will start at 8:15. . . . Tickets may be obtained in advance . . . on the mezzanine floor of the Arcade Building. . . . All members of the House of David club . . . wear beards and long hair. Grover Cleveland Alexander, manager of the . . . club will be the starting pitcher for the visitors. . . . If the game proves a success, it [is] possible [that] major league magnates may be influenced to allow an occasional night game during the regular league schedule next year.

So Medwick played in the first night game at his home park in only his third game there. (He would be invited to be there when the same park closed thirty-four years later.)

Medwick made two hits and scored against the Pirates on Friday. Saturday, before a year-end crowd of 750, Pop Haines was called in relief with one out in the first inning and pitched the rest of the game. Medwick supported his friend with a hit in the eighth, a double off the right field screen, driving in first baseman Ripper Collins, but the Cardinals lost 7-4 nevertheless.

The last day of the season was on Sunday, and it was the second doubleheader in four days. In center field again, Medwick, batting fifth, went 3-4 and then 1-4 in the second game, which the Cardinals won.

On this same day, as the Pirates defeated the Cardinals 7-1 in the first game, Pirate outfielder Paul Waner set a new National League record with his 62nd double. The record had been owned by Chuck Klein, who had made fifty-nine doubles in 1930 as a Philadelphia Phillies outfielder. (The Cardinal outfielder, Joe Medwick, would break that record in four years.)

In twenty-six games, Medwick batted .349, with thirty-seven hits, forty-nine total bases, and twelve doubles. His slugging average was .538, and his on-base percentage was .367. Playing in 16 percent of his team's games, he was nevertheless ninth in steals and tenth in doubles.

As he was cleaning out his locker, Medwick was told he would be sent a contract around Christmastime and after he checked out of the Forest Park Hotel, he rode the train back to New York and then to Carteret, while Frankie Frisch and a part-time infielder, Jake Flowers, drove back to New York City.

After Bottomley's off-season trade to the Reds, Ripper Collins would be the regular first baseman for the Cardinals and left field would belong to Joe.

7

Playing Left Field for the Cardinals, 1933

Medwick's contract apparently was the subject of much discussion among the Casaleggi brothers, Benny Zussman (now writing for the Carteret *Press*), pal John Szelag, and Medwick himself during the winter months at the dances at St. Elias and games at the Red Star Billiard Academy. Charles Casaleggi, nicknamed "Peanuts," did not talk as much as his brother, John, who was nicknamed "Beaner."

Beaner wanted to know what sort of salary Meddi could expect. Medwick answered "$3,000"—rookie money, paid from game 1 to game 154, with no money during spring training.

"What did Meddi know about the owners?" Medwick's buddies wondered. Sam Breadon was a good-time fellow—an Irishman from Manhattan, who sang Irish ballads and barbershop quartet songs with a thick New York accent. He loved his scotch, was a great salesman (reputed to have sold 280 Pierce Arrows in one year), and he didn't mind firing managers, including one who was now the other stockholder and vice president, Branch Rickey. After the club finished seventh in 1919 while on the verge of bankruptcy, Sam Breadon bought 72 percent of the stock; Rickey owned the rest.

Rickey did the hiring, buying, and contracting. Rickey may have been getting, in addition to his salary, 10 percent or more of the profits from the sales of ballplayers. (Rickey would average around $38,000 each year with the Cardinals.) So the less he paid you now, the more he could pay himself later when he sold your contract. Some said that Rickey was in the business of selling baseball players, not in the business of baseball. Because he was part-owner as well, he collected a piece of the profits of the team; some of the profits came from selling players' contracts.

If a player would not sign for the amount the club offered, he would be sent elsewhere through trade. The "elsewhere," if Rickey was vituperative, could be a city that would not earn any postseason money for the player. Rickey could also release the player to a minor league team. Or the player could be forced to leave professional baseball, labeled as "suspended" or "ineligible." These three choices were what the reserve clause meant.

"And what have you got to sell them?" Beaner wanted to know.

"I'll probably start in left field this year. Hafey is gone; the job is mine. That should be worth something."

"And what weapons do we have?"

"I can hold out for more money—not sign—and hope that they decide they must have me play for them, and then they'll offer me more money."

"Okay," Beaner must have said, "let me be your manager. Don't you talk to Rickey."

In his fifteen years of business dealings, Rickey's tough talk was often used to overpower, impress, confuse—to wear people down. Joe believed in action, in performance, not in words; he acknowledged his limitations in both education and language. "Let me do it," Beaner urged. "That way, if he gets pissed off, he'll be pissed off at me, not you."

"Go ahead," said Medwick.

And when the contract arrived in the mail that January, all that was needed was for Medwick to sign. Medwick would not sign; instead, Beaner would negotiate.

The salary offered was by now more than three times the annual pay of physical laborers. A new Dodge automobile could be bought for $585 dollars. It was unlikely that many people, if anyone in all of Carteret, was making the amount of money that was being offered to Medwick.

What Medwick was doing was scarcely practiced: he was a rookie and yet he was holding out. Some of his teammates cursed him for his arrogance—he was challenging the near-legendary Branch Rickey, who everyone called "Mister." Some admired Medwick for his conviction, his "pluck," as it was called. Some didn't concern themselves with anyone else's salary.

But Medwick either didn't know about all of this or he just didn't care. He wanted what he wanted. He wanted what he was worth, and he was worth a great deal, in both money and respect. Medwick would have his justice.

Meanwhile, second baseman Frankie Frisch's salary, which had been cut from $28,000 to $18,500 in 1932, was reduced further to under $10,000. The team had a new rule: there would be no salaries over $10,000 for that year.

At the end of January, Beaner Casaleggi must have been having heated telephone calls from the Red Star Billiard Academy, with Rickey, and Medwick and his pals must have been delighted. Then outfielder George "Pooch" Puccinelli refused to sign, so he was sent to Rochester, where he spent the entire year. (Sometimes players were paid more in the minors than a major league owner would be willing to pay.)

On March 1, Rickey announced to his newspaper pals that "He [Medwick] had a manager who was advising him against acceptance of the terms offered. As a result, Medwick had received an ultimatum from me which said that he can sign at the figure offered or he will be released, probably to Rochester. Medwick's manager offered to compromise but we replied that there was no compromise possible." The terms dictated by Rickey were reluctantly accepted, and Medwick began to make plans to go south. Rickey always called Medwick "Joseph," as if Medwick were his child and he, the stern parent.

The Orange Blossom Special that left New York's Pennsylvania Station at 10:05 A.M. took Medwick to Florida. The train, advertised as "the only all-Pullman train from New York to Miami," arrived in Tampa in twenty-nine hours. From there, Medwick traveled to Bradenton, where the Cardinals had trained since 1923, and checked in at the Dixie Grande Hotel, where the team slept and ate.

Spring training, called "the training season" in 1933, was still a time for players to accomplish two main things: first, they were to get rid of any extra weight that may have been put on during the winter, and second, they were to get their legs in shape. These two tasks were achieved by "running 'til you drop," which was the best measure of how much running a player ought to do. In the off-season in those days, most of the players had some kind of job. Their efforts to stay in shape were very casual, particularly in the north. Some would play basketball; some might do elementary exercises like sit-ups. To players of that era, getting in "shape" meant getting your wind and your legs ready for the season.

The rest was hitting and throwing. Hitting was worked on without a batting cage, since that device was another eight years away from its first appearance, and it would be many years after the 1941 experiment in Cuba before it came into general use. So at most, a wheeled backstop behind the catcher would be used.

Monday, March 13, work began, with exactly a month until the season began. Medwick was now a rookie in camp, with a very good chance at making the team. For years in baseball, as far back as the beginning of the century, a rookie player meant, to some members of the team, a man who was trying to steal a paycheck from a friend. This was true for Cobb, Medwick, and Jackie Robinson. And Medwick was a rookie who held out. The resentful players thought, "This guy was trying to send my friend down to the minors or off of this team!" This social organization, of course, was a company of men who lived together and shared a physical profession. So it was to be expected that the testing of the newcomer would be physical. Pour water in his shoes while he's in the shower. Take his razor blades. Throw at him. Tag him hard. Trip him when he runs. Make him earn his spot. See if he's got what it takes.

This rookie hazing, ostensibly waged to test the mettle of a man, his spunk, was also a way to be cruel to him for trying to alter the intimate social relationships of a team. Yet all the players knew the intransigence of playing for a businessman such as Branch Rickey; much of the mettle testing was simply an honored tradition, a rite of passage.

The ritual could become more complicated because a rookie might put money into your pocket while taking it out of your friend's. If the rookie was a very good player, he would help the team win. How well a rookie held up against the hazing would depend largely on how willingly he accepted this tradition of abuse.

Joe was a "private guy" practically his whole life, as Bing Devine told me. He was not unfriendly, just introspective. "Out of uniform, he simply didn't look for attention."

But Medwick got results. He was doing a job, and part of that job was to show his talent and be proud of it, not humble.

Medwick was twenty-one years old, the youngest player in the training camp. Only Burgess Whitehead, twenty-three, a well-educated southerner, was near his age. Everyone else, except for a few pitchers, was ten years or more older than Medwick.

Like many other ballplayers, Medwick had few social skills. He acted "cocky," his opponents would say; "assured" was what his friends said. Medwick was not skillful at accepting anything that resembled contempt being directed at him or at his abilities. So when tricks were played he tried not to show any reaction.

But then some went too far for Medwick. As he was about to step up to the plate for his swings, someone would grab at his belt or step into the batters' box before he got a chance to get set. Batters had a limited number of swings in batting practice simply because so many players needed to hit. Trying to stop Medwick from hitting was a mistake. He would shove, yell, and let his tormentors know that he would not be denied. Many who looked into his dark, flashing eyes decided to let him have his turn before he took stronger action with that black bat in his hands. Somehow the bat looked bigger in his hands than in someone else's.

In the wonderful book *The Gashouse Gang*, author Robert E. Hood quoted teammate Pat Crawford: "They gave him a hard time. The veterans rode him viciously. They wanted him put in his place, not to be too much of a take-charge guy. Right from the start, Joe wanted to be a big star. If he wasn't getting that publicity, he'd gripe about it. In those days, Crawford pointed out, rookies were 'to be seen and not heard.'"

Medwick may or may not have been aware that his manager (Gabby Street), Branch Rickey, and Sam Breadon were watching all of this baiting and testing. The other players were also watching it, gauging how Medwick was taking it. Other rookies were getting the needle as well. But Medwick did not take the hazing with equanimity; he took it with belligerence. He was not here to be razzed; he was here to be a star. This was the big leagues—this was where he belonged. And he began to understand how important it was for him to be in the big leagues, apart from the money.

Spring training was not entirely awful for Medwick; he began to sense the respect he was getting from the other players. His hits were somehow more impressive—those line drives he hit all over the park. He started so many games in left field that soon everyone knew that was where he would be on the opening day of the season. And if he helped them to the World Series and they won it, then he could help each one of them to add $5,000 or more to their wages. (Most of the players were not making $5,000 for the year.)

As the team moved north, Medwick stayed with them. He was the left fielder. And as the season got closer, the hazing continued (as he tried to sleep, there always seemed to be a lot of noise outside his upper berth), but it became less frequent, if not less severe. It was an annoyance nevertheless. Still, they had not stopped him from batting; they had not stopped him from playing; they had not stopped him from making the team.

The Cardinals finished spring training at 3-5 in interleague play, though they did better within their own league. Next would be the annual series, the City Series, with the Browns, the American League team that shared the park with the Cardinals. Both teams agreed on the segregation of the stands by races; African Americans were only allowed seats in right field. In fact, black professional baseball players, who were given free admission to every other major league park, and who had, in fact, played in those parks, were denied free admission here.

After those two City Series games, the Cardinals had an exhibition record of 14 and 8, the season to begin on Wednesday, April 12.

Medwick knew he was the only new permanent starter in the lineup. (Oskie Slade, playing shortstop, was new to the Cardinals, coming from Brooklyn that year, but he came to bat sixty-two times in 1933.) Of the sixty-four possible jobs in the National League as a starting position player (a player other than a pitcher), Medwick was one of only four rookies. Gabby Street had him bat fifth, a tribute to his run-making possibilities. Joe knew it was something of an honor on the team to be placed so high in the batting order. The other starting outfielders were Ernie Orsatti in center and George Watkins in right.

Opening day was April 13, 1933, in Chicago, the first big-league park that Medwick had played in. The uniform was the same one he had pulled on in 1932, except the stockings below the knicker pants were white on top, followed by bands of red, blue, and white, and all red at the bottom. The other change was the use of the word "Cardinals" on the chest of both home and road uniforms, which has continued ever since.

"Opening day ceremonies preceded the game," J. Roy Stockton of the *St. Louis Post-Dispatch*'s sports staff wrote. "There was a parade to the flag pole with a band leading the line of march, the flag was raised to the strains of the National Anthem, many pictures were taken, flowers presented and then the umpires, Charley Rigler and George Magerkurth, started the contest."

The team traveled home from Chicago to St. Louis for the first game at home that year with Medwick hitting 1-9. Some of the Cardinals reminded him of it. They likely read him his batting average every day. "The season is young," Medwick could answer. They didn't know that he was on his way to make 181 more hits that year.

Medwick was getting to know some of his teammates better. Pepper Martin was mostly called "Johnnie" in the clubhouse. Dizzy Dean was "Diz" ("Jerome" to Frisch), and sometimes Ernie Orsatti was called "Showboat." Everybody seemed to like Coach Mike Gonzales, who called Joe "Yoe." Gonzales was known for not being exact in the pronunciation of English, which was his second language, but he knew his baseball. Once, when asked for a report on a player, Gonzales wired the soon-famous baseball expression, "good field, no hit."

In *The Gashouse Gang,* Hood claims that Tex Carleton "considered himself a benefactor of the young slugger from Carteret. The tall Texan had played with him at Houston and knew what a great prospect he was and how much he could help a ball club. 'It wasn't easy to come up to the majors in those days,' Carleton said. Older players didn't lay out welcome mats for rookies. As Carleton put it, 'You kind of had to fight your way in.'"

The first game at Sportsman's Park that year for the Cardinals was on April 20. Medwick noticed the boys who were in seats where he warmed up in left. There were a lot of boys for a school day, but it was the opening game. The boys saw him at the plate, holding his bat high in the air and waving it like a weapon being shown to an enemy. As the pitch was being sighted, Medwick raised his front leg, and as the bat came down and around, he would stride solidly forward. He did not miss often. It may have been that power and strength that attracted the boys, but whatever it was, a strong affection developed between him and the boys, members of the Knothole club, an affection that would last decades. The boys began to notice his superstition of stepping on third base with his right foot and nicking it with his left on his way in from left field.

The triple Medwick hit was one of six hits that day, and he scored the only run. In his next twenty at bats to the end of April he hit .450 with nine hits and ended the month hitting .351. He was tenth in the National League in average, but led his team, which was in seventh place, next to last. By now the team saw clearly that Medwick hit pitches solidly, pitches that no one else was likely to be able to reach.

When he was ready to swing, he made an instant adjustment to where the pitch was, and sent it deep. He used a Jimmie Foxx-model bat much of the time, a bat that was thirty-six inches long and thirty-six ounces in weight. With a bat that long, Medwick knew he could get to many pitches. And he hit them, as his statistics show. He struck out only 9 percent of his times at bat. (Foxx would strike out 16 percent of his times at bat that year.)

Nevertheless, the attacks on Medwick continued. "Medwick was treated roughly in '33, too roughly, some of the Cardinals felt. The savage riding might break his spirit. Tex Carleton took his part. 'I almost had a fight defending him,' he recalled." It seemed odd that a .351 hitter would have to defend himself, or have someone defend him, but he had offended some people—Dizzy Dean, for one. Medwick's youth and brashness, as well as his talent and courting of the press, alienated some team members. Although the snipers seemed to be few, they were loud. Medwick didn't bother to figure out who his detractors were, perhaps because he couldn't do anything about it anyway or because he was too busy hitting.

In May, the Cardinals traveled east, and the weekly averages showed Medwick hitting .302, placing seventeenth in the league. The Cardinals, for one game in Brooklyn, were in third place. As the Cardinals were halving a doubleheader, Breadon and Rickey made an important decision to try to get the team into first place. Charlie Gelbert, the man who had been the regular shortstop since 1929, was not playing because in November 1932, he had almost lost a foot in a hunting accident. The Cardinal owners, especially Rickey, had disapproved of the living habits of pitcher Paul Derringer for some time, and probably the amount of his contract as well. Rickey, who was comfortable doing business with Sid Weil's Reds, knew that Weil was unhappy with the free-spending living habits of his shortstop, Leo Durocher. The trade for Durocher was announced from Rickey's bed, where he frequently took his meals and conducted his business. (It was his way of letting people know their place.) In describing the trade, the *New York Times* called Durocher "the greatest fielding shortstop of the day." Since Cincinnati was in New York to play the Giants, Durocher simply showed up at Ebbets Field in Brooklyn to begin his work with the Cardinals.

So the Cardinals got a great fielding shortstop, but they gave up a starting pitcher. Rickey, lauded in the press for his ability to judge baseball ability, traded away a 26-year-old pitcher who would win almost two hundred more games after he left the Cardinals, for a great fielding shortstop who only once would hit above .265 with the Cardinals, and only twice in his entire career. Medwick must have been rooming with Fish Hook Stout, a pitcher, or with Sparky Adams. Those players, being traded with Derringer, left an open spot to room on the road with Medwick, which was filled by Durocher.

Durocher was almost twenty-eight years old with five years' experience as a big-league shortstop, including the 1928 Yankees, with whom he was a part-time infielder, coming to bat twice in the World Series against the team he now played for, the Cardinals. The St. Louis newspaper's headline shouted, "Durocher at Short Gives Cards New Life," because Durocher was "one of the best defensive men the game had produced in a decade."

In Durocher's first game with the Cardinals, Medwick hit a home run against Freddie Fitzsimmons into the upper deck above the Polo Grounds' left field. "So I'm happy. Me, a rookie," Medwick recalled years later, "hitting a home run off Freddie Fitzsimmons. All around the bases, I'm grinning. But when I got to home plate, there stood Fitz. 'Why you bush so and so,' he growls at me. 'It's all right for you to hit a home run off me, but you ain't gonna laugh your head off at me as you circle those bases! You'd better be ready the next time you come up.' And sure enough, my next time at bat, Fitz tries to stick one in my ear and I hit the dirt. But quick." Tex Carleton got the win, side-arming his pitches, with Dean relieving for a 4-3 victory.

The next two days were rainouts, and then the team was off to Boston. During this time, Medwick had plenty of time to get to know his new roommate. There were likenesses between Durocher and Medwick. They both enjoyed pool, straight pool, which Medwick had become so proficient in back in Carteret; Durocher actually gave exhibitions in pool. Both men seemed to be fearless, and they also shared the Catholic religion. Medwick wore a rosary around his neck as a sign of his belief, and Durocher was known to go to daily Mass. And Durocher could always spot talent.

Medwick saw Durocher's ferocity in Frisch and in Pop Haines ("When his eyes grew wide, we all got out of the way," Hood reports Medwick saying), and he admired that passion for winning and for the game.

Brash young rookies usually got harsh treatment from the veterans. Mel Ott was no brash rookie. "He wouldn't open his mouth

... so everyone was happy to help him," Fred Fitzsimmons said in Eugene Murdock's *Baseball Players and Their Times.*

But Joe Medwick was a different type. He was a good one, but he was fresh. We're playing the Cardinals in the Polo Grounds. The count went to one-and-one and I threw one under his chin. Then I threw him a knuckleball which he popped to the second baseman. He ran down to first base and then cut across the infield to the St. Louis dugout. When he got by me he said, "Why don't you go and warm up?" I didn't say anything to him. Gus Mancuso was my catcher. The next time Medwick came up I got him out on a ground ball to Terry. I covered the bag on the play as he came running down the line. He said something else fresh to me, like, "you haven't got enough to hurt anybody." Now I replied, saying, "Next time up, if I'm still out here let's find out."

So the third time Medwick came up, Mancuso didn't give me a sign. He was just standing up. He was waiting for Medwick to walk into the batter's box. Then he yelled out, "Here he is; what are you gonna do about it?" I called back, "You just get down and tell me what you think I should do." So he kneeled down and gave me "the thumb." I threw one right up here. His bat flew, his hat flew, and he went down, dirt all over his uniform. He got back up, brushed himself off, got his hat on and the bat in his hands and stepped in there again. He didn't say a word. So I gave him another one and down he goes again. He never opened his mouth. I got him out, nothing-for-four.

The next day I'm working out at shortstop in infield practice. Both clubhouses were in center field at the Polo Grounds, so the players had to come right through the middle of the diamond to go to their dugouts. Now Medwick was coming in from the outfield and going right by me. I didn't know if he was going to take a pop at me or what. He put his hand on my shoulder and said, "I just want to apologize to you. I don't blame you. I shouldn't have opened my big mouth to you." I said, "I'm awfully glad you said this because if you hadn't, those other fastball pitchers, like Parmelee and some of the others, were going to throw at you and one of them was going to hurt you. They won't mean to, but they'll hurt you." "Well," he said, "I just had to tell you." And that was good enough for me. All the rest of the time he played against me he never opened his mouth—and I knocked him down a couple of times. And then later we were teammates with the Dodgers.

Two and a half weeks after the first All-Star game, the Cardinals' All-Star second baseman, Frankie Frisch, was named to replace Gabby Street as manager of the team. Breadon said, "He had been the spark plug of the team ever since we obtained him from New York." Nobody doubted that Frisch was the "hardest-boiled egg in the Redbird nest." The same day he was hired, Frisch told team members, "If I find a single man on my club who is contented to play out his games without trying to win—he's through with the Cardinals."

Frisch, thirty-five, was a wonderfully odd mix of a man. Educated in chemistry at Fordham, he never played an inning of minor league baseball, but was a winner almost from his first at bat with the New York Giants. He had already played on seven World Series teams and wanted another chance at big money.

Frisch's model for managing was his first manager, John McGraw ("Muggsy the martinet"). But Medwick respected Frisch. Robert E. Hood recorded Medwick saying,

> Frankie was a great manager. He never gave up. He was a good teacher. He never bothered you. When you made a mistake, he'd take you aside and talk to you. He never showed you up, which was a great thing. And the way I always felt was: When I made a mistake I wanted the manager to tell me, not the other players. A player's got enough to take care of his own position and his own job. And I would not allow anybody to tell me . . . that I had made a mistake. Frankie Frisch, my manager, would tell me.

The two men with the thick New York accents would come to admire each other's play greatly.

Joe knew that this was a man's game, a team's game. No women were ever allowed in the clubhouse at any time; in fact, apart from the players, very few people ever came into the dressing area. In the clubhouse, as well as on the field, masculine virtues were never questioned, never doubted. A man was brave, stoic, and free to do whatever he decided to do. A man would be valued for his endurance, strength, his stamina, and comradeship. Part of that comradeship was a dedication to winning, to helping the whole team. This way of behaving and playing came from the John McGraw school of the predominance of winning. For Joe, there was no one in baseball who was a winner like Frankie Frisch. Just as Frisch would be powerfully affected by his first big-league manager, John McGraw, so Medwick would be powerfully affected by the man who managed him for the longest time.

August began in Pittsburgh, and on the second, early in the game, Medwick popped up to the catcher, Bob Grace, on a good pitch.

Medwick was furious, particularly because he was in a slump, a period when he was getting no hits, so he slammed the catcher's mask with his bat, bending the mask. Grace was forced to go to the dugout to get another. In the ninth inning, shortstop Arky Vaughan grounded out and attempted to block the path of pitcher Bill Walker, who was covering first base. When Walker pushed Vaughan away to make his play on Paul Waner, the runner on third, Vaughan took a punch at Walker. Walker threw one himself and while the fight was going on, Waner scored. Frisch, Wares, and Gonzales screamed that Waner must be sent back to third. While that was happening, Walker and Vaughan were told to leave the field. When a soda pop bottle hit Walker, he dared the thrower to come out and fight him, but the umpire, Ernie Quigley, moved Walker away. Meanwhile, Umpire George Magerkurth sent Waner back to third and "the spectators in the left field stands showed their displeasure by throwing several dozen pop bottles to the field." Medwick drove in the game-winning run in the twelfth. (Because he went 8-17 in the rest of the series, Medwick began to believe that whomping catcher's masks was a magic cure for ending a slump. When Grace gave him a bill for $8 for the new mask that the catcher needed, that ended Joe's belief in the good luck of whomping a mask.)

By now it was clear to the team that Medwick was here to stay. His fielding ability, hitting prowess, and his hustle had all been apparent. The team saw that Medwick delivered on his promises, and much preferred his relatively quiet demeanor to the noisy banter of some of the others. There was no more "Ducky-Wucky" for Medwick among the players. Even the occasional "Ducky" by itself sounded more affectionate than taunting.

Some of Medwick's ideas were supported by various team members as well as by the team trainer, "Bucko" Weaver, who "ministered to the morale and muscle of the St. Louis Cardinals from 1927," as Bob Broeg described him. It was Weaver who used the term "buckerinos." Among professionals, money does count; among workers, money is important. "I have two good friends in the world, the buckerinos and the base hits. If I get the base hits, I will get the buckerinos." Medwick, at age twenty-one, got a lot of attention for saying this. No doubt he sounded sufficiently worldly-wise to himself; how much of it he really believed is impossible to say.

Medwick had made some friends on the team. While he was out of the circle of Martin and Dean, Medwick had probably enjoyed the company of Durocher, seeing another part of life. Durocher and Medwick both enjoyed the company of another flamboyant player, Ernie Orsatti. Orsatti, who the newspapers called "the Hollywood Wop," threatened to go back and join his Hollywood brother in the business of managing actors and actresses.

By the time the road trip was over, the team had won eleven times and lost eleven. Clearly, no ground would be gained. Returning back to St. Louis, they were in fifth place.

All the team had to play for now was first-division money. If the team finished second, third, or fourth in the league of eight, each player made extra money. Of course, the team that won the pennant went into the World Series, and each player then would probably make about $3,000 if he was on the losing team and about $5,000 if he was on the winning team.

Dean won his twentieth game on September 12 against Brooklyn, and now led the major leagues in strikeouts, but Bill Hallahan lost the next day. Syl Johnson's win in the first game of a Saturday doubleheader was aided by Medwick's three-run home run, as well as his other two RBIs and two runs scored. Medwick was also the last man on a triple steal as Watkins stole home, Frisch third, and Medwick second in the seventh inning. Pepper Martin hit a double, throwing his bat at the ball, and Terry Moore made his first major league hit in the first game. The second game was called a no contest because too few innings were played before dark.

On September 24 against Pittsburgh, Medwick hit a home run in the win. He was also struck by a pitch. The Cardinal win meant that if they won the two games left, they'd get third-place money. If they won one of the games, they'd get fourth-place money.

The Cardinals lost both, scoring just three runs to nineteen by the Cubs. Had the Cardinals won, "they would have received fourth-place money and would have received between $300 and $400 apiece as a cut from the series melon." They finished out of the money by three percentage points, .539 to .536.

John Thorn and Pete Palmer, in their 1994 *Total Baseball* report:

In 1957, formal guidelines were finally established for determining rookie status. A player could not have accumulated more than 75 at-bats, 45 innings pitched, or had been on a major league roster between May 15 and September 1 of any previous season. Shortly after, the guidelines were changed to 90 at-bats, 45 innings pitched or 45 days on a major league roster before September 1. Finally, in 1971, the guidelines were set at 130 at-bats, 50 innings, or 45 days on a roster.

Joe's time in 1932 was for 106 at bats, making 1933 his rookie year.

Total Baseball picked Frank Demaree of the Cubs for its 1933 "Hypothetical Rookie of the Year" award. Yet Medwick hit 34 points higher in 14 more games than Demaree, with 42 more hits and 47 more RBIs.

When the Most Valuable Player in the League votes were published, Joe Medwick was in eighteenth place with five votes. He was given these votes because he was in the top five in the National League in seven categories: runs scored, doubles, runs batted in, runs produced, slugging percentage, total bases, and home runs. His home runs equaled 4 percent of the league total. He was thirteenth in batting average, seventh in triples, and sixth in total hits. His batting average was 40 points above the league average.

Medwick was also fourth among the league's outfielders in assists with 17, and tenth in fielding average for outfielders. Even though he walked only 26 times, he was twenty-third in the league in onbase percentage, partly because he only struck out 9 percent of the time he was at bat. Medwick put the ball in play.

For a Cardinal rookie, Joe's 40 doubles and 296 total bases in 1933 stood as the team record until the 2001 season, after more than one hundred years of Cardinal baseball.

8

The Gashouse Year, 1934

If business manager Branch Rickey wanted to see what Medwick had done in the league when it came time to sign a contract for 1934, Medwick could show the executive his impressive contribution to the team in 1933: he was first in RBIs and home runs, second in batting average and times at bat. He batted in 14 percent of the team's runs, had hit 31 percent of their home runs, had produced 25 percent of the runs scored by the Cardinals, and led the outfielders of St. Louis with putouts and assists (seventeen), something that was usually reserved for the center fielder.

But no matter how well Medwick, or any other player, succeeded, the fact was that the team had finished fifth, and attendance had been 256,000. And Rickey had been complaining about attendance, which was something of a straw man for him, since he never did bring up revenues from selling players.

Frankie Frisch visited Ripper Collins in Rochester during the winter, and then went to see Joe. Frisch and Medwick had both been very good football players, Frisch a second team All-American at Fordham. Both had a low level of patience with indifference and underachievement. "If intolerance of mediocrity is a crime," Frisch loved to say, "I plead guilty." Frisch admired Medwick's hustle and his dedication to baseball; they stayed great friends for many years, Frisch being a kind of father figure to Medwick.

Frisch, like Medwick's mother, called him "Joey." So it was no surprise that their visit went well.

Medwick, who signed on February 10, probably got a $2,000 raise to $5,000. That is, $217.39 for each week of the twenty-three weeks of the season, or for fifty-two weeks, $96.15 per week.

The Cardinal training camp had a clubhouse that was really a wooden barracks building, its floor raised off the ground. Two practices were scheduled from 10 to 11:30 A.M. and 2 to 4 P.M. each day. None of the players were given any cash. Their room and board was paid by the team. The men walked back and forth to the team hotel, the Dixie Grande (later the Manatee), and they took all their meals as a team. After workouts, Joe played golf, swam, or shot pool.

"Before the Cardinals broke camp," as Robert E. Hood tells it, "manager Frankie Frisch made a fire eating speech: 'Don't let anybody push you around. . . . Your nights [are] your own, but your bodies belong to the Cardinals in the daylight. . . . Now if you'd rather go back to the mines and dig coal or ride around the country in Pullmans and live in the best hotels at the expense of the club, speak right up. We haven't any room for softies, no holds . . . barred. That's the way we're going to play ball.'"

The manager of the Giants, Bill Terry, claimed the loss of right fielder George Watkins would hurt the Cardinals and help the Giants, Watkins's new team. Though the Cardinals were known for their "swift-moving game," the team was picked to finish fourth in a before-season poll of ninety-seven sportswriters, receiving thirteen first-place votes.

The Cardinals finished their twenty-one-game exhibition schedule for 1934 with the City Series games with the Browns. Joe and many teammates moved into semiprivate rooms at the Coronado Hotel for the season.

As for the coaching staff, Buzzy Wares was an experienced coach who wore steel-rimmed glasses and liked to dance on the lines at first, and Gonzales was smart and noisy at third, a skilled sign stealer. Frisch led by example. He called many of the pitches using hand signals. While the team's speed promised to produce runs and extra-base hits along with steals, the Cardinal pitching was now much younger on average than it had been in 1933. Walker and Moon Hallahan were thirty, but Tex Carleton was twenty-seven, Dizzy Dean was twenty-three, and Paul Dean, only twenty. Pepper Martin was at third, Durocher at short, Frisch at second, and Ripper

Collins on first. Spud Davis and Dee Delancey handled the catching. The outfield was shaping up to be Rothrock in right, Orsatti in center (Chuck Fullis would substitute and hit against lefties), and Joe Medwick in left. Frisch named Durocher team captain. This was the Gashouse Gang.

By now Medwick's reputation as a hard hitter and a consistent performer was secure. When he was not being called "a one-man rampage," sportswriters summoned up "the Hungarian Rhapsody." Frisch said, "He can do everything—hit, run, throw, and think. . . . He's always got his head up, always trying." The manager acknowledged "that he hit too many bad balls . . . [but] figure[d] experience [would] curb the tendency." Said one reporter of Manager Frisch, "Frank does not try to change a natural hitter."

Medwick was working very hard at his craft. Sliding, bat selection, and base running were just three of the aspects of his game at which he was trying to become more skilled. He had ordered a bat to be his own signature model, a bat fashioned from a thirty-five-inch, thirty-five-ounce Jimmie Foxx model, but with a Chick Hafey-style knob. Coming to bat he carried his own resin bag in his back pocket at a time when most players used the dirt on their hands before coming to bat.

Medwick, hazed so often by some team members in 1933, was clearly accepted in spring training in 1934. And though remnants of the hazing persisted, the "Ducky-Wucky" label that he hated so much was almost gone. It was certainly gone from the mouths of his teammates. Now he was just "Joe." The mocking was over partly because Medwick delivered, and delivered under pressure. He was one of the gang now.

The only uniform change was in the stockings, a change from white to red at the top, and the Cardinals started their season with park announcer Jim Kelly using his megaphone when needed. At the end of April, the Cardinals were in sixth place with four wins in eleven games. Medwick did his best in that span, hitting .325, including three homers, and driving in nine runs.

On May 3, Medwick hit a bases-loaded home run into the left field bleachers in the fourth inning (the term "grand slam" was not yet in use at that time), and with five RBIs, he helped Paul Dean to get his first big-league win; the Cardinals got to fifth place.

The roster needed to be cut, however, so Burleigh Grimes was released on May 15. There was other news, including the following from a writer for the *St. Louis Star-Times:*

Yesterday Joe Medwick and Tex Carleton showed a new punch but not with their bats. They used fists. During batting practice, Carleton objected to Medwick taking a turn [during] the first fifteen-minute time that pitchers were hitting, and Medwick shouted, "I'm tired of taking your abuse!"

"Well, let's go," Carleton shouted back.

Round one was on. They both swung wild, Medwick leading with a hard right that grazed Carleton's left eye. The pitcher came back with a right hook that caught the outfielder flush on the chin. They sparred. Medwick connected with a hard right, and Carleton missed an uppercut. By this time, other players intervened and pulled them part. Both insisted the row arose on the spur of the moment and was not the aftermath of two defeats suffered by Carleton due to fielding mistakes by the man with whom he scuffled. Later the two men shook hands and agreed to bury the hatchet, but not in each other's head.

This story was often used to show how ruthless and belligerent Medwick was thought to be. Yet Carleton gave well, and maybe better, than he had received. The true origins of the quarrel were fourfold: first, Medwick loved hitting and would take any extra time that he could. For this, some players admired his hard work; some thought he was a pain in the neck. Second, some of the pitchers also loved to hit, but all of them were given a space of just fifteen minutes to hit. Third, there was a line on almost all baseball teams between pitchers and position players. Fourth, as Leo Durocher knew, "He [Medwick] was being paid by a magazine to pose. Carleton didn't know, or care, about that." When Robert E. Hood asked Carleton in 1974 about this two-punch fight—one per man—Tex commented, "hell—it wasn't serious. We became friends within fifteen minutes and remain friends to this day." Medwick knew that Carleton not only liked him but had stood up for him the previous year. Medwick also knew he had better not back down. Years later, Joe told Hood, "A young feller had to learn to protect himself. They'd run you out of there. They'd run you out of the batter's box."

While maintaining his friendship with Tex, Joe also knew that violence with a teammate could be useful to him. Later Medwick said about the incident, "They never stopped me again." Territoriality is important to everyone, and in Medwick's territory there was money to be made.

Joe told the story to Robert E. Hood this way: "I went to hit 15 minutes before the pitchers hit. . . . I hit him right there and that was it. They never stopped me again. I got permission from the manager and that's good enough for me. And no one said another word after that. That was it."

This incident was something that appeared from that day on whenever someone wrote about Joe Medwick. Research has revealed that Medwick had only three other fights in his nineteen years of professional baseball. (Two were with teammates.) Many people had confused Medwick's style of playing—his aggressive hitting, base running, and fielding—with his personality.

J. Roy Stockton wrote in the *Post-Dispatch* at the end of May:

> There was one man in the Cardinal camp whose war club played a most important part in the Redbirds' drive to the top of the National league. Joseph Michael Medwick was the slugger, and during the twelve games on the road he clouted the old American apple for 26 hits in 53 times at bat, including a home run, four triples, and four doubles. Hostile pitchers tried every trick in the bag. They pitched inside, and Joe whacked the ball against the left field fence. They pitched outside, and he banged extra base hits down the right field line. They pitched high and low, fast and slow, and they haven't found a weakness.

Medwick must have been pleased that his ability was being recognized. He was not merely a bad-ball hitter, a label that was often slapped on him. He did not hit only bad balls; he was an all-ball hitter.

Stockton continued his summary:

> Pitchers were calling Joe Medwick the most dangerous hitter in the league. Last year he tended to fold up in the pinches, largely because he was so eager he would swing at bad balls. Now he makes the pitcher get the ball within reach of the bat. It doesn't have to be in the strike zone. But he must be able to reach it. He won't swing any more if the pitchers roll the ball to the catcher or bounce it in front of the plate, but when it's within reach, he's likely to slam it against the fence.

But along with this positive, even flattering, comment on his play on the field were two other observations: "Other players in the league say that [the young Hungarian] . . . [is] a bit 'chesty.' 'Why shouldn't he be?' retorted a teammate. 'If I could hit as far and as often as he does, you would have to send your name into the office boy before I would speak to you.'"

"Chesty" here can mean many things. If "other players in the league" had that label for Medwick, they meant he was arrogant. Medwick was still establishing himself as a player. Humility was not the way to prove your worth. A teammate agreed that Joe was boastful, and that he should be; he had earned the right to be proud. Joe possessed a kind of swaggering cynicism for a man who had not yet reached his twenty-second birthday—a kind of bravado that athletes were notorious for.

"I just smell the lettuce," Joe stated. "I have two good friends in this world. Buckerinos and base hits. If I get base hits I will get buckerinos. I smell World Series lettuce, and I'll get my two or three [hits] a day." The term "Buckerinos" was borrowed from "Doc Bucko" Weaver, the well-liked trainer who wore floppy, brightly colored straw hats and loud neck scarves, and was fond of posting canceled World Series checks as a way of encouraging his players. Medwick always understood that he was being paid to play and that his pay would rise as his performance did. There were those writers who believed this was another ugly trait in Medwick. There have always been, and always will be, those who do not understand that players like money the same way that owners do and the same way that writers do. Baseball players are neither fools nor children, no matter how much some may want to believe that they are. Barney Schultz told me that "There may have been a little friction there between Joe and the writers. They'd look at Joe and consider him hard-nosed. Well, Joe was tough in his day. Ah, he played a hard game. He went all out. He didn't take a backseat to anybody. . . . He was his own man. They'd ask a silly question and he'd give a silly answer."

Jim Mooney remembered Medwick as very serious and intent on the game:

> Joe Medwick never did say too much. He was just quiet. He had a funny attitude. I never could figure him out. I hit fungoes to him all the time, and shoot, you had to hit them right in his hand almost. He wouldn't even run to catch them. But he was a pretty good fielder. . . . Funny thing about him and his hitting—you might fool him on the pitch, and come right back with the same pitch, and he would knock it out of the park. . . . He was a moody boy. . . . When Medwick was in a slump, you'd better leave him alone. As long as Medwick was hitting,

everything was fine and dandy. If he was getting his base hits, every-thing was fine, but if he was in a slump, boy, just leave Joe alone. He'd sit over in the corner and come in and sit by himself. His hittin' was where his bread and butter was coming from, I reckon. He had to have his hits.

The Cardinals believed in Medwick's seriousness, intensity, and pride. It was his eight RBIs in seven games that had gotten them past the New York Giants. It was his .375 batting average for May that had helped them past their weak pitching in the first month of the season. Medwick, though batting fourth, would lead the team in at bats for four consecutive years, and average 630 at bats a year. When he went up the dugout steps, he was ready to play hard. And now there was a sign in red saying "Win Today's Game" posted on the clubhouse door, which the team had to pass to get to the field.

June 26 was the date for the annual St. Louis charity ball game against the Giants, which was known as "Tuberculosis Day." For two hours before the game's late starting time of 4 P.M., there were foot races, wrestling, boxing matches, a bicycle pageant, and music played by nineteen brilliantly costumed bands.

When that was done the teams then took part in the filming of the motion picture *Death on the Diamond*, starring Robert Young and Madge Evans. The Cardinals, not the Giants, were first at bat. Or-satti was up and there were already two runners on base. Then Orsatti "hit" a long drive to center and tried to score. But he col-lapsed short of home, "shot dead," according to the script. "Who was murdering members of the St. Louis Cardinals?" the film's pro-mos asked. "Who poisoned the mustard that one of the players put on his hot dog? Three players bite the dust before the ending; but don't worry, we won't tell you who the culprit is even though you should figure it out by the end of the second reel. What you may find hard to believe, however, is the throw the hero pitcher makes to conk out the villain."

Then the real game began.

Announced the next day were the All-Star teams picked by the baseball fans of the country. Medwick was seventh in the National League voting behind Bill Terry; his friend, Frankie Frisch, who became team captain; Pie Traynor; Chuck Klein; Carl Hubbell; and Travis Jackson. He was second among outfielders, fourteenth in both leagues. Dizzy Dean was one of the three pitchers. The newspapers wrote that of the two teams of eleven men, these players wouldn't necessarily start the game; the starters would be chosen by the managers.

After some more movie filming on July 4, the Cardinals split a doubleheader at Sportsman's—Medwick getting six hits—and remained in third place and stayed there, while winning two of four against Cincinnati.

For the second All-Star game, Pepper Martin had been named as a reserve and joined Frisch, the starting second baseman, Dean, and Medwick, the starting left fielder, at New York's Polo Grounds. At the All-Star break, Medwick was hitting .352, fifth in the league, with a league-leading 111 hits.

After the players checked into the Hotel Commodore next to Grand Central Station, they attended a team meeting with Bill Terry at which they were each assessed $10 for the Professional Baseball Players Association, which "had the handling of the needy cases among members of the profession. . . . The All-Star Game was to be used for such purposes."

Over fifteen thousand fans who could not get tickets had the gates locked on them fifteen minutes prior to game time. As Medwick went onto the field at the Polo Grounds and looked at the bunting on the upper and lower boxes, most of the fifty-five thousand fans were already in their seats, probably for the same reason that Medwick had come out early: to see the batting-practice hitting of Ruth, Gehrig, and Dickey from the Yankees, and Gehringer and Cochrane from the Tigers—and all the others. (All but five of the thirty-four who played that day would be elected to the Hall of Fame.)

This was the well-known game in which screwball pitcher Carl Hubbell struck out five future Hall of Fame players in order. When Hubbell finished his three innings of work, the Nationals had a one-run lead. After two out in the home third, Traynor singled after Frisch walked. After a ball and a strike, Joe Medwick hit a home run into the upper left field stands, giving his team a 4-0 lead. ("How anybody can get so much power on a ball . . . high over his head . . . is a mystery.") Later Medwick said, "I hit a high outside pitch . . . it was a good homer. It went in over the bullpen in left field, in the second deck. Gomez said to me, 'You so-and-so Hungarian. I'll never give you anything you can hit again. I'll put 'em all right down the middle,' and I said, 'Lefty, your control isn't that good.'" After the game, Medwick was described as a player "whose fame was just beginning."

The Cardinals were still stuck in third place. Two games against second-division Brooklyn were won when Medwick drove in five with two home runs, one to left and one to right. The next day, Dodger players, in the Brooklyn *Eagle* of July 16, were talking about Medwick's performance the day before:

> The first homer hit off his ear. It was high and wide. "The only way to fool that guy," said [Buzz] Boyle [Dodger right fielder], "was to throw right over the heart of the plate. . . . His first home run went to left and his second hit the right field fence. What can you do with a fellow like that?"
>
> Medwick, besides being a hustling, rifle-throwing outfielder, seems to be the reincarnation of that fabled fellow who reached over and hit the fourth ball of an intentional walk over the fence for a winning homer. He swings at—and hits—anything.

The *Eagle* continued:

> The Cardinals may be sagging but Joseph "Ducky-Wucky" Medwick, former New Jersey semi-pro had the National league all heated up over his sensational hitting. Medwick, the son of a Hungarian mill-hand, was discovered by a St. Louis scout three years ago while the Giants, Yankees, and Dodgers slumbered.
>
> Yesterday's pre-game conversation in the Brooklyn dugout centered around Medwick. Ducky had just belted two balls (during batting practice) into the upper deck in left center and this got a rise from the Brooklyn pitchers.
>
> "I'd rather pitch to any other hitter in the league," declared Van Mungo. "He's bad news all the time. No game was ever won against the Cardinals until Medwick was out in the ninth. I'd rather face nine left-handed hitters all day than face Joe twice. He can do more harm with one swing than nine other guys."
>
> "If you think he's tough for you, what should I say?" piped Dutch Leonard. "I'm a relief pitcher. He's a baseball murderer. You can't let up on him for a second. And the harder you bear down, the harder he hits. I fooled him twice with knucklers at Sportsman's Park last month, and Sunday he hit the same pitch out into the street. I think the league should forbid his carrying a bat to the plate. Make Medwick use his fist to swing against us. Then he'd only smack out singles."

Even though Medwick doubled off the right field wall and hit a home run against the screen to the left of the scoreboard, the Cardinals lost again, 7-6.

The Cardinals, with Bill Walker starting, won the last game of the Brooklyn series, 5-3, on July 18, and Bill McCullough wrote, "Ducky Wucky Medwick has left Ebbets Field for a while. Thank goodness the National League schedule permits him to play only eleven games in Flatbush each year. . . . During the series he made ten hits, including four homers, a triple, and two doubles and knocked in eleven runs. On the strength of his showing, Medwick was rated the outstanding visiting player to perform at Ebbets Field this season."

Even though the team was unable to move up in the standings all through August 1934, it took as a good omen Hallahan's 7-1 win to begin September. But the Cardinals' satisfaction in getting out of third place was a pleasure that faded after an awful Monday doubleheader in Pittsburgh, which was lost by a combined score of 17-5. In those games, both Martin and Collins failed to cover their bases, Medwick didn't hustle on a pop fly and was thrown out, Paul Dean fell down, and the team was beaten by a pitcher they considered to be an old man, Waite Hoyt.

But, at the same time, something important happened. Medwick, who had been playing since July 23 with a painfully injured right shoulder that had been hurt trying to catch a short fly by Memphis Bill Terry, said that his "sore shoulder disappeared one day when he stuck a full swing at a pitch and missed. 'Something snapped in the upper arm,' said Joe, 'and I was all right after that.'" His average was .333.

Back in St. Louis, Roy Stockton took the opportunity to hand out blame for the team's weak showing this late in the season: "Joe Medwick, after a fine start, when he was among the league's leading batters, has been in a bad slump for more than a month. [The month he had been injured. Didn't Stockton know?] In the past twelve games he has batted .213. Due to inexperience and other things, Joe has to hit .350 to be valuable to the team." He *has* to hit .350? I can think of few things ever written about a player that were more extraordinary.

Frisch sensed the gloom among the team members but was aware of their strengths, so he called a clubhouse meeting at Ebbets Field one hour early before the game of September 5. "I stood before them and burned them like they had never been burned before. 'Were you fellows going to quit now? This race was just getting hot. It ain't over. Don't give up. Fight to the finish and if you do, I'm telling you fellows, we won't be beaten.'" The change on their expressions was remarkable. They started kicking the benches around. That day they beat Brooklyn and took over second place, as the Cubs lost to the Giants.

The September 16 Polo Grounds doubleheader seated the largest crowd in the history of the National League, the fire department ordering the doors locked while fifteen thousand fans watched from the Eighth-Avenue elevated train tracks or from Coogan's Bluff. Frisch drove in two in the first game, which the Cardinals won 5-3, Tex Carleton pitching in three-inning relief of Dizzy Dean. "Joe Medwick, whose work in the field had been slovenly through much of the season, was honored between games by a delegation of fans from Carteret, New Jersey, his home town." In the second game, Paul Dean won his fourth game of the year against Hubbell. Medwick drove in the only run the Cardinals scored in the first nine innings. The score was tied at one in the tenth when there occurred "the miracle performed in the gloom by Ducky Medwick, who went up against a [concrete] sign in left field and just got his glove between the billposter and Lieber's liner." The catch meant that the hit by the next batter, Blondy Ryan, produced no run, and so allowed time for Pepper Martin to hit a homer in the eleventh to win the game by 3-1. Two weeks later, Bendel wrote that "the Giants blame that [catch] for their defeat in the race. It was the break of the game and the turning point of the race."

After two days of rain in Boston, the Giants were four games up.

Medwick homered in the second inning to aid Tex's three-hit win in the first game (it was his sixth win against the Braves in 1934), and Bill Walker zeroed the Braves on eight hits in the second. Though the Cardinals won both from Boston, they gained only a half-game. Still, the players had "[remarkable] spirit and enthusiasm," and in their train car on the Patriot to New York, they chanted, "We can win the pennant!" Medwick knew he must pick up his pace in hitting. The Cards had done well enough in the nine games played since the eleventh, but Medwick had had only five hits in that span. He would do very well from now on. Somebody reminded Dizzy Dean that he had told a writer that after the games in Brooklyn, he and Paul will be known as "one-hit Dean and no-hit Dean."

Dizzy was wrong; he gave up three hits. With Collins hitting his thirty-fourth home run and driving in six runs, St. Louis won the first game 13-0. Medwick had two hits, two runs, and an RBI. Paul's no-hitter was helped by Medwick's two superb catches: in the sixth inning he took a double away from Buzz Boyle in left center, and in the seventh, caught Sambo Leslie's long drive near the wall, again in left center. He also doubled and tripled, scoring two of the three runs to bring the Cardinals to fewer than three games behind.

Close to the Giants now, the Cardinals went to dinner at 6 P.M. at St. Louis's Lennox Hotel, courtesy of Loew's management, and then to the theater to see themselves in the movie *Death on the Diamond* at 7:30 P.M.

In the last twenty games, the Giants were 9-11, while the Cardinals had played at .750. Giants pitcher Freddie Fitzsimmons had no runs scored behind him for thirty-three straight innings. Mel Ott was hitting .247 in September. And the "vengeful band of Dodgers" were waiting for the hated Giants. Every fan in the borough remembered what Giants manager Bill Terry asked eight months ago: "Is Brooklyn still in the league?"

"Just before the Dodgers were to leave the clubhouse, a telegram was delivered . . . with 50 signatures that said 'You'll win the undying gratitude of Brooklyn fans if you knock Bill Terry and his Giants flat on their backs.'"

On Saturday, despite the rain, many Dodgers fans traveled to see their Van Mungo go against Roy Parmelee with the pennant on the line. The Giants lost again, 5-1. The first-place spot that the New Yorkers had held since June 8 was about to be lost for good.

On a rainy Saturday in St. Louis, Sportsman's Park attendance was 11,500 paid plus 8,870 women and 2,671 girls. Frisch had picked Paul Dean to start against Paul Derringer, though the younger Dean had lost on Wednesday. In the third inning, Medwick tripled down the right field line with Frisch on second base; he also hit homer number seventeen in the fifth to knock out former teammate Paul Derringer. Stockton wrote that "Medwick . . . suddenly had remembered how to bat." Since September 21, he was hitting .415. Medwick delivered the .350 that Stockton had demanded. After the 6-1 win, Dizzy led a snake dance in front of the dugout. The Cardinals were one game in front, with one to play.

The ad in the newspaper that night read:

"DIZZY" DEAN
PITCHING THIS AFTERNOON
Cardinals vs. Cincinnati
Sportsman's Park, 2:30 P.M.
This game decides pennant
Box Office at Park Open at 9 A.M. Today

Winning by a score of 9-0 in the ninth inning that day, Dean loaded the bases and then struck out Pete Manion and Ted Petoskey, batting for the pitcher, "Fish Hook" Stout. When the scoreboard said that the Giants lost in the tenth, factory whistles and bells sounded. And then when Sparky Adams popped to Dee at 4:41 P.M., the St. Louis Cardinals won the game, and the pennant, by two games.

In the clubhouse, first baseman Ripper Collins sang "We're in the Money." In another part of the clubhouse, harmonizing on "I Want a Girl" were stolen-base champion Pepper Martin, first-base coach Buzzy Wares, and Joe Medwick, the league leader in triples; Joe was also fourth in total bases, fourth in RBIs, and fifth in slugging average and in hits. Third-base coach Mike Gonzales was grinning and exclaiming, "Mike, she tole you, we could do." Pop Haines puffed a cigar as he dressed. Pitcher Dazzy Vance, in and out of the league since 1915, was ecstatic that at age forty-three, he finally was on a championship team.

Later, a small party of Cardinals celebrated at the Grecian Gardens owned by Jim Mertikas, a native-born Greek. He welcomed and shook hands with Tex and Fanny Carleton, with Mr. and Mrs. Dazzy Vance, Bill Walker and his girl friend, and with bachelors Medwick and Hallahan.

> [They] had a festive evening, drinking Mestika [Metaxa?] and dining on egg-lemon soup, lettuce salad with feta cheese, shish kebab and stewed green beans. For dessert, they ate baklava. Then red-haired Dazzy Vance ordered a "Dazz-Marie." When the waiter looked puzzled, Vance mixed into an oversized glass filled with ice cubes the following: rye, bourbon and Scotch, one-half shots of gin, sloe gin, vermouth, brandy and Benedictine. Stirring in some sugar, Vance asked, "Anybody want some?"
>
> "Nobody could drink that," Hallahan said.
>
> Tex Carleton raised his highball in a toast. "Bring on the Tigers," he said.
>
> "We'll turn 'em into pussycats," Dazzy Vance said as he took a large swallow of his Dazz-Marie.

Later, when Bill Hallahan was helping him across the hotel lobby, Vance thought the chairs were jumping at all of them. Dazzy wouldn't move until Medwick walked ahead and told Dazzy he wouldn't let the chairs get him.

Years later, Vance said, "It was like bananas. Taken one at a time we could be skinned, but together we made a helluva bunch."

The Detroit Tigers had not played in a World Series for twenty-five years—not since Ty Cobb. The team featured six of the eight position players hitting above .300, and four of them with one hundred RBIs or more. "Not since the days of the mauling Yankees of the Miller Huggins era had a pennant winner come to the fore carrying such heavy artillery into a World Series," the newspapers said.

It was a series that attracted a number of fans from outside of Detroit. Will Rogers had become a fan of the Cardinals, and he flew to Detroit to see the series open.

Before the first game, Commissioner Kenesaw Mountain Landis predicted, "This Series should be bitterly fought and full of color." He was an excellent fortune teller.

When it was time for the Cardinals to go to Detroit's Navin Field on Tuesday for a workout, Dizzy Dean, who was in street clothes, took a bat from Hank Greenberg and said, "Here, Moe, let me show you how to do it," and hit one into the left field bleachers. "Right there," Medwick said later, "we almost had a fight." In infield practice, Frisch asked that balls be hit hard to him so he could see where a ball would roll when it bounced off his chest. Mike Ryba, thirty-three, from the Springfield team, and Cotton Pippen, twenty-three, from Houston, pitched batting practice.

The Cardinals had five hitters at .300 or above, and the starting lineup was hitting .301. Ernie Orsatti, still limping, was penciled in to hit against right-handers, and Chick Fullis was to take his spot in center against left-handers. Pepper Martin had painful bone chips in his elbow that would have to be operated on, but he insisted on playing nevertheless.

The four umpires (six were not used until 1947) were Beans Reardon and Bill Klem of the National League and Brick Owens and Harry Geisel from the American League.

The Cardinals knew that "Schoolboy" Rowe would not oppose Dizzy in the first game, but they also knew that "Tiger skipper" Cochrane bypassed his four top starters and gave the game-one ball to Alvin "General" Crowder, thirty-five, who had been picked up on waivers from the Senators late in the season (as if to say the Tigers were already acknowledging a Dizzy win—as if to say Dizzy was unbeatable).

In the fifth inning of game one, "with the count one and one, Medwick lifted a home run into the left field bleachers for his third straight hit, as a murmur of admiration came from the packed stands," making the score 4-1. Then "Medwick got his fourth straight hit, a sharp single to right, on which Martin scored." Dean struck out pinch hitter Gee Walker to end the 8-3 St. Louis win.

In its front-page story the next day, the *New York Times* began by saying, "a swashbuckling band of St. Louis Cardinals . . . paced by the mighty war club of Jersey Joe Medwick pounded Detroit pitchers for a total of thirteen hits. Medwick's contributions were four blazing hits."

After the game, while all the Gashouse Gang swaggered the way some team members were inclined to do, Dizzy told reporters, "I didn't have a thing. Those Tigers looked like pussycats." "'Out of my way, you big stiff—make room for a real hero,' said Medwick as he shoved Dizzy out of his path to the showers. 'Where would you be without me, big boy?' yelled Carteret Joe from under the shower. 'They're going to have their troubles trying to stop little Joey from now on.'" Medwick was not at all shy about what he had done. Medwick, soaping up, could enjoy his individual stats as well as his achievement in scoring or driving in half the Cardinal runs. His four hits went to all three fields. After showering, Medwick joined in with five others to sing "I Want a Girl Just Like a Girl That Married Dear Old Dad."

The next day Associated Press sports editor Alan Gould's interview was printed, quoting Casey Stengel: "As for Medwick, he was liable to blow more of the Tigers down than the Deans. He's one of the greatest natural hitters I have seen in years."

Before game two, "Medwick came out on the field garbed more like a fullback than a star of the diamond. Around his right wrist was a band of tape, covering a gash he received sliding last week when he was spiked. His socks were rolled down, revealing muscled legs, and he pranced and cavorted around left in practice."

In the October 6, 1934 *New York Times,* two writers, Drebinger and Dawson, reported on the subsequent action. Describing Medwick's coming to bat in game two, Drebinger wrote: "Yesterday Jersey Joe had hammered the ball for four straight hits and the crowd had a profound respect for him." In the third, Medwick drove in Pepper Martin with a single to left field and moved to second on the throw to the plate by Goslin. Collins singled to left and Medwick headed for home, but, as Dawson put it: "he was out at the plate on a perfect, rifle-bullet throw from Goslin to Cochrane" on one bounce. "It was a masterpiece and caught Medwick by ten feet." Medwick crashed feet first into Mickey Cochrane and sent the catcher sprawling. Drebinger wrote: "It looked like Cochrane was seriously hurt but he was just winded, and limped off favoring his right leg." The Tigers won the game in the twelfth inning to tie the series.

After the game, Dee came into the clubhouse and "fired his mask at a trunk that he hit so hard that it sounded as though it had crashed through it." Frisch, perhaps annoyed with himself for his error, said "You chowder heads blew the dammed ball game for Hallahan."

"'Frisch raised the roof,' Joe Medwick remembered, 'He called us a lot of names, and we knew we deserved them.'"

Cochrane, in the Tiger clubhouse, was found to have two deep spike cuts. "Phff, that Medwick," Mickey Cochrane groaned. "Where do they grow fellows like him?"

There was no day off for travel, so the team got aboard the Cardinal Special for the twelve-hour trip back to St. Louis for games three, four, and five. Joe Williams in the *New York World Telegram* wrote of Medwick's team: "They looked like a bunch of boys from the gas house district who had crossed the railroad tracks for a game of ball with the nice kids."

Joe's parents, their daughter Bennie, and their son-in-law, Bill Beisel, arrived in St. Louis, traveling by bus from New York City for the $36 round-trip on the Great Eastern Bus System, arriving at twelfth and Delmar. At the hotel, Joe's parents were thrilled to find out that the bed was a hidden fold-down.

The first inning of Paul Dean's performance in game three was marked by Medwick's catch of leadoff batter Jo-Jo White's foul along the left field boxes, described as "the fielding classic of the series. Starting with the crack of the bat, Ducky made a beautiful dash, squirmed his way alongside the boxes, and leaned far over into the second row to spear it with one hand. No one thought he had it until he rushed out of the melee exhibiting the ball." Paul Dean saw his win secured with Frisch's fine catch of Goslin's fly "after a spectacular race out into short centre field." The manager was mobbed when he entered the clubhouse, and everyone shook Paul Dean's hand. Rothrock and Medwick talked about Tiger Marv Owen bumping them with his knee when they rounded third.

When game four ended, the series was tied at two games each.

In game five, the Tigers pitched Tommy Bridges, known for sharp-breaking down curves. Diz started game five, but the Tigers won the game 3-1 and were 3-2 in the series as it moved back to Detroit.

The train, carrying both teams, left at 7:30 P.M. and arrived at 7 A.M. As the Cardinals checked into their hotel, a truck outside blared, "Hold 'em Tigers."

In the first inning of game six, with Paul Dean pitching to keep his team in the series, Rothrock doubled, and then Medwick's single sent Jack home. That good beginning ended with a Cardinal 4-3 win to tie the series. In the clubhouse, a sportswriter observed, "all the Redbirds from bat boy to manager were busy kissing each other like a lot of French Generals bestowing the Croix de Guerre."

Generals they may be, for this game in particular had been a kind of war. Cochrane had a long cut on his kneecap, caused by Paul Dean's spikes. He was sore from a collision with Orsatti.

The collisions continued after the game as well, when umpires Brick Owens and Beans Reardon were in a jolting taxi crash.

And then there was the seventh game of the 1934 World Series.

To begin the day, Durocher and Medwick put on a home-run show, hitting a lot of homers into the bleachers in left during batting practice. A floral horseshoe, given by some Detroit fans, was delivered to the Tiger dugout, but no player went near it; the players believed that flowers brought bad luck.

But the Cardinals were the bad luck. By the end of the third inning, St. Louis was in the lead, 7-0.

In the Cardinal sixth inning, Martin singled and went to second when Goslin fumbled the ball. Rothrock and Frisch flew out. Then Medwick, after getting some dirt on his hands, hit a 1-2 pitch off the right field bleachers wall to score Martin with the eighth run. Medwick later said, "When I rounded second, I could see Mike Gonzales give me the hands-up signal. But Owen was straddling the bag as if waiting for a throw, blocking me off, and I couldn't see behind me. I still don't know what he was thinking. It's common enough for a second baseman or a shortstop to give you a fake coming into second, but a third baseman, never. There was no point to it. So I went sliding hard" (into Detroit third baseman Marv Owen). But Owen did not have the ball; the shortstop, Billy Rogell, had cut it off. Medwick later called this "a phantom tag."

(Frisch said in his autobiography, "I admit he slid hard. Joe always played hard. But it wasn't a dirty slide.") The slide, in fact, was exactly the same slide it had been all season—all during the series. Tommy Holmes, in the Brooklyn *Eagle*, wrote, "So far as high spikes were concerned, anybody who didn't navigate into a base that way in this series carries a sissy tag."

In this way, Medwick got tangled up with Marv Owen, who almost tripped and accidentally came down on Joe's left leg. Medwick twice kicked back, and Owen was ready to fight. Then they were at one another, with Umpire Bill Klem in the middle as the coaches stepped in. Other players ran over, but very soon returned back to the dugout. Klem must have seen provocation for Medwick, for neither man was punished, and that seemed to be the end of it. Medwick put out a hand to Owen as if to apologize, and Medwick remembered, "But he said what I could do, so I said what he could do, and that was all." Frisch added, "I thought Joe was showing unusual self-restraint . . . you couldn't do any talking in a row with Medwick. He'd swing that right of his after very little jawing and down you'd go." The inning continued and Medwick scored on Collins's single; his teammates in the dugout congratulated him. Delancey struck out, ending the inning with the score at 9-0.

Joe jogged out to his position in left field and was welcomed by loud, angry boos. As he got closer to the bleachers, all seventeen thousand angry fans began screaming curses and waving their arms for him to get off the field. Then, from over the chicken-wire screen, a red apple landed and rolled at Medwick's feet; he let the apple roll into his glove and threw it back to the base of the stands. Joe seemed to take it as a joke; he was smiling, hands on hips.

But then, soaring out of the stands were oranges, bananas, beer bottles, and more apples and pop bottles, all of which landed, and bounced off the grass, and rolled or turned in the air before coming to rest. "A wind-blown orchard," the radio announcer said. Medwick looked up into the stands as the umpires ordered the field crew out to left field with hemp sacks. Medwick refused to retreat. The other outfielders, Orsatti and Pepper Martin, played catch with some fruit. The crowd was waving hats and newspapers. No one knew what to do. Frisch suggested that Joe come to the infield while the cleanup was going on. He agreed.

On NBC radio, the announcers were remembering that many of the spectators had been in their seats at 9 A.M., meaning that they had brought lunches, and more, with them. (No one seemed to remember the lemons thrown at Hack Wilson during the 1930 season, lemons hurled to remind Wilson of the two balls he dropped in the fourth game of the 1929 World Series.)

When Joe went back out to his position after seven minutes had passed, the noise rose again and Medwick saw arcing toward him tomatoes, cigar stubs, paper cups, scorecards, newspapers, and parts of hot dogs. Durocher came out from shortstop, put an arm around Medwick and told him to stand fast. Medwick had a better idea. "Why don't you play left field and I'll play shortstop," Medwick suggested.

A photographer came out onto the field to snap Medwick, and "Because of his audacity," as NBC reported, Joe picked up an apple and hit the cameraman with the fruit. ("The only thing I did was . . . throw an orange at a photographer," Joe said in the *Sporting News* after the Series, "and miss him. . . . [W]hen that fellow tried to take a picture, why, I just didn't feel like posing so I let him have the fruit.") When other photographers came out, Medwick turned his back. Paul Gallico of the *New York Daily News* wrote the most vivid account of this incident: "I watched the crowd and Medwick and the pelting missiles through my field glasses, and it was a terrifying sight. Every face in the crowd, women and men, was distorted with rage. Mouths were torn wide, open eyes glistened and shone in the sun. All fists were clenched." Umpires Owens and Klem walked out to judge the situation.

Ten minutes into the melee, field attendants again rushed out with gunny sacks to pick up the debris while Medwick, moving safely out of range, played "pop-ball" at the edge of the infield. Martin bounced the ball off his bicep to Joe, and Medwick returned it with a throw behind his back. Dizzy Dean was brought a sweater coat, since by now about twelve minutes had passed. "'If,' said Frisch years later, 'they just had let Joey go out there with that big black bat in his hands, the odds would have been even.'" The manager called Medwick into the infield again.

The four umpires met near shortstop to talk the situation over. As soon as they decided on the threat to forfeit the game, they asked for public address announcements to that effect, but announcer Ty Tyson's voice couldn't be heard above the roar.

Paul Gallico described the last four minutes or so. At thirteen minutes into the disturbance,

Again Medwick returns to the diamond while the field was cleared, and then for the third time he tried to take his position. And he did a pretty brave thing. He trotted out and turned his back on the stands. Mobs [are] rank cowards, and the sight of courage inflames them beyond all reason. By far the most dangerous peal of rage broke from them, this third time. Heavy milk bottles flew onto the field. The police stood quietly by against the fence along the bottom row and did nothing. "Take him out! Take him out!" The chant echoed and re-echoed like a football yell. Mickey Cochrane ran half way into left field, and with one gesture tried to pacify the mob. It had no more effect than throwing a pebble into the ocean. Cochrane returned to the diamond. The umpires walked around helplessly.

(Cochrane, by the way, walked out to left with a bat in his hand.) Joe stood there, hands on hips. The NBC announcer said in admiration, "He certainly seems able to take it—all the boos and jeers that they offer him."

There were now eleven groundsmen cleaning up, ducking the bottles that still landed where they worked.

After the delay had lasted sixteen minutes, Umpire Harry Geisel told Frisch he'd better take Medwick out of the game. "Nothing doing," said Frisch, "he plays." Then Geisel advised Frisch to talk to the commissioner. Judge Landis gestured to Medwick and Frisch from his box. A few years earlier, Heinie Manush had been thrown out of a World Series game for snapping the elastic on the bow tie of Umpire Charley Moran. Baseball Commissioner Landis later ruled that only he could eject someone during a World Series.

So the left fielder and his manager met Landis who was standing dressed in a topcoat and hat at his box between home and third base. Teammates tried to join Joe, but were stopped by the other umpires. Photos show Medwick with his back to home plate, his hand resting on the railing, listening to the commissioner. The radio announcer described the scene: "Joe Medwick over there with his cap off, gentlemanly." Frisch, wearing number 3, and furious that his Joey might be removed from the game, was in an almost belligerent stance, his gloved hand on his hip, keeping his distance from Landis. Umpire Klem joined them, as well as Detroit manager, Mickey Cochrane, and Marv Owen. Hank Greenberg came over, and soon all had their arms around each other in a protective arrangement. It was seventeen minutes into the mob's party.

"Was there any reason at all," Landis asked Owen, "why this man, Medwick, should have taken a kick at you?"

"No, sir," he said.

"Did you kick Owen?" the judge asked Medwick.

"No, I was just trying to protect myself," answered Joe, adding, "but if I did, I didn't mean to, Judge. I ain't mad at him."

"Did you boys curse each other?" said Landis.

Lying, they shook their heads.

Then Landis, who had said a week earlier, "This series should be bitterly fought and full of color," delivered his verdict.

"Mr. Medwick," he said, not ruling on the case's merits, "you're out of the game—to prevent bodily harm from the fans," adding, as he turned to Frisch, "Take him out and resume play."

Frisch talked about this moment in his autobiography. "What amazed me was his bellowing voice, as though Medwick and I had committed some great crime. 'Judge, would it be all right if I moved Medwick over to right field? There were no bleachers there.'" When Frisch heard Landis again scream his order, "I thought then and I still think if Medwick had to go, why not Marv Owen?" And why not forfeit the game to the Cardinals instead of punishing them?

But Owen stayed. "I'll never forget . . . Frisch . . . saying, 'That old son of a bitch. I'm going to take him,'" Umpire Beans Reardon recalled, commenting on Frisch's rage at Landis. "I told him to forget it."

Medwick stomped over to the Cardinal dugout, and with his left hand, threw his glove down into the dugout, angry, perhaps, that he now had no chance to tie the series record for hits—angry that Landis had caved in to a mob. "His [Medwick's] great sin . . . was that he was not as clever with his carving utensils as some of the others," wrote Tommy Holmes. "Jo-Jo White [Tiger outfielder], for instance, could carve his initials on a running jack rabbit with his spikes."

During the next inning, Landis even ordered Medwick out of the dugout. With a police escort of five, Joe walked across the field and into the Tiger dugout, the entrance to the clubhouse. Once more the boos rose briefly. One more bottle was hurled at him, and then he vanished; the crowd was satisfied.

As Medwick arrived in the locker room, Will Rogers left Henry Ford's box to talk to Joe. Rogers had been in the Cardinal locker room before and after each game. Medwick refused to speak with reporters. "Mr. Rogers . . . advised Medwick to tell his version of the story. 'It's no disgrace to fight hard to win, or to fight back when somebody's trying to put one over on you.'"

As the two were talking, the Cardinals scored two more runs in the seventh inning, and Cochrane took himself out in the eighth. Frisch recalled the following conversation late in the game: Frisch said to Durocher, "How about playing a little closer to second and giving me a hand? I'm getting pooped." Durocher responded, "Go get yourself a wheelchair if you can't cover your territory. I'm not going to make myself looked bad just to make you look good."

Dizzy Dean may be the only World Series pitcher ever to giggle at the hitters. He snickered with his glove up to his mouth the first two times he struck out Hank Greenberg, and laughed out loud the third time, not even waiting to see the finish of Greenberg's wild swing. At this point, Dean was actually bent over with his hands on his knees, shaking with laughter. The Tigers got three more hits in the game but the score of 11-0 was the final.

Almost all of the Cardinals were jubilant after the game. They threw Doc Weaver into the showers.

But it would take a while for a quiet, resentful Medwick to recover. Medwick told reporters, "I didn't mean to harm anybody, but I didn't want anybody taking a kick out of me. . . . I offered to shake hands with Owen at the time, and he refused. What more could I do?"

"Medwick was hard to talk to, uncertain as to just why he suddenly was popped into the middle of the nearest thing to a riot that the World Series had ever seen. At first, Joe declared, 'I don't know anything. All I know was that I hit a triple and slid to third base and then Commissioner Landis put me out of the ball game. . . . I don't want to talk about it at all, if I can help it,' said Medwick. 'I just got out there and hustle[d] and play[ed] to win. I don't want to say that Owen did anything to cause me to kick at him, because I'm not sure that he did. It all happened pretty quickly. About all I can say, I guess, was that I'm sorry it happened.'" Owen said he was sorry that it had happened, too.

"We had to get police escorts [for the team bus] to get back to the hotel and to get out of town," Frisch recalled. After the game, Detroit detectives stayed with Medwick and Bill Hallahan in their room, where they ate, until it was time to get on board the midnight sleeper back to St. Louis. The police went right to the train with the team.

Newspapers were full of reports of the game and the crowds' reaction. "I've never known a city to take a World Series defeat so bitterly," one reporter declared. (Twenty-five years later, Ernie Orsatti, in business and wishing to stay at the same hotel where the team had stayed in 1934 [the hotel now called in 1959 the Sheraton-Cadillac], was refused a room when the desk clerk saw him sign the name "Orsatti.")

One reporter summed up the series by saying, "It was the Gas House Gang playing the nice boys from the right side of the railroad tracks."

Carl Fischer, who had thrown at Medwick when Joe had a tryout with the Newark Bears in 1929, pitched for Detroit in 1934 and was on the World Series roster, but did not throw a pitch in the World Series.

"What a ballplayer . . . I'll say . . . for Ducky Wucky Medwick, the Cardinal Cossack, who plays the game up to the hilt of flying spikes," Grantland Rice wrote. "Did Detroit ever see Ty Cobb along the base paths?"

Some days later, John Kiernan, in a column titled "Fond Memories of a Great World Series" wrote these six sentences to sum up the games: "There was glory enough for all and money enough, too. The athletes won't have to worry about the cost of coal this winter. But they earned whatever they got. They put on a great show and carried it off with fire and fury. Muscles Medwick and Pepper Martin went around those bases like wild boars heading for a gap in the hedge. It was all in fun, but it was fierce fun, and the Tigers never did seem to like it."

Medwick was still blue and confused and angry when the train pulled into St. Louis. (After Joe signed a picture of himself hitting in the 1934 series, he told Bob Kennedy, "That's what you get for hustling—kicked out of the 1934 World Series.") But he was pleased by such an unmistakably joyous welcome in the victory parade, so by the time it was over, he was among the most enthusiastic of players.

The Cardinals arrived in St. Louis a few minutes before eight the next morning and were whisked right away for a downtown parade. The celebration had begun a day earlier and streets were littered with toilet paper, "Depression ticker tape," they called it, as the Cardinal caravan of fourteen cars proceeded slowly past thousands of grateful, cheering fans. Rickey, Breadon, and Frisch rode with Mayor Bernard F. Dickman in the first car and wore the smiles of Busby Berkley chorus girls on pay day. Breadon's personal take would be $80,000. There was so much in the pot because of the World Series that he even gave $500 bonuses to Diz and Paul for their heroic work of the past month and considered himself almost philanthropic to do so. But he was no Frank Navin, who was handing out star bonuses, too. Rowe had been given $2,500, while Cochrane got $10,000.

"They deserved it," said Navin.

The Deans were in the second car. Diz was wearing a pith helmet and twisting a stuffed toy tiger's tail.

"Hey, Dizzy," yelled a girl, running alongside, "yesterday we didn't have to go to school and we stayed home and heard you pitch on the radio."

"Did you like it, honey?" he said.

"You bet 'cha."

Joe Medwick, just behind in the fourth car, with Pat Crawford next to him, was asked, "Have a banana, Joe?"

Players with full shares were to receive $5,389.57 (or $5,821.19), which was enough to pay for the full price of a house at that time.

On October 10, Dizzy, Paul, and Joe, were signed to play in Queens, New York, for the semi-pro Bushwicks against the Black Yankees. Dizzy pitched three innings, Paul Dean played some right field, but Joe played the whole game in left, as a replacement for Martin who was injured. One fan, a young boy, begged Joe for his autograph until Medwick finally relented. The boy's name was Jack Lang, and thirty-four years later he would make an important phone call to Medwick.

About to leave St. Louis on October 11, "Medwick dipped into his earnings to buy an automobile. He made the trip aboard his horse-less carriage, the last lap of his journey from Columbus . . . in a day," and on October 14, 1934, "Carteret welcomed home Joe . . . in a royal fashion. . . . A large portion of the borough's 14,000 population turned out to greet Medwick as he arrived in his car at East Rahway, shortly after two o'clock. Transferred to an open car, the St. Louis outfielder sat with his father on one side and his mother on the other," the *Newark News* reported. "Mayor Joseph A. Herman, chairman of the reception committee, was also in the car. Heading the parade was the band of Fire Company No. 2, followed by the fife and drum corps of Fire Company No. 1."

On October 16 there was a dinner at the New York City Crescent Club at Pierrepont and Clinton Streets. Attending the dinner were a

Supreme Court justice, the president of the National League, "Alfred De Oro, veteran billiard luminary," Dazzy Vance, and Frankie Frisch. Joe was there, too, and the caption in the Brooklyn *Eagle* named him "the stormy petrel . . . in the series, tabbed as the 'Battle of Flying Steel.'"

"I have been in eight World Series," explained Frankie, "but I want to say the other seven were played with kid gloves compared to this one. It was a rough, hard series and no mistake, but I think it did baseball a world of good. For years the game had been entirely too tame, too friendly. It lacked the fighting spirit that I knew under John McGraw. In this series, you never knew when a base runner would bowl you out into center field, and I think we all got a kick out of this eat-'em-up stuff." Frisch then went on to disclose that the current Cardinals were the "gamest team he had ever known." He pointed out that they weren't a hard-boiled bunch the way many people thought they were. "They love baseball and they play hard with no handshaking, but that's all. They're a fine lot." The ex-Fordham Flash paid a special tribute to Joe Medwick at a nearby table: "There's a ballplayer who would have made a big hit with John McGraw when John was at his scrappiest. . . . I'm for him and everything he did in this series. I like the way he tears into the bag when on the paths. He never deliberately spiked any player. Medwick isn't built that way." At this, diners thundered applause for Medwick, who stood up and took a bow. They wanted a speech, but Joe sat down hastily, and stayed down. "He's a little bashful here, but he's not that way on a ball field," observed Frankie.

Frisch got another chance to praise Joe on October 18, 1934, when Medwick was given a testimonial dinner by five hundred admirers in the high school gym; more than one hundred were unable to get in.

"Joe, I envy you," Frisch said at the dinner, "your speed of leg, your throwing arm, your keen eye, and your noodle. You have made good in a game that can be mighty good to you, providing you keep yourself in shape and retain the same fighting qualities that have made you outstanding in . . . the big time." Frisch continued, " I love the game and I enjoy watching a player who likes the game as I do. There were some players who were satisfied to play fifty, sixty, or seventy games, but you want to play them all. And for that, I can only praise you. You play the hard, aggressive type of ball that I like."

Medwick attended a number of functions in the fall that year. In Troy, New York, "Joe Medwick was the guest of honor at a bazaar for the benefit of Hillside School. . . . Joe was greeted upon his arrival at the Union Station by Johnny Evers and the Hillside School Band. A parade from the station to the city hall followed, where Medwick was greeted by Mayor Cornelius F. Burns, and the procession continued to the school." Then New Jersey natives Joe and Bill Urbanski were honored at a dinner in Perth Amboy on October 24. "Both were given dressing robes," the *Sporting News* reported.

By November 1, 1934, Jerry Mitchell reported the following in the Brooklyn *Eagle:*

> Letters from all parts of the country poured in after the fruit episode. . . . "He got 71 the first morning," said his father, beaming proudly, ". . . and 11 telegrams. Thirty-six letters in the afternoon. . . ." Beaner Casaleggi, brother of Peanuts, proprietor of the Red Star Billiard Academy, Joe's winter manager and operator of Joe's official haunt, opened fire, "He's got lots of offers, including marriage, football and baseball . . . he's gonna make personal appearances for Joe Herman—he's the Democratic candidate runnin' for mayor, ya know. He's even got an offer to sing on the radio in Newark. . . ." The first visitor was Cornbread Paine, colored, 57, and ready with a welcome-home oration. . . . Did Joe expect a pretty good raise in his Cardinal contract next year? "We don't expect no trouble," said Beaner.

"Medwick had been besieged with offers since he stole the headlines. He had even had professional football managers seeking to have him play in National League games," reports Bendel. "There was nothing I could imagine that would be more thrilling than to see Old Ducky Wucky King of the Cardinals, rush down the field bowling over opposing players. . . . Medwick was considering an offer to go into vaudeville. And his first crack was to start the tour in San Jose (Cal.), home of Marvin Owen."

When the final figures for 1934 were printed, Medwick, as in 1933, was in the top five of the league in seven categories: runs, hits, doubles, triples, RBIs, slugging percentage, and total bases. He was also sixth in home runs and twelfth in average at .319. It was his first year with over one hundred runs batted in, and his second year of hitting over .300. There was no diminution of his abilities. He was, even with these numbers, not yet at his peak.

9

Ten in the Top Three, 1935

Medwick had also contributed much to his team. He was second on the team in almost every offensive category to Rip Collins, who was six and a half years older. Medwick produced 26 percent of his team's 799 runs; was second in team RBIs, homers, at bats, hits, and slugging; was first in triples; and tied for first in doubles. Would Rickey point out his 14 fielding errors? Or would he say he knew that Joe worked hard to get at some balls that were well beyond his reach?

Back on Union Street in Carteret, Joe offered to buy his parents (both now in their sixties) a better house, but they insisted on just making the one they had more comfortable. Joe did buy an Essex for them to travel in, although apparently neither of his parents drove, leaving it up to Bill to be the driver. Joe's off-season routine by now was to come home to New Jersey and then to play golf all over the state. Over the winter, Joe often traveled to New York City for dinner and a show. He also traveled to Asbury Park, where there were heated indoor pools.

Traveling allowed Medwick time to think about his future. Right now the Cardinals were a strong team with three excellent starters, a young outfield, and with good-looking players coming up. Joe could be with this Cardinal team for a long time. At age twenty-three, only centerfield prospect Terry Moore was as young as Joe, and only Paul Dean, at age twenty-one, was younger than Joe. Medwick said he would quit if he didn't get $10,000 from the Cardinals for 1935. "Club officials apparently believe that I can live for a year on the fruit and vegetables that thoughtful Detroit fans contributed during the last game of the World Series. Such is not the case." Later he was quoted as saying, "I should have a good season. I know more about the game than I did last year. I know more about the pitchers and the parks, and I'm ready for a great year. As a matter of fact, I wouldn't be surprised if I led the league in hitting." Joe said his contract was $2,500 short of what he wanted.

The column "Sports Salad," by L. C. Davis in the *St. Louis Post-Dispatch*, offered the following verse with a cartoon: "Paul Dean and Medwick still remain/Outside the fold and there's a pain/in Brother Rickey's neck/But when the Cards assemble he was confident that they will be included in the deck." Around the same time that the cartoon appeared, Medwick had his tonsils and adenoids taken out in Perth Amboy General Hospital, where he recuperated for three days.

After Joe was discharged, he was making appearances at smokers at St. Leo's in Irvington, New Jersey, and at St. Joseph's in Maplewood. He was also being paid to present the first prize for the Newark Kennel Club at the Sussex Avenue Armory.

By the third day of spring training, Medwick signed for $7,500, which was a $2,500 raise from his previous salary. By March 15, Joe was in camp, playing in his first spring game.

The *Sporting News* noted that "Joe Medwick . . . was doing a bit of shifting in his stance. He was a natural left field hitter but he was crossing up the opposition occasionally by smacking line hits to right field." Medwick himself said that at 168 pounds he was about 16 pounds too light; he tried to add some weight as the team moved north through Georgia, Alabama, and Arkansas.

The season began for the World Series champions on April 16, and in that opening game Diz had to be taken to a hospital after Cub third baseman Freddy Lindstrom lined a single off of Diz's left shin, just above the shoe, and Dean was carried off the field. The Cardinals lost 4-3, but were rescued the next day by Paul Dean's shutout of the Wrigley Field team and Medwick's homer in a 1-0 victory. Back in Carteret down Chrome, Mrs. Kolibas, wife of the tavern owner on the corner of Pershing and Union, across the street from Medwick's house, began throwing small cereal boxes from her upstairs window when Joe homered. Kids would scoop them up.

For the home opener, "There was a parade to the flag pole. . . . The National League pennant was hoisted with the flag. The players gathered at home plate where a silver horseshoe was presented to Leo Durocher by friends." Frisch, with his spike-wound stitches smarting, had decided to put Whitey Whitehead in his place at second base, while Medwick, again in support of Paul Dean, made three fine running catches and drove in four runs with a double in the first inning and a single in the third. They lost the next two games, and the team plodded on, as April ended with Pop Haines losing 12-2 to Cincinnati. The team was playing only .500 baseball as it finished its series at Crosley Field. There, Medwick went 3-3, hitting a home run and then being hit by a pitch. "I always felt this," Joe told Robert E. Hood in 1974, "if they threw at me they belonged to me. See?"

After a loss to the Giants, Medwick with two hits, the team looked at the season the next day in the rain and saw themselves in an embarrassing fourth place, behind even Brooklyn. On this day as well, May 14, 1935, again in the *World-Telegram,* a column by Tom Meany referred to the "Gas House Gang," as did a companion cartoon by Willard Mullin, who had dressed a group of hoodlums in Cardinal uniforms. They were carrying extra-large bats and looked determined and belligerent, yet somehow free and easy. By late summer, as other newspapers picked it up, the nickname had taken hold, and it would stay in use through 1937, and much longer.

The team traveled to St. Louis that night. Pitcher Ed Heusser, who said he liked to be called the "Wild Elk of the Wasatch," after a single win back on April 26, lost to Babe Ruth and his new team, the Braves, on May 17.

Attendance was expected to be high while Ruth was in St. Louis, but three unions tried to prevent that from happening. Their claim was that "Durocher made anti-union statements and appeared in City Court as a witness against a woman striker who attempted to board his automobile as he drove it through picket lines at a garment factory." In an interview with Bob Broeg, he recalled that "Joe went with Leo to pick up Grace [at the Forest City Manufacturing Company, where she worked as a dress designer], and Medwick also heckled the strikers, who recognized Medwick and were really pissed that he stuck his nose into the incident." The unions picketed the park and boycotted the game—ineffectively it seemed—while the Cardinals won 2-1.

Joe was capable of arrogance in other ways as well. Sometimes, when he wanted to hit in batting practice, he was known to say to rookies who were hitting, "Your time's up"; Joe wanted to get them out of the box to let him hit, to let them know who was boss. There was a good chance was that rookies already knew.

Medwick's two hits the next day helped pitcher Pop Haines win. The next day Joe had a two-run home run as one of his three hits that not only aided Will Bill Hallahan to a win, but also took the Dodgers out of second place in the league. Also in that game, Medwick showed why Frisch loved to have him on his team. In the sixth, his long fly, though not a difficult catch, was dropped; Medwick, unlike so many others, did not stop running hard on the balls that he hit, and he went to second base. This hustle was not only energizing to his own team; it was frequently discouraging—even maddening— to the other. Medwick believed throughout his career that you had to make the man with the ball make the good throw. Joe put his body in play. Even with that error, Medwick could see that he was hitting .302 after thirty-four games.

When the Reds came into town at May's end, the Cardinals won behind Walker, but Joe realized he had only two hits in the last four games. He knew he must do better in the doubleheader the next day, May 30.

He did. Joe doubled in the first, third, and sixth innings, and tripled in the seventh in game one; he singled and hit two more doubles in game two. As the Cardinals won both games, Medwick had hit 7-9, six of them extra-base hits, and five of them doubles. This was a record for extra-base hits in a doubleheader. The hits had driven in six runs and Medwick had scored twice. The Cards moved into second place in a Memorial Day doubleheader to remember; Medwick had raised his average up to .322, still a long way from the league lead with Arky Vaughan, the Pirate shortstop, hitting .403.

And then on June 4, going into the visiting fifth, the Cardinals were a run behind. In the game's play-by-play, the following was written: "FIFTH—CARDINALS—Whitehead flied to Jensen. There was a scuffling match on the Cardinal bench, Dizzy Dean taking exception to other players' protests because he had merely lobbed the ball over the plate during the fourth inning. Frisch separated Dizzy and a teammate, and escorted his pitcher to a corner of the dugout. Rothrock singled to center. Martin forced Rothrock. Medwick tripled to right center for his third straight hit, scoring Martin. Collins grounded to Suhr."

While St. Louis was at bat in the fifth inning, as Robert E. Hood told it, Diz cursed the weak fielding he saw and then berated the entire team as a

> "bunch of lousy, no-good ballplayers," who didn't belong on the same field with him. "You-all ain't good enough," he said.
>
> "Shut up," snapped Collins, angrily jumping from the bench. They were fed up with his "crazy shit," said Collins, and [if] he [Diz] didn't shut his "fucking mouth" somebody was going to do it for him.
>
> "You do it," said Diz, "If you're man enough and not yellow." Collins was about to swing when Frisch stepped between them.
>
> A few feet away, Joe Medwick, who had wanted to punch Diz on many other occasions, warned him not to say another thing. "Fuck you," said Diz, and they started for each other. They were in front of the dugout in plain sight. As Paul hurried to his brother's side, believing Medwick might be too much for Diz to handle alone, Joe picked up a bat. He intended to separate them, he said, and one swing to the head would get both. At that point, Pepper Martin and several others intervened. Everybody settled down and the truce held.

It held even later when Diz hit Vaughan and the play-by-play said, "Dean was merely lobbing the ball over the plate" because he was angry at the newly enforced balk rule. The Pirates scored four that half of an inning. In the Pirate sixth, "Jensen picked on a slow ball and hit into the right field stands for a home run." The Pirates were grateful, but the disgusted fans were not. They were yelling for Dean to bear down or get out of the game. By the time he finally left in the seventh, Pittsburgh led, 9-3.

Durocher, and others, would claim over the years that a few innings later Medwick hit a grand-slam homer and said to Diz, "Okay, see if you can hold that lead, gutless." But there were no home runs in the game by the Cardinals, grand slam or otherwise, and though they made two runs in the eighth inning, they never led after the third, and lost, 9-5.

> Frisch paced back and forth in the clubhouse while the boys were dressing before starting his discussion of the case with Dizzy, who was in street clothes, while Frisch only had on his socks [and] shoes. Frank was puffing on a big black cigar as he tried to decide what was best to be done.

Frisch said, "I told him 'in his own language of the clubhouse' that, 'you can't come on our bench and tell these young fellows that they're lousy or not hustling for you.'" Frisch said Dean, "made slurring remarks about the team, describing it as a lousy ball club. Naturally, the fellows who have been hustling their heads off, resented this, and they challenged him. He wasn't doing his best out there and he knows it. He had twice in previous games with the Pirates disobeyed my instructions and pitched wrong to Arky Vaughan with the result that we lost both games."

"It was an unwarranted display of temper on Dean's part," explained Frisch about the lobs which had started it all, "and I told him if he ever failed again to give his best, I'd fine him $5,000 and put him under suspension. That's all. It's a closed incident." Dean was on official probation.

Later Dean was quoted as saying, "As for Medwick, I'll crack him on his Hungarian beeper." Later, Frisch, flabbergasted at Dean's remark that Medwick wasn't hustling, was quoted as saying, "Imagine, telling Medwick he hadn't hustled."

Over the years this incident, like the batting-cage fight with Carleton, was used as evidence of Medwick's supposed intractability—his pugnacity, his viciousness. But what really happened? Was Medwick protecting Collins? Was Medwick the only team member who could put a stop to Dean's childishness—to Dean's willingness to give away a game because batters are hitting him hard—a game that could mean more than $5,000 to each man on the team? Does anyone believe Dean should have kept pitching the way he was and that everyone should have kept silent? No punches were thrown; no harm was done.

Medwick went 4-4 with two RBIs and a run scored in Dean's loss. Joe wanted to play hard and he wanted to win. He may have gotten angry at himself, at other teammates, or at the other team, but despite the anger he didn't stop trying to win. And he didn't make statements to the press; he just played harder.

Dizzy Dean was met first by silence and then by boos at Sportsman's the next day as he went to the mound to pitch; "two customers" threw a dozen lemons when he came to bat in the bottom of the second. Nevertheless, he got three hits, the Cardinals scored in every inning, and the Cubs were beaten for the third straight time. The Cardinals liked their 13-2 win, and Joe went 3-5. He also caught the last out.

During that game Joe had his eye on a girl in the stands who was sitting behind the Cardinal dugout with a classmate. The girl, age seventeen, named Isabelle, was finishing her junior year in high school. This game may have been her first baseball game.

After thirty years had passed, Isabelle Heutel Medwick remembered that "after the game Joey and Terry Moore played catch as they came in from the outfield, and when they got to the bench, Joey tossed the ball toward me. I caught it." One of Isabelle's friends later said to her, "Oh, Isabelle, he must have liked you," to which she answered, "I don't even know the man."

But Joe was clearly attracted to Isabelle.

After the Cardinals lost at the Polo Grounds, and then at Cincinnati's Crosley Field by 4-2, the June 29th game was the one in which Medwick hit for the "cycle." Not yet called by that name, in the history of baseball there had been many more no-hitters pitched than there had been players who had hit for the cycle. Medwick supplied most of his team's runs in the 8-6 loss with a double, a triple, a single, and a homer in the ninth. He had made fifty-six hits in the games played in June.

Against the Cubs in Chicago for the Fourth of July doubleheader, before a holiday crowd of 38,100, Orsatti made five hits and Medwick hit a low line drive through an exit gate below the center field bleachers.

The team traveled four hundred miles that night to play in St. Paul, and then they traveled seven hundred miles after the game for a two-day series with the Reds.

On the night of July 7, the Cardinal 1935 All-Stars made the 250-mile trip to Cleveland for the 1935 game. "Frisch, who will direct this team, based his choices on the recommendations of other managers and club owners," and so he picked Collins as a reserve first baseman, himself as second baseman, Johnny Martin as third baseman, Whitey Whitehead as a utility infielder, and Joe, who by game time had accumulated 107 hits and a .358 batting average. Bill Walker and Diz were picked as pitchers, while Doc Weaver would serve as the All-Star trainer.

The game was played on July 8, but unlike other years, Joe could only contribute a walk. After the game, the weary All-Stars traveled the miles home for games with the Phillies, the season starting again on July 11. The Giants, at almost a .700 winning percentage with forty-eight wins and twenty-one losses, had completed 45 percent of their games and were eight ahead of the Cardinals in losses, eleven losses ahead of the Cubs, and thirteen ahead of Pittsburgh.

The Cardinals had a six-game winning streak and an odd second half schedule for 1935 since almost all of July (and all of September) were home games.

Isabelle Heutel, accompanied by her mother, began to be a regular at the games. It was during this extended period at home that Joe started dating the girl to whom he had thrown the ball back on June 9. He first asked her out by asking Mrs. Heutel's permission and then having a note asking for a date delivered to Miss Heutel in the stands. She accepted. Isabelle Heutel grew up in southwestern St. Louis County, an area that natives now call Sunset Hills. Her grandfather and father were the businessmen who opened Sunset Automobile Company, a company that still exists in St. Louis but is now called Sunset Ford.

Sunday, July 14, 1935, was championship day at Sportsman's Park. Commissioner Kennesaw Mountain Landis had traveled to St. Louis to hand out the diamond rings for the 1934 World Series win to each Cardinal team member, and along with twenty-three thousand fans, watched "the world's championship flag . . . hoisted to the centre field flagpole." Medwick went 4-8 in the doubleheader. Paul Dean pitched a seven-hitter in game one, with Medwick getting one hit but scoring twice; in the second game, Willie Walker gave up sixteen hits but only one run as Medwick went 3-5 and stole second base.

Joe Williams wrote:

> The Cardinals seem to be the type of team that can turn the pressure on any time the mood strikes. Appropriately dubbed the Gas House Gang, they play the game up to the hilt . . . have more color, fight and verve than any club since the old days of McGraw. They have a fiery manager in Frisch and their play reflect[s] his rugged characteristics. They fight among themselves and with others. Some of them hate Frisch; Dizzy Dean laughs at him. They [are] anything but one large happy family, but when the chips [are] down, they get together and play baseball.

Manager Frankie Frisch admitted, "You've got to be profane with this bunch of mugs, otherwise they think you don't like 'em."

As the first-place Giants came to St. Louis, John Kiernan wrote the following about Joe's team: "They're fast and rough and they boast about it. They swell with pride when they're referred to as 'the galloping hoodlums.'" Hallahan pitched them to an 8-5 win, helped by Medwick's three hits to bring the Cardinals to just one half-game from the lead.

In the first game of the July 23 doubleheaders, Medwick had home runs number thirteen and fourteen. His "spectacular catch" off Bill Terry's drive helped his team into first place.

But not for long, though Medwick went 4-4 in the second game, making half of the Cardinal hits and scoring half of the Cardinal runs, when Walker lost 8-2.

Some of the Cardinals were hitting very well: Medwick was second in his team's batting average, first in hits with 131, tied with Johnnie Martin for runs, while Martin led in stolen bases and doubles, with Ripper Collins second in home runs. But there was something about the team pitching that just wasn't right.

The team, in second place now, and three and a half games behind, traveled East the night of July 25 to play an exhibition in Rochester, New York (eight hundred miles from St. Louis). When that was through, they went another three hundred miles to Pittsburgh. In the first ever Sunday doubleheader in Pittsburgh, Dizzy won and Paul lost, followed by a 3-2 loss on the 29th pitched by Bill Hallahan. Roy Stockton wrote: "The Cardinals continued this afternoon to show the devastating attack of a second division club in the Junior Bloomer Girls League." But Medwick continued his focused hitting, with 2-4 that day, his average now .380 to Arky Vaughan's .393.

July 31 was one of the seven night games played in the major leagues in 1935, all held at Crosley Field. Before the game, "there was a band concert and a dandy fireworks display. [There was also] a baseball field meet. . . . Babe Herman hit the longest fungo, Delancey won the 60-yard dash for batterymen, Terry Moore won the open 60-yard race and Virgil Davis was the most accurate thrower, hitting a barrel at second base twice out of three tries." By the fourth inning, a boisterous, over-capacity crowd of many more than the twenty thousand the park was built to seat, forced its way onto the field in right and center fields, along the foul lines, and behind home plate—so close that batters had to shoulder their way to the plate. Some fans even sat in the dugouts, slapping the players on the back and kidding with them. Some fans fought for baseballs in foul territory. "Thousands of beer and soda bottles were strewn about the field. Pop flies to right and left field were made doubles by the ground rules."

Earlier in the game, a blond nightclub entertainer named Kitty Burke engaged in some joking with Medwick as he was in the on deck circle. She was razzing Joe, shouting that she was a better hitter than he was. In the eighth inning, the Cardinals were winning 2-1. With the Reds' Sammy Byrd on first, Goodie Goodman flied out to Terry Moore, but Frisch collided with Moore, and as Frisch was being tended to, Burke made her move. With Commissioner Landis watching, and Umpire Bill Stewart dumbstruck, Burke took a bat from Cincinnati outfielder Babe Herman, came to the plate, and motioned for Paul Dean to toss one. Paul, after hesitating to see if his team was in position, threw an underhanded pitch. Burke swung, knocking the ball down the first base line; Dean fielded the ball, and stepped on first. Burke took a few steps, and then went back to her seat. Since the umpire had not objected, Frisch argued that her at bat ought to count as an out, but Stewart called Herman up to the plate for his at bat as though nothing had happened. Babe hit a double into the crowd in left, helping the Reds to take the lead, 3-2. The Cardinals lost 4-3. Medwick went 2-4 with a double; he had made nineteen hits in the last fourteen games of July.

August began in Cincinnati with a game played in ninety-five-degree heat, during which at least two odd things happened: Umpire Dolly Stark had to leave the game due to the heat, Riegler moving behind the plate, and Joe and Ripper hit back-to-back triples in the first inning. Medwick also had two walks, a single, with a run scored, and two RBIs.

Soon, the Cards moved East for their last away-games of the season. While they were gone, Breadon gave a picnic at his farm in Fenton, Missouri, for 120 members of the Cardinal Boys' Band. The Giants still led the National League on August 11, but both the Cardinals and the Cubs were very close. Medwick was still 16 points behind Vaughan's .395, but 32 points ahead of the American League's best hitter, Joe Vosmik. Medwick's 156 hits led both leagues. He was also first in runs and RBIs.

There was an exhibition against the Red Sox at Battle Creek, Michigan, where the Cardinals, playing hard, rallied for eight runs in the seventh inning to win, 9-8. After being guests at a testimonial dinner for Branch Rickey in that Michigan city, it was onto the train for a seven-hundred-mile trip to New York, stopping off in

Rochester for another exhibition with the farm team, before the actual twenty-four-day road trip began.

Though Martin gave his all, they could only win two of the five games at their first stop, the Polo Grounds, with both wins given to Dizzy. On the fourteenth, with 50,868 spectators watching, they lost to Hubbell, 6-4, and then Hallahan zeroed the Giants, beating Slick Castelman 3-0, during which Wild Bill hit his only major league home run. After that game, the *World-Telegram* commented that "Medwick broke his batting slump by singling to right." This was a slump that lasted seven games. The newspaper also went on to say that "Joe Medwick believes it's an accident anytime he doesn't get a hit. Derives real pleasure from insulting opposing players during batting practice, or during the game, if they show a disposition to carry the kidding further." The paper also noted that Jimmie Foxx picked Joe Medwick as the best left fielder in the game. On the fifteenth, Martin hit an inside-the-park home run to right center over Ott's head in the seventh, finishing with a great slide. But Medwick struck out twice.

The *New York Times* said, "An entertaining, picturesque bunch, these Cards, who seem to have captivated New York as no visiting team has done in many years. Crowds totaling 94,438 saw the four days of battling on the Harlem." The Giants' lead was two games. The Cubs had as many wins as the Giants, but five more losses.

In a doubleheader in Brooklyn, Medwick got four hits, one to right was another triple, and Ed Heusser won the first, Phil Collins the other, as the Cardinals outscored the Dodgers 17-6, and the two wins were summed up as "the rough and ready champions from beyond the Mississippi trampled all over the Flatbush flock." On Saturday the twenty-fourth, the newspapers told the story of the umpires punished for yelling at fans; of Frisch signed to another contract; of Medwick hitting .370 with 173 hits and 96 RBIs. In that day's game against the Dodgers, in the fourth inning with Jack Rockroth on, "Medwick touched [Ray] Benge for his 18th homer . . . it was an unusual circuit blow, the ball bouncing out of the corner in left over Taylor's head, Medwick completing the circuit before it could be returned. [Frenchy] Bordagaray stood in centre field watching the ball." It was Joe's 100th run scored. In game one in Sunday's doubleheader, Joe had a double and a triple. Medwick's average of .370 was 29 points behind Vaughan. Even so, with the Cardinals still in the race, Medwick was a close second in the preliminary voting for Most Valuable Player.

After Medwick's twentieth homer, the Cardinals were 77-46, the Giants were 76-47, and the Cubs were 77-51. The Cardinal team had won 23 and lost 6 in August; Medwick had made 44 hits for a .355 average for the month. He had hit in 16 games in a row, and in 26 of the 29 games. For the season, Medwick had played in 122 games (and one of five players to have come to bat 500 times), and was hitting .368 to Vaughan's .398.

Although the Cardinals lost to Paul Derringer on September first by 4-3, Medwick made a hit for the seventeenth game in a row, and the team happily traveled home to finish the year.

On the way, a letter appeared in the *Sporting News* from a fan in Brooklyn, who claimed "inasmuch as we have books of autographs, we asked Joe Medwick if he would kindly sign his name. Instead of obliging, as most players would, Medwick insulted all of us with remarks that would not be fit to print. . . . I . . . hope you publish this letter so other fans may know how the Cardinal player feels about his public." It may be that someone had been rude here, but to whom was unclear. In any case, "Joe Medwick received a letter this afternoon from Commissioner Landis stating that a Brooklyn fan had written a complaint alleging that Joe the Duck had addressed him disrespectfully. It would be interesting to know what a Brooklyn fan considers disrespectful."

It might be equally interesting to know whether Joe really was asked in a "kindly" manner; perhaps Joe had been asked to sign his name for that particular fan many times before—perhaps he was on his way to work (it could have been his turn to hit, for example).

September 2 was a doubleheader against the Pirates; they were games eighteen and nineteen in a row for Joe. On September 4, Walker won the team's third in a row, beating the Braves 6-3. Joe, alert to how deep third basemen around the league were playing him now, had a bunt single in third inning. It was game number twenty in a row for Joe.

Regarding the Most Valuable Player award, the "Poppin' Off" column with Dizzy Dean's byline said, "the experts won't be makin' no mistake if they pick Joe Medwick. Joe sure has done his share to put the Redbirds where they are. He can hit a ball as far as anybody and he has become a great outfielder along with it."

Since July 1, the Cardinals had played .705 baseball and had picked up eleven and a half games on the Giants. Collins won over the Braves 15-3. Medwick had two hits and a sacrifice, and Terry

Moore went 6-6, giving them a three-game lead. Meanwhile, the Cubs had a win and almost made it to second place. (It was game number twenty-one in a row for Joe.)

Diz beat Boston 6-4 on the sixth, and the Cubs also won. (Game number twenty-two in a row for Joe.)

Paul beat Boston, as Joe went 3-4, driving in two and scoring two (half the runs), along with stealing second base in the fifth inning; he was hitting .369. The Cards won six in a row and all four from the Braves, putting the Cardinals up five games in the loss column. (Game number twenty-three in a row for Joe.)

On a Sunday Medwick extended his streak to twenty-five. That night the major league All-Star team was announced, a team that was once again called "Babe Ruth's All-American team." Medwick was the left fielder. (The left fielders on the team go back in 1922 to Cobb, then Goslin; since 1927, the pick had been mostly Al Simmons, including in 1934.)

September 9 was Frankie Frisch's thirty-seventh birthday, and players gave him flowers and sang a birthday song. The lead was one game as the Cubs won. Moon Hallahan won the third game of the series against the Phillies. Joe's streak stood at twenty-seven games.

In the last game of the series against Philadelphia, Joe singled in the second and stole second base. In the third, he was struck by a thrown ball. As Joe ran toward second, Collins grounded to second baseman Lou Chiozza, whose throw hit Medwick when Chiozza threw to shortstop Gomez to start a double play. Medwick's bruise produced a Frisch score, and Joe later scored. After the game, in true sportswriter fashion, Medwick was described as "no mental colossus, this lad from Carteret, New Jersey [but he] is quite a hitter and a much improved outfielder. . . . Pepper may be the spark plug but Medwick is the dynamo."

Paul Dean beat the Phils on a seven-hitter 10-2 in game number twenty-eight in a row for Joe.

On September 12, the Giants came to town and the league chose to have four umpires rather than the usual three work the game. Against Carl Hubbell, Medwick struck out in the first inning, and flew out to Ott in the third and fifth. Then he was intentionally walked. Dizzy beat Hubbell 5-2; the Cubs also won.

There is not a single word in any issue of the *Post-Dispatch* about the end of Medwick's hitting streak, a streak that was not matched by Ruth, Gehrig, Williams, Mays, or Aaron. He had hit in thirty-eight of his last forty-one games.

During the game against the Giants on the fourteenth, the Cardinals scored in the first inning and went ahead in the seventh, but the Giants tied the score in the eighth. In the eighth, Medwick hit a pitch so hard back to pitcher Hal Schumacher that the ball deflected past Hughie Critz at second base; running hard as usual, Joe made it to second base, and moved to third on Collins's infield out. When Spud Davis also hit one hard to the pitcher, Medwick slid under the tag at home to break the 2-2 tie. But the Giants tied it in the ninth and went ahead in the tenth. Once again, Medwick came through. After he walked, he moved to third on a fielder's choice and an infield hit, and scored on Durocher's fly. In the eleventh, relief pitcher Castleman doubled off Phil Collins and scored on a single to left by Joe Moore. When the ball got through Medwick, Moore tried to score, but Medwick recovered and threw him out. But the Cardinals couldn't get a runner around in their half, and "Silently the crowd trooped out of the park. For the second successive afternoon it had seen its Cardinals beaten in the sort of ball games the Cardinals usually win." The loss dropped the Cardinals to second place behind Chicago, who were in the lead for the first time.

The Sunday game on September 15 drew forty-three thousand spectators, the largest crowd ever for a single game at Sportsman's Park, with some of the crowd standing or sitting all the way across the outfield "in a solid bank from foul line to foul line." By the time Medwick homered in the sixth inning for the first Cardinal run, the team was five runs down and Dizzy Dean had been replaced by Willie Walker. But the Giants scored two more in their seventh, and some in the crowd, seeing that the Cardinals had lost all three to the Giants as the Cubs kept on winning, were angry. Joe Moore in left had a soda pop bottle thrown at him, and then one was thrown at right fielder Mel Ott. At the end, it was Hubbell on the mound to get the win, his twenty-second, while Dizzy took his fifth straight loss. Joe was 2-5, producing two of the three Card runs.

Cincinnati and Pittsburgh both slapped around Joe's team, and when the Cardinal team was shutout, a fan played taps on a bugle. The loss was the Cardinals' third in seven days. Joe hit into two double plays. "The way he's going now," Red Bird Notes proclaimed, "he probably couldn't even hit a grapefruit even if he did get to Detroit."

The Cubs, who were on an eighteen-game winning streak, came into town needing only two of five to win the pennant, whereas the Cardinals would have to beat the Cubs all five times to get to the World Series, or four to get to a tie and a play-off. Frisch was quoted as saying, "We were almost this near the Valley of No World Series Parsnips last year and we pulled through. We'll cut and slash right down to the finish—that is, we'll be out there trying to cut and slash."

After a 1-0 loss and a rain day, Dizzy was sent out to stop the Cubs in the first game of a Friday doubleheader, but the Cubs scored six, Medwick went hitless for the third straight game, and Diz lost to Big Bill Lee, who won his twentieth, bringing the Cubs the pennant; it was also their 100th win and their 20th in a row, a streak that began on September 4. In the first three losses to the Cubs in the series, the team produced five runs. The *World-Telegram* commented, "[Medwick] slumped badly at bat in the stretch run and . . . Ducky Wucky can be had at the proper figure along with any of the other Cardinals excepting the two Deans." Medwick had a twenty-eight-game hitting streak stopped on September 12, and though he hit .277 for September, he hit .355 for the first eleven games of the month. He had produced, so far, 228 runs for the team. The only other player in the league who had produced more than 200 runs was his teammate Rip Collins. Why was it that no one blamed Collins?

Medwick came to work the next day and made four hits: a single in the first inning, a triple in the fifth, and two home runs. In the eleventh, with Jack Rothrock on, he homered to win the game for Willie Walker. "Joe, back in the best hitting stride [was] just about too late to butter any World Series parsnips." The Cardinals still played hard, trying to stretch doubles into triples—trying to extend double steals. Dean didn't show up for the game. The Cubs lost after twenty-one consecutive wins. Frisch signed to manage for another year.

Joe finished in the top three in the National League: first in total bases; second in runs, hits (224), doubles, batting average, RBIs, and slugging percentage; third in triples, home runs, and runs created. Among all major leaguers, he was second in hits made and in runs scored, third in RBIs, fifth in slugging, seventh in triples, and ninth in home runs. This wasn't even his best year in baseball, but it was the start of a remarkable five-year span in his career from 1935 to 1939.

A full share of the Cardinals' World Series money was worth $1,149.09. Medwick picked up some money when the owner of Philips Delicious Tomato Packing Company in Cambridge, Maryland, was offered a bet of $500 from a Buick dealer in the same city to play his team. The dealer's team, nothing but ringers, included Athletics' future outfielder Bill Nicholson, Wally Roetger from Cincinnati, Maxie Bishop with the Red Sox, Bud Thomas, who had played with the Senators, Jimmie Foxx with the Athletics, and Billy Werber, who related this story. Dick Porter called Joe, since Porter had been chosen to get Philips's team together. Joe agreed to play in Maryland to finish out the year.

10

Sixty-Four Doubles, 1936

Joe signed early for the 1936 season, just after Frisch had signed in December. Going to St. Louis to sign his contract may not have been Joe's only reason for visiting the city where Isabelle Heutel lived. Strangely enough, Frisch, having returned from the winter meeting at the Palmer House in Chicago, met with Joe, Leo, and Dizzy, and they all had a chat in the Cardinal offices.

By March 1, Joe read an Associated Press (AP) release that claimed, "The General Manager [of the Boston Bees] tried to trade Wally Berger for Ducky Medwick yesterday when he visited the Cardinal camp at Bradenton." Joe was probably paid $9,000 that year, so Rickey might have been tempted to make the trade.

The St. Louis newspaper of March 4 told its readers that "28 Redbirds will be hobnobbing with muchachos of the Pearl of the Antilles." The team boarded a steamship to play some games in Cuba. There, on March 5, Luis Tiant, Sr., pitched for the Havana team of the Cuban Winter League and each team won a game.

After returning by steamer to Miami, and then to Bradenton, the Cardinals played a notable game on St. Patrick's Day: it was the major league debut of a rookie right fielder, Joe DiMaggio, who tripled over Medwick's head.

On March 26, an overflow crowd of one thousand spectators watched the Cardinals at their home field play the Tigers. Before the game, Joe and Marv Owen were photographed shaking hands, but during the game, Medwick once again went into third with spikes high, but there was no throw, so Owens had to step aside.

On the way north, the odds for the baseball season appeared; they favored the Cubs, with the Cardinals in second, followed by the Giants and Pittsburgh.

In St. Louis, the night of April 13 was marked by a dinner to salute the Cardinals and the Browns at the Hotel Jefferson. The next day, to draw attention to the sixtieth anniversary of the National League, horse-drawn "hacks in which visiting ballplayers were conveyed from their hotel to the baseball park" were used to carry the Cardinal players in uniform to the park for opening day. The new electric public address system was manned by George Carson. Also new was baseball's antifraternization rule, which carried with it a $10 fine if a player talked to a rival on the field before or during a game.

In Medwick's year for doubles, he drove in his first run of the year with his first two-base hit of the year. Medwick also got four more hits and an intentional walk to end this opening series.

Joe apparently decided to show off his physique: "Joe Medwick certainly can shellac the old American apple, but cutting his undershirt sleeves doesn't make him Jimmie Foxx and too, it wouldn't detract from his appearance to get back in the collar and tie league."

Of the first eleven games played, Joe had had hits in ten of them, nine being multihit games, for a total of twenty-one hits. Against the newly christened Boston Bees, Medwick's defense helped: "Joe charged in and over toward the foul lines. He raced to the bleacher wall for a seemingly impossible catch. He was everywhere in left field. The Braves [*sic*] must have thought there were a dozen Medwicks out there."

On May 5, in the ninth, his team down by a run, Joe singled to center and on the next play Chile Gomez at second threw wild, and Joe raced all the way in to tie the game. On May 7, in Chicago, as Ryba picked up his first win in an 11-9 game, new teammate Johnny Mize hit two home runs and Medwick drove in five with three hits: a single in the first inning drove in two and his first home run in the fifth drove in two more, so the Cards took over first place.

The Cardinals needed Joe's bat because there were one hundred points between him and the rest of the team's regulars. More than half of the position players were hitting at .266 or below. Medwick had produced 26 percent of the team's runs and drove in 19 percent.

He made forty-three hits in the first month of play, along with twenty-one RBIs.

Frisch said the reason for Medwick's success was "due to the fact he makes pitchers pitch to him nowadays. . . . I believe he is slated to be the best player in the National League this year."

The *Sporting News* article of May 28, 1936, admitted,

> This ought to be as good a time as any to pin a few posies upon the manly chest of Joe Medwick. . . . Joe is a one-man rebellion against National League pitching. . . . One pitcher may throw high inside to him, make him look like a sucker on one pitch. But Ducky-Wucky is liable to unleash his big bat on the next delivery and hit it over the outfield escarpments. . . . Medwick was not regarded as a top in fielding last year or the season before. But his defensive play has improved steadily. This year he has been racing far and wide to take down drives that might otherwise go for base knocks. And there isn't a better arm in the league.

The team was doing what it had to do, winning at a .654 percentage against first-division clubs.

There was a note on June 11 in the *Post-Dispatch* revealing that "wedding bells were chiming in the distance for Joe Medwick. The gal was a St. Louis Mary Institute grad of last week. She's 17." The day of that story, while running from second to third base in the fifth inning, Joe was hit on the left leg near the hip on a wild throw by second baseman Chile Gomez, and the left fielder was forced out of the lineup, replaced by Lynn King.

Joe homered the next day, leading off the second, and on June 13 he put the ball in play and ran hard, reaching second base when Gomez dropped his fly. This pop-fly error caused Stu Martin to score and Pepper Martin to reach third, and forced the Phillies to walk Collins. This in turn led to Mize forcing Collins at second, which allowed Pepper to score. And then, on a double steal with Mize, Joe scored on his steal of home. All of this happened in a six-run second inning on the way to Dizzy's twelfth win, 7-1.

After the team traveled to Rochester for an exhibition, they moved on to Boston. During the doubleheader the next day, June 17, Bunker Hill Day at the Bees' "Hive," a typically Gashouse Gang thing happened. Before the first game, Pepper Martin was replaced by Lynn King in right field because Martin, imitating professional wrestler Ali Baba, injured his left hip while wrestling with Paul Dean, the starting pitcher, in the clubhouse.

In the Polo Grounds on June 19, in the first with Prince Hal Schumacher pitching, "Medwick hit a tremendous line drive against the façade of the left field stands [between the upper and lower decks] for a home run." Just to be safe, Medwick was walked in the ninth with two out. Dizzy won his ninth in a row, 7-5. In this Saturday game, Joe was 1-5 against King Carl Hubbell and his "butterfly curve." But Joe always found a way to influence the game. In the third inning, though Medwick forced Pepper Martin at second, Pepper upset Whitehead after Burgess had thrown to first trying for a double play. Then first baseman Bill Terry held the ball, protesting that Martin's slide had interfered and Joe should be out as well. During Terry's protest, Medwick raced safely to second. Medwick also got an infield hit in the loss. That loss, combined with the Cubs' fourteenth win in a row, put the Chicago team only one game back. Joe had fifteen hits in the last nine games.

The Cardinals traveled to Brooklyn for a weekend series, during which they split two games, one win with the help of Medwick, who "fell away from the plate and maced a bad inside curve ball" for his eighth home run. For the month of June 1936, he had thirty-two hits including ten multihit games.

The July 4 doubleheader at Crosley Field in Cincinnati showed Joe's determination: "Medwick played despite a spiked foot which was swollen and bandaged."

For the 1936 All-Star game, Joe's third in a row, Medwick traveled to Boston's Braves Field. There, the National League won for the first time 4-3, and Joe, batting cleanup as usual, played the whole game along with teammates Ripper Collins at first and Leo Durocher at shortstop. The important hits were Gabby Hartnett's triple, Augie Galan's homer, and Joe's game-winning RBI single off Schoolboy Rowe in the fifth.

"There [are] two sides to a story and that seems to be true in the case of Joe Medwick, who was the target for indignant columnists while he was in the East with the Cardinals recently [June 16–July 5]," J. Roy Stockton wrote in his "Extra Innings" column of July 10. One side of the story was that

a committee [arranging for a benefit in Perth Amboy] called on Joe Medwick and . . . that the Cardinal slugger refused to talk to the members. . . . This drew the following blast from a columnist in a New York newspaper: "He was too busy to talk about such trivial matters. . . . Joe used to know all the members of the committee when he was playing sand-lot ball over around Perth Amboy, but, shucks, an important big leaguer like Joe had no time to waste on small town rubes. So Joe turned heel on the boys and refused to sign. . . ." Now listen to what happened as told by Medwick: "Mr. Paden of the Perth Amboy newspaper . . . said they were having a benefit game and wanted to get three autographed baseballs. . . . So I told him I couldn't get any baseballs for him, tough as Coach Buzzy Wares was—he's the keeper of the baseball bag—but . . . if Mr. Padden would get the baseballs I would be very happy to get them autographed for him. . . ." Because Joe Medwick would not take $3.75 out of the Cardinal strong box and give it to a young man from Perth Amboy, he was attacked as a high-hatted big headed galoot. Joe made mistakes during his first big league year, but he had learned rapidly. He is well-behaved, lives a clean life and is good to his mother. The last time we saw Joe's mother was in Brooklyn, where she journeyed to Ebbets Field to see her boy play against the Dodgers. When she entered a front row box, Joe left the dugout, leaned over the railing and they embraced. He stood there with her until duty of the game called. Proudly, she put her arm around her boy and patted his shoulder as they stood there. Baseball had enabled Joe to do a lot for Mother Medwick. It's too bad if anybody showed her that unwarranted dig at her boy, Joe.

Joe's off-the-field life continued in the press on July 10 with the "Announcement of the engagement of Joe Medwick, Cardinal outfielder, and Miss Isabelle Heutel of Sappington, Mo., a suburb of St. Louis. The prospective bride was 19 years old and was graduated from Mary Institute, St. Louis, this year. Medwick . . . corresponded with her from his home in Carteret, N.J. during the winter. According to Miss Heutel's mother, the marriage will take place some time in the fall."

Against the fearsome Carl Hubbell the next day in the humid 102-degree St. Louis summer weather, Joe scored two and drove in one in the following performance in thirteen innings: he doubled off Hubbell in the fourth; he beat out an infield hit, and when the throw went into the dugout, he claimed second base, from where he scored on Durocher's single for the first run for his team; his second double of the day drove in Terry Moore in the eighth, and then he came around to score the tying run, 4-4. Frisch doubled in the thirteenth to win it 5-4.

Against Brooklyn, Medwick hit in consecutive games number ten and eleven and also hit doubles number twenty-nine, thirty, and thirty-one, but Walker and Winford lost when Cardinal pitching allowed seventeen runs in the doubleheader. Joe made his first error of the season after seventy-eight games when his throw went into the dugout in the fifth inning of the second game. Days later, Medwick's single in the sixth made the streak sixteen games in a row; the newspapers took note of the streak.

The second and third games against Boston were a doubleheader quietly marked by Joe, who scored twice and had three hits in three at bats in game one. In game two, Medwick scored once, drove in three, and had a walk and four hits in four at bats. He was 7-7: six singles and a double in the doubleheader.

The next day, Carl Hubbell was awaiting the Cardinals yet again (some people consider Hubbell the best pitcher of the 1930s). Hubbell didn't disappoint; "King Carl" gave up nine hits, but only one run. And Joe singled in the second, doubled in the fourth, and singled again in the sixth against the finest pitcher of his time. Medwick's ten hits in a row meant he had tied the league record; only five National Leaguers had ever done that before Medwick. (In the next sixty years, this feat would only be accomplished six times in the major leagues.) Though he grounded to Bartell in the eighth, Medwick took over the league lead, raising his average to .372, sixteen points ahead of Waner of Pittsburgh.

> With 10 straight hits Joe Medwick tied
> The N.L. record and with pride
> We tip our hats to Ducky.
> He tried for the eleventh clout
> To rub Tris Speaker's record out
> But he was a bit unlucky.

At the same time, someone noticed that in the eighty games played so far, Joe made 181 putouts and 9 assists, with only 1 error.

Medwick kept hitting; now he had hit in twenty games consecutively. He scored and drove in one with his single to extend his streak to twenty-one games. But then in Boston on July 25, Deacon Danny Macfayden ended Medwick's hitting streak (which had started on July 1), beating Winford in a game shortened by rain. Joe, with seventeen more hits than Paul Waner, led him by ten percentage points at .369.

On August 7, Joe hit double number forty in a 14-5 loss. The team was glad to get home for five days with a two-game lead.

Fans were expecting a battle when the Cubs came to Sportsman's Park on August 10, but the teams tied the first game due to darkness, and though the Cardinals could only get five hits the next day, they won 5-3. Joe scored three of the runs in the following way: a lead-off double in the second inning, followed by an infield out and a long fly, produced the first run. His 374-foot homer in the fourth produced the second, and after Terry Moore singled in the sixth, "Charlie Grimm believed it wise strategy to walk Medwick." Mize homered them all in for runs three, four, and five, and Si Johnson earned his first Cardinal win.

On August 23, which was Joe's "last day as a bachelor," he got four straight hits. This was during a two-week heat wave in St. Louis, with heat so extreme that a circus camel had to be tended to by the humane society.

The next day, Monday, August 24, was an off-day by the original National League schedule, but for the Cardinals it was to be used to make up a rain date from April 27. It was an extremely hot day: eighty-six degrees at 9 A.M. and one hundred degrees during batting practice. Making three straight hits and driving in two, Joe took over the National League lead from teammate Johnny Mize. It was also Joe's wedding day. Joe made seven straight hits in the two games before his wedding, a ceremony delayed for two hours because of this unscheduled game.

The formal picture of bride and groom was taken at "the home of the bride's parents, Mr. and Mrs. Joseph H. Heutel, Geyer Road, Sappington." (Bob Broeg recalled, "I don't think her [Isabelle's] family ever did like him [Joe]—her father particularly.") Isabelle, a debutante, was one of the second-tier elite of St. Louis. Joe appeared only slightly taller than his bride and was dressed in a white suit and white shoes. The bride, six years younger than her groom, was often described as "lovely [and] olive-skinned." She resembled movie star Dolores Del Rio. After the wedding, from which "Frankie Frisch stayed away so his team could have fun," there was another photograph showing most of the men in white suits including Joe's best man, Leo Durocher, as well as Charlie Gelbert, Ed Heusser, Jesse Haines (with his hand on Joe's shoulder), Terry Moore, Buzzy Wares, Bud Parmelee, Spud Davis, and Mike Gonzalez. The bride looks enormously happy, as does the groom. A wedding photo that was printed years later said, "Ducky Joe, the poor kid from the wrong side of the tracks . . . at the time he married lovely Isabelle Heutel of a prominent South County family."

The next day bridegroom Joe was 3-7 in a doubleheader against the Bees, but even with his three RBIs, the Cardinals lost both.

In the last games of the month for St. Louis, Joe contributed four hits in a doubleheader against the Dodgers. He hit one single and two triples in game one, and a double and an RBI against Van Mungo in game two. Joe scored on "daring base running, when he came home after [second baseman Lonny] Frey took Gelbert's pop fly in short left."

On September 6, game one was lost to old teammate (and Joe's roommate), Bill Hallahan. In that game, Joe had two interesting innings: "Medwick made a fine throw to the plate to cut off a Cincinnati run in the third inning. Cuyler opened with a single to left and after Goodman and Herman had flied out, Scarsella hit the left field line with a double. The ball struck a pole supporting the awning over the Reds' bullpen and stopped, and Medwick had to sprint in for the ball. His throw reached Davis on the first hop and Cuyler was out on a close play" for the third out of the inning. Medwick, leading off the next inning, doubled to center. When he tried to tag up and go to third on Mize's fly to Rihhs, he was called out. "Medwick questioned the decision and Umpire Klem dramatically repeated the gesture that means the man was out." Then, in the Reds' half, "Medwick made a brilliant catch. . . . With Riggs on second, Thevenow on first and one out, Kampouris hit to the left field wall, but Medwick plucked the ball out of the air just as it was about to hit the concrete."

On the way to Pittsburgh, the newspapers announced that Joe had been picked as the All-American baseball team's left fielder and number six hitter (after Appling, Gehringer, DiMaggio, Gehrig, and Averill, and followed by Dickey). Typically for the 1930s, National Leaguer Joe was the only National League position player, with Dean and Hubbell chosen as the pitchers.

At the same time, "Babe Ruth, Chairman, All-American Board of Baseball," who had been "advised" by ten sports editors, all of whom had one vote, picked his "1936 All-Star team." Joe, with all ten votes, was the unanimous choice in left field. His selection "merely confirms a belief which generally prevails." He was the only National League position player except for Frank Demaree in center.

The last game of the series in the Polo Grounds against the league leaders was played on August 14, and Ed Heusser (who loved being called "the Wild Elk of the Wasatch") was the fourth pitcher of the day. At 6 feet, 187 pounds, Heusser had a bully's reputation and a history of professional boxing bouts in his past. Heusser, who was taken out in the sixth, losing 7-1 (Heusser hit a home run for the only run) complained as Medwick came into the dugout, saying either that Joe should have hustled more to get to a run-scoring single by Dick Bartell in left center in the bottom of the third or should have made a better throw to the plate.

"You Hungarian bastard, why didn't you catch that ball?"

"You can't say that to me," Medwick answered, and they swung at each other. Mike Ryba, Joe's Scottdale teammate, got punched in the ribs trying to break it up. Some reports said that Joe knocked Heusser down with a right to the mouth. (That's one version, anyway.)

In 1968, Joe said, "[Ed] popped me on the chin. I'd been playing over in left-center for a left-handed hitter and he sliced one inside the full line in deep left. Heusser didn't think I hustled enough chasing it and told me so . . . and finally he hit me on the chin. I told him I took a riding from the manager, but no one else."

Heusser, an invitee to Joe's wedding, said no more. Joe had had a terrible group of games since September 7, making only ten hits in eleven games. Being four and a half games back wasn't helping his disposition—or anyone else's.

People had different memories, and of course, inconsistent stories about Joe from this time period. "Truthfully," Gutteridge said, "Medwick had a sour disposition. He was just not a real likeable guy. He was a bit of an egotist. . . . But nobody liked Joe . . . I liked him because he drove me in all the time. I liked to score runs and he'd drive me in." So Joe was liked because he made money for others. Should Joe also like other players because they made money for him or dislike others when they prevented him from making money?

In any case, team members liked Joe enough to play jokes on him. Joe said, "You never knew what would happen. You might go to sleep and find a match in your shoe. We'd open the paper and there'd be a hole burned right in the middle of it." Don Gutteridge talked about how Dizzy Dean and Johnnie Martin "liked to agitate Medwick all they could." They "agitated" so easily because Medwick was so serious about the game, far too serious for some. Gutteridge admits to immediately feeling partial to Pepper Martin and

Chapter 10

Dizzy Dean. "They never did anything to me. I was a meek little lamb." Joe certainly wasn't meek.

At Baker Bowl in Philadelphia in mid September, Medwick joined a group of five other men who had hit sixty doubles or more in a season. Since 1936, no one has made sixty doubles in a season.

At home against the Reds for four games, Joe hit his National League record-tying 62nd double in the sixth inning on September 22. Joe's competition for the batting title, Paul Waner, had set the National League record for doubles on the last day of the season in 1932, breaking, in his turn, Chuck Klein's record of fifty-nine doubles in 1930.

A day of rain was followed by a Thursday doubleheader, and Mike Ryba got another win when he relieved in the ninth inning of game one. Joe scored the winning run for his old Scottdale teammate, and hit a National League record-breaking 63rd double in this game in the third inning.

On Friday, September 25, Joe came up in the second inning and hit his 64th double.

It would be seventeen years before a National Leaguer, Stan Musial, would get within even eleven doubles of Joe's record. In 2001, the National League record had stood for sixty-five years, one of the oldest records in hitting.

Bill McGee's 3-2 loss meant that the Cubs were coming to town two games down. But before the last game, there were two contests on the field. Mike Ryba won $25 for "accurate throwing to second base." Then, Cubs pitcher Lon Warneke won his sixteenth game, even though Dizzy gave up only seven hits to Wrecker's twelve. The goat of the game, said the St. Louis newspaper, was "Walter Alston, a recruit plucked from the Cardinals Huntington, West Virginia farm who was sent to first base."

When the Cubs won both games, the Associated Press saw that "The defeat cost the Cardinals about $10,000, for they must now split second and third World Series money with the Cubs." The Cardinals full share would have been worth $1,800, but because of the tie it was worth $1,000. Dizzy, who was blunt as usual, said the team was "a bunch of bushers except for four guys"—he and his brother, Johnnie Martin, and Joe Medwick.

Hubbell and Gehrig were voted most valuable players in their leagues by a poll in the *Sporting News*. Medwick came in fourth in the league behind the Giants pitcher. Hubbell had 60 votes; Dizzy, 53; second baseman Billy Herman of the Cubs received 37; and Medwick, 30.

Medwick's year was marked, then, by the following achievements: first in hits, doubles, total bases, runs produced, and runs batted in; second in triples and batting average as well as putouts for National League outfielders; third in slugging percentage in the league and third in assists and in double plays for a National League outfielder; fourth in runs scored.

During the last four years, Medwick had, at one time or another, led the league in every offensive category except home runs. In what's called the "stretch run," Joe hit .333 for September. There are few players who can lead a league in slugging percentage, doubles, and triples. No mere slugger, Medwick played in every game and he led his team in everything except for home runs and on-base percentage, including being struck by a pitch, and he drove in 19 percent of the team's RBIs, and produced, through runs scored or RBIs, 28 percent of the team's 795 runs.

11

A Triple-Crown Year, 1937

In 1937, Medwick got an early start for Florida. Beginning in 1937, right after the first of the year, Joe and Isabelle drove from their home in St. Louis to Sarasota and rented a cottage (on Lido Beach that year). Medwick's parents and his sister Bennie and her husband, Bill Beisel, came to see them and stayed with them often. Two months later, when the training season began, Joe and his wife moved into the team hotel.

But until then, "Medwick . . . had fallen heavily for golf and observers were wondering what effect it [would] have on his baseball . . . there were persons who wonder[ed] if a man [could] be as interested in golf as Medwick was, without it interfering with his baseball. Joe played golf daily during his winter in St. Louis and with coaching from Johnny Manion, Sunset's capable instructor, Joe had become one of the best golfers in baseball. He shoots in the low seventies . . . and . . . it may be just what he needs if and when he gets into a slump."

By February 10, "in match play in the Ormond beach golf championship, Joe Medwick won his first round match 5 and 4 and will meet Leo Durocher in the second round."

The new Daytona Beach facility for the Cardinals included "a fine clubhouse with twenty-five showers, sixty lockers, trainer's quarters and a manager and coaches' room." Sometimes, in those rooms, Pepper Martin's noisemakers, called the Mississippi Mudcats, had begun to pluck and yowl.

After ten days of workouts, and without the unsigned Dizzy Dean, the team left on March 12 by train to Miami, and then by boat that night to Havana to play the Giants, who were training in Cuba. While the Giants had moved up from third to first in 1936, the Cardinals had dropped from second to third. As in most places in the baseball world, the Cardinals were well known, and a crowd of ten thousand (including Colonel Fulgencio Batista) saw Warneke, Smith, and McGee pitch to a 4-3 win against Schumacher, Melton, and Castleman. The next day "one of the largest baseball crowds ever seen in this quaint metropolis of the Antilles"—twenty thousand—watched the Cardinals lose 5-4 against Hubbell, Fitzsimmons, and Gumbert.

"Joseph Michael Medwick one of these years will go through a National League season without a batting slump and when he does, the slugging son of Carteret [is] likely to capture the hitting championship without a struggle. . . . Medwick was a great ballplayer during the late weeks of the 1934 pennant race, great on the attack and great defensively. He did as much as either of the Deans. Observers who were with the club can still remember several fine catches he made near the outfield walls."

"There once was a man from Nantucket," L. C. Davis wrote in his "Sports Salad" column in the *St. Louis Post-Dispatch*, beginning a limerick that was addressed to Al Simmons, but fit Medwick just as well, "who hit with his foot in a bucket/but he swung a mean bat/and the fans noticed that/the ball took a ride when he struck it."

Dizzy Dean signed about this time, and just as Medwick was making $2,500 less than Joe DiMaggio and Paul Waner, Dizzy was now making that same $2,500 less than left-hander Carl Hubbell.

By the end of March, the Cardinals' team exhibition record was 2-7, including six losses in a row, which led Rickey to pronounce that his team was overrated. Whether the team was angry with its play, or whether Dizzy Dean was stirring things up again in the clubhouse, it was apparent that the line between team and writers had become a hard, thick line because of an episode on April 2, which came to be known as "the Battle of Tampa." This incident took place at the Tampa Terrace Hotel, when the Cards were staying in town to play the Reds. Waiting there for the team were writers, among them Joe Williams, Irv Kupcinet, and Jack Miley. Entering the hotel lobby at the head of eighteen teammates was Patricia Dean, Dizzy's wife, who pointed out Miley, a mountainous man who wrote scathing prose for the New York *Daily News*. Miley wasn't the only writer questioning Dizzy's play. As a Dean biographer, Curt Smith, described it in *America's Dizzy Dean* (1978),

> Diz's skill and staying power, previously unquestioned, came under growing and frequent debate. Some critics . . . savaged him without remorse. Among the most acerbic was Jack Miley. . . . "Dizzy was a big man now, especially between the ears," he wrote. "For a guy who was picking cotton for fifty cents a day a few years ago, Dizzy had an amusing idea of his own importance. Dizzy was full of prunes," Miley continued, "and my answer to him was—pfooey!"

Miley also commented that Patricia (Dean's wife) was the real boss in money matters.

Near one of the hotel's elevators, Dizzy said to the *Daily News* writer, "I don't want a $120-a-week man writing those things about me," to which Miley replied, "What are you going to do about it?"

"Why, you son of a bitch," said Dizzy. Dean took a swing and missed, but someone swung around Dean and hit Miley in the eye.

Then, Irv Kupcinet stepped between them. Kupcinet was a 6-foot-tall, 200-pound former pro football player, and he growled at Diz, "Why don't you pick on somebody your own size?"

"Stay outta my way, you New York Jew," snapped Dizzy, pushing Kup aside and letting go with a right hand that missed Miley's head. But Ryba found the mark, hitting Miley with a fist (or maybe a pair of spikes) that opened a gash above the writer's right eye, and Miley fell to the floor. "Nobody can beat up a sportswriter when I'm around," Kup cried, swatting Paul Dean and lunging for Diz's throat.

"Joe Medwick," wrote Roy Stockton, "never to be left out of a fight, public or private, sent a right hand [or a left hand] over Mike Ryba's shoulder that sent Kupcinet, a former All-America football player from North Dakota . . . sprawling into a potted palm tree that [resulted] in a domino effect, started by knocking down floor lamps, plants, a sand urn, chairs and four other palms." "Medwick's meaty fist landed flush on Kupcinet's jaw and the scribe went down for the count," as one newspaper described it. With Miley on the floor and Kup trying to get his bearings, and with "cigar girls and bell boys . . . very much excited," Diz took cover behind an overturned sofa as Coach Mike Gonzales tried to restore order.

Miley finally got up, wiped blood from his forehead, shook a fist at Diz and thundered, "Come outside you ignorant bastard and we'll finish it." Kup, with his puffed eye discoloring quickly, sneered not at Medwick but at Diz: "I'm going to give you a beating you dirty son of a bitch if it takes a lifetime," reported Joe Williams. "The Deans were pop-offs who can dish it out but can't take it. Mr. Patricia—I mean, Dizzy. . . ."

This "battle" would have serious ramifications for Medwick and Dean later on.

Moving north, "The Cardinals were Onkel Franz Frisch's problem children. Nobody can even guess what those fellows were going to do," the season preview in the *New York Times* said. Even so, "Jack Doyle, Broadway betting commissioner," picked the Cardinals to finish first with 8-5 odds, with the next three teams being the Cubs, the Giants, and the Pirates.

The starting lineup was Terry Moore leading off in center, Stu Martin at second, and Frenchy Bordagaray at third. Then Joe cleaned up, Mize followed at first base, Pepper Martin played right, though he had an arthritic knee to begin the season, Durocher was at short, and Brusie Ogrodowski caught with J. Dean pitching.

Joe Medwick in left field was starting a season that was not to be matched for sixty-five years in the National League.

On Tuesday, April 20, in the first game of the 1937 season, Joe doubled at Crosley Field. Dizzy Dean, the game winner, pitched ten shutout innings, as did Peaches Davis for nine innings, but then Joe's double came in the tenth and he scored the winning run when Johnny Mize doubled behind him. "Babe Ruth, sat in a box at the opening game and . . . when he caught a foul [he] stuck the ball in his pocket like any regular paying guest."

Back in St. Louis, "Opening day ceremonies began twenty minutes before the scheduled starting time of the game, a drum and bugle corps was going through maneuvers on the field. The Musicians Post Band then entered the field though a gate near the Cardinal dugout. After the flag raising, the marchers continued around the field to home plate, where the band gave the first public presentation of 'The March of the Cardinals,' composed by George M. Cohan especially for the Gas House Gang."

Medwick got three more hits, and the next day, still hot, he hit a double and a homer, drove in three, and scored two in a 13-12 loss; after six games, he was 13-26 with six RBIs.

On the way home, Joe would often stop on Grand Boulevard and buy a newspaper from his favorite newspaper boy, Larry Berra, now age eleven, who already had the nickname "Yogi."

The team lost by seven to start May, though Medwick got two hits and sacrificed once. But Joe bunted when Frisch's sign was for Joe to take. Frisch was very unhappy and resolved to make some sort of change in giving signs. So "Frisch brought a red and white checked napkin to the park with him to wave for signals because Medwick declared he misunderstood a signal. . . . 'They oughta be able to see that,' snorted Frisch."

L. G. Wray, sports editor of the *Post-Dispatch*, discussed the beaning of Mickey Cochrane, a career-ending injury, and reflected on a ballplayer's life:

> The ball player, besides being an extra hazardous risk (to the insurance fraternity) and therefore able to protect his family only under high premiums, confronts a limited professional life in that he seldom [is] active longer than 15 to twenty years, counting both major and minor league activities. Nor [does he have] the privilege of other professional men, since he cannot peddle his services to the highest bidder. He [is] tied fast to the club to which he [is] under contract and can no more leave it than a serf of the Middle Ages could leave the soil to which he was bound. During his playing career, his social life [is] broken up; even his place of residence [shifts] around. He spends 50 percent of his season on the train or in hotels. In some cases, he even faces the risk of having his skull cracked by some wild heaver like Feller or some "duster off" trying to force the batsman to hit the dirt—Did you say "The Life of Riley"?

There was some hand-wringing after Cochrane's beaning, and a few brief experiments. In the end, nothing changed. That failure would cause Joe Medwick to pay dearly.

The team caught The Patriot to New York on May 7 and got a chance for a good night's sleep before battling the Giants.

Lon Warneke won the May 8th game as Joe contributed five runs with four hits. With Pittsburgh leading the league playing .769 baseball and with St. Louis at .643, the Giants were the only other team over .500. Tom Meany saw how few Gashouse Gang players were left from the 1934 team and how many were the newer Cardinal players—Bordagaray and Siebert from Indianapolis, Stu Martin a year out from the Piedmont League, and two players from

Rochester, Brown and Weiland. Frisch, thirty-eight, would not be a factor this year, playing only seventeen games with thirty-two at bats.

When the team shifted over to Brooklyn for a Saturday game, Medwick took over the league batting lead from outfielder Gibby Brack, as Joe made three hits against Brack's Dodgers. But Joe's third in a row multihit game and home run couldn't do enough against the nine runs the Dodgers scored on Sunday. He homered again the next day, and the team left for Philadelphia.

In the Baker Bowl on May 12, Joe Medwick tied a major league record with four extra-base hits: a pair of doubles and two home runs, "one a powerful blast over the left field wall ['more than 450 feet'], duplicating a feat heretofore accomplished [in thirty-four years] only by Cliff Lee, Wally Berger, and Jimmie Foxx." The Phillies knew to fear him: he was intentionally walked in the first inning. "Not Bad. Hats off to Frankie's Senior Team/who hit the apple on the seam,/and started going places./Joe Medwick didn't do a thing/but on the pesky pellet swing/and sock it for twelve bases."

At Forbes Field, though Joe was 4-5 with a homer, Dizzy lost on May 14, but then won on May 15 by 4-2, as Joe got two more hits, one a homer to right, another intentional walk in the ninth, and a steal. "A fan who caught Medwick's home run in the right field stand yesterday traded him the ball for a new one. Joe has a habit of trying to collect balls which he hit for home runs." The Sunday game drew 39,571 spectators—Pittsburgh's largest crowd ever—which filled the aisles, ramps, and the outfield, and Joe got two more hits. Still, it was Joe being hit by a pitch thrown by Pirate starter right-hander Joe Bowman that contributed to the only Cardinal run in a 2-1 loss for Lefty Weiland.

Against the Giants at home, Dean, who was irritated at the new balk rule, simply let the other team hit, throwing fastballs right down the middle, as he had done on June 4, 1935. The Giants made four hits and three runs in the inning.

"Then . . . Ripple bunted down the first base line, and when Dizzy blocked the line to the bag, the two almost collided. Quickly Dean and Ripple were swinging fists and both dugouts emptied in a tempestuous fifteen-minute battle. Lou Chiozza reached over Ripple's shoulder and punched Dizzy. Fist[s] flew in all directions and . . . Freddie Fitzsimmons grabbed Joe Medwick. 'I'm just trying to break it up. I don't want to fight,' said Joe." Maybe Joe was tired of defending Dean, tired of fighting his battles. Mounted police were put around the outfield.

Meanwhile, the Cardinals tried to catch Pittsburgh, but to no avail. In fact, when Harrell took the loss on Memorial Day, the Cardinals found themselves in fourth place.

On a rain day, June 3, Stockton assessed the team's chances. "Two ace pitchers [Dean and Warneke] can't carry six or seven weaklings. Unseasoned catching doesn't gibe with championship aspirations. A sick second baseman [Jimmy Brown] doesn't help any. And a star pitcher who is mentally or otherwise out of sorts certainly can't improve team morale. Even that great hitter Medwick is not physically at his best."

Saturday, June 5 began a weekend series in the Baker Bowl. Joe started the series by driving in a run in the first, and then getting two hits and two RBIs in game one of the Sunday doubleheader, which Warneke won 7-2. In the second game, the Cardinals built a 6-2 lead on Medwick's home run, and in the fourth, the Phillies began to stall, trying to prevent the game from going the official five innings before darkness canceled the game. After Jess Haines, the reliever, struck out, Phillies manager Jimmie Wilson ran out to the mound and gave instructions to both catcher Earl Grace and pitcher Hugh ("Losing Pitcher") Mulcahy. The first pitch to the next batter was high and wide, and so were the next three pitches. Jimmy Brown was next up, but Wilson changed pitchers to stall some more. Brown flied out, though by now the fans were yelling for the fielder to drop it. Pepper Martin, trying to be put out, then stole second, and "Grace's throw was particularly leisurely." After Padgett was walked intentionally, Medwick "tried to break up the stalling with a well-directed grounder to short," which was waved at. Joe, of course, kept running, and the "ball reached Leo Norris before Joe reached second, but Norris declined to tag his man, and Medwick was very angry about it and gesticulated to the umpires about it. It was a case of a double forced upon a man." This continued with wide pitches being thrown and batters throwing their bats at them until the "overt act that brought the struggle to a conclusion," the AP reported, "was [right-hander Syl] Johnson's wild pitch to [Pepper] Martin that allowed Durocher to score from third. Umpire Klem, veteran of the National League, who was standing behind Johnson, rushed to the plate. After a few moments' conference, with two out in the fifth [thus, not a regulation game], Sears declared the game forfeit." This apparently meant that none of the hits made by anyone in the game now counted. When "a chorus of boos and a shower of cushions and other missiles . . . greeted the forget announcement, . . . Cardinals . . . rush[ed] from their dugout to protect the umpires. . . . One [pop bottle] narrowly missed Frisch and Klem who were walking together."

Did the hits count? The next day, "Official statistician of the National League, Al Munro Elias, said . . . that he thought it was a point for Frick to decide. Elias said that he was in favor of incorporating all such hits into the record in games which counted officially in the league race." (The rule that covers such goings-on was 4.15[b]. Where the box score would have appeared, this notice was printed: "No box score as game was forfeited before legal duration had been reached." Rule 10.03[e], instructions to the official scorer read, "If a game was forfeited before it was a regulation game, include no records. Report only the facts of the forfeit.") Joe Medwick had hit a home run in that game; it mattered. (The home run counts now, under the revised rules.)

After the June 14 off-day for all major league teams, which for Joe's team only meant another exhibition game in Monessen, Pennsylvania, with the Pennsylvania State League team, the Cardinals traveled home to meet the Phillies. The Cardinals found that they had moved up to third place, one half-game ahead of the Pirates. Joe got nine hits in the next three games and drove in five. Mike Ryba won the first game, Pop Haines won in relief in the second, but Dizzy lost the game on June 17, even though Medwick and Mize hit successive home runs.

When the Boston Bees came in to play, Joe made four hits in nine at bats in the first two games, including two homers on June 19. The first homer, his thirteenth, was "a smash into the right field pavilion," which tied the score in the sixth. Just before that long home run to right, he had hit a foul home run to left. At game's end, "The heavy hitting Joe Medwick," the AP wrote, "was the hero of the rally. After two were out in the ninth, Jimmy Brown and Don Padgett [the right fielder] singled." The St. Louis sportswriter then reported the following:

And now there was a roar of expectation from the crowd. For that meant Joe Medwick, the Hungarian rhapsody, would have one more chance to swing his big war club. Joe rubbed a bit of resin lovingly on the business end of the bludgeon, took his stance carefully and measured his bat against the far corner of the plate. . . . [After] a pitch inside, Turner pitched . . . once more. Only once. . . . It was in there and then, presto, it was out of there . . . the ball sailing merrily on its way. Out it soared over the head of outfielder [Roy] Johnson. Far above Johnson. It cleared the bleacher walls. It cleared the heads and outstretched arms of the sun seat customers and, as it crashed against the scoreboard . . . a bedlam of cheers broke from the stands. A little girl in turquoise blue . . . jumped from a front row box down beyond the Cardinal dugout and jumped up and down in her glee. And she kept dancing as Joe jogged around the bases. . . . The little girl in turquoise blue . . . was Mr. Joseph Michael Medwick's bride of less than a year and nobody blamed her for dancing. . . . All the girls at the Mary Institute where Joe found Isabelle would be talking about it. And didn't she have reason to be proud and to dance and to grin through tears of happiness? It was only a ball game, only a home run, but then it isn't every girl that catches a boy like that, who can hit home runs against score boards and change gloom into joy for a ladies' day crowd of 10,000 men, women and children. . . . Yes, it was quite an afternoon for the slugging son of Carteret, N.J.

The Cardinals completed the sweep in a Sunday doubleheader on June 20, as Lon Warneke ("the Arkansas Humming Bird sang a sweet pitching song") and Dean gave up only three runs in the two games and Joe went 5-8, a home run and two doubles. That is, Joe hit .529 for the series with four singles, three doubles, two home runs, and nine runs batted in, a third of the team's total. Joe's hitting had helped the team win fourteen of seventeen, good enough for second place—just one game behind the Cubs. They had moved up without "a dependable fourth starting pitcher."

Then, after the Dodgers came and went, the Giants arrived and "The rampant Cardinals . . . crushed the Terry forces 9 to 4 in the opening game of a three day series." In the third inning, "Medwick almost uprooted the park with his terrific blast. . . . Medwick's blow, his sixteenth of the campaign, was a tremendous clout which actually cleared the left field bleachers and crashed high up on the scoreboard. It was the second time this year Jersey Joe had hit that scoreboard, with today's smack landing even higher than the first one. Joe, in fact, was confident he will clear it in the very near future." Still, Ryba lost 5-3 the next day (June 26).

Before the game on June 27, "ropes were stretched from deep left all the way round to deep right a half hour before game time," and

Hubbell bested Dean 8-1 before "a gathering that overflowed the playing field from foul line to foul line . . . and totaled 39,719. . . . The result virtually tied the National League flag race into a bowknot." "After the game, the fans showed their displeasure by throwing at least a thousand [rented] cushions on the field."

At the 1937 All-Star break, Medwick had produced 105 hits, 83 RBIs, and a .404 batting average in 67 games. He was tied in the league for homers with Mel Ott of the Giants, and Paul Waner had one more hit than Joe.

The All-Star starting lineups of position players had Medwick batting cleanup. President Franklin Roosevelt, one of 31,391 spectators, attended the July 7 game to throw the ritual first pitch, "The Rooseveltian arm swept back, the players surged forward and as the white pellet arched through the air a football scramble ensued. . . . When the heap of players untangled themselves, Jo-Jo Moore of the Giants had the ball tightly clasped in his fingers." During the game, Gehrig homered and doubled, and Charlie Gehringer had three hits to lead their American League team to an 8-3 win. Gehrig's home run was hit off Dizzy Dean in the third, and the next batter was Earl Averill, the right fielder from Cleveland, who "hit the first pitch off Dean's leg, the ball bounced to Herman and the latter threw Averill out" to end the inning. That third inning was the end of Dean's work in the game.

And what about Joe? His first at bat was turned into an out when Charlie Gehringer moved to cover second on a hit-and-run, so the ball went up the middle, right to him. But then Medwick doubled over the head of third baseman Red Rolfe, driving in Billy Herman; in the sixth Joe singled to right center and scored; in the seventh, he hit a double past Gehrig to right, Lou falling as he missed a stab at the ball; and in the ninth "he was cheered as he came to bat and . . . then connected for his fourth straight hit, a single to right."

Only Ted Williams and Joe have ever had four hits in an All-Star game.

After the game, John Kiernan of the *Times* wrote, "Anyway, Muscles Medwick showed that all the big hitters weren't going around in American League circles. Gomez was the only pitcher who got him out all afternoon. When Muscles got a single, it means he half missed the ball."

Bill Terry said, "Medwick, I thought, was the best player on the field, certainly the best hitter." Wray's column, under the heading of

"Our Joe Makes Good," said, "our Joe prove[d] that he was no false alarm as the league's leading clouter."

Returning to St. Louis, the injured Dizzy consulted with Dr. Hyland, who found not an injured leg but a fractured toe. Dizzy was told not to pitch.

On July 17, with one out in the fourth, "Medwick whisked a terrific drive into the upper tier just alongside the foul pole. Umpire Ziggy Sears called it foul and the Cards raged. Finally Medwick compromised by slashing a single to left. . . . About the only satisfaction Medwick got out of his near home run," John Drebinger wrote, "came when he took the field in the latter half of the inning and the fans overhead assured him the ball had entered the stands just inside the foul pole. At the time the blow was struck, however, it was difficult to tell whether the crowd in that section was waving its derisive signals at Umpire Sears for calling it foul or at the Cards for contending it was fair." In the sixth inning, "the Cards' wonder clouter, Joe Medwick, unloaded his twentieth circuit blast of the campaign." July 18th meant games 76 and 77—the halfway point. The team dropped into fourth again, almost 100 points behind the leading Cubs. Joe added 4 more hits to his total so that he had 127, making an average of .417 after 300 at bats.

In Boston, Bill McKechnie, manager of the Bees (and manger of the Cardinals, 1928–1929) saw Dizzy trying to pitch warmups on July 20 and warned him not to throw that day. Dizzy chose to pitch anyway. McKechnie saw that Dizzy had changed his delivery, and when he pitched against Bill Urbanski, he ruined his pitching arm. "When I pitched in Boston, I was unable to pivot on my left foot with the result that I was pitching entirely with my arm. During the game I noticed a soreness in the old flipper, and it has been sore ever since."

"Somethin' snapped up there in my shoulder. Why, my arm was so sore I [couldn't] even lift a glass of beer," Dizzy said a month later. At the age of twenty-seven, Dizzy, who had averaged almost two hundred strikeouts a year, would strikeout only sixty-seven in average the next three years; he had twenty-four wins per year from 1932–1936, but would average only five wins in the next three years.

Then, Joe had gone 4-15; no doubt he brooded about this on the way to play Brooklyn at Ebbets. There, when number 44 Pop Haines pitched a six-hitter in the July 23 game, "Joe (Muscles) Medwick led the Gashouse Gang assault . . . with a double, a triple and a single," and an intentional walk. The triple was Medwick's hit number 1,000. He had used 702 games to make 1,000 hits.

At the end of the road trip, the team traveled home to St. Louis to play three games against the Giants. "I like to hit against teams with infielders like Herman and Whitehead of the Giants," Joe said, his craft evident. "Both great ballplayers, but it doesn't pay ever to try to be too smart."

When the team left for New York at 9:30 on Saturday night, L. C. Davis wrote the following for the evening paper: "We don't believe the theory that Joe Medwick's weakness was hitting bad balls will stand up. Now, if he missed them that would be different. Even the pitchers were complaining. They say that trying to give Joe a base on balls was pitching to his batting strength. Unless the catcher stands somewhere in the vicinity of first base it can't be done." After seventy-five games, Medwick was hitting .410.

The team did well against Hubbell, and though the Giants came back to tie the first game of the series with eight in the eighth, "deviltry was still afoot for the sorely distressed Terrymen," John Drebinger reported, and "in the last half of the ninth inning, with two out and nobody on, Joe Medwick, demon clouter of the Cards, rifled a homer off Al Smith just inside the foul line and into the left field bleachers" to win the game. Stockton wrote:

> It's great to have a Medwick. Too bad there aren't more of him. A Medwick can make such a difference. You get a seven-run lead and can't hold it. Your pitchers were as baby rabbits to hungry hounds. Your infield was a sieve. . . . The leering enemy was preparing for the kill. And then the muscles of the Medwick boy go into action. He measures his bat against the far corner of the plate. That bat, a big, brown flailing thing, flashes through the air. It meets the ball and the ball sails on a line toward left field . . . it zooms with such speed that you're not certain where it hit . . . but [the umpire] was letting the Medwick boy run around the bases. Yes, it's a home run and the Cardinals, despite woeful assorted weaknesses, have won a baseball game 9-8.

"Week by week," the AP reported on July 31, "the belief was growing that the National League's various competitions should be run on a handicap basis. . . . The Cardinal clouter should either spot them hits and runs or with his right arm tied behind him."

Another loss by Dizzy in the first game of the August 1 doubleheader put the Cardinals back in fourth place. Joe's triple in the second inning of the second game drove in his 100th RBI in his team's 90th game.

On the off-day, Joe's average was listed as below .400 for the first time. The next day at Sportsman's Park was Joe Medwick Day, so before the game he tossed two dozen autographed balls into the stands in left to the knothole boys and then went 1-4 against Boston. Bill McKechnie explained his attempts at handling Medwick: "We don't pitch to him as we did a few years ago. In the old days, we'd side arm Joe and get a strike on him and he'd . . . try to hit almost anything we threw. He's improved tremendously since then. He doesn't hit so many bad balls and the result is it's pretty tough to know just how to throw to him." In sixty-seven at bats that year against the Bees, Joe was hitting .373. The team that had dealt with him the most successfully was the Reds, against whom he was hitting .341; against the Pirates, Joe's average was .621.

Joe came back again on August 4, tying the major league record with four extra-base hits (four doubles) in a game. It was the third time he had performed the feat, and it raised his average to .403.

Soon, the team optioned the other sore-armed Dean, Paul, out to Houston. Pop lost that day 4-1 while Joe, 2-4, got hit number 150 in game 93. He drove in two, runs eight and nine, in a 10-7 win against Philadelphia. In that game, Frisch hit into a double play because he couldn't get down the line fast enough anymore. It was his last at bat (of a total of 32) in 1937. It was his last at bat of a total of 9,312 in 2,311 games. Soon he would begin to refer to himself as "The Old Flash."

When Cincinnati came to town, "The National League's great one-two punch—Johnny Mize and Joe Medwick—drove in three runs in the third inning today," the AP wrote, "to give the Cardinals a 3 to 2 victory. . . . With two out and two on base, Mize singled off Lefty Lee Grissom to score one run and Medwick tripled to drive in two." The triple in the third put him at .401. Yet careless base running—trying to take second on a passed ball—embarrassed Joe.

Medwick by now had been gathering his home-run balls. The St. Louis newspaper noted this in a picture captioned that he was "exchanging with fans a new autographed ball—costing him $5 each time—for the home-run ball." Joe took the balls home and put them on display in his den.

There was now talk around the league that Durocher was to be traded. The lack of cooperation between Frisch and Durocher was palpable, and though Breadon was fond of Frisch, Rickey liked Durocher. Frisch could point to the ear infection that had plagued Durocher, along with both indigestion and a low batting average. And Durocher's growing ambition to be a manager needed to be fed.

On August 16, a day when all the major league teams were idle, the Cardinals traveled 511 miles to another exhibition game, this time a charity game in Charleston; after the West Virginia game, they traveled another 253 miles to Cincinnati for the eighteenth night game ever played. The team produced eight runs "in the fourth floodlit contest of the major league season" against the Reds on August 17. It was the first major league night game to start one day and end the next, when the game's last out was made at 12:02 A.M. They played a doubleheader against the Reds on August 19 and won both. In game two, when Joe had four hits, including his forty-fourth double, he singled in the sixth inning. "With Frenchy Borda-garay at bat, the ball got away from Gillie Campbell behind the plate. Medwick went to second and then to third. Umpire Sears threw in a new ball and Medwick was safe at home when Campbell apparently made no effort to tag him with [third baseman] Lew Rigg's return." It was three bases and a score on a passed ball, something Mike Schmidt would repeat many years later. "Looks Like Joe Had It" the "Sports Salad" column said. "There's quite a bit of opinion as to the respective ability of Medwick and DiMaggio. There may be little to choose between them."

On August 20, Joe remained right at .400, with 174 hits and 121 RBIs. But he only got 2 more hits in his next 13 at bats; August 22—game 110—was his last day at the magical number. "The fans [in Forbes Field] booed Medwick because he wasn't getting his share of hits, and in the late innings of the second game a dozen or two pop and beer bottles were thrown into left field from the left field bleachers. Joe returned a few of them, shattering them against the bleacher wall."

The team, without the two Deans and Pepper Martin, and without third starter Jim Winford since All-Star break, now had to play three games at the Polo Grounds against the Giants, tied for first place. Joe drove in two of the eight runs and had eight total bases with his three hits, including a home run. He also seized the chance to advance when an outfield throw from Hank Leiber died in soft dirt in the infield, an advance that led to a run. Mel Ott hit homer twenty-nine the next day in support of Prince Hal Schumacher, and in so doing passed Medwick for the home-run lead, though Joe got two more hits in a 7-3 loss. Joe was on by an error in the sixth, and then he walked with the bases loaded in the eighth. When he singled in the tenth, he was tagged out as he "wandered off." Ott homered again, beating Si Johnson in the last game of the series while Joe doubled (number fifty) in the 5-4 loss. "Silas was soaking wet from perspiration. But major league groceries were much better," Stockton wrote, "than those the clubs in the International League buy for you, and Silas didn't mind the heat. . . . Joe Medwick came to his help in the first inning with a good catch of a line drive with runners on first and third and two out." Joe was 6-14 against the Giants.

Though Joe was hitting .392 and Waner was at .375, Medwick's feared slump now began with another night game at Crosley Field. Beginning with that Friday game in Cincinnati, until September 10 in Chicago, Joe went 6-34, or .176. Because he made only one hit in sixteen times up for four days, his season's average dropped from .399 on September 3 to .377 on September 10.

But back home in front of 4,583 fans on September 11, Medwick, now 0-11, began hitting again and when he hit a double to right center against the Reds in the fourth inning, he had reached the 200-hit level. It was his third straight year at that level. Medwick would hit in twenty-two of the remaining twenty-five games for a .371 average when the team was fighting to stay in the first division—fighting to win a share of the World Series money.

Once again, Joe was selected as the left fielder and cleanup hitter of the All-American team, which had Paul Waner in right and Joe DiMaggio in center.

Medwick had the game winner on September 22, and he got hit 224 on September 23, which was a Dodger game, after which the Cardinals were mathematically eliminated from the pennant race. There were only 915 paid fans in the stands to see the double play from Medwick to Mize on Lavagetto on September 23. Joe had driven in 23 runners in September.

So the season ended in Chicago. Joe's first hit of two was number 235, as Si Johnson won and went to 12-12 for the season. An apparent hit up the middle struck second and became a double play in the fifth. In the field, after catching a fly, Joe doubled a runner off first. The next loss knocked the Cardinals out of third place for good, as Medwick went hitless against Peaches Davis in the 5-1 loss to

Chicago (only five batters got a hit). They lost again for the seventeenth time to the Cubs, though Mize drove in two with his twenty-fifth homer. Down 6-1, Joe got his final hit of the year against rookie pitcher Kirby Higbe from Moline of the Three I League as the team unsuccessfully tried to rally. This last hit was hit number 237.

Since then, only Don Mattingly, Rod Carew, Wade Boggs, and Ichiro Suzuki have had more hits in a season, all in longer seasons by eight games than Joe had. Only seventeen players have ever made more hits in a season. Medwick even tied a player from the Boston Beaneaters, Hugh Duffy, who made 237 hits in 1894.

"That year," Terry Moore said later, "there wasn't any place to pitch him. Not only would he hit it, but he would hit it well. His eyes were great, his reflexes were great, he was a great athlete and he was such a great competitor." Being a great competitor included "being hard to get along with," Moore continued. "He didn't joke a lot. Everything he did was pretty serious." One writer claimed, "They say the good-natured youngster can 'go' when they press him too hard."

In an interview with Fred J. Bendel from the *Newark Evening News,* Medwick was quoted as saying, "I guess ambition had as much to do as anything else in a ballplayer's success. Ambition keeps a fellow hustling, keeps him in condition, keeps him studying pitchers." He also studied bats. "I hit better this year because I switched bats. When a fastball pitcher was in there I used a light stick; when the slow boys worked I used the heavy timber. I carry a bat 36 inches long, weight 36 ounces, for ordinary pitching. I use one maybe four to five ounces lighter when a Mungo works."

The Most Valuable Player award was announced in a press release written by Henry P. Edwards, secretary of the B.B.W.A.A, which read: "Three of the eight committee members making the award named Hartnett first, two voted for Medwick and one each for Hubbell, Dick Bartell and Harry Danning. Joe and Gabby tied for second place but when they counted the third-place ballots, Medwick took the play away from the Chicago players." "A member of the committee said . . . that if he had waited another two weeks he would have dropped Medwick . . . because Joe went down the stretch in a bad batting slump."

AP writer Sid Feder announced:

In well-deserved recognition of baseball's classiest clouting since the palmy day of Ty Cobb, The Baseball Writers Association today selected

Ducky Medwick as the most valuable player in the National League for 1937. . . . As a result, the No. 1 Gas House Gangster won . . . The Sporting News Trophy.

Because he was a member of a fourth-place club, there was a question whether Joe could get enough votes to go over. . . . Medwick's tremendous clouting during the greater part of the season was a major reason why the disintegrated Cardinal team with only one ace pitcher and a lot of unproved youngsters in the lineup was able to make a fight for the flag. That Joe gained the verdict by two points over Leo Hartnett of the second-place Cubs was a real tribute to Joe's efficiency.

In 1924, Rogers Hornsby hit .424 and did not win the Most Valuable Player award—Dazzy Vance got it. Ted Williams's .401 in 1941 did not win him the award.

Medwick's achievements in 1937 included the following:

- highest fielding percentage of regular outfielders;
- top in the majors in batting average, hits, and doubles;
- 97 extra-base hits (a number that has since been topped only rarely);
- 406 total bases (a number that has been topped few times since—once by another Cardinal, Stan Musial, in 1948, and then again only beginning in the home-run-crazy-year of 2000);
- third straight time leading the league in total bases;
- third straight year played in every game;
- 56 doubles (making him eleventh all-time; sixth all-time in the National League);
- 154 runs batted in (which only a few players have topped since, and only in the home-run-crazy years).

To this day, Medwick is one of ten National and American Leaguers to lead the league in both at bats and batting average during the twentieth century. Among right-handed National Leaguers, his .374 mark has never since been topped.

The Baseball Writers of America quickly voted to change the method of selecting the most valuable players. The writers saw that the system that was being used did not reflect the deeds of the players.

On December 13, the Associated Press award for the outstanding male athlete for 1937 went to tennis champion Donald Budge. "Chief contenders for the runner up honors were those two rivals for all round honors, Outfielders Joe Medwick of the Cardinals and Joe DiMaggio of the New York Yankees. Medwick finally outpointed the Yankee sophomore, 39 to 35, but each received three first-place votes and the margin was not enough to settle an argument that raged all year between their partisans."

On December 14, 1937, Medwick attended a dinner in his honor at the Hotel Jefferson at 6:30 P.M., with one thousand attendees, including Joe Schultz, Grimes, Grimm, Frick, Max Carey, Durocher, Sunny Jim Bottomley, Bill Walker, Heine Mueller, Terry Moore, Bill McGee. "A number of orphans . . . attended as guests of the Knights of the Cauliflower Ear. . . . The *Sporting News* presented Medwick with a watch for winning the most valuable player award."

"Joe, as usual, had little to say. . . . Medwick did little talking but prior to the dinner he had expressed it as his desire that the proceeds intended for a present for him should be given to the hospital for Crippled Children and this was done."

"Sports Salad" memorialized the event with the following verse: "Though fabulous amounts of dough/In the market he would bring,/We wouldn't part with Jersey Joe/For the ransom of a king."

Joe said repeatedly, "I gave my wife the triple crown in 1937."

Medwick was first in his league in batting average, at bats, runs, hits, doubles, RBIs, slugging percentage, total bases, and runs produced. These numbers were so high that each placed him in the top thirty of all time. He came to bat, including walks, 674 times; he put the ball in play or got on base 624 times— 92 percent of the time. He had a third of the team's home runs, and 21 percent of the team's RBIs.

To measure further, in the hard-hitting American League, the leader in doubles had two more than his closest rival, whereas Joe in the National had sixteen more. The American League leader in hits had three more than his closest rival; Joe had eighteen more. The American League leader in RBIs had sixteen more than his closest rival; Joe had thirty-four more. The American League leader in slugging average had five points higher than his closest rival; Joe won that title by forty-six points.

12

Three RBI Crowns
in a Row, 1938

In addition to his beloved golf, Medwick spent some time hunting with a local sheriff in the Ozarks around St. Louis before his annual trip to Florida around New Year's Day.

Not long after he arrived, he read "January 4, St. Louis (AP). Somewhere there were two members of the Baseball Writers Association who would leave Joe DiMaggio off an All-Star 1937 baseball team and there were four writers who would pass up Joe Medwick of the St. Louis Cardinals. . . . An All-Star team named by 247 baseball experts . . . announced by The Sporting News [had] DiMaggio [getting] 245 votes and Medwick 243."

In light of this vote, an AP report on Medwick said, "He declined to say how much he received last year and how great an increase had been offered for 1938. . . . 'My salary demands were based upon my actions on the field and I feel that I am entitled to a substantial increase.' He . . . would keep up with golf and enter the baseball players' tournament at Sarasota Thursday [January 20]." According to Bob Broeg's account in Bob and William J. Miller's *Baseball from a Different Angle* (1988), the following happened during Medwick's holdout in 1938:

> Head-to-head confrontation with Rickey was difficult, but they met before breakfast in Rickey's spring-training suite at Bradenton, Fla. Rickey, sartorially a rumpled bed, jawed with Joe while shaving with-

out lather. Years later, Medwick would reflect in disgust, "He bled so much I thought I'd met Count Dracula." The thrust was the out-fielder's sarcastic comment, "All right, Mr. Rickey, every year you've been telling me what I did wrong. What in hell did I do wrong this time?" Coughingly, the master communicator suggested that this time Muscles better see club owner Sam Breadon. He did.

At one tense moment, the boss suggested it was a matter of princi-ple rather than principal. "I'd just as soon throw those $2,000 out the window," Sam said.

Medwick scoffed. "If you did, Mr. Breadon," he said, "your arm still would be holding on to it."

All of these statements, of course, were bargaining techniques. That Rickey would talk business while in bed or while shaving let the player know his status, not unlike Lyndon Johnson, who sometimes talked to an underling while seated on the toilet. Max Lanier related stories of negotiating with the Cardinals. If a player sent back his Cardinal contract offer unsigned, he would get sent back a Colum-bus contract, a clear sign that he was on his way to the minors again. Sometimes, Lanier said, a player needed money during the winter and Rickey would offer to loan him money to pay off his debts as soon as he signed.

So Joe continued to play golf in the Lido Beach area. He played in the second annual Dizzy Dean golf tournament at Bradenton Coun-try Club. "Medwick who got $12,500 last season was holding out for $17,500 which he considers a modest figure. . . . [T]he Yankees had offered $25,000 to Joe DiMaggio." DiMaggio wanted $40,000. "On his recent trip to New York, he had heard much about the kind of dough Joe DiMaggio was holding out for [$40,000]. It made Med-wick's demands seem modest in contrast and while the Carteret boy admires DiMaggio, he [is] unwilling to admit that the San Francis-can can do anything that he cannot do."

When asked about the two outfielders, Rogers Hornsby said, "DiMaggio had been up there only two years. I'd rather have Joe Medwick of the Cards. He's showed he can stay there. Joe Medwick is a better hitter than Joe DiMaggio."

On March 2, 1938, the first day of workouts, the Cardinals had moved from Daytona Beach to St. Petersburg. At this point, the Car-dinals had not signed their two most potent hitters, Medwick and Mize. "The conference between Medwick and Breadon was held in the clubhouse at Waterfront Park [in St. Petersburg] and Medwick quickly donned a uniform to join the Cardinals for their morning workout." Medwick said later, "I'm glad it's settled. Now I can get out and play ball." Sportswriters tend to believe that Joe signed for $20,000, but since the newspapers were also guessing that the team manager was making that same amount, and because Joe didn't even ask for that much, $20,000 was an unlikely figure. Sportswriters also tended to connect the birth of Joe's son, Joe, Jr., back in St. Louis, with his agreeing to sign.

On March 23, on a day off from training, something that could jeopardize the Cardinals' success finally happened. Murray Polner, Rickey's biographer, related the following complicated story in *Branch Rickey* (1982):

> In the third week of March in what came to be known as the Cedar Rapids case, Landis charged that Rickey and Breadon had tried to obtain "complete control of the lower classification clubs through secret understandings," had broken the law banning a club from contracting away "its right and obligation to get competitive playing strength as needed and whenever obtainable," and had violated the order not to have any working agreement with more than one team in any one league. Donald Ray Andersen, who wrote a doctoral dissertation on the Cardinal farm system, noted that "further investigation by the Commissioner's office revealed that Rickey and the Cardinals even controlled entire leagues."

Because of the ruling, Judge Landis released from their contracts as many as one hundred players from minor league teams under Rickey's control in Cedar Rapids, as well as in five other towns. (Outfielder Pete Reiser was one of the players released.) This ruling would affect Joe Medwick as well, but in odd and secret ways; Rickey was not through with his scheming.

On April 16, the first game of the St. Louis City Series was played on a Saturday and Joe homered to the pavilion roof in his fifth at bat with two on base, to break the 7-7 tie; the team won, 10-7. After the game, "Sam Breadon, president of the club, making the announcement at five o'clock . . . handed the newspapermen typewritten statements" saying that Dizzy Dean was traded to the Cubs for two pitchers (Curt Davis and Hardrock Shoun) and outfielder Tuck Stainback, along with $185,000. Pepper Martin guessed that the $185,000 profit on the deal could be used to buy strikeout pitcher Van Mungo from the Dodgers. [Once you subtract Rickey's $18,500 as his percentage of the deal per his contract.]

In the *Times*, John Kiernan quoted a neighbor of Frisch who said, "with Dizzy gone, Frank must feel like a fellow who had just lost a couple of abscessed teeth."

So as the 1938 season opened, only Joe and Johnnie Martin remained as players from the 1934 championship team. But "[a]n attack of lumbago . . . caused him [Medwick] to miss his first game in a Cardinal uniform. . . . He had a total of 485 consecutive contests to his credit." Joe would miss seven games because of the affliction.

The 19,865 fans got a new scoreboard—an electric one—"including official decisions on doubtful plays." The scoreboard had two light towers (but not the lights) built into it, ready to go.

The Cardinals lost to a new National League power—Pittsburgh—in the first game. "Paul Waner's double in the first inning, a high fly that fell in front of Padgett, probably would have been caught by Medwick. . . . All the Pirate pitchers of the day formerly were in the Redbird organization." When the team went on to Chicago on the night of April 21, Joe stayed in St. Louis for treatment on his back.

Without Joe, the Cardinals lost six of the first seven games. Joe left his home in suburban St. Louis on April 26 to join the team in Cincinnati, and though his "condition had greatly improved, [it was] not entirely cleared." Medwick's first game back was on April 27 in Cincinnati; his single was one of the hits in the second win of the season for the team with Warneke getting his first win, a shutout. For Weiland the next day, Joe made two hits (one a triple) and drove in two in a 5-3 win.

Meanwhile, Dizzy Dean, in Chicago, told his "version of the affair" that had occurred in the hotel in Tampa in the spring of 1937 when two sportswriters were slugged. Dean and Irv Kupcinet finally appeared to have made peace, shaking hands for a page-one newspaper picture; indeed, they became good friends. The reason may have been that Kupcinet was based in Chicago, Dean's new hometown. By then, Diz was denying he had even been in the fight, and certainly not in one with his new pal, Irv. Dean blamed Medwick for instigating the fight.

The *New York Times* addressed Dean's statement with the following headline: "Medwick Pops Off, Dean the Target."

PITTSBURGH, Pa., April 28. Joe Medwick was hardly in camp an hour, before he fell into Gas House Gang character yesterday in Cincinnati with a blast at Jerome Herman Dean. It seems that Dizzy, in a chapter of his life story, recently published in a New York paper, said that Medwick was the Cardinal who started that row with Jack Miley and Irv Kupcinet a year ago this spring in a Tampa hotel. In the same story, Dizzy said he wasn't in the fight at all.

"He's right in one respect," Medwick wrote to Chicago newspapers. "He wasn't in the fight after fists started to fly. He usually does a craw-fish act about that time. He starts a fight and then somebody else had to protect him. That's what he did at Tampa, and it's true he was running away. The same thing in the fight with the Giants. He tried to bean somebody and when the Giants rushed him, he ran and let us fight his battles. Dean was about to be taken apart in that Tampa hotel when I entered the lobby and saved his life. That Kupcinet was too much for Dizzy. In fact, any man-sized boy is too much for Dizzy. You notice any time he throws a bean ball it's at some little fellow. If he ever gets into trouble while with the Cubs, watch him hide behind Hartnett. The trouble with Dizzy is that he can't take it, and he got to thinking maybe Kupcinet, who lives in Chicago, might look him up and take him apart."

It must have felt good to the Cardinals to hear somebody talk in Gashouse Gang terms. Perhaps Medwick was just what they needed in more ways than one.

Medwick also said that if Diz had the nerve, they could settle their misunderstanding with fists, but Dizzy dismissed him, saying, "All that Hungarian bastard wants to do is fight." Dean claimed that he spoke to Medwick on the phone on April 27, and Joe told Dizzy that owner Breadon forced Medwick to say those things about Dizzy.

Home again in Sportsman's Park with a record of 3-7, the Giants were leading the National League with a record of 9-1, and the Cubs beat the Cardinals for the third time while scoring eleven runs. Joe, picking up speed, was 2-4 with a triple and two RBIs. But the team was seventh in batting, though newcomer Enos Slaughter was tied for the league lead in hits, with Mickey Owen right behind him.

Max Lanier told Peter Golenbeck the following about that game:

> We had some tough guys on that team. Joe Medwick was hard to get along with. . . . The first game I went in to relieve [Medwick] was going out as I was going to the mound [from the bullpen alongside of the left field stands]. He always stepped on third base going to left field, and we met, and he said, "Come on, Lanier, get them out or you'll go back to Columbus." That was a heck of a thing to say. He was a great hitter, and he knew it, and he could do anything he wanted, just about.

Joe had paid his dues as a rookie, and evidently he felt that Lanier should also have to prove how tough he was.

A tie with the Bees in early May didn't erase Joe's home run when he became "the first batter to hit the new scoreboard with a batted ball."

While the team was in New York, Medwick's brother-in-law, Bill Beisel, would go get him at the ballpark. Players, hearing of Mrs. Medwick's famous cooking, would come with Joe to Carteret, including roommate Bill Hallahan, Johnny Martin, Durocher, and Mike Gonzalez.

Sportswriters wondered why the management was not looking for a way to help the team. From the time Joe had walked on the field in 1932 until 1946, the team spent money on fifteen players, all of whom were forgettable—most for the waiver price. Many of those players were immediately sold. Could it be that since Rickey only got a percentage of the profits of a sale, he was not willing to pay much for a player?

A joke going around in St. Louis was this: Do you know the difference between the Cardinals and the Cardinals' Boys Band? The Cardinals' Boys Band only blows *between* innings.

Up in Boston, the St. Louis team began to slide down. Padgett in right field was just above .200. "Only Jersey Joe Medwick remains [of the 1934 team] in active service. Joe is still one of the all-time hitters in baseball but he can't put on a show all by himself, even though he hasn't stopped trying."

When the Cards played in New York long enough to be beaten 9-4 and 2-1, John Kiernan said, "The Gas House Gang seemed completely deflated." As a telling story, "it was recalled that a bellboy in the Cardinal hostelry here went up to Muscles Medwick and asked that pipe-smoking hero where he could get a group picture of the Cardinals to add to his private gallery. 'There was no group picture of this club,' said Muscles. 'They can't make any. We change players too fast.'"

By the end of the first week in June, the team was eight games back, and four games below .500.

The first two games with the last-place Phillies resulted in two wins by Curt Davis and Mike Ryba as Joe hit five singles. That night, the story goes, sportswriter Ray Gillespie of the *St. Louis Star-Times* bought a handful of different-sized hairpins from a chambermaid at the Bellevue-Stratford Hotel: short pins were for small hits, longer pins for longer hits. Gillespie left them for Pepper Martin to find, but Joe scooped them all up. "Let 'im find his own hits," Medwick was heard to say.

That night, June 15, the Cardinals lost 3-2 and Joe drove in one of the runs; he would never drive in another at Baker Bowl. Only three more games would ever be played there since the Phillies had signed an agreement with Connie Mack to play at Shibe Park.

At the Polo Grounds, on June 19, 1938, Medwick was given a plaque from the Newark Athletic Club as New Jersey's best professional athlete. "So awed was the Duke of Carteret by the presentation jinx that he was held to a measly five hits."

The Cardinals played five games on the three days before the All-Star break and lost four of them. The now second-place Pirates beat them three times when the St. Louis team could only score eight runs to Pittsburgh's seventeen. St. Louis split a doubleheader with the Cubs on July 4, leaving the team six games under .500 and thirteen games behind the Giants. Joe was now second in hitting at .342, while fourth in RBIs and fifth in homers.

Two hours before the 1938 All-Star game, the managers met their teams and "impressed upon them the gravity of the occasion." The Nationals won 4-1 with only Joe Cronin and Schnozz Lombardi getting more than one hit. In the ninth inning, Bill Dickey, the Yankee catcher, came to bat with his teammate DiMaggio on base. Dickey "lifted a long fly toward the scoreboard in left center" as Medwick and Ott "tore in pursuit. Medwick finally caught up with it as he raced up the embankment, speared the ball in his outstretched glove and went down in a heap. But he held the white pill and there was one out." Medwick's catch was described as "spectacular"—one "that prevented serious trouble for his team." Indeed, the catch was blazoned in a colored Wheaties ad—like a comic strip—within weeks. In addition, there was a story that Larry MacPhail of the Dodgers offered to buy Medwick's contract for $200,000 at that All-Star game.

The Brooklyn series and the Cardinals home stand ended with a Sunday doubleheader, which the Cardinals split before 14,491 spectators. Before the first game, there was a long-distance hitting contest. "The great George Herman Ruth [now a Dodger coach] proved that he still was the 'Sultan of Swat.' . . . Babe topped all competitors with a drive of 430 feet, the ball landing in the second car tracks of Grand Avenue. Medwick was second with a clout of 425 feet over the left field barrier into Sullivan Avenue. . . . Ruth got $50 and Med-wick $25." Brooklyn catcher Merv Shea was the pitcher for Ruth, and Mike Gonzales helped Joe to the prize money paid by the Car-dinals. Men with the title of army range finders determined the length of the hits, and Joe was unhappy with their decision. "No wonder the enemy looks at you and laughs," he said to them. Dur-ing this home stand, the team was 7-14, which caused them to drop back six more games. Joe was now second in hits to McCormick and hitting .349, second to Lombardi.

In July's thirty-one games in twenty-five days, Joe made forty-two hits, scored twenty-one runs, and had twenty-six RBIs.

August 2 was a doubleheader marked by the use of colored base-balls in game one. A "Special Correspondent of the *Post-Dispatch*" reported that "a yellow baseball, advocated by color specialists . . . was tested in the game. Yellow, according to the spectrum scientists, was the most highly visible of all colors and had been recommended in baseball to decrease the possibility of bean-ball injuries."

Mize liked the ball well enough to hit it into Bedford Avenue in the seventh inning, and the next day, August 3, the Cardinals saw a crowd forming early for a rare night game. The Ebbets Field gates were closed a half hour before game time, by which time there were a number of competitions going on. In another long-distance hitting competition, Joe again came in second, this time to his teammate Big John Mize. The lefty hit one 391 feet into Bedford Avenue to win $50, and Joe hit one 380 to left to win $25. The Babe and first baseman Dolph Camilli were out of the money. And with the season almost half over, Joe was the only full-time player on the team hitting over .300. The team was last in fielding. Weiland, at 10-8, was the only pitcher over .500.

As the team rode the train back to St. Louis, J. Roy Stockton reported:

There can be no complaint about the outfield. . . . It was expected that this would be a very tough year for Joe the Duck Medwick. . . . It's something to lead both leagues in batting and to be selected as the Na-tional League's most valuable player. A young man wouldn't be hu-man if it didn't impress him a bit. Just as all ball clubs try a little harder against the league leaders or world champions, so all pitchers bear down a little harder against a batter of outstanding reputation. They've been bearing down against Joe the Duck this year. Pitchers had changed their style in an effort to throw Medwick off stride. He had seen more side arm curves than in two or three previous seasons. But

I don't think the pitchers had Joe's number. He's still one of the great batters of all time. And regardless of how he finishes this season, he'll be a favorite to lead the league next year. And with not so many laurel wreaths hanging over his Magyar brow, it will be easier for him to swing his war club in 1939.

After Max Macon pitched a complete game 7-5 loss against the Cubs, it was announced that Paul Dean was coming back from the Dallas Steers, and would pitch very soon. In fact, he pitched batting practice on the 8th, having reported to Frisch early in the day. Weiland lost on September 8 by 7-4 in ten innings, with Medwick having yet another single-hit day. Medwick may have been tired or disgusted the next day, which was a Friday; the game description said, "Medwick loafed on a roller down the third-base line in foul territory and when the ball rolled in fair territory before reaching the bag, Hack still had time to throw him out, Medwick thereby losing a base hit."

It was true that Joe lost that base hit, but he had also won something. Ads three columns wide had been appearing now for weeks:

Help your favorite left fielder win a big, new Buick!
KELLOGG'S ALL-AMERICAN BASEBALL POLL
More than $5,000.00 cash prizes weekly
Kellogg's Corn Flakes Oven Crisp Flavor Perfect
The All-American Ready-to-Eat Cereal
The Lineup to Date:
First Base . . . Gehrig
Second Base . . . Gehringer
Third Base . . . Ott
Shortstop . . . Cronin
Left Fielder (To be announced Monday)
Complete Instructions and Official Entry Ballot at your Grocer's

On September 10, "Before the game . . . Miss Marie Taylor Spink, daughter of J. G. Taylor Spink, publisher of The Sporting News, drove [the new Buick] onto the field and Edgar Brands, editor of the same publication, made the presentation . . . to Joe Medwick as a reward for his popularity among the fans of the country who selected him as the left fielder on the Kellogg All-Star team." Joe and his wife, Isabelle, accepted the car together at home plate.

September 11, two days after his birthday, Frankie Frisch was fired shortly after noon, effective after the day's game. Mike Gonzales was picked to run the team for the rest of 1938. For Frisch's last game, Paul Dean had returned and the team was glad to see him. A photograph showed Paul in the dugout with his arm around Joe. Before that game,

> there was a long-distance hitting contest with Medwick, Mize and Padgett representing the Cardinals and Paul Waner, [rookie Johnny] Rizzo and [veteran first baseman Gus] Suhr, from the Pirates. Medwick won the competition with a drive of 430 feet. The mechanical pitcher, invented by Bryon Moser, the St. Louis banker, did the pitching. It took some time to get the machine adjusted and . . . Medwick pocketed $50 for his drive.

After the game, "when [Frisch left] the room . . . [h]e was half choked in an affectionate way by Joe Medwick," the *Sporting News* reported. At least one of the many reasons Frankie "had to quit the St. Louis club was because he wouldn't kow-tow to Branch Rickey. Branch possibly wanted a manager who would accept all his suggestions."

During an eastern trip, on the train from New York to Boston, Medwick read that he was picked for the fourth consecutive time to "Babe Ruth's All America" team "In collaboration with the All American Board of Baseball." Of the ten major leaguers picked, four were National League men: Joe, Mel Ott, Ernie Lombardi, and Paul Derringer. Red Rolfe, Joe DiMaggio, and Red Ruffing were from the Yankees. All but Rolfe would be chosen for the Baseball Hall of Fame.

At home against the eager Cubs, Joe, back in left field, hit two doubles in a 7-7 tie. Joe came up with the bases loaded in the ninth inning but popped up. For the season, Medwick was still four RBIs in front of Ott. This tie still left the Cubs a game and a half ahead, with three to play while the Pirates played at Crosley Field. Lefty Weiland won on October 1 in game one on Mize's eighth-inning homer, and McGee lost in a game that ended 10-3. It was the game that won the pennant for the Cubs, who had taken twenty of the last twenty-four games. Before a surprising twelve thousand fans, Paul Dean won again, 7-5, and Joe did well again, with two hits, two runs, and two RBIs in the game to finish the season—a game that took one hour and thirty-three minutes.

Again, Joe was in the top five in the National League in many categories: runs, hits, slugging percentage, total bases, and fielding percentage for outfielders. He led in doubles again, and it was his third straight year as league leader in RBIs. Ernie Lombardi was named Most Valuable Player by the Baseball Writers; Mize was twelfth and Medwick was eleventh, playing for a sixth-place team.

13

In the League's Top Five in Five, 1939

Two new managers would have a great effect on Joe's professional life. When Dodger manager Burleigh Grimes learned that Larry MacPhail planned to fire him before the 1939 season, he told Leo Durocher to ask for the job. On October 11, 1938, Larry MacPhail hired Durocher, Joe's sartorial mentor and friend, as manager of the Brooklyn Dodgers under a one-year contract.

The other new manager was the one hired by Branch Rickey, and the hiring got very complicated. To begin with, Burt Shotton was Rickey's first choice, but he settled for Ray Blades. Second, Blades was Rickey's man. The 43-year-old Illinois man had served as the de facto, Sundays-only manager of the Cardinals in the 1920s when Rickey was the manager; that is, on the Sabbath, when Rickey would not work, Blades was the manager for Rickey. Whereas Mike Gonzalez and Frankie Frisch were certainly loyal to the players, Blades was more apt to be loyal to his mentor. Medwick, when asked by the Associated Press, commented judiciously, "'We hated to lose Frankie but the ball club owners want a winner and when you don't win, somebody has to suffer. . . . From what I hear, Blades is a smart fellow and we'll all be plugging for him.'"

A reporter was covering Medwick well before the season started: "Driving with Medwick in the automobile he won in a popularity contest last summer were Mrs. Medwick, their small son Mickey and a maid. . . . He said he would keep fit by golfing, fishing and hunting until the rest of the team gets here [St. Petersburg] next month." Joe did play golf throughout January, sometimes at the two courses in the St. Petersburg area leased by Jimmie Foxx. When he wasn't playing golf, Medwick worked as an instructor at Joe Stripp's (another Jersey Joe) baseball school in Orlando.

At the end of January, Joe sent back his unsigned contract. As a full-time player from 1933–1938, Medwick averaged 618 at bats. As far as he was concerned, he had played hard for his team. Rickey pointed to the Cardinals home attendance of 291,418 spectators in 1938 (fewer than 4,000 per game), which left the team seventh in attendance in the eight-team league. The *New York Times*, seemingly in support of Rickey's contentions, decided to use "the all-time high" as a way to measure batting average each year. So Jimmie Foxx, at .349, had a feeble year, since he batted ninety-one points below the all-time high of Hugh Duffy's .440. Medwick could argue that he averaged forty-nine doubles during the last six years. For his part, Rickey could point out that the team got the fewest dollars for a radio contract of any major league team ($33,000). Rickey didn't get tired of negotiating—that was his job. Besides, it would not cost him money if Joe didn't sign for awhile. It would cost Joe money, however.

"Medwick, his wife and infant son, and the family maid were quartered at the Detroit Hotel which also housed the baseball club," when the reporting date of March 1 arrived. March 4 was motion picture day for the team at training; Medwick stayed around the hotel and wondered about a new offer from Rickey. He had been doing some throwing on the beach. On March 5, Medwick "was gentlemanly and polite" about his contract, though he and the team were $5,000 apart to begin with. "Breadon reasons [Medwick] ought to be a good boy and take a cut." Breadon sounded as if he believed that it was the job of an employee not to make trouble for his boss. When the team was out of the usual poverty arguments, they used that one. Joe was clearly tired of waiting and wrangling—tired of empty promises.

"When Joe was coming up the ladder in rather spectacular jumps, they kept telling him on Dodier Street that he was a young man and to please be satisfied to climb the ladder slowly. . . . They told him all that, but Joe had read the papers and books. He knew the record books and he knew that ballplayers had only a brief career in the big money. 'Get the buckerinos while you can,' was his slogan. Nobody will take care of you when you can't make the base hits. It'll be up to Joe to pay the grocer and the meat market. Joe saw Jess Haines pass out of the picture. Haines was kept long on the Cardinal pay-roll. There was much sentiment there. But finally he went, to a mea-ger salary as a Brooklyn coach and Joe saw no sentiment. He only saw Jess Haines departing out of the baseball picture with only Jess Haines to take care of Jess Haines. And what if he did slump from .374 to .322. The entire Cardinal team bogged down. . . . The Cardi-nals made money in other years. . . . It wasn't his fault" the team fell apart in 1938. No, Medwick in Joe's eyes was still a very valuable ballplayer with many good years ahead of him.

The club's idea of a fair offer was to cut Medwick's 1938 salary of $20,000 by only $2,500 dollars, which was probably the true number Rickey had in mind all along. The team did argue that Joe did not do as well in 1938 as he did in 1937. Of course, it was hard to think of many players in the history of baseball who ever had a year as dom-inating in the league in every category as was Medwick's 1937. In Medwick's first six full years, he had averaged 209 hits.

"I want to play baseball," a Stockton profile of Medwick began in the *St. Louis Post-Dispatch*, "My mind is on baseball. . . . I came to Florida after a winter of daily golf and right now I weigh 183." When Stockton asked him about his 1938 "slump," Joe answered, "They were lucky last year. . . . In 1937 I was lucky . . . the pitchers didn't pitch any different to me. I can look back and remember many a base hit that was taken away from me. I mean drives that almost went safe, on which somebody made a spectacular stop. Camilli took enough to make a difference of several points." Asked if teams changed the way they played him in 1938, Joe said,

No, they play you different in different towns and on different days. And each time you go up there you take it as a separate time at bat. One time the third baseman may be near the line and the shortstop may be playing you on that side of the diamond. The next time you go up, perhaps against the same pitcher, they'll be shifted a bit toward right. Each time I glance around and get a picture of what I figure they're trying to do. Then I try to cross 'em up. That's what batting was. Try to hit 'em where they ain't and they try to make you hit where they're playing. Look what it means to a fellow if you can cross 'em up. They always played Lombardi to left field, the third baseman and the shortstop, well over toward left. He was a dead left field hitter. Last year he suddenly found out how to hit to right and what does he do? He led the league. It's all a game. Maybe I'll cross 'em next year and maybe they'll get the breaks again.

Stockton also said that Medwick was "generally regarded as one of the great hitters of the decade."

On March 8, Breadon offered what he called "a substantial increase" over the $17,500. It was unlikely it was more than $18,000. During the last six years, Medwick had averaged 124 RBIs.

Joe missed the first exhibition game and missed Rickey's decree in the clubhouse that there was to be no more of the Pepper Martin's Mudcat Band. Meanwhile, Rickey, MacPhail, McKechnie, and Medwick "foregathered at an exhibition game" and Rickey, Blades, Durocher, and Dressen had dinner together. Was Leo thinking of his friend?

By March 21, day twenty of Medwick's holdout, the team offered $18,000—sort of. "Rickey said that while Breadon would not give more than $17,5000, he, Rickey, would dig into his own pocket for the extra $500 if Joe would sign."

Let us look into Rickey's pockets for a moment. Never mind the sales of minor league players. Looking beyond his $50,000 salary, let us look at the year 1938 for Rickey. In that year alone, he accepted in trade three players for Dizzy Dean. The combined salaries of all three would not equal half of what Dean made. Since Rickey saved the team about $10,000, he received a portion of that money. In addition, the $185,000 that Rickey negotiated for the team became $166,500, because Rickey put into his own pocket $18,500. The public moralist who said he believed in justice and fair play seemed privately to believe in paying himself while hosing his lessers.

Joe was tired of being denied money in salary while being promised that World Series money, a sure thing this year, would be coming his way. All Joe wanted this year was not to have his salary cut.

Westbrook Pegler, a few years before, wrote, "The individual . . . ballplayer . . . was one toiler who was positively not done right by being denied the right of collective bargaining and even forbidden to shop around for another job with a more liberal employer than the one to whom he finds himself rather agreeably enslaved."

On March 21, "Medwick motored to Branch's beach cottage with a friend," probably entertainer Johnny Perkins, where the contract was signed. "Joe Medwick had signed his contract but he was not exactly a happy warrior." In fact, Joe would say insulting things about owner Sam Breadon all season. Medwick had included in his contract a laughable attendance clause that called for the team to draw 142,000 more fans at home in 1939 than they drew in 1938. The reason Medwick signed was that "Joe was afraid the club would fine him heavily . . . for not being in condition . . . [and] the club could make a decision as to his condition and Joe could easily be fined a month's salary or at least enough to reduce his salary for the year to the $17,500 the club wanted to pay. When Joe saw that the club had the upper hand and that he would be the one to suffer, he decided to take the $18,000. . . . So you can guess for yourself if the Cardinals will have a satisfied ball player in Joe Medwick."

Then, while the Cardinals moved north, so did the Dodgers. Pete Reiser, freed from the Cardinal farm, was playing short for the Dodgers in the spring, and his performance had the sportswriters hoping he would be the Dodger shortstop. The management was saying he would go to a farm team.

On Opening Day, Joe, with a fine running catch on Billy Herman, went 2-3 with two RBIs, but those were the only runs the team scored. "You won't see better outfielding very often than the fly-chasing by Joe Medwick . . . in the third inning."

Lon Warneke, with two shutouts, pitched to a large Crosley Field crowd on Sunday in a game that saw some unusual plays from the beginning. In the first inning, after Stu Martin was forced by Pepper Martin, Pepper stole second, and when Medwick hit a pop fly so high between home and third it was not caught, Pepper came all the way home. In the seventh, Stu Martin doubled, Pepper was hit by a Derringer pitch, and Medwick singled in Stu. On that play, third baseman Billy Werber cut off the throw from left and tried to get his throw in time to tag Joe, who was stretching his hit on the outfield throw. When the throw went wild, Pepper scored and Joe went to third, from where he scored on a force out. Once again, Joe put the ball in play.

During this time, the newspapers were reporting on a resolution introduced by a state senator from New York City, Democrat Charles Perry, "disapproving 'discrimination' by major baseball leagues against colored players." Rickey's biographer, Murray Polner, recounted that Vice President Rickey recalled "an incident in the 1930's when he had tentatively raised the issue of desegregating Sportsman's Park with Breadon":

"I had made that effort in St. Louis only to find effective opposition on the part of ownership and on the part of the public—press—everybody." Forget it, ordered the Cardinal owner and president. The white fans would never sit in the stands to watch blacks perform, he insisted. Well, Rickey persisted, would Breadon permit black customers to sit anywhere they chose in Sportsman's Park without making any formal announcement? Breadon said he personally didn't give a damn about desegregating seating but the fans would never allow such liberties. Business, he said, was business. Rickey later discovered after questioning a municipal official that no city ordinance demanded black fans be seated apart from white fans. Even so, he backed away, unwilling to offend Breadon or white customers.

June began for the team at the Polo Grounds, and Joe's slump deepened. On June 3, 1939, three Cardinals drove to the New York World's Fair and were shown to the National Youth Administration exhibits in the Consumer Building where they gave baseball instruction at 10:30 A.M. First, Mayor LaGuardia spoke to the crowd of three thousand Boy Scouts and Girl Scouts. Next, Manager Ray Blades, Pepper, and Joe served as instructors at the Court of Sport at the World's Fair. "After the instructions, [Medwick was] presented a certificate and a sweater . . . for being named on the 1938 All-America baseball team."

After two consecutive doubleheaders in Philadelphia, there were two days that were not part of the championship season. Most of the Cardinals went on to play an exhibition game each day in Grand Rapids and Kalamazoo, where Paul Dean would pitch against a team of local All-Stars. Terry Moore and Joe Medwick traveled from Philadelphia to Cooperstown, New York, for the baseball centennial game. "Thirty-two star players selected from both circuits and the living immortals of the game came to Cooperstown to present the great Centennial program."

At 12:15 P.M. on June 12, 1939, the National Baseball Hall of Fame was dedicated. "Then the names of the twelve players elected to the Hall of Fame were announced." After a parade and the dedication of Doubleday Field at 2:30, a colorful pageant was presented. Called "The Cavalcade of Baseball," the development of the sport was pictured from the days of town ball, down to modern times. The climax of the Cavalcade, which was held at Doubleday Field, with every seat filled and many fans sitting on the grass, was a seven-inning exhibition of the modern game by teams of major league players captained by two of the "immortals," Honus Wagner and Eddie Collins.

Eight players in that game would later be selected for the Hall of Fame. Collins's team included Hank Greenberg from Detroit on first base; Billy Herman, Cubs, second base; Mel Ott, New York Giants, left field; Lloyd Waner, Pittsburgh, center field; and as a pitcher, Chicago's Dizzy Dean. Playing for Wagner's team were pitcher Lefty Grove, from the Red Sox; Detroit's Charlie Gehringer, second base; Arky Vaughan, Pittsburgh, shortstop; and Joe Medwick, Cardinals, left field. "Medwick came to bat to the rousing cheers of the crowd who wanted to see 'Ducky' hit a homer." The final Hall of Fame player that red-letter day in 1939 was "the Babe." Retired four years earlier, Ruth pinch-hit by popular demand for Boston Braves' pitcher Danny MacFayden. (It was twenty-five years ago that Ruth had pitched his first major league game.) Each team made six hits, and Joe's team won, 4-2.

In a later year, Joe would be back in Cooperstown, back to the Hall of Fame.

Two rain days followed on June 9 and 10, and the Cardinals then did very well against the last-place Phillies, scoring twenty-five runs to the Phillies seven, as Joe hit a homer in each game. At .321, Medwick led his team in at bats, hits, RBIs, and average. Manager Blades, naturally, dropped Joe to sixth. It was the first time Joe had batted anything but fourth in many years. One writer, Tommy Holmes, said that Blades was "continuing Spring training until about July 1."

It was around this time that a well-known incident took place— well-known because the batting practice pitcher was young Bing Devine. Devine told me that in 1939 he was a hopeful ballplayer working as an office boy. Because of Devine's connection with the club, he was given permission to work out with the team, which he called "a thrill." Part of the workout was to earn his keep as batting practice pitcher. But back then there were "no protective screens," so that batting practice pitchers were a "convenient target and it was a kind of a game to try to hit them."

Bing Devine told Peter Golenbock:

> I think back now, You got to be crazy. There were a bunch of guys who could hit the ball hard enough to hurt you, but Joe Medwick was the only one who looked upon you as an adversary. Medwick liked to hit balls at batting practice pitchers. And particularly at me. He liked me less than other batting practice pitchers because I worked for the front office, and Joe Medwick was one of the early enemies of the front office.
>
> A couple of times he met me at the door going in and out of the club- house and said, "What are you doing here today?" I told him, "Pitch- ing batting practice." He said, "You better look out. I'll get you." A

couple of times he didn't even take his turn at bat when I pitched. But he never did fulfill his threat to hit me.

So this was a ballplayer having his fun with an administrator. Devine seemed to take it as good-natured razzing.

As Devine told me, "But I didn't mind—or I wasn't very smart— I never got angry or scared. In fact, I pitched batting practice for the whole season." But Bing Devine told the Medwick stories to another summertime Cardinals employee, a junior at the University of Missouri by the name of Bob Broeg, whose long career was capped by his selection to the writer's wing of the Hall of Fame. Consequently, this Devine story was retold many times.

The All-Star Cardinals traveled to New York for the July 11, 1939, game at Yankee Stadium for the first televised All-Star game. It was a low scoring game, 3-1, and DiMaggio's solo home run was described in this way: "Ironically, the ball sailed over the head of the National League's lone DiMaggio rival, Joe Medwick, the Cardinals slugging outfielder."

For a month afterward, it may have been Joe's play that inspired the Cardinals. He had two hits and a sacrifice fly at the Polo Grounds. In the sixth inning of a close game, Joe had an infield hit that advanced Mize to second. But on the next play, Mize, rounding third base, was caught in a rundown, after which pitcher "Mountain Music" Melton strolled back to the mound, ball in hand. Catcher Harry Danning, also daydreaming, woke up in time to see Joe sprint home to an unguarded home plate for a steal of home. He just kept coming; it was one of three Cardinal runs.

Danning, in a letter to S.A.B.R. (Society for American Baseball Research) member Ace Parker of California, initially described Medwick as a great hitter and good outfielder: "He was a hustler from the word go, before Rose was Charlie Hustle." How did the Giants pitch to Medwick? Well, that was easy: "fastballs low and outside which he would rifle down the line at a third baseman playing deep." Danning said that "I have always been happy to have him as a friend—not on the field but after," because on the field "he gave no quarter and he didn't expect you to give him one." Joe, by the way, was on Danning's list as the All-Star left fielder from 1933–1942.

Home again, Joe got two hits and scored twice while making a diving catch on July 27, helping Curt Davis to a win. This was not enough for Ray Blades, however, who felt he needed to put Lynn

King in left field to replace Joe for the Giants' last at bats in two games. At this point, King had played in about sixty major league games and made about one hundred putouts. Blades, it appeared, considered King a defensive specialist—at least a better one than Joe.

Ending the month with the Dodgers, the Cardinals lost the first game, though Medwick homered; they also lost the second game, 7-4. Before the doubleheader, Joe was "one of the guests of honor" at a party at Durocher's apartment in St. Louis. Ted McGrew, Brooklyn Dodger scout, told Leo that the Dodgers needed to get Medwick. There were writers who believed that Larry MacPhail had an offer of $10,000 on the table for any sportswriter who would help to buy Medwick's contract, and with that kind of money, many writers were working to try to complete that deal. MacPhail had apparently offered $200,000 for Medwick's contract the previous year. In the doubleheader on July 30, Sunkel won again, as did Bowman, with two complete game jobs. Joe was hitting .322, was fourth in the league in RBIs (with 60), and had 107 hits in 85 games played. Yet this was not enough for Ray Blades—not for "hard-bitten," "short-tempered" Blades.

"It was quite true," Dan Daniel wrote, "that at times this season Medwick had looked none too eager. A salary reduction . . . after a big year and the certainty that diminishing attendance in St. Louis would bring another cut for 1940 with developments which have spawned a feud between the player and Ray Blades. [When] Blades removed Medwick . . . that was a studied insult."

Here's what happened: in a previous game, Medwick had loafed on a roller that would have put him on first if he had hustled. The incident cost the Cardinals the ball game. On two other occasions, Medwick had loafed on hits to the outfield.

August 1 was an important day for Joe Medwick. He was again replaced in left field, this time with two out, a count of 1-2, and the score at 4-3 with a runner on first base. As Joe saw Lynn King, glove in hand, running toward him, he knew what was happening. Ray Blades was taking him out of the game with one strike left to play. Joe knew when he was being demeaned. In a fury, he threw his glove high in the air, and stomped after it. After he picked it up, he left the ballpark through the vehicle gate near third base.

Who knows what made Blades so angry? Even with Blades' famous quick temper, Stockton didn't think that he had any "axes to

grind." It would seem, then, that Blades was inept in handling players; he said, "I don't care how mad Medwick gets, just so we win."
But was it wise to attempt a win by replacing the best player for one
pitch? What about the ramifications of making the best player, and
his friends, angry? Was Blades acting on orders from management
to punish a hostile employee?

During this time period, writers were reminding their readers that
Joe was angry about his contract negotiation; he wanted things his
way. He thought he deserved better, and would find a way to get
his due.

Medwick and Blades talked things over in a Sportsman's Park
ticket booth before the August 3 doubleheader. At this point, it was
clear that Joe had cooled off and was accepting his situation—for
now. Medwick, hitting fifth, was loudly cheered each time he came
to bat, and in his first at bat that day, he homered to right. The home
run broke a 1-1 tie and gave Lon Warneke the winning runs. Later
he doubled and walked. Mort Cooper won game two.

All of this was not over, however, although in the peacemaking
photograph the newsmen had asked for, Joe's smile at Blades seems
sincere enough. "With his second substandard season in succession
staring him in the face, he probably had had many things to contend
with." L. G. Wray of "Sports Salad" from the *St. Louis Post-Dispatch*
gave his half-baked guess that "Johnny Mize had been stealing
much of the hitting spotlight . . . and there [were] such up and coming swatters as Don Padgett and Enos Slaughter to cast shadows
over him." Yet Stockton wrote, "On a recent eastern trip, Mrs.
Johnny Mize and Mrs. Joe Medwick accompanied the team and the
Mizes and the Medwicks went to picture shows together, dined together, and in other ways passed the time in each other's company."

Later, Wray wrote, "Blades exploded [about Medwick's apparent
lack of hustle], 'I don't care who Medwick is, he can't do that on this
club.' Personally, we think Blades was right. It should have the effect
of bringing Medwick to his senses." Writers did tend to side with the
management; Wray certainly seemed to. It was a long-standing
problem in baseball: writers, believing themselves superior to
"dumb jocks," treated the players as children who spent their time
playing a children's game. But the reality was that the players were
grown men supporting themselves and their families. Many writers
in this era seemed to have a hard time acknowledging that reality.
Dan Daniels was not one of them, however: "On the ridiculous at-

tendance there this season, St. Louis does not deserve a Medwick." The *Sporting News* report on the incident said, "Your reporter personally feels that Joe had been giving the best that was in him." Another asked if it was a good strategy to take out a productive star for a rookie, a player who would have a lifetime average of .208. L. C. Davis's "Sports Salad" column said this: "We have no quarrel with playing the percentage out to the vanishing point, but if Joe McCarthy ever took out Babe Ruth for a pinch hitter, we don't recall it."

Second in RBIs in the league now, Joe ended the month with two days of rain in New York, from where the club returned to St. Louis. Joe played in twenty-seven games in August, going 37-109, a .339 average, while driving in twenty runs.

In the first ten days of the September pennant race, Joe hit .436, producing twenty-five runs for his team. At home against Philadelphia, the Cardinals celebrated an important victory. Bob Bowman won 4-3 with the help of Joe's homer in the second inning, a bases-empty long ball that was Medwick's 100th RBI; it was his sixth consecutive 100-RBI season. Medwick had another great day for the crowd of 1,423 on September 13: 4-5, a double and a home run, three runs scored, and three RBIs. The team kept winning against Boston—they had to keep winning because Cincinnati was playing well, too.

In a doubleheader, the Cardinals took game one behind Curt Davis's 6-3 win. In the fourteenth inning of the second game of the series, Joe drove home Enos Slaughter with the only run of the game. The Cardinals then won their fifth in a row in the third game by scoring a run in the ninth inning to give Clyde Shoun a victory. Joe had hit in ten straight games.

When the Giants split a doubleheader in St. Louis, Joe drove in Slaughter again with the winning run in game two. Medwick's streak of games ended at game thirteen the next day during a split with the Giants.

With eight games left, the Cardinals had to find a way to close the space between themselves and the Reds; the Reds would have to lose when the Cardinals won. Three of these games were against the Reds. Manager Ray Blades would not be replacing Joe in this series. In the first game (game one of a Tuesday doubleheader), Joe threw out a runner at the plate, made three hits, and scored once, but that run was all the team could show in a 3-1 loss. In game two, McGee's four-hit shutout and an RBI single by Joe, as well as four by others, gave them a 6-0 win. With five games to go, they were three and a half back. McGee, under pressure, gave them another shutout, and with four games to go, they were two and a half back. But Paul Derringer, winning his twenty-fifth, was too much for the Cardinals, who lost 5-3. Joe's 200th hit, a double, was no solace, because as usual, he went all out, in this game trying to stretch his two-base hit into a triple to help tie the score (trying as usual to take the extra base). "Ival Goodman, rightfielder, . . . whipped a perfect peg to Bill Werber at third. Werber dived like a fullback to make the putout as Medwick came up cursing his impetuosity." With three games to go, the Cardinals were three and a half back. The Reds had won.

In the twenty-nine games played until the pennant was settled, Joe had been everything people had been saying about him. He hit .424 in the twenty-nine games, with fifty-three hits. He drove in twenty-nine runs.

But there were three games left. Rain canceled one and forced a doubleheader on September 30. Joe's team was 90-59 and could not lose their second spot.

It was a year of second-places for Medwick: second in hits, second in doubles (60th all-time), second in RBIs (only four hitters were above one hundred), second in runs produced. In addition to his third spot in batting average, Joe was also third in total bases. He was also fifth in slugging percentage (eight players were above .500) and at bats. This meant he was in the top five in seven traditional statistical categories. He was also ninth in triples, tenth in homers (Mize was first), and fourteenth in on-base percent. He finished eighth in fielding average among National League outfielders, and second on the team to the amazing Terry Moore, who made but two errors and had sixteen assists. And in the Most Valuable Player voting, which then included pitchers, he finished seventh, his fifth straight year in the top ten.

Joe drove in one hundred runs for his seventh consecutive year. He drove in 16 percent of the team's runs, scored 12 percent of the runs, tied for the team lead in steals, and struck out in only 7 percent of his at bats, or once every fourteen times. Medwick had missed only twenty games in his seven full seasons. For the third year, he walked more than he struck out.

And for the seventh consecutive year he had struck forty doubles or more. No one else was able to accomplish that until Wade Boggs more than forty years later. No one has ever done it in the National League.

After the season, Joe took his place on two more major league teams, which were called the All-Star team and the All-American team.

That October, at the Downtown YMCA Club in St. Louis, a father and son affair had as its speakers Joe and Leo Durocher, both St. Louis residents. Durocher talked on the topic "My Success with the Dodgers," and Stockton reported Leo's words in a column:

> Durocher said that one of his great problems when he went to Brooklyn was to toughen up the team. His pitchers, he said, didn't want to throw at opposing hitters. . . . But he finally got his pitchers to realize that it was dangerous to let batters stand at the plate with spikes dug in and that finally he got them to throwing at opposing batters and that then the team began to improve. Durocher pointed to Medwick and said, "This fellow doesn't escape either, just because he's my friend. We set him down almost every time he comes up to the plate. . . ." Durocher also said his base runners weren't tough enough and he had to teach them to slide into enemy basemen to break up double plays. He said he finally got them to sharpen their spikes and keep them high as they crashed into bases.

These ideas were not new; they reflected a style of baseball played when Durocher was a young man. Some managers used these techniques when necessary. Durocher seemed to think they were always necessary. There were drawbacks associated with this attitude toward the game: Dodger team members were penalized for not playing Durocher's way, and the other team was forced to play the way Durocher played.

Medwick would pay for Durocher's words.

14

Traded, 1940

New York writer Dan Parker very early saw the future for Joe: "Medwick openly criticized Breadon all season for that slice in salary he was forced to take and Sam seemed bent this time on unloading his balky star." Medwick felt that he was being cheated while others continued to profit from his services. Peter Golenbock added up Rickey's sales, for example, in the summer of 1940, to be $385,000. This meant that, beyond Branch's salary, in sales commissions alone, Rickey made more than twice Medwick's salary. Rickey could afford to throw his shirts away after one wear. (Rickey loved to tell people that he threw his shirts away.)

On March 2, players attended the first Cardinal workout in Florida. Joe was saying he would go back to St. Louis rather than pay "a hotel bill when I have a perfectly good home in St. Louis." His wife, Isabelle, was more than eight months pregnant, and she had gone back to her family doctor some time ago.

On March 17, Joe's second child, a daughter, was born, and after noting that, sportswriters looked around for something else to comment on. J. Roy Stockton mused about salaries at a time when the major league average salary was $7,000 a year. The average factory worker was making about $100 a month; the average major league salary was $583 per month, based on a 168-day work schedule. But the average major league player was at the top of his profession; the average factory worker was not. Average salaries of players in the minors were the same as those of average factory-worker wages. Two St. Louis Browns players, Ed Cole and Johnny Bernardino, drew $15 a week in unemployment cash.

Joe returned to Florida on March 21 and asked permission to work out with the squad, but Rickey refused. By March 26, Medwick "surrendered at 8 o'clock . . . after a brief note from Sam Breadon informed him that he would be 'on his own' after the departure of the squad from its St. Petersburg hotel and that if and when he did choose to sign a contract, the club would require him to train without salary until such time as Manager Blades decided he was in condition to play." Within forty-eight hours, Medwick was under contract.

The outfield of Medwick, Terry Moore, and Enos Slaughter that arrived back in St. Louis for the championship season was one of the best in the league. Joe was now taking very early batting practice (at 11 A.M.). As he hit, many things must have made him angry and tired. The club still didn't furnish a jock or a sweatshirt, and the clubhouse boy was pressured not to give out hats. There was no food between doubleheaders; no drinks were provided—ever. From where he was hitting, Joe saw the new lights in place all over the park. From where he was hitting, he could sometimes see uniforms spread out on seats in the stands to dry in the sun. Joe and Butch (the clubhouse man) both knew that the uniforms did not always dry out before game time.

The team played its final games of exhibition against the Browns at Sportsman's Park. After a tie game, the Cardinals lost 7-3. After the game, both teams attended the annual Chamber of Commerce banquet at the Hotel Jefferson (the 1940 version) with a crowd of 906, including Senator Harry Truman. The newspapers that covered the event had some new features: European maps showing the Nazi advances and sidebars on the front page of "War News."

And Joe? "Those who run the St. Louis club had a chance to make Medwick once more the No. 1 ball player of their league and a tremendous power in their pennant drive. But they left Medwick disgruntled over mere chicken feed. When fans boo, Medwick yells at them and they yell back."

No one was booing Pete Reiser, who once again was playing very well for the Dodger organization, though in the minors. MacPhail was worrying because of his secret deal with Rickey, even as the newspapers praised Reiser repeatedly. The Brooklyn sportswriters wondered when Pete would be in the Dodger outfield or infield, if Durocher could do what he said—turn him into a second baseman. MacPhail and Rickey both knew that something was going to have to be done about Reiser, who was now "hidden" in Elmira, New York.

For the month of April, Joe was 33-103, or .320. But he had driven in only fifteen runs in twenty-four games, which equaled a pace of ninety-six RBIs. Something was wrong when Medwick, hitting fourth, batting .320, drove in only fifteen runs. The problem may have been fewer extra-base hits than average for Joe, or it may have been the weakness of the Cardinal order (not enough men getting on base in front of him).

Rickey was thinking about Medwick's declining production. (Rickey's reputation as a player salesman—since he made a percentage of the sales—was well known.) Rickey had three very powerful beliefs about a ballplayer's worth to the team. To Rickey, there was a connection between ease of negotiation, the size of the salary the player took from the club, and the player's continued employment by the Cardinals. This convoluted equation had nothing whatsoever to do with the team's success on the field. It didn't seem to matter to Rickey at all if the team failed at the pennant race as long as it could win for Rickey's bank account and the corporation's. Since Joe arrived in September of 1932, Rickey and the corporation in charge of deal making had only bought two kinds of players: ones who were very old and very cheap (bought for the waiver price) and/or players who were bought and then sold before they played a game.

On June 4, the second-place Dodgers came into town for the Cardinals' first home night game. The game itself saw the Cardinals beaten badly once more. Joe, in another odd game, had five hits in five at bats, including three doubles using his thirty-six-ounce, thirty-five-inch-long bat—yet he had no RBI.

Leo Durocher invited Joe to a party for Dodger players at his apartment after the game. Joe had a great time, and Rickey found out his player was there.

Meanwhile, Breadon flew to Chicago to talk to Commissioner Landis about the All-Star game in St. Louis in 1940, and then called the president of the Rochester team and told Oliver French to go to New York for a meeting. Without Rickey being asked, Breadon hired Red Wings manager Billy Southworth to manage the Cardinals.

Bob Broeg said that "[w]hen the club got off to that lousy start in 1940, it would be typical of the Cardinals trying to retrench when they had a bad start. Breadon fired Blades . . . since Rickey did not want to fire, or hesitated to fire, Blades." The Cardinals, with a record of 15-26, dropped to seventh—fourteen games behind the Reds.

The game with Boston was rained out on Tuesday, June 11. Larry MacPhail had contacted Branch Rickey. When MacPhail was unable to secure an airplane reservation, he rode a train toward Philadelphia, only to get off in Camden, New Jersey, where he boarded a plane to St. Louis. Rickey met the Dodger owner at the airport, and they began to negotiate for Medwick. MacPhail stayed at the Jefferson Hotel, and met with both Breadon and Rickey on Wednesday, June 12. By that night, the deal was done. For Rickey, who seemed to be a man in love with his own voice, the deal was, in one of his favorite phrases, "an addition by subtraction"—as if the wit of the diction took care of the sense of the logic.

MacPhail announced in a midnight call to the New York newspapers that the Dodgers now owned the contract of pitcher Curt Davis and outfielder Joe Medwick. The Cardinals were sent Bert Haas, a 26-year-old first baseman; Ernie Koy, a 30-year-old outfielder; Carl Doyle, a pitcher who would never play in the majors; and Sam Nahem. They also got $132,500 in cash. A reasonable estimate is that Rickey personally made a minimum of $13,000 from the deal. He had originally paid $500 for Joe.

In Harold Parrot's *The Lords of Baseball* (1976), as well as in Peter Golenbock's *Bums: An Oral History of the Brooklyn Dodgers* (1984), the hidden figures were exposed. For this story, it is necessary to remember the performance of Pete Reiser. As Harold Parrot wrote in *The Lords of Baseball*, whenever Reiser played against major league pitching in 1939, and in the 1940 spring training season,

> the baseball writers had gotten another glimpse at Reiser . . . and they had fallen in love with him all over again. They were starting to ask embarrassing questions: When was Pistol Pete going to get his chance? MacPhail realized by then that he had to renege on returning Pistol Pete. He called Rickey, pleading, almost in tears: "Branch, they'd lynch me here if I traded Reiser away for Medwick right now, even up. Durocher had talked too much, and the reporters have written every word. The fans here were so excited about the kid, there would be a scandal. I just can't give him back to you."

Naturally, Rickey was in no position to complain, being a co-conspirator. But the Old Man would have to get cash, lots of cash, instead of the superbaby. They couldn't pass the money under the table; and to partially explain the $132,000 that would appear on the Cardinals' books after coming out of the Brooklyn Trust vaults, Rickey sent Coonskin Curt Davis, a thirty-eight-year-old pitcher, to the Dodgers along with Medwick.

Now it was clearer what MacPhail and Rickey had talked about on June 11 and 12: the money Rickey demanded for the loss of Reiser.

Joe was aboard a train heading for Rochester for a June 13 exhibition game. Outside Buffalo he was awakened by pitcher Jack Russell, who told him, "Congratulations, you lucky stiff. You've been traded to Brooklyn," and Joe was shown a newspaper for proof. He and Curt made plans to go meet old teammates Leo Durocher and Tex Carleton that day.

Years later, Red Smith wrote, "He [Medwick] was one ball player who recognized early the advantages of playing in New York. He wanted the spotlight, he wanted the financial opportunities that accrued to a star in the big town, and most of all he wanted to challenge Joe DiMaggio's position of eminence. . . . 'Get the Giants to trade for me,' he told Toots Shor after the 1937 season, 'and I'll give you half my salary the first year.'"

Perhaps he had, in effect, traded himself. He had gotten out of a bad situation and was going back to the area where he grew up, where his parents were.

Leaving Rochester on an American Airlines flight, they landed in New York at 2:44 P.M. When the two new players came down the steps, photographers made them climb up again, and took pictures of them at the doorway of the plane. Joe, in a double-breasted suit and broad-brimmed fedora, mostly said he was glad to come to a first-place club. He was questioned on the coach that took him to the Hotel New Yorker where he would live away from home. He said nothing harsh about the fans in St. Louis, or about the team. Southworth in Rochester said, "There comes a time when all players outlive their usefulness in any one city." Another writer said, "The Cardinals . . . have slipped into the second division. Medwick felt that he was above it all. There was no great incentive to exert himself and no doubt his attitude toward the Cardinals was as instrumental in the club selling him as anything else." And yet during that year, he was second on the team in average, at bats, games played, and RBIs.

He led the team in doubles. He had produced in RBIs and runs scored, 20 percent of the team's runs. Must Medwick lead the league in every category every year, as he did in 1937?

Joe knew, too, because he had seen it happen, that the Cardinals refused to pay well; Cardinal players weren't being paid as much as comparable players on other teams. Cardinal books from those years suggest that all of the money didn't come from attendance alone.

Joe had never liked being either cheated or put upon. The tryout in 1928 with the Newark Bears, the candy bars incident at Houston, the holdout in his first full year of major league play were all proof of that. If someone did not give him what he was convinced he was worth, Joe would find a way to get what he wanted.

The *Times* said, "the Cardinals have surrendered [the pennant]."

That's what the newspaper said, but a fan who wrote to the paper put it differently: "All I can say [is], I hope the boys at Grand and Dodier don't decide to build a new park. Where would they get another Medwick?" A drawing underneath the letter had two price tags: the first said, "Install One Scoreboard. Price: *Dizzy Dean*"; the second said, "Install One Light Plant at Grand and Dodier. Price: *Joe Medwick.*"

Nevertheless, Joe had gotten himself traded to the Brooklyn Dodgers. Joe made the trade to where Tex and Leo awaited, where possible World Series money awaited—where big-market money awaited. He was confident and said so as the days passed: "I haven't really been playing the way I really can play for the past two years. I just couldn't. They ruined my incentive out there."

In Joe's seven full seasons from 1933–1939, he had averaged 616 at bats, 123 RBIs, and 204 hits. From 1935–1939, he made 1,075 hits. He drove in 14 percent of his team's runs in that period. The newspapers called him "the National League's premier batsman" . . . "super slugger" . . . "a tremendous clouter with an accurate throwing arm." He was "the hustling Hungarian," and "jolting Joe." A drawing of Medwick that took up 25 percent of page thirteen of the Brooklyn *Eagle* had around its borders the following statements: "Happy Surroundings, I Sure Like It Here, Watch My Batting Figures Climb, Dodgers Can't Lose!" Delirious Dodger fans distributed thousands of throwaway cards reading "Don't Worry. We've Got Medwick."

There were doubters, however.

Jimmy Powers, the acid-penned columnist of the *New York Daily News*, described Medwick as "a cross between the Most Valuable

Player and the Most Valuable Jerk." Bill Terry, the Giants' manager, thought that Medwick's speed was greatly diminished and that he would hit into a lot of double plays. Joe replied that he would make Terry "eat those words, with mustard." In fact, Joe's highest total of hitting into double plays came in 1937, with twenty-one. In 1941, Medwick hit into sixteen.

Medwick was second in the National League, with twelve doubles. Joe was thought to be an "old" thirty (Joe would be thirty in five months). People were saying the same thing about Frank Robinson in 1965, but in 1966 he won the Most Valuable Player award and the Triple Crown. Joe was thought to have a constitution that delivered before age thirty rather than one that would allow him to remain near the top for a long period of time (like Mel Ott did, for example). The sportswriters tended to think that Joe's lower average, for example, was psychological in cause. Phrases such as "not in the proper frame of mind" and "his attitude" appeared frequently in sportswriters' predictions.

Joe himself thought his problems might be partly psychological, partly circumstantial. "In 1937 I hit .374. The next year I dropped to .322 and the boss . . . said I was a big disappointment . . . this year things were worse. Poor Blades was experimenting."

On the way to the Hotel New Yorker, Joe talked about his state of mind. "'If busting my back for the greatest guy in the world, Leo Durocher will help,'" Hy Turkin recorded him as saying, "'I'll just do that every day in the week and twice on Sunday. . . . My weight now [is] 182, just about my best playing poundage. Boy, am I happy to be here! I've always wanted to play for Leo Durocher and the Dodgers. They play my game—fight!'"

Durocher said, "I don't think I exaggerate when I say Medwick will increase our power 40 percent. . . . I expect him to be the Medwick of 1937."

The *Daily News* simply said the trade was "a deal which will probably bring Brooklyn its first pennant in 20 years." And one of the front-page headlines in the June 13, 1940, Brooklyn *Eagle* read "Hang Up the Pennant! We've got Medwick!"

As Joe was settling in, Pee Wee Reese was returning from Louisville, where he had been recovering from his June 1 beaning. The Dodgers were on top in the National League at 30-13, but only by .007. The team was trying to separate itself from the Reds in the pennant race. And Cincinnati had just arrived for four games.

Medwick was assigned to uniform number 7, the same number he had worn throughout his career. Joe had gotten off the train and onto the plane to New York in such a hurry that he brought no bats. But there were at least six Dodgers who used his model, including first baseman Dolph Camilli and shortstop Leo Durocher.

The two pitchers who started the most games for Durocher were Whitlow Wyatt, a 32-year-old right-hander, and another right-hander, 35-year-old "Hot Potato Hamlin." Hamlin and Wyatt both pitched against Joe in the Texas League. The next two starters were Freddie Fitzsimmons—"Fat Freddie," who was still effective at age thirty-eight—and, lastly, Joe's first protector on the Cardinals, Tex Carleton, who had thrown his first no-hitter for the Dodgers earlier in 1940 at age thirty-three.

Medwick joined a team that in 1940 was primed to win a pennant. The Dodgers, with their three veteran starting pitchers, gave the Dodgers winners, something that Branch Rickey, for all his genius, did not do from 1935 to 1941.

The Dodgers had on their roster what *The Cultural Encyclopedia of Baseball* ranks among the best sign-stealers in the history of the game: Durocher, Coach Charley Dressen, and Freddie Fitzsimmons.

The newspapers were ready to have the pennnat delivered: "Joe Medwick, husky Hungarian, who'll be the Moses to lead Leo Durocher's troupe into the promised land—they hope . . . singled to right in the third and drove in a run."

The next morning, June 15, Medwick, Curt Davis, and Leo appeared at 10:30 at the "weekly session at the World's Fair baseball school. . . . Durocher [spoke] through an amplifier. . . . Davis and Medwick acted as models for the hour-long talk by Durocher, who spoke to 1,000 youngsters." Photographed in front of a banner that read "Academy of Sport" with their coat jackets off, suspenders showing, Davis showed his pickoff move and Joe "furnished examples of the various batting stances used by different major league hitters."

Then, on Saturday, they went to the ballpark, where the Dodgers won again, 11-6. Tommy Holmes wrote:

As more than 21,000 cheered, the Medwickized Dodger legions smashed their way to a fourth straight triumph. . . . Big Day for Medwick. The colorful Joe Medwick had a whale of a day getting a single and a double in three times up, scoring three runs and knocking over one. . . . Medwick lined the first pitch into the right field screen for a tremendous single and Walker scored the first run. Phelps hit a home run smash over everything in right, completed a jubilant journey around the base paths, with Medwick leaping up and down and applauding at home plate waiting for him.

In *Nice Guys Finish Last* (1975), Leo Durocher remembered the morning of June 18:

Joe and I had always been great pals in St. Louis, and he had taken a suite at the New Yorker where I was staying. As we were leaving for the ball park, we found ourselves in the same elevator with Bob Bowman, who was going to be pitching against us. Given that opportunity, I made one of my lovable remarks about his chances for survival, which gave him a perfect opening to tell me that he was sure of at least one automatic out in the lineup. Me.

"You won't last long enough to get to Leo," Medwick snarled. "You'll be out of there before you get down that far."

The usual baseball byplay, sure. But also a little more than that. Bowman, like so many other St. Louis pitchers, had had a run-in with Medwick after accusing him of loafing after a fly ball and there was bad blood between them.

"I'll take care of both of you guys," Bowman said. "Wait and see."

In his book, *Country Hardball*, Enos Slaughter recalled the beginning of the game: "Once the game got started, each of the first three Dodgers greeted Bowman with a base hit. It turned out that third base coach Charlie Dressen, who had an uncanny ability to steal signs, noticed that Bowman was twisting his glove whenever he threw a curve ball. Then Don Padgett, who was catching for us that day, noticed that Dressen was whistling every time Bowman threw a curve. With Medwick coming up to bat, Padgett went to the mound and told Bowman to hold the glove the way he did when he was throwing curves, but to fire a fastball in high and tight.

"Up came Medwick. When he heard Dressen's whistle, he leaned towards the plate and reared back in anticipation of belting a predetected curve. Pow! Bowman's fastball caught him right on the temple, and he dropped to the ground like a stone. Out like a light."

Newspaperman Hy Turkin wrote that Joe was "solidly whacked right under the button of his cap. Medwick went down as though shot, landing on his shoulder blades so hard that his feet flew into the air. He settled with his arms outstretched and his face to the sky.

There was a sharp sob from just back of the dugout. It was Mrs. Isabelle Medwick who had just come from St. Louis to watch her husband for the first time in a Dodger uniform. She buried her head in the shoulder of Mrs. Grace Durocher beside her and kept it there while every else stared horrified at the fallen hero."

Durocher and Van Mungo and Cookie Lavagetto of the Dodgers rushed over to Joe, who was stretched out, as Bowman and Padgett looked over him

Dr. Henry Claasen, who worked out with the Dodgers each spring, jumped from his box and rushed to Medwick's side. Joe's face showed terrible pain, and his left hand covered the left side of his face, hiding. Durocher said, "I went for Bowman, the benches emptied and there were fights all over the field. That was to be expected."

Slaughter characterized it this way: "That's when all hell broke loose. The Dodgers charged at Bowman like a mass of hornets. They were not only led by manager Leo Durocher, but general manager Larry MacPhail. From right field, I rushed to the mound in aid of Bowman, along with the rest of the Cardinals. When I reached the scene of the melee, I grabbed the first Dodger I could reach, which happened to be Van Lingle Mungo. I had Mungo by the hair and my arm was around his neck when Freddie Fitzsimmons came along and collared me. Terry Moore jumped in and, in turn, collared Freddie."

In a letter describing the event, Ernie Koy recalled the following: "I was in left field during the game. When the accident occurred, I ran in and helped take Bowman to the dugout. Brooklyn people came on the field."

Durocher recalled that "MacPhail came running down from his box, and while Medwick was being carried off on a stretcher, MacPhail was standing in front of the St. Louis dugout challenging the whole ball club. Screaming at them. Out of control. The fiery Brooklyn boss shook off attempts of Dressen and Babe Phelps to restrain him, walked to the end of the St. Louis dugout, unloaded a tirade at the Cardinals team, inviting any of them to step under the stands. Johnny Mize and Pepper Martin tried to cool him off. It was a miracle that there wasn't a riot." In fact, a police department emergency squad of about one hundred arrived very quickly and spread out on the field.

When Medwick was carried off the field on a canvas stretcher by a teammate, Joe Gallagher, the trainer, and two policemen, writer Hy Turkin headed for the clubhouse under the stands.

As your correspondent entered the clubhouse, Medwick was on a stretcher a few inches above the floor. First to enter the clubhouse after Medwick was his wife. Her pretty face still tear-stained, she forced a smile when Joe assured her he was all right. Fully conscious, Joe said, "Remember the rabbit's foot you gave me in the dugout just before the game—to change my luck? Well, I knew it wouldn't work. The rabbit had four of 'em and they didn't help him. Ha! Ha!"

MacPhail entered, still fuming. He calmed down as Joe said he was better. But Medwick wasn't moving his head at all, and didn't try to roll his eyes upwards. "Take care of him," said Larry. "Give him a bourbon, if he wants it. Tell that ambulance to hurry."

"I'm O.K. Let me off this stretcher. I want to go back and play," Medwick said.

Just before the men in white came for him, Medwick, fingering his thick black hair, murmured, "They told me you can have bad days in a row, but I didn't know they could pile up like this. It's funny," he said. "That makes two bad days in a row. Yesterday I couldn't get a base hit and today this thing happens." Just to be certain that Medwick was all right, MacPhail asked him to repeat what he had said and the player did.

"What did you do, lose the ball?"

"No," he said. "He threw the ball behind me. I couldn't get out of the way."

"He threw the ball behind you?"

"That's the way you hit a batter. If they want to hit you they throw behind you: Your natural reaction was to fall backwards."

"Fall right into it?"

"That's right," Medwick said.

"That wasn't my fault," [Bowman] said in another Durocher book, *The Lip*, "Dressen was stealing the signs and tipping off the batters." [Dixie Walker also was good at spotting signs from second base and re-laying them to the batter.] The Dodgers had decided that when Bowman gripped the ball tightly he was to throw a fast ball but looser when a curve was about to be thrown. He'd [Dressen] whistle when he thought a curve was coming. So Bowman and catcher Don Padgett decided to cross up Dressen—and whoever happened to be batting. Padgett would signal for a curve but Bowman would come in with a high, hard one. "Poor Medwick was looking for a curve and he couldn't get out of the way," said Bowman.

Letters written by Terry Moore, Max Lanier, and Whitlow Wyatt support Bowman's version. Moore recalled the following: "when Dressen was calling the pitch, our club said to stop it. . . . Joe was looking for the ball to curve." Lanier said, "Medwick stepped into what he thought was a curve and it happened to be a fast ball. . . . I was Bob Bowman's roommate and I never heard him say anything about throwing at Medwick. There were a lot of brushbacks from both teams." And Whitlow Wyatt's letter said, "There were a few high inside pitchers in my day. And still is."

The first intern to arrive in the clubhouse was told by MacPhail that he wanted Medwick taken to Caledonian Hospital. As Isabelle Medwick walked out, leaning on Mrs. Durocher's arm, she sobbed, "Wait till I see that Bowman. He's the only Cardinal who ever throws at a batter deliberately. I'll punch him in the face myself." Mrs. Medwick and Nellie Durocher, Leo's stepdaughter, taxied to the hospital.

After the game, Larry MacPhail issued a signed statement in the press box in which he called Bowman a coward. Then, according to Harold Parrot,

> The beaning of old Muscles caused a riot on the field, charges brought and counstercharges off the field, even an investigation by William O'Dwyer, then district attorney in Brooklyn. MacPhail demanded that Bowman be barred from baseball for life; he came up with affidavits from everybody who had been in the elevator about the "threats" Bowman had made. Do you know that within twenty-four hours he had the District Attorney, Bill O'Dwyer, conducting a criminal investigation. O'Dwyer had just broken up Murder, Inc. MacPhail demanded that he now go after "Beanball, Inc.," which he described as a conspiracy among National League pitchers to kill off the Dodgers' pennant chances by eliminating our leading players. Burton Turkus, the man who had been in charge of the Murder, Inc., investigation, was assigned to the case and he actually had us all in a couple of days later for a hearing.
>
> X-ray examinations by Doctor Daniel A. Mcateer and Dr. Jeff Browder, the latter a brain specialist called in by the Brooklyn management, showed definitely there was no fracture.

Although Joe didn't have a fracture, he was ordered to be observed and rested for at least a week.

Medwick's beaning was followed first by demands for helmets to be worn by batters. There had been four minor league players who had died from beanballs, the last one on July 4, 1933. (The National League was fifteen years away from requiring a batting helmet and the American League, sixteen. Earflaps on helmets were thirty-four years away.) These demands were replaced by the backlash in articles such as "Dust-Off Pitch Part of the Game. . . . Batters expect it after a long hit." It was Durocher's fault, Pepper Martin suggested, since Leo considered beanballs an important tool for a team. In fact, Hugh Casey had hit Padgett, Mize, and Slaughter in the space of two innings at Sportsman's Park on May 7. Quite simply, using anything you can to diminish a player's ability at bat was the common trade of baseball for some managers.

And since it was common, batters must learn to deal with the fear that was always there when you come to bat. Fearlessness in the batter's box was a batter's tool.

"It was virtually impossible to refrain from thoughts of retaliation and some of the boys were saying today that Brooklyn's own pitchers do not do enough dusting off. Outside of Hugh Casey, who'll take no guff from anyone, the Dodgers haven't had a really good knockdown specialist and they've wound up with the worst of the decision in a long succession of feuds as a result," wrote Tommy Holmes.

After the beaning, while he was lying in a hospital bed, and suffering from awful earaches and blurred vision, Medwick received the kind of telephone call you could only get in Brooklyn. Medwick remembered it this way:

"Do you want his arm?" the guy asked.

"No, it was just one of those things," said Medwick.

Then the guy said, "I'll get Bowman's arm for you and send it to you."

Now Medwick shook his head in wonder. "That was Brooklyn. They were rough then."

On June 21, three days later, after going over thirty-two pages of testimony, National League president Ford Frick telegraphed MacPhail, Bowman, Billy Southworth, and Cardinal president Sam Breadon: "After careful consideration, the National League office finds no proof of the charge brought by the Brooklyn club that Pitcher Bob Bowman of St. Louis 'deliberately' and 'with premeditation' beaned Joe Medwick in the game played at Ebbets Field June 18. The charges, therefore, are dismissed."

The *Times* wrote:

Medwick told the prosecutor that he . . . paid very little attention to the conversation [in the elevator] and that he did not participate in it. He added that he knew of no threats by Bowman or any other Cardinal

July 20, 1936, Metuchen, New Jersey. Betty Barrett is sitting in the lap of Joe Medwick. He and the team came to town to play an exhibition game against the Metuchen B.B.C. before 4,000 fans on the New Jersey high school field. Also in the photo are Dizzy Dean, Johnny Mize, and Frankie Frisch.

BUFF OUTFIELDERS SET
FOR SEASON'S OPENER

Skipper Joe Schultz's fly chasers are rearing to go, and should get their share of the base knocks Wednesday at Beaumont. At the top, left to right, are Homer Peel and "Pooch" Puccinelli. At the bottom, left to right are Joe Medwick and Jimmy Sanders.
— Staff Photo by Andy Moss.

April 21, 1931. Four Houston Buffalo outfielders, three of whom would make it to the majors. They were Homer Peel (who had been in the big leagues and would go on to play 100 games with the Giants), Pooch Puccinelli (who played 187 games with the Cardinals and Athletics), and Jimmy Sanders.

September 5, 1939. Bat rifles—Don Padgett, Joe Medwick, Enos Slaughter,
Johnny Mize, and Pepper Martin. Joe, as usual, refuses to go along with the gag.

Early 1932, Houston, Medwick and his candy
bar—the Duckie-Wuckie was sold for a nickel.

The Cardinals gather in Tampa, Florida, radio station for baseball news to be broadcast back to St. Louis: Leo Durocher, Charley Gelbert, Martin Haley, and France Laux (broadcasters); Spud Davis, Sal Fleishman, Joe Medwick, and Bill Hallahan (players).

1934. The Gas House Gang before the World Series began: Dizzy Dean (pitcher), Lip Durocher (shortstop), Showboat Orsatti (center field), Dee Delancey (catcher), Ripper Collins (first base), Ducky Medwick (left field), Onkel Frank Frisch (second base), Jack Rothrock (right field), and Pepper Martin (third base).

1942. Four All Stars: National League stars Medwick, Ernie Lombardi, Mel Ott, and Johnny Mize pose in the polo grounds dugout.

Five Cardinals: Frankie Frisch, Pepper Martin, Ripper Collins, Joe Medwick, and Dizzy Dean. Taken early in Medwick's career, circa 1934, this is one of the few at-ease photos of Joe on a baseball field.

The Joseph Medwick Park in Carteret, New Jersey, is a handsome complex of athletic fields and picnic facilities.

Hall of Fame weekend, 1968. Chester "Jack" Wielgolinski (Carteret High School coach), Frank Tomczuk (Legionnaire), Joe, John Medwick (Joe's brother), Michael Joseph Medwick (Joe's son), and Joseph Comba (principal of Nathan Hale School, coach, and Legionnaire).

An undated photo that seems to be taken
during spring training in 1934.

Photo courtesy of Lt. Col. John Feltham.

Medwick and a young boy posed
for this picture in Ebbets Field,
circa 1941. The zipper for the
plastic insert that served as an
early batting helmet can be seen
over Joe's left ear.

This photo may have been taken
when former Cardinal teammates
Joe and Pepper Martin
were both managing in the
Florida International League
during the 1949 season.

Photo courtesy of the National Baseball
Hall of Fame Library, Cooperstown, New York.

July 1, 1945. This cartoon by Gene Mack
chronicled an early game with the
Braves when Tommy Holmes was
on his batting streak.

June 17, 1945. Medwick's first game
as a Boston Brave is recorded here
by cartoonist Gene Mack.

With Ripper Collins to his right, Joe is talking to Ken Boyer. There's a copy of Stockton's The Gas House Gang *on the table.*

1943. Advertisement for Whistling in Brooklyn *with Red Skelton. The Dodgers and Medwick appeared in the movie.*

*Three hundred of New York's most beautiful models were asked to pick
the man they would want to be stranded with on a desert island.
Victor Mature, movie and stage star, received the most votes; Joe Medwick
of the Dodgers was second; and Dodger manager Leo Durocher was third.
The selection was made at Sherman Billingsley's annual Artist, Models,
and Celebrity Party at the Stork Club.*

*Joe at work in Florida as a
hitting coach in the early '70s.*

Thomas Barthel, 8 Canterbury Drive, Clinton, NY 13323, 315-853-3485

Dear Mr.Wyatt,

I am the author of three essays of biography for the standard reference work *The Dictionary of American Biography*. One of my subjects was Joe Medwick.

I am currently working on a piece of writing concerning the beaning of Joe Medwick in 1940 and the development of the batting helmet. Since you are one of the players who was there on June 18, 1940 at Brooklyn, I would be very grateful for any information you could supply about the beaning. A return envelope is enclosed.

I would also very much like for you to enclose an autograph addressed to my son Mike, but if that is too much I will certainly understand. I do not want to be a pest.

1. How did the beaning happen? Was there one thing that caused it? I have read that there was an argument just prior to the game between Bowman and Medwick. Is this true? Did you witness it? What was said?

I dont know about any argument. There was a few in my career 16½ years

2. Some writers think that Mr. Medwick had made enemies on the St. Louis team. What can you tell me about this?

Medwick was a great fellow on the Club and off.

3. Some writers attribute the beaning to a fierce rivalry between the two National League powerhouses. Can you confirm this?

There was a few high inside pitches in my days. and still is.

4. Anything you wish to add can be written on the other side.

Yours,

Tom

Tom Barthel

Whitlow Wyatt was a teammate of Joe's on the Dodgers and knew him from the Texas League in 1931.

"DUCKY" MEDWICK

A 1930s Diamond Stars baseball card.

1937 Wheaties advertisement.

1938 Wheaties advertisement.

Cartoon depicting the three-way game in 1944 between the Giants, Dodgers, and Yankees.

THE HARD FIGHTING, HARD HITTING, JOE. M. MEDWICK, OF THE ST. LOUIS CARDINALS

1934 photo of Joe.

*Another 1930s baseball card depicting
"Big League Joe."*

Advertisement for Faust pasta, with mail-in offer for a Cardinals baseball cap, circa 1936.

H. E. CRAMER
PRESIDENT AND TREASURER

BRANCH RICKEY
VICE PRESIDENT

EDWIN H. DYER
MANAGER AND SECRETARY

The Scottdale Base Ball Club

THE YOUNG CARDINALS

MIDDLE ATLANTIC LEAGUE

SCOTTDALE, PA.   June 30, 1930.

Mr. Elmer M. Daily, President,
        Ebensburg, Pa.
Dear Mr. Daily:-
        On June 23rd, I forwarded for promulgation, contract of
Joseph Medwick alias Mickey King. Upon advice that this player was a
Minor, I asked him to sign another contract over the signatures of his
parents, John Medwick and Lizzie Medwick, Father and Mother. I am enclosing
herewith the second contract which has been witnessed by Geo. W. Massey
which should be properly substituted in regular way and promulgated to
Mr. Farrell, replacing the original contract.

        Now Mr. Daily this young man appears to be a wonderful
prospect and seems to have all the natural ability necessary to become
a great ball player, with the proper coaching. I do not want to slip up
on anything that would make our title to his services doubtful; also I
do not care to hamper him in his proposed future college career. If in
your opinion, there is anything further to be done to assure us of a
proper claim or title to him, I would thank you to advise me of same
at once, by wire collect. As formerly stated in my letter of the 23rd,
King is an absolute Rookie and his salary is $200.00 per month.

        I am also enclosing, for promulgation, contract of player
Creth B. Hines; Salary $225.00 per month. From the information I now have,
this player is an absolute rookie. Should further information develop
otherwise, I will advise.
                Yours very truly

                                President.

Special Delivery.

Copy to B.R.

1930 contract from the files of the National Baseball Hall of Fame Library in Cooperstown, New York.

Photo of Medwick with autograph, circa 1935.

player to do him injury. In his description of the Ebbets Field incident, Medwick said that he went to the plate, looked about to check the Cardinal outfield, decided in which direction he would attempt to hit, got set to await the pitch and then faced Bowman. The outfielder said that he saw Bowman deliver the pitch and the next thing he knew he was lying on the ground with a number of players grouped around him. Medwick said that he didn't recall seeing the ball, but that he must have ducked instinctively because he was struck on the left side in the rear, indicating that he turned.

Reese, beaned at Wrigley Field on June 1, played his first game in three weeks on June 21, and after the game,

> a number of St. Louis players, headed by Southworth, attempted to see Medwick at Caledonian Hospital. . . . Southworth said, "The people at the hospital . . . let me in to see him. I was pleased to see that Joe looks all right and glad to hear that he was getting along fine. I gave him the best wishes of the gang and told him how upset Bowman was . . . especially a former teammate like Medwick who Bob feels helped him as he broke in. . . ." Southworth was told by Joe that the beaning was an accident; that invariably he would easily duck such a pitch but that he somehow lost sight of the ball as it approached him. . . . Bowman did not appear at the ballpark last night. Southworth said that he thought it unlikely that Bowman would come to any physical violence but that it seemed better to take no chances.

Joe left the hospital that night at 7:10 to go back to his apartment at the Hotel New Yorker. He still had throbbing earaches and blurred vision—and worse. But he wanted to play, especially in the 1940 All-Star Game he had again been picked for.

Medwick didn't tell anyone what his true problem was. He had double vision for many, many, months. He didn't even tell his wife about this.

Robert Creamer's book quoted the Dodger president: "'Medwick was badly hurt,' MacPhail said, 'worse than we ever knew at the time. We rushed him back into action too quickly, partly because Ducky insisted on playing. A doctor told me later that Leo and I should have been arrested for sending him back that soon.'"

Joe was in uniform for the game on June 22, having missed only two games. He pinch-hit in the eighth but grounded out against the Frank Frisch Pirates. The Dodgers lost 7-2. The team needed to start hitting, since it was seventh in the league, a pallid .254.

MacPhail said he wanted both Reese and Medwick to wear helmets from now on. ("Some players think the wearing of helmets would be a 'sissy' move, but . . . no one regards umpires or catchers as sissies for wearing masks, protectors and shin guards behind the plate.")

More than a week after he returned, Joe singled and scored. In the crucial eighth inning, with Dixie Walker on second, Medwick could only hit the ball back to pitcher Bill Lee, but Joe hustled down the line, and Lee threw to Cavarretta at first while Walker got to third with the tying run and then scored on Camilli's single. Joe did not hit for power, but he did his job as a hitter, though at just 9-32 since he was struck by Bowman's pitch. This was an average of .281, which was downright marvelous for a hitter with dizzy spells, ringing ears, and double vision.

Joe said nothing about his problems; he was a man. He was a star.

The All-Star game for Joe was a return home to St. Louis and Sportsman's Park. He heard cheers amid the boos the first time up, and boos among the cheers for his last at bat. Joe Williams's column in the *World-Telegram* on July 12 commented that Joe "had not been the Mighty Medwick of old for a couple of years now, but there was a tendency to discount his relatively modest hitting in St. Louis last season and the season before on the basis that he was not happy in his surroundings. . . . It cannot be said that Medwick isn't hustling. . . . On the contrary, he was trying so hard, it may possibly be . . . what was wrong with him. Sometimes he appeared to be over-swinging, and other times under-swinging. Anyway, it was plain that his timing and co-ordination were faulty, and instead of meeting the ball squarely he was merely getting thin pieces of it." Double vision will do that. And since no one else was hitting on the Dodgers, the offensive weight fell on Medwick.

Talking to Tommy Holmes, Medwick told "the nearest thing to a confession of weakness ever emitted by the Hammering Hungarian. 'I've been pressing, swinging too hard for the best interests of timing,' said Joe. 'Sure I know what causes it. This business of being a $200,000 purchase was a lot of responsibility to be carrying on your shoulders, but I'll get going.'" And, for luck, "Going out to field his position each inning, [Medwick] stays clear of home plate; returning to the dugout, he always spikes the plate."

Very soon, Joe pushed his average up to .289 while his RBI total showed him eleventh in the league and second on the team. Back in

St. Louis again, Medwick was heavily booed when he came to bat "for the first time in his career as an enemy player." With Lavagetto on first and Warneke pitching, Joe hit a long home run to the foot of the left field scoreboard. "Mike Haley, veteran St. Louis sports writer, thought that the home run was the longest, fastest traveling ball he ever saw Medwick hit." The homer produced all the runs for his team, this time for Curt Davis in a 3-2 loss, a loss that kept them four back.

In July, Joe in July had hit 39-134—.291—and had driven in twenty-four runs. Most mangers would settle for a hitter who drove in twenty-four runs a month.

Tommy Holmes said, "Medwick had been in a long slump because he was all tangled up at the plate. Every one on the Brooklyn bench knew why Medwick wasn't hitting. So did every fan who remembers the Hungarian's terrific reef at a pitched ball in the old days. Medwick must know it himself. Involuntarily he had been pulling away from pitches and merely waving at them. There was a common suspicion that Joe had become plate-shy since he was put in a hospital by a fast ball pitched by Bob Bowman, his old St. Louis pal. If that's the answer, he'll get over it or he won't."

If a batter has double vision, can he see that a ball is coming at him? Maybe if he held his head at a certain angle, the double vision would go away. Maybe not. Joe's insistence on playing even though he was suffering dizzy spells, ringing ears, and double vision was all too typical of him, to his credit and to his shame. He knew he was being counted on to produce, to play every day—to win the pennant by himself. Daniel ended his August 13 column with "There were extenuating circumstances in the Medwick situation. He hasn't been himself since he was beaned. . . . Joe still suffers dizzy spells on arising and it took him nearly half an hour to recover his bearings."

"The fans of St. Louis came out to the ball park to razz their one time Hungarian hero," Tommy Holmes wrote from Chicago,

> and remained to gloat ghoulishly as Muscles found himself completely handcuffed in the series. . . . Some of the explanations for the Medwick slump were fantastic. One story suggested that Medwick sulked because the Dodgers refused to give him a high contract when they obtained him. . . . "Bunk," said Mr. Medwick. "I knew I wasn't going to work for cheapskates and that I'd be taken care of. But first I knew I had to produce." There was a suggestion that Medwick's personal friendship with Skipper Durocher caused dissension among the rest of

the team and that Joe's slump was cheered by team-mates on the bench. Your agent can testify that this is plain bunk. . . . Medwick, underneath his brusque, rough exterior is a pretty good fellow. No explanation, in fact, fit the situation as well as Medwick's own, which was that his slump was caused by a combination of a return to action too soon after he was beaned in June, plus over-anxiety to win the pennant for Brooklyn.

August ended as well with various views of Medwick's slump, mostly with Durocher talking about his own responsibility for Joe coming back too soon after the beaning. According to Pat McDonough, Leo said, "Jurges was hit on the head and he's still out. Pee Wee Reese was hit on the head and was out three weeks. Medwick was hit and was back in the lineup in four days. I figured then he was a big, strong fellow and was ready. But I was wrong. He still hasn't recovered for the effects of the blow and probably won't until he has an entire winter to forget it. Joe weighs only 173 pounds now whereas his playing weight should be about 185." To Holmes he said, "Ducky was stronger than the other two but he probably was hit harder. I know now he wasn't strong enough to return after only three days on the sideline."

During Medwick's era, it was typical for people as poor as Medwick's family to have no dealings with doctors, believing that doctors were ridiculously expensive and not to be trusted. Doctors bring only bad news, it was thought; doctors will tell the club not to play Medwick and then where will he be? (Baseball players have always been afraid of receiving a bad report from a doctor.)

Medwick's version via Holmes was the following: "I went against the advice of my doctors and begged to get back into the lineup. I wanted to make good in Brooklyn but I should have stayed out longer. I kept getting loads of mail from Dodger fans all rooting for me and that probably pushed me into trying harder than ever. You know how it was. Anyway, I [felt] that I [could] make a comeback."

He was about to show the National League what he could do even weakened, underweight, with or without blurred or even double vision, dizzy spells, and throbbing headaches.

Medwick began the month of September 1940 with twelve games that started with the Giants and ended with them as well. First the Dodgers took a doubleheader at home as Joe went 2-4 in each game, making three runs for pitchers Lee Grissom and Whit Wyatt. At that game, a Brooklyn fan, seated behind the Brooklyn bench, popped balloons and bellowed at the Giants. This fan also carried and put on the rail in front of him a rubber duck, a kind of tribute to Medwick.

A few teammates skipped the team airplane and rode the train to Boston, where the next day, Joe, hitting third now, was 4-10 in another doubleheader that was halved by his team. In the sixth inning, he hit his twelfth home run. In all of 1939 he had totaled fourteen.

Next it was four games in Philadelphia. Joe was 1-4 on the fourth of the month and hit "a prodigious triple to the deepest part of center field; Joe was 2-6 on the fifth, 2-2, on the sixth." Then when he was "plunked in the ribs by one of Kirby Higbe's fast balls . . . Joe Medwick of the Dodgers made a dash for the Phillie pitcher but was detoured to first base by his manager, Leo Durocher." Higbe offered to hit Joe in the ribs again if Medwick came after him with the bat. Durocher had to take the bat out of Joe's hand. He was hit, Higbe said in his book, because Joe laughed as he ran the bases after he hit home-run number thirteen in the third inning. Medwick continued to shout and gesture at Higbe from first base. In Medwick's next at bat, the first pitch from Higbe was a fast, high, inside pitch, which Joe evaded. Had Higbe hit Medwick, it would have been the fourth time he was hit since mid June.

A man had to be tested; a batter had to show he was not afraid. That was the code.

Then Medwick lined a single. In game two, a 3-5 showing, Joe hit a grand-slam home run. In the series he had hit 8-17 and driven in nine runs, scored eight, one on a home run. No wonder Higbe threw at him. The Dodgers swept the series. Joe now led the team in triples, at bats, and was second in homers, hits, and RBIs. No one had played more games than he had. Medwick had dragged his average up twelve points to .291.

On September 7, Joe's 16-game hitting streak ended. No Dodger had a longer hitting streak that year. The 4-1 loss put the team 8 games back once again, after 130 games. But then when rain canceled the game on the September 10, Joe was 23-54, .426, for the first ten days of September.

But the Reds won the pennant on September 18. The closest team to the Dodgers for second-place money was now the Cardinals, and they were five games behind, with nine to play.

In the game on September 24, Joe helped his team to secure second place in the league when "Muscles Medwick greeted Mountain Music [Melton] with a 400-foot drive to the center field fence that

[Johnny] Rucker caught with his back against the barrier. Reiser trotting home" with the run that won the game 5-4.

After a rain day and a doubleheader against the seventh-place Bees, Dixie Walker, Joe, and others were sat down by Durocher, and many new names were in the Dodger lineup. Neither did Joe play in Philadelphia, except in the last inning of the last game of the year, a game that took one hour and thirty-six minutes. While the Reds finished at 100-53, the Dodgers ended with a record of 88-65, twelve games behind. Each Brooklyn player made about $1,200; that is, $4,000 less than each Reds player.

Joe's production for his team when he was having an "atypical" Medwick year made him first in hits, second in triples, second in homers, tied for second in being struck by a pitch, and second in RBIs. Medwick was one of two hitters on the Dodgers with a batting average of over .300, the other being Dixie Walker, whose average was seven points higher.

In the National League, Joe was fourteenth in doubles; fourteenth in runs scored; eleventh in RBIs; eleventh in average; eighth in home runs; sixth in triples; sixth in slugging percentage; fifth in hits; third in total bases; first in outfield fielding.

Who would not take these accomplishments and be proud of them? Who would not take these statistics and say he had a superior year?

"Medwick came to me after the last game and said, 'Draw a contract for next season and pay me what you think I am worth. I have not had any spring training in three years and want to report with the early birds at Havana next February' said Larry MacPhail" according to Daniel's report in the *World Telegram*. "The belief was that Joe would receive $20,000 for the 1941 season, an increase of $2,000. 'He offered to sign at the club's terms. We fixed the matter up in a couple of minutes.'"

But there was still some guessing going on, and John McDonald, the public relations man for the Brooklyn club, tried to make his guessing sound like science. At the end of October, Daniel reported the following statement from McDonald: "all through September, we had a crew of three men in the center field stands at Ebbets Field taking movies of the Dodgers. . . . Won't Joe Medwick's face be red when he saw what he was doing at the plate. The pictures show that Joe was batting with one foot in the bucket. . . . Medwick was normal until the pitch came right up to him. Then, out went that left foot and he was completely off balance. I am confident that you will see a different Joe next season."

Yet what did Joe do in the time of the filming from September 1 to season's close? He hit .390, drove in 27, and made 48 hits. That's 48 hits in one month, which would extrapolate to 264 hits in a season. MacDonald was just another non-baseball man who thought he knew baseball. Back in September of 1932, Roy Stockton wrote, "Medwick was a right-handed hitter who steps in the bucket, much after the fashion of Al Simmons. . . . and few batters were successful when they swing while stepping backward from the plate. However, Simmons was an exception and Medwick seems to be another. He steps backward with his left foot as he swings but he [has] so much power that he hits left and right field fences, despite what [is] generally considered a handicap to a batter."

It was true that Medwick was not getting as many marks in the top five as he had been, but his production had been declining since 1937. When you lead the league in everything, what awaits is decline.

Look at Medwick's extra-base hits by year:

1934: 76
1935: 82
1936: 95
1937: 99
1938: 76
1939: 70
1940: 59

In *The Politics of Glory* (1994), Bill James says flatly, "Most players' best years were behind them by the age of 28." Medwick's decline, which began in 1938, was not due to the beaning—it was age. In November of 1940, Joe had finished his eleventh professional year and was age twenty-nine. His lifetime average was .335.

On November 27, 1940, "Three members of the Brooklyn Club— Manager Leo Durocher, Joe Medwick and Pete Reiser—were making a tour of the Mayo Clinic today. . . . The trio arrived . . . by plane from St. Louis. They expect to stay several days."

The results of the testing were printed on December 10, 1940, in a special to the *World-Telegram*:

Medwick was suffering from double vision that traces to having been beaned by Bob Bowman. That Medwick had double vision became known to Durocher when Joe, Leo and Pete Reiser were examined at the Mayo Clinic in Rochester, Minn. Medwick told Durocher the trouble was clearing up. The double vision now came only on objects seen from the side. After Joe had been beaned, he had double vision on all angles. He saw two pitchers whenever he came to bat and two sets of infielders. But he never said a word and kept right on fighting. . . . "The eye specialists at Mayo's were amazed that Medwick had risked playing after he had become aware of the double vision," said Durocher. "However, this Medwick was one game guy. We are confident that by Feb. 15 when Joe report[s] at Havana his trouble will have disappeared."

15

The Bums Go
to the World Series, 1941

Joe began 1941 by changing his schedule slightly, staying in St. Louis longer than usual during the winter. Because of the war in Europe, the government had restricted air travel, so baseball required that the Dodgers travel by train. What other changes the war, or the threat of war, might bring, no one knew.

How much better did Joe have to be? How much weight of the team must he carry? How productive must his year be? Joe was not satisfied. His confidence, though, remained high, and he was eager to show what he could do.

More than eager, perhaps; after eleven years of professional baseball, Joe's back was suffering from lumbago and he was beginning to see how fragile his body might become. It takes time for young men to learn mortality. Joe had said repeatedly that he understood that in all of the teams he had been on, much of the weight for that team's success rested on his performance. For example, Dodger fans expected the pennant to be theirs in 1940 once Medwick arrived. For Medwick not to deliver what was expected of him—failing to deliver as he had always delivered—must have been a cruel blow to him.

Medwick arrived in New York for the annual Baseball Writers Dinner with Durocher and "let it be known that he hoped to win the batting title this season. 'I'm not blaming that knock on the head for my failure to win it last year,' said Joe. 'I just had a bad year. But I'm going to make up for it this year.'" Later Medwick confided, while joking with 41-year-old Waite Hoyt, "There were days . . . when I couldn't have hit *you* if I stood on my head. Might just as well have left my bat in the rack."

Then it was on to training in Cuba. The players who arrived by steamship in mid February got to Cuba at 9 A.M. After they checked into their luxurious rooms at the Hotel Nacional, they hurried out to practice at La Tropical Stadium, a 27,000-seat park with very distant fences. "A hot sun shone and turned many a Dodger face red during the work, which lasted an hour and a half. Muscles Medwick, who had acquired a deep tan in Florida, took his exercises stripped to the waist. Durocher banned golf for Medwick from now until the season ended, but said all others could play on off-days or at other times by asking permission." Meanwhile, Tom Meany wrote, "First to benefit from the ban against Medwick was pitcher Bill Swift, who borrowed Joe's clubs."

Roscoe McGowen took note of Joe. "Medwick's great enthusiasm in hitting had a painful aftermath. He was counting blisters in the palms of his hands later on. 'No wonder,' commented Pee Wee Reese, 'you were up there hitting every time I looked up.'" While he was hitting, newsreel cameramen roamed the field and filmed number 6 (Joe's new number), working out.

Eight hard days of training were followed by a day off. Joe was one of only four players who had their wives with them.

February 24 was the anniversary of Cuba's successful revolt from Spain and President Batista came to the ballpark to be posed for photos with owner Larry MacPhail and manager Leo Durocher. The day after, many of the Dodgers frolicked "as soon as they returned from the workout. . . . Freddie Fitzsimmons was the ringleader of the group, including Muscles Medwick and Herman Franks, that had great fun catching players and throwing them into the water. Fitz and Cookie Lavagetto threatened to toss Pee Wee Reese in with his clothes on but relented and permitted him to get his trunks on before giving him the heave-ho."

March 3 was the day for Mickey Owen to sign his contract, though boils had cost him fifteen pounds of needed weight. "Mickey waved a hand," McGowen saw, "toward Muscles Medwick in the batting cage. Muscles, his torso covered only with a deep coat of tan, was swinging viciously at the overhand offerings of Southpaw Howard

Mills. 'I'd like to see that fellow hit 'em like he did when I first came up with the Cardinals,' said Mickey. 'Boy he sure could powder that ball.' If earnest effort will bring back that slugging ability, Medwick will have it this year. He's the busiest man on the field, never inactive for a moment. Today, for instance, while waiting for his turn at bat, he grabbed Dolph Camilli's glove and gave a peppery, if ungraceful, exhibition of left-handed first basing. Joe [wasn't] through when the team workout was ended, either. No sooner did he return to the hotel than he was in the swimming pool and after a couple of hours of diving, swimming and pushing other players into the water he repairs to the tennis courts."

When the Cleveland Indians came to Havana to play on March 7, both Reese and Medwick wore the new head protectors without anyone noticing. The protection devices were regular baseball caps redesigned so a zippered pocket could hold a plastic shield that was inserted on each side of the cap. Roscoe McGowen from the *Times* reported that "Medwick said . . . he actually forgot he was wearing the protector. He kept it on all the time he was in the game, whether in the field or at bat. 'You'd never notice you had it on,' said Joe. 'There's not enough difference in the weight or the feeling to bother anybody.'"

On March 25, Tommy Holmes saw "the old Medwick up at the plate. . . . Now hitting with one foot in the bucket, now stepping into a pitch . . . or again reaching up and whacking a wild pitch off his ear. . . . 'In those early games,' Joe explained . . . 'I've concentrated more on just meeting the ball than on giving it a long ride.' . . . He hit a mere .301 last year but only four hitters topped his total of 175 hits and Medwick missed a dozen ball games and had no spring training whatsoever."

When the team returned to New York, Arthur Daley of the *Times* reported on the talk about "Medwick's Resurgence." Tommy Holmes commented, "Of course, Joe will run into better pitching once the seasons starts. Right handers . . . will pitch him tight, knock him down and then throw side arm fast balls. . . . Even before Bob Bowman skulled him last June, pitchers worked on him that way and couldn't stop him because Medwick, like Rogers Hornsby, had the knack of hitting that outside pitch and the muscular strength to hit it hard . . . the hammering Hungarian ought to do all right." Holmes continued by saying, "Medwick had a reputation for truculence that was undeserved off the ball field. There isn't a cleaner

living, milder mannered fellow on the Brooklyn team than this ace
of National League pitcher pests."

It was the hated Giants who started the season at Ebbets for 1941's
Opening Day—April 15—a day full of flags and bands. After the
game, Tommy Holmes, mindful of Nazis in Paris, ended his remarks
by saying, "And does any one else worry that there may not be an
Opening Day next year?"

Against Philadelphia, Reiser was hit in the right cheekbone by Ike
Pearson. "You could plainly see the imprint of three stitches where
it hit him," Dolph Camilli reported. "When he came back a few days
later, Durocher let him sit on the bench for a while, perhaps thinking
of the haste to get Medwick back," Robert Creamer wrote years later.

And as the Dodgers continued to win, a streak that started on the
twenty-second at the Polo Grounds, Joe started a new streak at home
against New York. His double was part of a 7-5 win that left the
Dodgers two games behind St. Louis. With hits in all three games
and wins in all three games with the Reds, the Dodgers moved to
just .04 behind the Cardinals. Joe hit a 380- foot center field homer in
one game, and in the next game, "Joe Medwick," Tommy Holmes
reported, "floundered all over the batter's box missing one Vander
Meer pitch by no more than two feet, then hit another into the left
field orchestra seats to tie the score. 'That was the pay-off,' exulted
Durocher in the clubhouse, 'anytime they make a bad pitch to Medwick, no matter how he's slumping, you're back in the ball game.
He'll lose the ball.'" Joe's "slumping" consists of only one hit in each
game.

Later, after a rain day off at the Warwick in Philadelphia, the
Dodgers put runners on second and third in the first inning, and the
Phillie manager, Doc Prothro, decided not to walk Medwick. Joe's
single drove in two in Wyatt's win against the Phillies. "That was
Joe's only hit and he drew a chorus of Bronx cheers from most of the
3,344 fans the rest of the chilly afternoon." The fans probably didn't
know that Joe's hitting streak was now twelve and that he had hit in
twenty-two of the Dodgers' twenty-five games. Or maybe they were
just Philadelphia sport fans. Higbe won again the next day and Joe
hit again. But while Roscoe McGowen pointed out the hitting streak,
he also noted, "he had batted in eleven runs but had left seventeen
men on base in scoring position and hit into three double plays" in
the thirteen games. McGowen didn't say that Joe was first in the National League in at bats, eighth in runs, second in hits, fourth in

home runs, and fourth in RBIs, though McGowen's newspaper printed the statistics. Once again, through runs scored and RBIs, Joe was making over 20 percent of his team's runs.

After a Polo Grounds doubleheader on May 30, Eddie Brannick, the Dodger-hating secretary of the Giants called the Dodgers, "Strictly hotel lobby and Pullman car champions. They talk a great game, all of them. . . . All that Leo had left was his voice. . . . Reese will weaken. . . . Medwick! See where they had him hitting . . . Seventh! One more drop and he's off the list. Next thing you know they'll have him outside the ball park chasing fouls hit over the fence." John Kiernan, who was quoting Brannick, interrupted with "Well, well! Muscles Medwick once stood high in Mr. Brannick's estimation. They were pals. Mr. Brannick was a Medwick booster around the league. 'He was with St. Louis then. . . . He looks different in a Dodger uniform. Anyway, I'm not knocking him. Brooklyn was. You don't suppose putting Medwick in the seventh slot was any compliment to him do you? That's a big knock if you ask me.'"

The next day, still seventh in the order, Joe came to bat in the third inning, "which Medwick opened by ramming one of Hubbell's deliveries against the parapet of the left field . . . the blow landed with such force it seemed to knock the Giants apart at all points." He was knocked down the next time up, and then "Casey at the first opportunity knocked down Harry Danning who presumably had called for the pitch to Medwick." Then, "with Johnny Wittig pitching the eighth for the Giants . . . once more it was Medwick who did the most damage. Finding Lavagetto on second base . . . Muscles pounded a triple to right center and the Dodgers had another run." Holmes said, "he almost drilled a hole through Billy Jurges for a single" as well. He even caught the last out of the game in a 5-2 win, Hugh Casey getting some help from Mace Brown.

At month's end, the Dodgers were 30-12 and the Cardinals were 31-11, with more than 70 percent of the games yet to be played.

Left fielder Medwick had hit .280 for the month, and among hitters in the league, he was first in at bats and in games played, sixth in hits, homers, and runs, and seventh in RBIs. On his team, Joe was first in at bats, second in hits, third in total bases, homers, RBIs, and batting average.

After a three-game series against the Cardinals, Holmes wrote, "It was the devil-may-care swagger too that Medwick had in his palmy days when he 'owned' all National League pitching. 'He's discouraged,' admitted Leo, 'and every little thing that happens to go wrong makes him more so. But I know that all Medwick needs to become the Ducky of old is a little boost, a little start. . . . I know he still has it . . . When sportswriters say he looks bad, they may be telling the truth; but remember Medwick often looked bad judged by ordinary standards when he was hitting .360. A lot of people forget that. . . . But in another little while . . . the pitchers who put another hitter on base to get a Joe will be wondering if they were just plain screwy.'" Joe was hitting .272

After two rainouts, the Dodgers beat Chicago. But Medwick would play only one game in the next fifteen. Most of the games in which Joe was out of the lineup were because he had the mumps, but not all of them. After being forbidden to even leave his room ("the doctors will not let him mingle with his mates until danger of contagion was passed"), Joe tried to come back on June 18, and did so, hitting a double and a home run, but he could not continue and was not put back in the lineup until June 22.

Medwick lost ten pounds during his illness in 1941. But on June 22 in Cincinnati, in game two, he singled and with Higbe pitching. There were only "two threatening gestures made against Kirby and Muscles Medwick took care of those," McGowen wrote. "In the sixth, Frank McCormick [first baseman] hit a liner toward the left-field corner and Joe snared it with one of his running 'sit-down' catches. In the eighth, he raced back against the left-field barrier to rob [third baseman Billy] Werber of a two or three base hit."

By the end of June, Joe led the team for the year in triples and was second in homers and hits, third in RBIs and at bats. His average, raised 25 points to .297, was fifth for the full-time players.

But after a day off and a rain day (Larry MacPhail had bought $10,000 worth of rain insurance for $1,900) on July 4, Joe was sat down during a 2-1 win against Boston that put the team up by two games. "Medwick apparently was kept out of the lineup because of Wasdell's good hitting for Camilli," who had a cold. "But Muscles seemed to be a bit puzzled. 'Maybe they're resting me for the All-Star game' he wisecracked."

The doubleheader the next day gave them win number fifty but not fifty-one since it ended in a tie. Joe's 1-6 hitting in the two games seemed all too typical of the year for him. Tommy Holmes recorded a "complaint . . . from Joe Medwick and we'll side with it as the soundest of the day. With a man on in the fourth, Medwick hit a screamer which [second baseman Sibby] Sisti went into a tailspin to grab for the third out. Next time up, Joe belted a scorcher with two on and one out. This one knocked [shortstop] Eddie Miller flat on his face but he held it. 'It's a wonder Miller didn't get up and double Lavagetto off first,' complained Medwick later. 'That's the way things were going for me. When you're getting your hits, you don't mind these things. But that's the way my luck's been running ever since I came to Brooklyn. When's it gonna change?'" Joe neglected to mention the "duster" thrown at him by Johnny Hutchings in the sixth of game two.

The Dodgers led the league at the All-Star break by three games at 50-24.

So Joe returned to Detroit, where fans remembered him well from the 1934 series. Medwick had played in every All-Star Game except the first in 1933. He played in this 1941 one, too, batting for Bucky Walters in the seventh and "Just to show that seven long years scarcely tax the memory of a baseball fan, there was again a fine round of boos for Muscles Joe," who grounded out to Lou Boudreau. This booing stayed with Joe for a long time.

After the All-Star break, Cincinnati visited Ebbets Field. Joe's second run, a home run into the center field seats, made the score 3-0 and Higbe got the win 8-3, a win repeated just as the homer was repeated on July 11 with Curt Davis pitching the team to a 12-2 win. That home run in the sixth was predicted by Joe, who said to Jackie Bodner, the batboy, "I feel I'm going to catch one and ride it high . . . you notice I got to hit 'em where they can't reach 'em, to get a base hit though," laughed Joe. But he was hitting the ball hard, and almost bowled Eddie Joost over with one shot to shortstop. Joe would call another home run before he was through. In that game as well, "Medwick gave one of the better demonstrations," McGowen judged, "of his famous 'sit down' catch when he snared Werber's line drive to open the game."

The team stayed around awhile after a big win, and after "the game had been over for an hour, Fitz drove his car up Washington Ave., across Eastern Parkway, the gals still lined the street, looking for an autograph, praying for a red light to stop their heroes who always drive home that way. But no luck. The Medwicks in their car, then Fitz and Mrs. Fitz and the Billy Hermans, and then a cab with Curt Davis, Vito Tamulis, Jimmy Wasdell. . . . Particular darling of the gals, of course, was boyish Pee Wee Reese. He and roomie Pete

Reiser have a tough time of it in that hotel into which most of Dodgers have moved, turning it into a sort of college fraternity. The Medwicks moved in the other day and the rest of the crowd . . . have told 'em they'll have to submit to an initiation."

That apartment was a source of yet another superstition. Medwick stopped his wife from opening the apartment entrance door one night saying, "Isabelle, I opened the door last night and I got three hits today. I've got to open it again." And when fans sent him hairpins, Mrs. Medwick remembered, "I had to let him find them when they arrived. It wasn't the same if I handed them to him." According to his wife, Medwick could discard the serious demeanor he wore so intensely while in uniform. "Joe only brought home the funny things of baseball. He never came home angry. I just love baseball and that's because the men were like boys."

On the next day, in the ninth, the game scoreless, Joe singled, Camilli sacrificed, Walker's bouncer to first baseman Babe Dahlgren was mishandled, and then Owen was walked to bring up the pitcher Kirby Higbe. But Durocher pinch-hit himself for the pitcher, and on the second pitch, dropped a bunt. "Olsen fielded the ball but never had a chance to throw out Joe Medwick, charging across the plate with express-train speed for the only run of the game. . . . With a muttered series of curses, Olsen wound up and threw the ball completely over the grandstand," Holmes gleefully reported. Joe was now fourth on the team at .296, second in RBIs to Camilli's fifty-seven, and second in homers with eleven. "In all," Harold Parrott wrote, "Joe had smashed nine hits in his last sixteen trips. Now he's at .306, quite a revival for a benched hitter who had swooned to .262 in early June." Perhaps his double vision was finally gone.

Early August was marked by the lead alternating almost daily between the Cardinals and the Dodgers. On August 11, Goodrich of the *Eagle* quoted a Dodger fan: "Take that Ducky Wucky. . . . Why he's a changed guy. He's friendly with everybody now and he autographs books and everything for the kids—a la Babe Ruth. He was tired, that's why he was slumping. Durocher gives him a rest and now look at him."

With an off-day, *Times* writer Pat McDonough began his column with the headline "Medwick in Comeback—Dodger Fielder Like Joe of Old with .373 Mark for Last Month." According to McDonough's report:

One of the major reasons for the Dodgers' success in the last two months and one of the reasons they were a good bet to fight the Cardinals tooth and nail down to the wire was Joe Medwick's return to his hard hitting Cardinal form. Joe today is hitting only .317 but that represents a tremendous advance from his mark of mid-June. In a nutshell here's what Medwick has done: . . . he's hit .353 the last two months, during which time he tacked 45 points onto his season mark, lifting it from .272. Joe was much like the slugging Medwick of his big years, he even looks like a great hitter on his hitless days. . . . Afield Medwick had been playing an excellent game, cutting off base hits and fielding ground balls flawlessly. When Joe's hitting, he looks great on the defense too. Medwick was only eleven points behind Pete Reiser in the averages and at the present pace will soon overtake the brilliant rookie who was benched because of a hitting slump.

Joe had had to climb the batting tables the hard way. Opposing pitchers having been throwing "tight" to Joe and he had to be on his guard for bean balls. . . . He's just about the best hitter in the league right now, but his earlier season troubles may prevent him from winning the batting title.

After a rain day, with Ethel Barrymore in the stands eating a box lunch, Joe was 5-7 in the doubleheader. In game one, "Joe Medwick's smashing triple to the center field fence . . . brought a roar that citizens of Canarsie must have thought was a distant air raid barrage." This doubleheader was also a split, so that after four games between the two top teams, nothing had changed.

Against the visiting Giants, former Cardinal Curt Davis won yet again on September 6 against former Cardinal "Fiddler Bill" McGee, with Durocher at short, as Medwick still rested his "lame back." Now it was time for Joe's back to recover.

A Dodger fan came to the games wearing a grotesquely horrible mask, which he said would be a jinx to the Giants. In game one of the series, the visiting Giants were beaten 13-1 by Kirby Higbe, his twenty-first win. Joe hit two singles, a double, and a triple—four consecutive hits—scored twice and drove in three. Game two saw a three-run seventh for the Giants to break a scoreless tie, and bottle throwing at Umpire Tom Dunn when he called a strike on Camilli, who had ducked out of the way of a "Mountain Music" Melton pitch. With the scoreboard posting a Cardinals loss, the Dodger game featured a ninth inning that began with the Dodgers down 3-1. In that inning, Billy Herman, the dependable second baseman, led off with a single to right. Reiser, in the third spot, hit next, and "Bad News Hale," the New York second baseman, couldn't handle Pete's hit; Herman ran to third while Reiser made second. Joe was next, hitting cleanup. His single drove in the tying runs. McGowen described the fans' reaction to Joe's hit:

> There never had been such a scene in Ebbets Field as was unfolded in the game following Medwick's hit. Seemingly every fan present rose and all began sending a storm of paper onto the field. It came in cascades of torn bits as well as whole newspapers and score cards. Telegraphers, in the din, could not hear their sending machines click. . . . Chief umpire . . . called a halt and instructed the announcer to inform the hysterical fans that unless they ceased throwing paper the game would not proceed. Then it was necessary to call out the regular ground crew as well as every available usher from the lower stands.

Reiser, former Cardinal, finished the job by driving in former Cardinal Mickey Owen in the tenth inning for a 4-3 win. The Dodgers were up two games. Holmes, in the next day's *Eagle*, called the ninth inning roar "the loudest noise these ears have ever heard . . . the torn paper almost concealing the Giant outfielders from the stands."

The Dodgers would not be at home again until September 27. As they neared their train, "Crowds of fans turned on the cheers for each new arrival. The cowbell of Hilda Chester, cheer leader of the Ebbets Field bleachers, led the din." The Dodgers now had three regulars hitting over .300: Reiser, Medwick, and then Dixie. The Cardinals had five. In the National League batting average contest, Reiser placed first, Johnny Hopp second, Mize third, and Joe tied for fifth.

The first game at Sportsman's Park ran eleven innings, partly because Reese again made a woeful error, and again behind Fitzsimmons, so that the Dodgers' four-run fourth inning was matched by the two runs in the third and the two in the seventh. A St. Louis run scored on Reese's error; Medwick's throw home on right fielder Crabby Crabtree's single to put out Don Padgett was in plenty of time, but Owen dropped the ball, tying the game. "In the ninth, Fitzsimmons was furious about a call made by umpire Al Barlick on Mize. When Fitzsimmons saw Mize smiling, Freddie said, 'Three fastballs and then you're outta here.' He was." The game stayed tied until the top of the eleventh, an inning that Joe began with a single hit so hard that second baseman Jimmy Brown couldn't contain it.

Cookie Lavagetto walked. When power-hitter Camilli bunted, Mize fell while fielding the ball and kicked it into foul territory, so the bases were loaded. Billy Southworth brought his infield in with none out and Dixie Walker bounced a single through to the outfield to score Medwick and Cookie. Hugh Casey prevented the Cardinals from scoring in their half, and the Dodgers were up by two games.

In the series' second game, twice Joe failed to drive in a runner in scoring position, but in the fifth inning he drove in Reese and scored himself on Camilli's single. These two runs and one other were all the Dodgers produced. Max Lanier came into the game and was pitching when Crabtree in right threw out Owen by ten feet. Then in the ninth, Lanier "threw a curve that seemed to explode. Reiser fell flat on his face . . . but the thing broke out and cut the middle of the plate for strike three."

The three games were won by a total of four runs.

Tommy Holmes wrote, "Each afternoon they've torn one's heart out, placed it on home plate and jumped on it with their spikes." Following a game against Pittsburgh on the eighteenth, some of the Dodgers—Wyatt, Camilli, Coscarart, Franks, and Medwick—sought out Umpire Magerkurth under the stands after the game and used what Ford Frick labeled "vile and profane" words to talk to the big umpire. The indecorous language cost each man $25.

The lead was one game. Joe was fourth in the league in batting average.

A doubleheader at Shibe Park awaited and Dodgers fans wanted to be there. There were nine games left. The Brooklyn Dodger Victory Committee chartered thirty-five "streamlined motor coaches" and six transport planes to bring fans to the game. Tickets for the planes, which included lunch on the way and dinner on the return, were $9.95 each, with a seat in a Dodger section in the Philadelphia ball yard included.

Sitting behind the Dodger dugout for the game in Philadelphia were George Raft and Betty Grable. Jack Benny had a seat in the press box. Also attending were Eddie Bittan "tooting a whistle, wearing a big-game hunter's hat . . . and with two horseshoes dangling from his belt. His echo, Bill Fleischer, wore a crew coxswain's megaphone strapped to his mouth for rooting convenience." And there was more of what Harold Parrott called "the Greenpoint Band," with members Jo-Jo Delio, Jerry Hammer, and Stonewall Sorrentino. Fan Jack Launce also had a megaphone. Three of the signs for the Dodgers said "Yea! Dixie Ducky Dolph Cookie Reiser" and "Bring on Those Yankees" and "Yes! We Are from Brooklyn." Young boys were seen wearing small Dodger uniforms.

As the Dodgers were playing in Philadelphia, someone wasn't satisfied with Medwick or his performance: "While Reiser and Camilli continue to carry the Brooklyn club toward the World Series, Joe Medwick just cannot fire the spark of another year. Time was when Ducky Wucky was the hero of the Gas House Gang . . . he became the terror of the league . . . soon a beaning and now the Superbas pray for the Medwick who used to be. Time was when Joe was a grand money player . . . that day is gone for Medwick. The Dodgers would like him to recapture it." Medwick was currently fourth in average and RBIs in the league. He had twenty more RBIs than Reiser and five more home runs. In his Most Valuable Player year, Camilli had scored ten fewer runs and made thirteen fewer hits than Medwick. The lead was one and a half.

There were four games left for both teams. The Cardinals continued to play at Forbes Field in Pittsburgh and the Dodgers traveled to Boston for two games with the Braves. There, on an off-day, the players gathered in their rooms to listen "avidly to the account of the Buccos' 4-0 defeat of the Cardinals in the first game of the double-header in Smokytown." In Brooklyn Supreme Court, Justice Lee Parson Davis stopped a negligence hearing to announce the Cardinal loss. In Brooklyn, nine chartered planes bound for Boston had sold out. Harold Parrott, who was traveling with the Cardinals, said the team talked a lot about Moore being beaned on August 21 and the powerful negative effect that had on the team. "Most of the Cards, too, know that other ball players, almost to the man, were rooting for Brooklyn to win. They think it will hurt their interests if the underpaid Cards win and World Series dough becomes an accepted part of the salary check."

More Brooklyn fans were noticed arriving in Boston, including "Mike Smith, the Brooklyn undertaker and his pal, Harry Metcalfe," both of whom traveled on the entire Western trip with the team. Also present were Dr. Trench, a Philadelphia brain specialist who was in Clearwater during the training season; Dr. Labredo from Havana with his wife and son; Monchy, a Dodger fan had also come. Tony Martin, singer and movie star, had refused to change his shirt or suit until the Dodgers won. Kirby Higbe hadn't shaved in so long that teammates had begun to call him a House of David player.

Durocher was wearing the same black knitted tie for the whole Western trip. Leo's mother had come across the state from Springfield for the Boston games.

The first game in Boston was a 4-2 Brooklyn win that maintained the one-and-a-half-game lead, as the Cardinals shut out the Pirates. The next day, September 28, with three games left, Whitlow Wyatt was picked to pitch what might be the pennant winner. The lineup included Dixie Walker in right as the only different player in what had been the lineup almost from the start of the season, Billy Herman excepted. Joe was batting behind Walker, Herman, Reiser, and Camilli. He was followed by Lavagetto, Reese, and Owen. Walker singled to start off the game and Joe beat out an infield single with two out to bring Walker home with the only run the Dodgers would need. Reiser drove in two more with a home run in the seventh, and three more runs were unearned. In the third inning, Medwick's grounder was mishandled by Bama Rowell, the second baseman, and Camilli scored.

Back in Brooklyn, most activities stopped for the time it took to finish the bottom half of the ninth, which began at about 4:45 P.M. On Bedford Avenue and Flatbush Avenue, in Coney Island and Red Hook, in Williamsburg and Brooklyn Heights, all radios were turned up—in cabs, candy stores, clothing stores, and supermarkets. Red Barber's voice was caught by passing trolleycar motormen who paused their machines longer than necessary at stops.

In Boston, Gene Moore grounded to Pete Coscarart, who had replaced Billy Herman and his bad leg. Buddy Hassett flied out to Joe. But then Paul Waner singled. When Max West grounded to Lavagetto, he threw to Camilli and the pennant belonged to the Brooklyn Dodgers. The team carried Wyatt off the field.

At the end of the twenty important games that led to this game, a sportswriter stated, "When the Dodgers fought their way through the final tour of the West, Ducky Wucky was not one of their Grade A producers." What the sportswriter had written was nonsense: beginning with the September 7 doubleheader, Medwick hit .355 for the next twenty games.

Nobody cared about any of that in the locker room as bottles of beer in clenched fists were swung about the room. Congratulations, embraces, and attempts at group photographs followed. "In a corner of the locker room Medwick and Camilli were hugging each other like long-lost brothers."

In this remarkable pennant race, the Cardinals were in first place for seventy days and the Dodgers for seventy-five. Brooklyn and St. Louis were never more than four games apart.

Then fans began their plans to go to Grand Central terminal to meet the team train.

In *Bums,* Leo Durocher remembered that the team drank $1,400 worth of beer, scotch, and champagne in five and a half hours. "The lid was off. That train must have wobbled. There wasn't a shirt on anybody's back. . . . We bums were on the gravy train." Medwick remembered, "We were riding bareback until Durocher said we'd better dress up again on account of the crowd that was at the station." Also, they stopped drinking and started eating a steak dinner.

In Grand Central, ten thousand maddened Dodger fans had been waiting since 9 P.M. Jack Pierce, wearing his jinx mask, blew up balloons and dropped them to the crowd below, where they were batted. The Dodgers Rooters Band showed up. Banners reading "Durocher for Mayor" and "Camilli for President" were seen. "Then, at 11:30, the train pulled in and the players tumbled out."

Durocher returned to the Hotel New Yorker where he was met by a furious MacPhail—so furious that he fired Durocher. The manager was told, "the newsreel men were waiting below and I refused to come down. . . . They had to use Joe Medwick."

The last game of the season, the first major league game for pitcher Bob Chipman, was attended by 12,870 spectators. "Dozens of happy fans . . . scampered out into left field in the pauses between the last three innings," Roscoe McGowen pointed out, "to get Muscles Medwick's autograph . . . few failed to get Joe's signature." Joe, again, played the whole game, as did Cookie Lavagetto at third and Augie Galan in center. In win number 100 for the year, 6 more than any other Dodger team since 1884, Joe got 2 hits, drove in Camilli, and the Dodgers won 5-3. Joe was eighth in the major leagues with 171 hits. (Those 171 hits, by the way, were 4 fewer than the year he was beaned.) He was one of three National Leaguers to score 100 times.

The next day belonged to all the Dodgers, and to all the Brooklyn fans. The police said that one million people watched the parade. While the Dodgers rode in cars, tens of thousands of Brooklynites walked along with them. "Ducky Medwick called out to the chic and pretty Mrs. Medwick that the fans had swiped his hat. However, Mrs. Medwick still had hers—her lucky hat—which she brought new with her to Brooklyn when the season started, a huge bright green corduroy banded in red, which she wore with a glen plaid suit and a camel's hair topcoat. She made the most of the occasion with her camera and should have a good series of parade pictures."

After the parade, the *Eagle*, under an editorial headline that read "Why Slam Our Own Heroes by Calling Them the 'Bums'?" argued "that there is nothing suggesting admiration or affection in the word 'bum' . . . we happen to know how Brooklyn's champion players themselves regard it—Camilli, Reiser, Wyatt, Walker and the rest. They loathe it and resent it."

Mostly the team heard "Murder Them Yankees," and may have believed they could, though the Yankees had not lost a World Series game in some time. The Yankees won only one more game than the Dodgers in the 1941 season. In batting average statistics at least, the Dodgers had the edge at second, third, right field, and left field. The only significant difference between the two teams was the edge in home runs, with the Yankees having hit a third more than Brooklyn did. The Dodgers had it over the Yankees in shutouts and earned run average (ERA) while the Yankees led in saves and complete games. On defense, the fielding percentages were .001 apart. The Yankee catchers had six passed balls; the Dodger catchers had six passed balls. Some of those passed balls were given to Mickey Owen, the catcher who made only six errors all year, even though his legs had not fully healed.

The *Times* put six writers on duty. One of them, John Drebinger, picked the Yankees in six games, and in his analysis said, "Joe Medwick may not be the hitter of five or six years ago, but 1941 saw him come back a long way, packing plenty of punch, especially in the clutch, and a match for any hurler." Yankee right fielder Tommy Henrich recalled in *Baseball Chronicles*:

> I got a big bang out of the 1941 Series. There was a lot of drama in that baby. Both teams were full of professional talent. Leo Durocher (the Dodger manager) would rip the Yankees in the papers, saying they would run us into the ground. But they won 100 games and we won 101, so the thing was up for grabs and I had a tight feeling all the way through. McCarthy told me he was so nervous he couldn't eat. (Pitcher) Marius Russo was so tense he wobbled. This had to be the emotional high point of my career. Now, it wasn't the most important thing in the world to win, but just the same, it would kill me if we

didn't beat them. They were a great team, but I knew we were just as good, maybe better.

On game day, Drebinger said that "blasé New York" was thrilled about the series, though Yankee fans had never filled Yankee Stadium for a World Series game. His colleague, John Kiernan, characterized the 1941 series as "the common people against the aristocrats; the unwashed against the precious," and "if they win," Kiernan supposed, "Durocher's Dandies will reach a peak of baseball popularity. If they lose, they may be torn to pieces by their disappointed followers and the remnants cast into the Gowanus Canal." Two players, Camilli and Rizzuto, were to "write" columns for the series. Camilli predicted that the Dodger fighting spirit would be more important than the Yankees' experience. To those who were saying that the World Series was just another game, Rizzuto answered, "That's the bunk."

Game one in the series saw the Dodger's last opportunity come in the ninth inning when Joe ran out an infield single and then Reese got his third hit of the game. But a foul out and a double play ended the game, the Dodgers taking the loss. The other play of note in this game happened in the Yankee fourth when DiMaggio "blasted the first pitch toward the lower left field stand," as the play-by-play in the *Times* described it. "Timing the ball accurately, Medwick was waiting in front of the stand for it to descend, leaped high, speared the horsehide with his gloved hand, then toppled over, holding grimly to the ball despite his fall." One writer thought Joe hit his chin on the concrete wall. The catch was called "gorgeous" . . . "outstanding" . . . "acrobatic" . . . "magnificent." Arthur Daley said that before the catch, "Muscles leaned against a box with all the nonchalance of a man waiting for a streetcar."

"Even if they had won, it couldn't have delighted Mrs. Joseph Medwick more than her husband's spectacular catch. A lovely and charming woman, who claims St. Louis as her home, Mrs. Medwick started the series very calmly, but soon was pleading with her husband to 'show them Brooklyn's best.' Ducky Medwick . . . received a wire just before he went to bed. It read 'That was a sensational catch you made. You saved me from getting hit right on top of the head.' It was from a Bridgeport fan who was sitting right behind Ducky when he snared the liner."

The Dodgers the next day, Harold Parrott reported,

> bounced out of their special bus and into Yankee Stadium this morning just before 11 o'clock . . . the crowd piled into the locker room to get dressed but Joe Medwick lolled behind in the little Harry Stevens lunchroom under the stands. An attendant poured Ducky a cup of coffee and said, with a Yankee grin, "Last time up here for you guys this season, Joe."
>
> "Yeah," laughed Medwick, "you think we can win it in four straight from here in, huh?" The fellow started to explain, but Joe, with a mouthful of cruller and coffee, said, "No, I'll give it to you straight. We win today, see, and we win two of three over in our park. Then we come back here. We like it here, see? We're coming back."

In game two, Joe's double in the fifth, his second hit of the game, sent first baseman Camilli to third on a perfect hit and run. Lavagetto's walk was followed by Reese's fielder's choice to second, which scored Camilli. Mickey Owen's hit, driving Joe home, was the other run of the inning, tying the game. Owen also crashed into Yankee shortstop Phil Rizzuto. Camilli broke the tie in the next inning when his single off "Grandma" Murphy, the Yankee reliever, scored Dixie Walker. As in the game the previous day, the Dodgers made six hits (and the Yankees made nine) but the final score was Dodgers, 3, and Yankees, 2.

"Whitlow Wyatt was . . . mobbed by his mates," Louis Effrat reported, "Cookie Lavagetto, in full view of the crowd, . . . hugged the veteran right-hander and planted a big kiss on his right cheek." Harold Parrott, eager for an opinion on the collision at second, reported the following: "Medwick, hitting the ball well and always a more affable, talkative and dangerous citizen when doing so, had something to say too. 'What do those guys want?' asked Joe. 'Do they think Mickey's going to run around Rizzuto and bow as he passes?'"

When game three, the first Ebbets Field World Series game since 1920, was rained out, a *World-Telegram* column appeared under the heading "That Catch by Medwick," reporting that

> A few words should be said about Joe Medwick, who had been around long enough to grow a fine, luxuriant beard. Nobody had torn down any fences in this series, but Mr. Medwick had got his share of hits, a total of three, one of which, a double, figured in the Bums' vital

two-run rally in the second game. But the item which makes Mr. Medwick stand out was his catch of DiMaggio. . . . Indeed, we can still see him leaning over the concrete barrier waiting for the ball to drop into his gloved hand. Even so, any time an outfielder converts a home-run ball into a simple putout it was a rarity—and when he did it before the gaze of the largest crowd that ever saw a World Series game, the performance took on added dramatic values.

Bing Miller, the Tigers' coach, said, "If Medwick hadn't caught that ball . . . the homer that would have resulted might have done more than just clinch the first game. It would probably have put Joe [DiMaggio] in stride. Now, having been horse-collared, he appears to me to be pressing."

Harold Conrad of the *Eagle* investigated Joe's .375 average in the first two games. "This may have something to do with Ducky Wucky's batting average. . . . Last week he ordered a dozen new bats. They were 46-ouncers, the weight he used to use a few years ago. He had been using 35-ounce clubs since. They arrived just before the series started and the morning of the opener Joe stenciled each bat with these words, 'Get Hot.'"

Joe's parents had come to see him play in game three on October 4 and Joe was photographed with his "Moms" near the first-base dugout during batting practice. It was during the practice before game three that Dodger bad luck began to appear. During batting practice, Billy Herman pulled a rib and couldn't play beyond the fourth inning. In the game, the Dodger couldn't make more than four hits against lefty Marius Russo. The Yankees had only made four hits off Freddie Fitzsimmons, who was determined to win after being 0-3 in 1933 and 1936 World Series play. One of those hitters now stood on second base with two out and Russo at bat. Russo hit a line drive off Fitzsimmons's knee, a ball caught in the air by Reese for the third out. Fitzsimmons had to leave the scoreless game, his knee beginning to swell. Hugh Casey, who completed only one-third of an inning, gave up two runs, enough to lose game three. What else could happen to the Dodgers?

This: "Brooklyn's Millions Plunged into Darkness by Dodger Collapse in Ninth" the *Times* headline blared. The nine hits by Brooklyn had led them to a 4-3 lead in the ninth. With Casey pitching, the first two batters were out on grounders. With a 3-2 on Tommy Henrich, the third strike got past Mickey Owen, and

Henrich reached first. DiMaggio singled "and right here was where I really have to give it to myself," Durocher said in *Bums.* "The next batter was Charlie Keller, a left-handed hitter. I had Larry French, a veteran left hander . . . warming up in the bullpen . . . the situation screamed for me to replace Casey with French. I did nothing. I froze . . . DiMag (Joe DiMaggio) hit the doggonedest line drive . . . for a double that never was more than six feet off the ground, and Charlie Keller hit a 0-2 pitch for an Ebbets Field double." Keller doubled off the screen to tie the game and then break the tie, Casey still pitching. Nor did Dickey's walk or Gordon's double or Rizzuto's walk cause him to be exchanged for French. Fans, numbering 33,817, sat silently.

After the game, Owen accepted the blame. Lefty Gomez claimed that "It was just the way we planned it. We've been working on that play for months."

In 1989, Owen said, "What's odd about that play was the three people involved. Hugh Casey holds the record for the highest winning percentage among relief pitchers, .709. He lost the game. One of the most reliable clutch hitters ever—Henrich—struck out. And the catcher in the midst of setting the league record for consecutive chances without an error, made an error. All three failed miserably in doing what they were best at doing."

John Drebinger, writing about the next game (game five) said, "the crowd . . . was larger than either of the gatherings that had turned out for the two week-end games in Flatbush. The appearance of the additional five hundred was inspired by a desire to see whether the Dodgers could conceive of still one more way of losing a ball game." During the game, Joe DiMaggio came so close to a fight with Wyatt after DiMaggio had to duck a pitch that both teams came out on the field. Tiny Bonham won game five and the series, when the Dodgers made only four hits.

Minus the radio rights, the Yankees' full share was $5,917.31; the Dodgers' was $4,808. Someone from Flatbush wrote to the *Eagle* with the suggestion that sixty thousand Dodger fans could donate one dollar each and then the nineteen Brooklyn full shares would equal the thirty-two Yankee full shares.

Among the full-time 1941 Dodgers, Joe placed fourth in at bats, slugging percentage, and fewest strikeouts; second in RBIs, home runs, triples, and hits; first in doubles and runs.

Joe Medwick took a lot of abuse that year for not being the Medwick of 1937. Yet how many players would be willing to settle for these league accomplishments? In the league, Medwick was third in runs and batting average, fourth in triples, fifth in hits and doubles, seventh in home runs, and ninth in RBIs. He was also second in outfield fielding percentage.

For nine full years, Joe was averaging 203 hits per year and 119 RBIs.

16

The Best Clutch Hitter
in the League, 1942

Since December 7, 1941, the country was completely absorbed in the declaration of war. Everyone was expected to contribute to the war effort, and in many ways. Everything was directed toward survival first, and victory at the last.

Medwick, examined for the draft at the Brooklyn Navy Yard, was found to have perforated eardrums, probably from the beaning, which made him ineligible for military service. In addition, he was above the current draftee age level of twenty-eight and he had two children and a wife, so it was unlikely he'd be called for some time, if at all.

Individual games changed because of the war. Exhibition games were to be against military-base teams. No inning of a night game would start "after 12:50 A.M. (new war time) to be sure that workers [would] not lose sleep."

As they returned to Havana, the Dodgers got set to become the first team to train outside of the United States during a war. On February 16, on the next-to-last crossing of the ship *Cuba* as a non-government vessel, locker room men Dan Comerford and Johnny Griffin tended to the twelve large equipment trunks. Just before the team left Florida, Medwick, Walker, Allen, French, and Arky Vaughan all signed for 1942. Joe was to earn $19,000.

Within a week of the team's arrival in Cuba, Tim Cohane of the *Herald-Tribune* quoted Joe:

> "I'll admit," the Carteret product conceded as he waited to take his batting practice turn at Tropical Stadium this morning, "that I haven't got all the power I had. . . . I found out that I couldn't lift a ball as high as I did at Sportsman's Park. There were little tricky wind currents at Brooklyn which in St. Louis was always that dead humid air. . . . So I have tried to hit more on a line. . . . As far as that beaning two years ago, it affected me only for a short time, mainly because I got back into uniform too soon after it. I'm positive that I'm the same hitter psychologically as I was before." While not the terror of old, Medwick must be regarded as among the league's hitting elite. . . . Had he not missed 21 games, Medwick might have gone over the century mark [in RBIs] for the seventh time. . . . When not in baseball togs, Medwick divides his attention between the dining room in the Nacional Hotel, the salt water swimming pool on the hotel terrace, and a detective story magazine, with emphasis on tales that deal with the machinations of Adolf's Gestapo.

According to Cohane's report, "If there was a fist fight between Medwick and Dolph Camilli, last summer as alleged, and both vigorously deny it, it might have soon been forgotten, for both spend plenty of time together with Lew Riggs around the swimming pool here."

After seven games in Cuba, the team moved north. Tommy Holmes saw "an outfield situation that finds Walker, Reiser, Joe Medwick, Augie Galan, Johnny Rizzo and Frenchy Bordagaray scrambling for jobs."

The day before the season opened, Harold Parrott's column started off with an item called "The Kennel Club." The "Latest dope from the doghouse was that Joe (Double Chin) Medwick and Dixie (People's Choice) Walker will emerge from there in time to get into tomorrow's opening lineup. . . . This was . . . The Lip's way of commenting on the Medwick diet. Joe was roughly 20 pounds overweight. . . . Where the diet calls for grapefruit and black coffee, Muscles compromised on ham and eggs and cafe au lait. In yesterday's chill gloaming, Medwick was probably mad enough to bite the knob off one of his bat handles." (Wasn't it Durocher who said Joe was more than ten pounds underweight after his beaning?)

But opening day found Joe in his usual place in left field; the lineup was the same as in 1941, except that Arky Vaughan was at third in place of the newly drafted Cookie Lavagetto.

Holmes filed the following report: "Joe Medwick . . . the one time terror of National League pitching had had a melancholy time this Spring. He never did find his batting eye in the South and when the season opened, the fact that he found himself relegated to a part-time job didn't help a bit. Right now Yussel the Muscle was a problem. Chances [are] he won't hit unless he plays every day, but how can Durocher play him every day when he's in a slump while other outfielders are hitting?" The month of April ended with Joe at .250 in twelve games out of the seventeen played.

The Dodger game at home on May 8 was notable for many reasons. The game marked the first contest to contribute money to wartime relief. (Relief meant money for people who became widows and orphans because of the war.) Everyone at Ebbets Field—on the staff and on the teams—had a paid ticket.

Was Joe thinking still about Giants' secretary Eddie Brannick's crack from last May 30? It seemed that, indeed, he was.

After a rain day, "unbeaten pitcher Ed Head had Joe Medwick to thank for his fourth victory of the season. And Mr. Medwick, whose troubles at home plate this Spring have caused some unkind souls to remark that he was living in the past as a great hitter, truly rates a medal for meritorious service." The play that was so noteworthy was not a hit from Joe's sixth spot, although he did have a hit and a run scored; it was Medwick's play on Bartell's bases-loaded line drive to left center in the ninth. "Pete Reiser took one look and faced back to field the ball off the fence. But Medwick, disregarding caution, kept pounding over on his stumpy legs. As the liner started to sink, Medwick sank with it, doing his peculiar, copyrighted slide. . . . He was on his haunches when he caught the ball inches above the top of the grass. The Giant runner had to go into reverse and tag up. Medwick rebounding to his feet, fired the ball to the infield in time to prevent anyone from scoring." The *Herald-Tribune*'s Tim Cohane interviewed Joe after the game: "'As soon as I had that ball in my mitt,' Medwick chortled later, 'I looked around for Brannick. But he had disappeared. Probably into a hole in the ground.'"

Against the Pirates, Joe homered on the fifteenth, a 7-4 win for Larry French. As he rounded the bases, Red Barber, from his radio booth behind home plate, let a carton of Old Gold cigarettes slide down the protective screen—"the customary reward for batting prowess from the Dodgers' radio sponsor, Old Gold cigarettes." In *Spartan Seasons,* Red Barber remembered, "We called homers 'Old Goldies.' . . . There was a hole in the screen and the batboy grabbed them for the player."

The team celebrated the next day before the game as they marched out to the concave cement wall in right center. There, beneath the scoreboard sign that said "Buy U.S. War Stamps" and in front of the three signs advertising Lifebuoy, Coca-Cola, and Botany ties, Dolph Camilli raised the white triangular flag with blue lettering, which read "Champions National League 1941." By the time the visit by the second-place Pirates was over, Joe went 5-12 and the Cardinals were 14-14, and the Dodgers were 21-6.

Joe hit his fourth home run that year at the Polo Grounds on May 22 in a 5-1 loss, which loss moved the Cardinals into second place. Medwick's average was now .291 and he was second to Reiser on the team in most hitting categories. He was also fifth in the league in RBIs. Medwick's double to the wall the next day started a streak for him in a 5-2 loss that left the Brooklyns up five in the league. "'I know they think those beanings last year and two years ago made me pull away from right handers,' Medwick asserted. 'but that's not my answer. Some day I'll start meeting the ball and getting my share.' It was not long after that that Medwick began to prove himself a fair prophet."

During the first game against the Cardinals, after Joe had singled earlier, Max Lanier walked Medwick in the sixth. On a passed ball, Joe tried to go to second base, but Walker Cooper's throw to shortstop Marty Marion beat Joe, "and Joe went into the bag with spikes flying." Joe got up and he and Marion went for one another, but Frank Crespi came in between them and Joe and Crespi wrestled to the ground. First to reach the wrestlers was Camilli, who was at bat, "closely followed by Dixie Walker. Dolph dove onto Crespi who was over Medwick then, and before anyone could see exactly what was happening the spot around second base was a mass of players and umpires," McGowen wrote. You could see Walker's flying tackle of some Cardinal player. Crespi and Medwick were thrown out of the game with Galan going to left. (Later, Joe was fined by the league.) Whitey Kurowski had a shiner and Walker hurt his ankle. The Dodgers had a 5-2 win. The Brooklyns won the next day, too, 4-3, a game featuring Reiser's steal of home and Joe's two hits to take him to game number twenty-two in a row. The Dodgers won again on the May 20: "Walker Cooper [catcher] appeared to be needling Medwick on Joe's first at bat. . . . They exchanged words, and after Joe fouled out to Cooper, he took a belt at the Card catcher's mask with his bat." After that, "With the cheers of 21,284 fans rising higher each time he came to bat, Medwick hammered four straight hits . . . batted in three runs and boosted his season average to .350 to take the league batting lead from his young team-mate, Pete Reiser." The Dodger lead over the Cardinals reached seven and a half games.

Tommy Holmes interviewed Joe for the *Eagle:* "'I'll talk about my hitting, if you like. . . . There was nothing to it,' said the muscle man, 'except I've come out of the worst slump of my life. For some reason, my timing was all off this Spring and I had all kinds of trouble correcting it. It happened overnight. I suddenly found a stance I liked. They're pitching to me now exactly the same as they were when they were getting me out this Spring. But now I'm pickling the ball instead of popping it up.'" Joe had gone 35-89 in the last twenty-two games, scored ten, and batted in seventeen. "He had been directly responsible for an average of more than one run per game over the streak and the number one reason why the Dodgers have won 16 of those 22 games."

The June 21 doubleheader was split by the two teams, and when Joe got one hit in each game, his streak reached twenty-five games. Joe conceded that he had been using an Augie Galan model, which was thirty-five inches long and weighed thirty-four ounces; his usual bat was thirty-five inches long and weighed thirty-three ounces.

Joe's hit against the Phillies and his hits against Cincinnati were the end of his streak. Hardrock Shoun, a former teammate, helped to end it. At twenty-seven games, it was the fourth longest streak (he owned the third longest as well) in National League history at the time, behind Keeler's forty-four games and Hornsby's thirty-three.

In the next two games against Cincinnati, all Joe managed was a sacrifice fly to drive in a run, and so he finished the four-game series at Ebbets with a hit in each game of the doubleheader and his 50th RBI.

Medwick, hitless for the day, was now 0-10, but Medwick made two of those sliding, sit down catches, one on Harry Craft in the sixth that was one of Joe's super specials.

Joe Medwick's triple to win the decisive third out of five games from the Reds. It developed today that among the benefits assimilated by Medwick during his recent 27 consecutive game hitting streak was an occult prescience possibly unequaled since the early Egyptian times of Imhotep The Magnificent. "When the score of the second game was tied, 1-1, and the Reds were at bat in the first half of the eighth," said Joe today, brushing some magic powder off his left shoulder, "I looked up at the clock on the scoreboard. It was 5:53 P.M. I said to myself: 'Joe, you will break up this game at exactly six o'clock.'"

"Well, when I reached third base after hitting that triple to right center off Bucky Walters to score Pete Reiser from first, with what turned out to be the winning run, I looked at the clock again. It was 6:01 P.M." It was pointed out to Joe that if the moon had been in the proper phase, the triple might have come at exactly six o'clock, and he was rather inclined to agree.

At the 1942 All-Star break, lasting from July 6-8, Joe was second in the league in hits, RBIs, and average (.344). Going down to New York with Joe were Pete Reiser, who was also in the starting outfield, and Mel Ott. Teammates Arky Vaughan and Mickey Owen joined Joe and Pete on the train as starters with Billy Herman, Pee Wee Reese, and Whit Wyatt rounding out the group of Dodger players.

Two home runs in the American League first yielded three runs, but this was all they scored, and Mickey Owen hit his only home run of the year to give the National League their only run. Joe went hitless and his replacement in left, and former teammate, Slaughter, went 1-2. The American League won the right to play a service team in Cleveland on the seventh. The League team won 5-0.

After two series, the Dodgers arrived in St. Louis after midnight on July 14 and were taken to the Coronado Hotel. Tommy Holmes's story began with a bold headline: "Dodgers in St. Loo Move in for the Kill." The pitchers were rested; the team had a streak of 12-4. Although the Dodgers' Larry French was beaten 7-4 in game one, the Dodgers' Max Macon won 2-1 in game two. Medwick, 1-8, heard the same boos he heard before he was traded in June 1940. The next day, the Cardinals won two more, but not before Webber threw at Musial twice and Stan went to the mound with his bat in hand. "That [is] the way the Dodgers play ball, and apparently they were best at this sort of stuff. There was nothing coy about the way they zing a duster at you," Harold Parrott wrote, "but was it good baseball for Durocher and the Dodgers? They make too many enemies—when they should be coasting in. . . . The Cards, having sold Lon Warneke, were beginning to wave the white flag. . . . Although the Card owners surrendered, the Card ballplayers were so mad, they didn't." Mad enough to take three games from the league leaders.

And then a series of awful things happened to the Brooklyn team. Hugh Casey's finger was fractured. Wyatt's arm was hurt and he probably wouldn't be able to pitch for two weeks. But worst of all, in the second game at Sportsman's Park, when the score was tied 6-6 in the eleventh, center fielder Pete Reiser, trying desperately to catch up with a long drive by Enos Slaughter, crashed head first into the wall. Reiser bounced unconscious off the wall and the ball dropped out of his glove as Slaughter raced around the bases for a game-winning inside-the-park home run. As Reiser was being taken to St. John's Hospital, Joe described the accident: "'It might have been the greatest catch I've ever seen,' said Joseph shaking his head. 'I'll swear Slaughter hit the ball beyond Reiser and Pete overtook it. He was traveling like a bullet when he hit the fence.'"

In the July 27 *World-Telegram,* Daniel acknowledged Joe's contribution to the game:

> "Medwick Appears Headed for Valuable Player Prize . . . Ducky, in Remarkable Comeback, Real Spark of Dodger Attack," [s]aid one of the Dodgers today and it wasn't Ducky himself. "If the season were to end now the baseball writers would have to vote Joe Medwick the most valuable player in the National League. . . ." [When] the pennant race got under way, rival clubs got the impression that the Dodgers were vulnerable against left-handed pitching. This plethora of southpaw hurling encouraged a good start by right-Medwick—and he had been at it ever since, poison to lefties and right-handers alike. He had more hits than any other player in the National League and was outranked in major totals only by Start Spence of the Senators and Johnny Pesky of the Red Sox. The other evening Medwick came out of Ebbets Field with a new glove. "This was for a sick kid," he explained. He toted no mitts for ill youngsters in 1941. The change in Medwick was more than meets the eye. He was positively beatific.

Medwick seemed to understand more about himself with age. He had seen the respect he got from players on his team and in the league— in all of baseball. He had succeeded, and continued to succeed.

"The Greatest Crowd Ever to See a Single Game at the Polo Grounds," the *Times* labeled its photo of the August 3 Army

Emergency Relief game. The gates opened at 4 P.M., and "fences ordinarily used for football games were planted across the outfield
. . . holding the standees back [and making] necessary a two-base
rule for the first time in the history of the park," that was, since 1911.
After the anthem, buglers at home plate and in center played
"Taps." At the end, at 9:10, due to wartime dimout regulations, the
umpires left the field even though the Giants had two men on and
the crowd of 57,305, "the greatest crowd that ever saw a single game
in the Harlem arena [made] a storm of boos and jeers that drowned
out the opening bars of 'The Star Spangled Banner' [again] in a dark-
ened park. Some of the fans, as had been requested, stood with
matches alight in an eerie scene" as the anthem was "sung by a
choral group under Bob Shaw." A single light illuminated the American Flag and this seemed to quiet the fans. Officially, at the end, the
Dodgers won 7-4. The box score read, "Game called, dimout regulations, none out for the Giants in the ninth" with the cleanup hitter
Babe Young about to hit.

The next game ended in a 1-1 tie. Peewee Reese had hit an inside-
the-park bases-loaded home run in the tenth inning, and then Galan
walked and Walker flied out. Joe came to bat, the count went to 1-2,
and the umpires called the game. All that had happened in the tenth
was erased since that inning was never finished and the score re-
verted to the score at the end of nine. This was the first major league
tie game under the lights. Reiser, still not feeling well, had been having headaches, dizzy spells, and nausea so intense that he could not
play.

"Possibly," suggested Tommy Holmes on August 8, "this was the
start of the Dodger slump that Billy Southworth of the Cardinals
had been talking about all summer." If it were, the Cardinals had to
win, and this day they didn't do that, so the Dodger lead was nine
and a half games.

In mid August, after a game, owner Larry MacPhail decided to
have a stern talk with the team in front of reporters, including
Roscoe McGowen, whose report of the meeting with the team said,
"in Roaring Red's opinion, they weren't playing the kind of baseball
they ought to be playing. Muscles Medwick was gently chided because, in the boss's view, he might have thrown out Danny Litwhiler
on the latter's second inning double . . . 'if he had hustled,' and
MacPhail added a general statement to the entire club that he didn't
like 'this club as well as he had the 1941 club when they were a half

game out of the lead.'" MacPhail, not Medwick's manager, was crit-
icizing Joe's play—in front of others, outsiders. No one did that to
Joe with impunity. This had been a rule with Joe for a long time.

Durocher remembered it this way. "As usual, Larry pulled no
punches. 'You were not hustling,' he accused us. 'You should be
twenty games in front of the Cardinals, instead of only eight. Right
now, only six men in this club were carrying their gloves out there
every day: Reiser, Reese, Medwick, Owen, Casey, and Davis." But it
was too late for Joe to forgive MacPhail.

Boston, which was currently thirty-four games back, came to
Brooklyn. and after a rain postponement, was beaten in a doubleheader by the combined score of 17-3. The Brooklyns made only fifteen hits in the two games. Joe went 4-9, making four runs, and "a
ladies-day crowd of 17,031 (10,367 paid) gave Medwick the first big
cheer of the day when Muscles made one of his famous 'sit-down-
slide' catches of Waner's liner in the first inning. Joe added a leaping, gloved hand catch of Sibby Sisti's drive off Wyatt to draw more
applause." Larry French got the win on August 15 when Camilli hit
his twentieth home run with two out in the ninth. "As Camilli came
trotting across the plate, Muscles Medwick, who had been on base
via a single [to score the tying run] leaped for Dolph and hugged
him, with Larry French joining in the back-slapping."

After a Max Macon loss to Philadelphia, Curt Davis almost shut
out the Braves, winning 11-1 for his thirteenth win and Wyatt beat
the Giants 2-1 for his fifteenth win. When Joe reached third base in
the second inning, he thought he had a triple, but the official scorer
called it an error on Babe Young and Medwick held his nose when
the error sign was turned on. Joe's anger and frustration with his
weak hitting was very apparent in the next game, a 10-5 win in
seven innings when Medwick slid hard into second baseman
Mickey Witek, knocking him down. Both men got up, exchanging
unpleasantness. Shortstop Billy Jurges tried to make peace, but
when third baseman Billy Werber arrived, Medwick wanted to attack him and had to be restrained. "Even the normally placid Whitlow Wyatt," came out to scream at Werber. Joe, hitting sixth, was
2-3 with three RBIs. Don Gutteridge told me, "Joe was ferocious during the game and docile afterwards."

The next day's doubleheader won by Brooklyn was followed by a
police escort to Pennsylvania Station, where the team caught "the
Victory Special" on the way to St. Louis to begin their final road trip

of 1942, with five weeks to go and a seven and a half game lead. It was the first time in league history that a team played in New York and St. Louis on successive days; the distance between the two is one thousand miles and takes about twenty-two hours to cover.

As they dressed before the game, the players sensed that these games could be important. These three games, followed by two more in September, were the only ones left against the Cardinals. The Dodgers had not played well in St. Louis and "maybe the fact that the Dodgers would rather show up well here in old St. Louis than almost anywhere else in the league had something to do with the fact that they don't," Holmes wrote on August 25. "Durocher makes his home here. So do Pete Reiser and Joe Medwick. Moreover, this was the spot where the fans dish it out to Medwick, the one time slugging idol of Sportsman's Park. The Magyar muscle man would give a month's pay to break up a couple of games in this series, but all year long his efforts have been futile before his razzing jeering Winter neighbors."

The Dodgers were futile again, Medwick without a hit, in the 7-1 loss to Lanier, a four-time winner over the Dodgers this year. Joe was still second in RBIs in the league but his average at .316 was now below .320 for the first time in a long time. Holmes continued his description of Medwick's razzing, but this time with a difference: "What a ride Joe Medwick got from the same St. Louis fans who used to cheer him to the echo. Nor did Joe make it any easier for himself here in his old stamping ground with his swashbuckling mannerisms. His gesture of disgust last night, for example, after Marion's wild throw on a slow hit ball to short was scored as an error brought a large assortment of raspberries. It was a close scorer's decision all right, but the fact that Lanier had a no-hit game up to that moment made it inadvisable to lean backward in Medwick's favor."

Daniel wrote that Medwick "indicated by a series of gestures for the next two minutes that he thought the official scorer was very wrong. . . . He also complained last Thursday [August 20] when a ball he hit to Babe Young in Ebbets Field was called an error." Some writers discussed Medwick's suitability for the Most Valuable Player award after what they considered to be graceless gestures— the sportswriters were generally fascinated by what they called "class."

It was, by the way, this fascination with "class" that had the writers value DiMaggio over Medwick, as if that trait had anything to do with achievement. "Class" seemed to indicate something about the manly virtues: determination combined with stoicism; if you were silent in the face of injustice, it appeared, you had class. To fight for what you thought was yours, it seemed, was not class. It seemed that this preoccupation with "class" spoke a great deal about the writers themselves— their desire to have readers think that writers could spot and judge class, since the writers themselves were so intimately familiar with it. As if they alone had class "meters"—as if class were some attainable goal. As if it mattered.

The next night, Joe was three for six before the largest night-game crowd ever at Sportsman's, but neither the Dodgers nor the Cardinals could score for twelve innings. Owen, Wyatt, and Lew Riggs combined for one run in the thirteenth, "but Wyatt, his gray uniform stained with perspiration hadn't enough to stagger across the finish line." In the bottom of the thirteenth, Wyatt walked Slaughter, Reese's leap was just not enough to catch Musial's single, and Walker Cooper, the catcher/brother, singled Slaughter home. St. Louis fans tossed their rented seat cushions all over the outfield, delaying the game. In the Cardinal fourteenth, an infield single, a misplayed sacrifice bunt, and a walk finished French, and with the infield in, Webber made Terry Moore hit to Riggs at third, but Lew slipped, making his throw home too late. Mort Cooper, Cardinal pitcher, won his sixteenth. The Dodgers could not win scoring one run per game. Joe wanted to win, as he always had, and was angry when he didn't. At the end of the inning, Slats Marion made a fine play that stopped a runner from moving up a base. Because of Marion's sharp play, Joe had to settle for a fielder's choice, and running to his left field position, kicked Marion's glove high and far.

To end August there were three games in Pittsburgh, two of which were wins. When Wyatt won game one by 3-1 on August 30, Joe produced two of the runs. In game two, Medwick drove in two without any hits, but the Pirates scored nine to win. Curt Davis won on August 31, and Joe drove in two more. Those two RBIs tied Medwick with Slaughter for the league RBI lead at ninety. And though Joe's average had dropped again to .311 (from .325 at the end of July), he was still fifth in the league since others were as tired as he was, and he was tenth in games, sixth in at bats, and second in hits. Brooklyn had gone 12-11 while the Cardinals were 20-3, so the Dodgers had obviously lost games off the lead.

Harold Parrott was willing to say that "it could be that the Dodgers have been traveling over their heads, and were now being debunked by a team that had been slighted all along. It could be that the Cards, hanging on to the Dodgers' coattails all season when other clubs would have been discouraged and folded, have too much innate class to be denied. It could be, but I don't believe it." (Here we see the obsession with "class" once again.)

At the same time, Tommy Holmes was saying that "our guys look tired and, without getting panicky about it, there was a growing fear that the Cardinals had too much youth and vitality if the campaign resolves into a neck-and-neck drive down the September stretch." At the end of August, it was clear that it was a two-team race in the National League. The Dodgers, 88-40, were ahead by three in the win column and four in the loss column over the 85-44 Cardinals. Joe was still trying to do what he could to help the team. His average had dropped fourteen points in August—he hit .264 during that month—and yet in August's thirty-one games he produced 19 percent of the team's runs by driving in 18 and scoring 8 of its 131 runs.

Kirby Higbe beat Pittsburgh at Forbes Field and the team moved into Cincinnati. Wyatt won his seventeenth in relief and then Bobo Newsom won with a four-hitter. Joe was not hitting, starting the month 2-12; his average was down to .308.

When Wyatt lost against the Giants, and Joe only got one hit and left too many men on base, Durocher ordered Galan to replace Medwick in game one of the September 6 doubleheader. "When an ambulance presented to the Army rolled around the field between games, someone suggested that Medwick's wounded feelings were inside." (After all, ridicule is the price of celebrity.) Joe's recent 9-42 hitting was something he was very much aware of; he was very much aware of how much the team counted on him. Then Parrott wrote that there were nine players on the team who qualified for the Most Valuable Player title. First on his list was "Joe Medwick, whose long hitting streak carried the attack of the club for a solid month in mid-summer."

In game two, Joe scored twice, once when he drove himself home on a fourth-inning home run. And how was that rewarded? "[C]ustomers chucked citrus at him when he went back to left field."

And the Cardinals kept coming, winning twenty-six of their last thirty-one games. Leo Durocher recalled the following in his autobiography: "Other disturbing things happened. Medwick, a cocky gent when he was hitting, and morose and ill-tempered when he wasn't, had just about worn out his welcome on the club. A lot of the boys had begun to growl at him. Joe had fistfights on the Cardinal team. When things went bad, I had to step in several times to avert them on our club. I still had faith in Joe, but perhaps I humored him too much." Fights happen when players are angry about losing. Perhaps having fistfights on a team doesn't do it any harm; it didn't hurt the 1934 Cardinals, the A's of the early 1970s, or the Yankees of the late 1970s. But it was true that much of Joe's professional behavior was centered on his hitting. He depended on his hitting to keep him balanced. With just a two-and-a-half-game lead, the team needed him to hit.

The day of September 11 was a Cardinal day in Brooklyn. At Sportsman's Park against the Cardinals, the Dodgers were 3-8, while at Ebbets they were 6-3. It was 6-4 after Mort Cooper, wearing number 20, won number twenty with a 3-0 shutout. Wyatt, the loser, explained, "it was the breaks . . . the hard-hit balls [that] our side hit were straight at somebody or just foul." The Dodgers only made three hits, one each by Galan, Vaughan, and Reese. On September 12, the Dodgers lost again when Max Lanier gave the Brooklyns but one run. The attempt to tie the game came in the eighth when Billy Herman was on first and Joe singled. Medwick's 2,000th hit came just days after Herman's, although Billy had begun playing in the league a year before Joe did. The hit moved Herman up, but Camilli grounded out to end the inning. The 2-1 loss tied the two teams. Although there is no mention of Joe's hit number 2,000 in the newspapers, Joe was aware of it, and kept the ball.

Cincinnati was next against the dispirited Dodgers and they lost a doubleheader that dropped them a game behind the Cardinals, the first time the Dodgers were out of first place in four months. They had lost four games in three crucial days, while scoring a mere five runs.

As for that slump, and the coming loss of the pennant, while it was time to dish out some praise, it was mostly time to assign blame, because "the collapse of the Dodgers had assumed the proportions of a civic tragedy here [in Brooklyn]":

1. Frankie Frisch, Pirates manager, "was laying down to the Dodgers because he hates Branch Rickey [of the Cardinals]."
2. Bill McKechnie, Braves manager and former manager of the Cardinals, "saved his aces to pitch them against the Dodgers

when their ship was sinking," and threw his weaker pitchers against the Cardinals.

3. Durocher had made too many enemies.
4. The Dodgers had thrown too many beanballs.
5. The Dodgers did not have enough right-handed hitters in their lineup, which made them prey to left-handers.
6. Higbe wasn't doing well—he hadn't won since September 1.
7. Durocher's cockiness: a large part of "Durocher's stock in trade," had been ripped away by a vicious magazine article that "opened up an ugly door into the past," as Harold Parrott described it, and damaged Leo's "ability to get a group of athletes that many called misfits to produce tremendous results. . . . More important, perhaps some of the Dodgers lost a little of their confidence in their nervy pilot." The team seemed to lack confidence and a sense of togetherness—"teamness," as Stan Musial calls it.
8. The jitters: "[The players] were . . . white faced and tight lipped and waving at pitched balls in such a way that you [knew] the muscles in their stomachs were tied in hard, unyielding knots."
9. "The Cardinals were lucky in having violent rooters in the right places," Parrott said from St. Louis. "One might have been the Pirate outfielder who did not even move after a fly ball which fell for the base hit," which led to a big Cardinal inning in their 9-3 win. "He was the same outfielder [Vince DiMaggio] who had a violent argument with Durocher in a Dodger Pirate game. And Monday he missed the bunt sign twice with two men on and none out and eventually he flied out."
10. Of the players who had been in more than 120 games, the shortstop, the catcher, the second baseman, and the first baseman were hitting below .260. Only Medwick was hitting over .300.

Intended to be the difference in the pennant race, Medwick, still burned to win, but remembered being singled out by MacPhail the month before for not hustling. Harold Parrott, writing years later, said, "MacPhail announced that Medwick should be benched. The bankers down the block hopped on the Redhead with both feet: Imagine spending all that cash for a bench-warmer. They didn't know the inside of the Reiser story. Durocher still refused to believe all the thunder had gone out of his pal Medwick's bat." Riggs and Galan, who were held up as a threat to replace Joe, didn't have as many games played as Joe did, even when they combined their total. In his nine full seasons, Medwick had been absent from, on average, fewer than six games per season. Up until now, in 1942, he had only missed four games.

On September 20, the only reason the Dodgers won against Philadelphia (last-place Philadelphia), was because the winning run was walked in at the end of the bases-loaded eleventh. When Joe went hitless in this game, he drove in a run; this put Joe at 5-30 in the seven most recent games. When he was 21-102 so far for September (.205), he knew he was not helping the team. It seemed that no one, except Wyatt, was helping the team consistently. There were nine games left for the Dodgers. The Dodgers couldn't win, and the Cardinals, who couldn't seem to lose, scored three runs in three games and yet won two of them.

Joe did not play in the September 20 doubleheader, which the Dodgers split. His replacement, Augie Galan, was 1-7. "Joe Medwick remained out of the doubleheader with the Phillies at his own request." Dan Daniel's interpretation was that Medwick was "replaced by Augie Galan because Joe had not been hitting recently. He asked to be benched. . . . Even if Medwick had come up twelve times without a hit, it was considered poor spirit for the left fielder to beg off. It was almost without a parallel."

This was the logic? MacPhail thought Joe wasn't playing hard enough, and said so in front of the team and in front of reporters. Then MacPhail said Joe ought to be benched. Medwick was 0-12. Could it be that Medwick had the team at heart, so he volunteered to be benched? Was he pouting? Was MacPhail abusing him? Had Leo asked Joe to volunteer to be benched? Had MacPhail ordered Leo to bench Joe? Who can say?

Galan got a hit the next day as Joe sat again. Did he sit because Durocher sat him, because MacPhail ordered Durocher to sit him, or did Joe request it? And if he did, would Durocher sit his cleanup hitter without some other reason than that Joe asked him to? Did Joe have another of his painful back pains and not talk about it? Who can know?

For some reason, Joe was back in the lineup on September 22 against the Giants and went hitless in his first three at bats, though he scored and drove in a run. During this game, as well, Reese threw wild for one of his thirty-five errors for the year, Herman fumbled a ball at second, and Walker dropped a ball he had in his glove. But, Holmes said, "MacPhail almost scalped himself on a girder as Medwick booted Bartell's single to left and he ambled after the ball with all the speed and grace of a rheumatic bear." As Parrott recalled in *The Lords of Baseball*, during this game, MacPhail "blew up because Medwick's . . . in the starting lineup . . . after all his lectures to Durocher. Larry stormed into the press bar yelling that he wanted a paper and pencil. He moved down to the far end of the bar, away from the prying eyes of the writers, who would have given anything to see what he was putting into this war communiqué. Larry was so mad he ground his teeth as he bore down hard on the paper, printing the words. He folded it so hard he almost tore it in half. Then he summoned Benny Weinrig, the press box messenger, and bade him take it down to Durocher on the run."

Durocher, in his book, told of receiving the note: "MacPhail sent me a pencil-written message in the dugout. 'Leo: Medwick was a nice fellow (this was sarcasm because we were pals) but, why let him rule the club? Larry.' As I look back now, I think we would have won the pennant that year if I had yanked Medwick sooner, and gone along with Augie Galan in left. But that's second-guessing."

In Parrott's account, "That afternoon, the late editions of the New York *Journal* reached Ebbets Field before the ballgame was over; a scare headline screamed that Durocher had been fired again. The reason: keeping Medwick in the lineup."

(Medwick was asked about this note in 1943. "'That's rich,' grumbled Joe, 'me trying to run the club. Ain't I got enough trying to get back into left field and staying there?'" Then, Parrott reported, "John McDonald, trying to shed new light on the discovery, was asked about Leo's reaction to the note. 'He never saw it,' laughed McDonald. 'I still have the note [at] home in my archives.'")

Who can know?

The next day, MacPhail officially turned in his resignation to the Brooklyn owners. He had other plans. The Dodger board had other plans for him, that is—he would be fired, and he knew it.

By season's end, the Dodgers had won 104 and lost the pennant to a team that won 106. The last time a National League club won 106 or more was in 1916. Only nine teams had won more than 106 games in a season. While the Dodgers were 16-10 in September (62 percent), the Cardinals were 21-4 (84 percent).

The Cardinals, for instance, over the whole of the season, outscored the Dodgers by thirteen runs, had two fewer home runs, and two more RBIs. Four points separated the teams in average and the on-base percentage was exactly the same.

And if the Dodgers had won three more one-run games, or if the Cardinals had lost three more one-run games; if Lew Riggs had not slipped and if Max Macon had not slipped. . . . Dixie Walker's summary was apt: "They won it. We didn't lose it." John Kiernan wrote months later that the Cardinals were "embodying the unbridled spirit of youth that was sweeping the land."

Who would be the hero among these losing Dodgers?

Here was what Joe did for his team, even when they sat him down for eight games at the end: he finished sixth in runs; fourth in games; fourth in slugging; third in on-base percentage; second in RBIs; second in batting average; second in fielding average; first in fewest strikeouts; first in doubles, and first in hits. He also scored and drove in 11.5 percent of the team's runs; drove in 14 percent of the team's runs; and made 11.8 percent of the team's hits. In the National League, Medwick yet again placed high: second in doubles, third in hits, fourth in RBIs, and sixth in average.

In the year's beginning, Medwick said, "I found out that I couldn't lift a ball as high as I did at Sportsman's Park. There were little tricky wind currents at Brooklyn . . . in St. Louis [there] was always that dead humid air. . . . So I have tried to hit more on a line. . . . As far as that beaning two years ago, it affected me only for a short time, mainly because I got back into uniform too soon after it. I'm positive that I'm the same hitter psychologically as I was before."

Is this an excuse? Is this the explanation of a very crafty hitter? According to Bill James's account in *New Historical Baseball Abstract*,

> After he was traded to the Dodgers in 1940 Medwick was hit in the skull by former teammate Bob Bowman of the Cardinals. Accounts of this event invariably state that Medwick was never the same player after this, or that he was not as aggressive a hitter, and lost his power after this. This is untrue. It's another case of park effects being misinterpreted as actual changes in ability. The National League ERA dropped sharply in 1941 and dropped further in 1942, plus Medwick, in moving from Sportsman's Park to Ebbets Field, was moving to a much tougher home run park. If you adjust for those things, Medwick's value in 1941–42 was almost exactly the same as it had been in 1938–39.

And according to the measure in *Total Baseball*, Joe was the top clutch hitter for the year in the National League and third in all of the majors. His clutch hitting even placed him forty-third lifetime for a single season. Medwick was voted seventeenth in the Most Valuable Player election.

In August and September, Joe's forty-nine hits were more hits than Camilli, Reiser, and Owen had, but fewer than Walker, Reese, Herman, and Vaughan had. Joe's twenty-six RBIs in those two months were more RBIs than anyone else produced except Camilli, who had fifty-three.

With MacPhail gone from the Dodger organization and Branch Rickey about to enter, the Dodger organization came up with a plan in which the team would be 25 percent owned by the older Dearie and Jim Mulvey; the other part of the team was owned equally by John L. Smith, attorney Walter O'Malley, and Branch Rickey, brought in from St. Louis to run the team. Each man paid $82,000 down (Rickey's salary in 1942 was $80,000), with the remainder financed by the Brooklyn Trust Company.

The Dodger owners believed in Rickey; he had just come from a team that took the World Series from the New York Yankees, and he continued to be regarded highly by many baseball people. Just as a baseball player who read books was quickly adjudged an "intellectual" by sportswriters desperate for any kinship with players, so an owner (such as Rickey) who used Latinate words and spoke in sonorous generalities was labeled a genius. For purposes of controlling salaries, Rickey loved to use polysyllabic words on his mostly uneducated players, making them think that he was smart and they were unintelligent. One of his major contributions seemed to be the employment (but not the invention) of the farm system, but Rickey himself admitted that he had little to do with the farm system by 1935 or so. "In recent seasons, I depended largely on scouts, minor league managers, club observers," Rickey said in September of 1938.

Perhaps people forget as well that Rickey convinced Breadon to invest his money; that is, Breadon's money, not Rickey's money. Rickey may have seen that more players meant more sale opportunities, which meant more 10 percent allocations into his pocket.

Parrott wrote: "The Dodger chieftain indicated that he had grave fears about the Dodgers' chances of winning the pennant next year, although he denied having said the club would not finish one, two, three. 'There were an amazing number of 10-year veterans on the

Brooklyn club . . . and the rate of disintegration or fall which set in last September and enabled my Cardinals to win, must be checked." Every ten-year man, of course, will have a ten-year man's salary.

Parrott's later series on Rickey said that "Rickey had a horror of what he calls a 'veteranized' ball team. He shudders as he looks at the Brooklyn roster which shows thirteen individuals with 133 years of service in the big leagues. 'We were sitting on a volcano of complete and sudden disintegration here in Brooklyn.'" (Rickey was sitting atop an "income from baseball [which] had rivaled and sometimes surpassed the $75,000 wage of the game's high commissioner.")

Joe, of course, was one of those ten-year men.

At the same time, only Dan Daniel in the *World-Telegram* was telling stories such as the following. On October 24, 1942: "The dope was that in the last fortnight of the season the other players gave Joe the silent treatment." On December 3, 1942: "Medwick would appeal to [the Cubs] only as a waiver price ball player. Medwick who became persona non grata with his fellow ball players in Brooklyn late last season." Many players from that time deny these stories. Tommy Holmes reported on December 10: "the prospect of losing Reiser [to military service] from his outfield led Rickey to say that for the present he was entertaining no notions of trading Joe Medwick. Muscles Joe lost favor with the Flock during the closing of the ill-starred 1942 campaign and it generally had been expected that he would be offered for sale. Rickey now was confident he [could] build up the veteran outfielder, who at one time was the league's outstanding hitter. 'If I can have a talk with Medwick . . . I am confident I can convince Joe he still can be the Medwick of old, the Medwick who runs out hits and played the game for all he's got. Actually he ought to be right in his prime.'" So now all "sonny boy Joe" needed was a good talking to by "Dad."

Rickey, traveling to see his family, went to St. Louis announcing, in typically religious terms, "Now I am going to begin the job of redemption with Medwick, who [is] only 32 and should still be a great player. He has got to run out his hits. Managers around the league told me he took a cut at the first one last season and from them on, protected himself. However, Joe did hit .300 and if persuasion will do anything he will reform. I am going to see him in St. Louis next week," Daniel reported. "Reform" and "redemption"—the words of Mr. Rickey.

When Rickey got back, he said, "I had a long talk with Medwick. . . . I got Joe to open up. He said he sensed a feeling here that he had not done his best last season but pleaded that he had not done any 'conscious' loafing."

Medwick's so-called loafing produced 166 hits, which were 22 more than anyone else on the team, just as his "loafing" made him first in doubles on the Dodgers. Everyone else on the team must have been "loafing" to make Joe second on the team in triples. It must have been Medwick's "loafing" that put him in the outfield of a 1942 all-defensive team, along with Danny Litwhiler and Tommy Holmes. The top pair in RBIs in 1942 was Pete Reiser and Medwick, who were higher than Mize and Ott for the Giants. Rickey's accusations of Medwick's "loafing" appear to be (once again) driven by the tactics of contract negotiation.

Rickey must have been thinking back to Joe's rookie year, when he hired an agent to negotiate his contract. How could Rickey help but think about the lack of respect that Medwick showed Breadon. Rickey knew Joe was more than capable of doing the same thing in Brooklyn. Rickey needed respect. He was used to admiration from everyone around him—he demanded it.

Though still averaging 197 hits for his first ten years, Joe must have known how short his stay with the Dodgers was liable to be.

17

Rickey Again, 1943

The war, of course, occupied all of the front-page news, particularly when citizens read that U.S. casualties now approached 100,000. With troops needed, Red Ruffing, the Yankee pitcher with four missing toes, was drafted for noncombat service.

In the sports pages, Rickey's idea of a good contract for Joe in 1943 was (surprise for Medwick) to take a cut of $7,000—from $19,000 to $12,000.

On January 2, 1943, Stanley Frank wrote an early column reflecting on Medwick:

Joe Medwick has been called many names, classic and common—a stormy petrel, Clubhouse lawyer, cause celebre and bum—but no one forgets to mention, in an afterthought, that he was one of the great natural hitters baseball had seen in the last decade. . . . At 31 and healthy as a horse, Medwick should be at the peak of his career and regarded as one of the first five standouts in his profession. . . . Medwick had not been a holdout in Brooklyn and, in fact, had expressed himself as being satisfied with the money offered him, yet he was, once again, persona non grata. Even Durocher, his most ardent booster, seemed to have soured on him. It had been said that Medwick was an Individualist, a guy strictly for himself and his batting average. He had been described as a man who feels he didn't need friends as long as he can hit .300 and when he cannot, friends won't help him anyway.

Whatever the cause of the dissatisfaction that follows him, Medwick seems to [have] a peculiar talent for losing friends and alienating people. . . . [On] a certain day in St. Louis, he hit a sharp infield grounder that was juggled momentarily and he beat the throw to first base . . . the official scorer elected to call it an error. Medwick made a gesture of disgust toward the press box. The customers in Sportsman's Park promptly booed him fervently and the newspapermen, who had been considering Medwick a candidate for the most valuable player award, said he had disqualified himself by his action. . . . Nobody really knew how or why Medwick's latent greatness was detoured. His few remaining boosters say he had not been handled with sympathy. His detractors report, with much logic, that a mature man who was well paid should require no treatment different form that accorded anyone else. One thing was certain: Medwick was a funny Ducky, all right.

As was often the case, sportswriters seemed to have some powerful attitudes: first, the owners, the educated grown-ups who bought the drinks, were always right. Second, ballplayers ought to have well-rounded personalities to match the excellence of their athletic ability, so they could provide colorful and readily available copy. Third, ballplayers—children in funny suits—could never do enough and always wanted more. Never did one read that Horace Stoneham or Sam Breadon or Branch Rickey was making too much money.

Meanwhile, the baseball world kept adapting as best it could to wartime circumstances. For the Dodgers, the training season would now start a month later than the previous year and the men would not travel to Florida, 1,350 miles south of Brooklyn, but rather to Bear Mountain, New York, fifty miles north.

On January 9, 1943, Rickey said, "I would still like to trade Medwick."

Since some writers printed that Joe kept himself out of the lineup in the stretch in 1942 to keep his .300 average, Medwick's reply, by way of Harold Parrott in the *Eagle* was, "No player asks to be benched. I wasn't going good and Augie Galan was, so Leo made the shift. Why, as far as my batting average was concerned, I would much rather had been in there every day. I certainly could have kept it above .300 against the Phillies pitching." Once again, Medwick knew what he was talking about when it came to his craft, to hitting. The Phillies pitching was last in the league, and fourteenth in the majors with a 4.12 ERA (league average being 3.31), and it was a staff that had given up more earned runs than anyone in the league and more walks as well, with just two shutouts, the fewest in the majors.

At 1 P.M. on Saturday, March 13, the main group of Dodgers players and ten sportswriters, left New York's West Forty-second Street slip, and boated past chunks of ice to the New Jersey side of the Hudson on the ferry so they could board the West Shore Day Coach for the trip to the Bear Mountain Inn. Joe was being kidded by other players for his very short, almost military-style, haircut.

The Bear Mountain Inn, resembling a luxurious hunting lodge, had been picked because it offered access to the spacious field house at West Point Military Academy. The team took its meals together at the inn, and here Dixie Walker, accompanied by Bobby Bragan on piano, would sing at night after the workouts.

On March 27, seven Dodger outfielders posed for a photograph. They were asked to pretend their bats were rifles, so all but one were holding the bat to their shoulders and sighting down the barrel. Joe would not. Baseball was what he was good at and what he loved. In photo after photo, while others around him clowned around, you can see that Medwick would not demean the game, and especially not his part in it.

Durocher talked to the press about his seven outfielders, Waner and Johnny Cooney being the elders at ages forty and forty-two. "I expect Medwick to have a great year," Leo told Arthur Daley. "He's hustling more, the players like him better and he seems to be enjoying himself more. It's up to him and he can do it." This seems a miraculous change in the attitude of the players who hated him only a few months ago. Or did they not really loathe him? Or had Joe changed completely over the winter, learning social skills, courting his teammates?

Before two weeks were done, one exhibition game was played on the inn's picnic grounds, attended by twenty-five hundred fans who sailed up the Hudson River to see the game on Saturday, the twenty-seventh. After that, the picnic grounds field was abandoned because of too many rocks and too much wind, and all work moved into the field house.

April 2 was the last night spent at Bear Mountain, the Dodgers leaving there to play their first exhibition game at Ebbets Field in April, a game in which Medwick was the only Dodger player in the same position as in 1942. That date also marked the beginning of bond-drive activities for the team members, who had been assigned to teams of two players each, along with a baseball writer and a Treasury Department worker. On the field before the game with the Red Sox, the players were sworn in as special agents of the Treasury Department. As part of the "Dodger Spring Offensive," each player was urged to generate at least $500,000 in bond sales by appearing at factories, schools, and theaters.

Also as part of the war effort, Medwick and seventeen other Dodgers donated blood at the Brooklyn Red Cross headquarters. Afterwards, Joe, Mickey Owen, Paul Waner, and Dixie Walker along with pitchers Wyatt, Higbe, and Fitzsimmons, and writers Holmes, Meany, Turkin, and Patterson "addressed a total of about 5,000 employees of the Todd Shipyards, A. Schrader's Sons, Vulcan Proofing and the Brooklyn Union Gas Company."

The next day, after the workout with Camilli and Vaughan, members of a team called the Battling Beavers including the bearded Galan, Dee Moore, and Frenchy Bordagaray (he no stranger to beards) worked on the Red Skelton movie *Whistling in Brooklyn*, which was being filmed at Ebbets. In the afternoon, the war-bond visits continued, and Joe and Dixie Walker addressed the workers at the Brooklyn Union Gas Company.

The next day was the Civilian Defense Volunteer Office benefit game, a three-way set of games labeled an "elimination double-header." At Yankee Stadium, all three New York City teams appeared on the same day. A crowd of 35,301 showed up for the two games while 20,000 tickets bought to give to servicemen were not used. Yet the crowd was the largest ever to see a preseason exhibition game as "a pair of lusty two-baggers by Joe Medwick and Dolph Camilli . . . crushed the Yanks in the opener." Medwick appeared only briefly in the game against the Giants as the Dodgers placed an outfielder on first, and catcher Bobby Bragan at third.

Team members were also working on the Skelton movie each day, beginning at ten o'clock, for an hour and a half. Durocher, of course, appeared on radio shows frequently and was pals with many entertainers. Joe, Leo's pal, met them too, but was clearly not awestruck by them. In fact, for Joe, it was just the opposite; he was thinking about hitting all the while. Parrott's column recounted Joe asking questions as he was reading the script:

"Who pitches for them Beavers?" asked Joe.
"Red Skelton," said the director.

A maniacal gleam came into the Medwick's eye. "That's all, brother," said Ducky, swishing his bat.

Ray Hayworth and Max Macon, wearing beards, were supposed to be in the Beavers' infield. "Where do we play," they asked.

"The deeper the better, with that guy pitching," said Medwick. "And in a suit of armor, if you can"

And Ducky wasn't fooling. In rehearsal, Skelton threw the ball up there and Medwick drove it back through the box. Red had to skip rope to save some broken bones.

"Hey," shouted the director, "take it easy, he's our big investment."

Arthur Daley's column, "Play Ball," also reflected on Medwick: "Joe, now a half year past his thirty-first birthday, hit .500 with a triple, a double, and three singles, with three RBIs in the three team exhibitions, hitting to all fields, hustling, sliding." Branch Rickey was the cause for Medwick's sliding and hitting since, as some wanted to believe, and as Cohane wrote, "Branch had a long talk with Ducky Wucky in St. Louis last December and it seems to have borne fruit off that Yankee series." So ballplayers—athletes—were children who just needed a stern talking to, not only to behave, but to excel at a craft as difficult as hitting a baseball. Yet, Holmes wrote, since Medwick was essentially an ignorant child like most ballplayers, talented though he may be, "the boys generally agree that Medwick's batting average will climb again if he continues to hit and slash. That's reasonable enough since Medwick and his mace never seemed designed to outsmart anybody." These remarks were all too typical of sportswriters, who were ambivalent about their own work—writers writing about baseball instead of writing novels. Medwick was not an educated man and did not claim to be. Neither was he glib or a good interview like Dizzy or Leo. Nor was he garrulous like Rickey. Like many American men, to Medwick, action, not talk, was the paramount measure of a man. Ballplayers were often labeled as "naturals" or "instinctive"—that is, the ones who blindly swung their bats and got lucky a lot—those were the ones writers called "stars." The hours of hard work, the constant practice, the study of pitchers and of bats and of air currents, the conversations with batters, not only on a player's own team but in other leagues as well, were all ignored and discounted by writers. Talking about all that work and study was not something that a man like Medwick would discuss with writers, even if they had been interested. Hard work was what was expected of him; it was the norm.

Still, hitters talked about hitting with each other, and since writers were not hitters, there was no reason to talk about hitting with reporters. Medwick had hit .300 or better since he played in Scottdale in June of 1930. Sportswriters would quickly credit other sportswriters who had written well for thirteen years, just as they would credit a fiction writer like Hemingway or Lawrence or Steinbeck—writers who had written well over the same thirteen-year span. Anyone who credited such excellence and consistency to luck in any difficult craft—fiction, baseball, carpentry—was speaking as a fool. But there have always been those who think that Twain was a clown, Picasso, a child, Hemingway, a drunk and so on.

Rickey was quoted as saying that this team was "too veteranized." (Tom Tresh talked about his father's trades: "In those days they felt you were an old man as soon as you turned thirty and you'd better not have a bad season.")

One of Rickey's more expensive veterans said, "'I think we'll be in this pennant fight all the way,' Medwick said, 'just as we were last year. Sure, we'll miss Reese and Reiser, but the Cards will miss Moore, Slaughter and Beazley. We figure to have strong pitching all the way down the line.'" Rickey called the National League race, "a scramble in the field of prophecy." A prophecy scramble? Again Rickey used mellifluous language to impress or confuse listeners—listeners such as Pepper Martin, who were apt to become impatient, and were therefore vulnerable to being hustled. Language that is euphonious isn't necessarily clear, and rather than battle out the meaning, many gave up and let Rickey's words stand; Rickey counted on that.

This was a crucial problem between Joe and Rickey. Since his rookie year, Joe had known clearly how Rickey worked, evidenced by Joe in 1933 asking his Carteret pal, Beaner Casaleggi, to negotiate his contract with Rickey. Medwick knew about Rickey when he had himself traded to Brooklyn, and he knew he was one of those "veteranized" players—an "anesthetic"—that Rickey had been dwelling on since he was hired in October of 1942. Rex Barney, who was to have four decisions in 1943, said it this way in *Bums:* "If we had a guy who was the least [bit of a] troublemaker, he was gone."

But for now, Joe stayed.

There was evidence from all over showing the ineffectiveness of the baseball used early in 1943—the balata ball. To begin the 1943 season, of the first eleven major league games, seven were shutouts.

Next was the following description by Tommy Holmes: "the lone extra-base hit in yesterday's game was Joe Medwick's double. . . . Medwick really belted this one, but it died completely for a blooper hit behind third base." The same hit, according to Arthur Daley, "had as much speed, life and resiliency to it as a grapefruit falling off a kitchen table."

May began with a Saturday doubleheader at the Polo Grounds, and though Joe broke his hitless streak at seventeen at bats, by day's end he was one for his last twenty-six. Holmes wrote: "Yussel the Muscle had been having a terrible time, languishing in one of those inexplicable slumps . . . and in the cool of the evening, the fans have been giving him a terrific ride." The next day, Holmes talked to Medwick. "'I just don't get it,' said the muscular left-fielder of the Dodgers. 'I feel all right and if there's anything wrong with my timing, I don't know what it was. I've hit some balls pretty well, too, but they're not dropping where they'd do any good.' Medwick pointed out that he had been hitting right-handers all right but that the southpaws, for reasons unknown, have got him out."

Moved to the number six spot, Joe got a hit in four at bats in Higbe's win on Monday, and two hits on Tuesday to drive in the only Dodger run in a 3-1 loss. Then Joe was hurt.

"'I landed on my right shoulder diving for that ball that Pinkie May hit Monday. . . . It didn't bother me Tuesday when I pitched some batting practice. But then I couldn't raise my arm and Leo took me out when I told him about it.'

"'Kind of tough to be sitting the game out with so much hitting going on,' someone suggested.

"'Not at all,' said the new Medwick. 'It was fun watching the guys hit.'"

The guys hit the new balata ball, which was touted as being livelier than the 1942 ball, but it was also one that "after one good sock," pitcher Johnny Allen claimed, "was knocked all out of shape. You could wear it as a wristwatch."

While the team was in Boston, Holmes said, "The team's best fourth place hitter—when he's hitting of course—was Joe Medwick. But Joseph wasn't likely to start a game until a left-hander starts against the Dodgers. At present, there was no reason to bench either Walker or Waner or Galan against a right-handed pitcher."

Leo's powerful belief that Joe was not able to hit right-handers was put to an interesting test on May 13 against the visiting Pirates.

In the ninth, with the winning run on third, left-handed batter Dixie Walker came to bat. Left-handed pitcher Preacher Hebert, out of the majors since 1933, took Dixie to 0-1 and Durocher called time. Why? Parrott's interview with Durocher had Leo saying, "Well, I thought Walker could hit that Hebert if the old guy didn't sidearm him. . . . So I said to Dixie, 'You go up there and have a look. If he sidearms you, you will be on the spot and I will lift you.' So what happens? Hebert came in there sidearm, Walker fouled the ball into the stands, and I yelled for Medwick. Joe took a ball, then slashed a hit between third and short and it was curtains." Joe was sure he could hit anybody, right or left, sidearm or overhand, and he must have begun to wonder why he was being told he couldn't. He must have begun to wonder if Rickey was just looking for some way and some reason to trade him yet again. A few days later, Newsom was heard to say, "If a man was a .300 hitter, he gets his hits somehow, sometime."

The strongest complaint seemed to be that Joe was not driving in runs. Medwick was driving in runs at a higher rate than Galan, Bordagaray, Vaughan, and Camilli. Frequently, Bordagaray was sent to left field.

The sometime shortstop of the 1943 Dodgers, Bobby Bragan, told me that Medwick had respect from the other players and that Camilli had the same kind of respect that Joe got. Joe was kidded, of course, as teammates were, and in Medwick's case, it was about how he always took more clothes on a road trip than anybody else except Durocher. On those trips, Joe never or rarely played cards, though card playing was clearly something that many team members did. Yet camaraderie on the club was good, and if Joe was not put into the lineup for a game, he, like other reserves, would pitch batting practice to the reserves. These men who played with him were pros, Bragan said, and that meant they did their jobs.

And Bragan vehemently denied the stories that Daniel had been telling about a "silent hazing by his playing associates." "No one disliked Joe," Bragan said in an interview. Everyone could see that Joe was "independent, his own man," a man who was "confident, not abrasive or arrogant," and considering his achievements in baseball, "players looked up to him." Bragan concluded, "he was not making enemies; he was his own man." Not unlike Arky Vaughan, Joe was quiet, by now rarely seeking the spotlight.

The war-bond work Joe and the team were doing continued. There were appearances at movie theaters, defense plants, and businesses where employees might buy bonds. Local businesses also got in on the Baseball War Bond League. At the Waldorf-Astoria, players were auctioned off and "sold" to companies who bid for them, the bid being what would be purchased in war bonds. Arky Vaughan and Dixie Walker were the only players from New York teams who brought in double figures in bids—that is, eleven million dollars. "The original stake in this War Bond drive will be augmented by the additional pledges of sponsors for all kinds of base hits and victories as well as fan subscriptions at the ball park." Both catcher Bill Dickey and Medwick brought in bids of two million dollars in bonds.

When the team traveled to Mitchel Field on Long Island for an exhibition game played in front of the Administration building with two thousand spectators, the sound of airplanes was never absent. That was the day that Joe read he might be traded for Reds shortstop Eddie Miller. Holmes wrote, "It's fairly obvious that the Reds would attempt to solve their ever-present outfield problems with Joe Medwick and probably get one of two other players." Joe must wonder why he was worth, in effect, one third of a player. But the Dodgers did need a shortstop, a fact highlighted by Leo's attempt to play that position and letting Medwick hit for him on June 13. Just one and a half games ahead on June 2, by June 15 the Dodgers were three back, six down in the loss column, and during that time Medwick started four games. Joe, who never took losing well, and who got so much pleasure from hitting well, had this said about him: "[he] was genuinely heartbroken over being locked in the Dodger doghouse; doesn't realize how bad he looks in the field, when his hitting falls off." About the doghouse, Arthur Daley later wrote, "Nor had Leo the Lip closed down that commodious doghouse. . . . The Brooks shuttle in and out with bewildering rapidity."

Still, one of the requirements for good hitting was playing every day. Tommy Holmes said, "I don't know why this was so, but when any ordinary mortal was benched because of a hitting slump it was accepted as just that. But whenever Medwick had troubles with the Louisville lumber, the boys insist on serving him kennel rations." The animosity from the newspaper boys was partly due to Joe's surly moods when he was not hitting well. That was a clear trait in Medwick; unfortunately, Medwick also could be impatient with questions he judged stupid and impatient with the same question asked repeatedly. The writers he liked, he liked; the ones he did not like didn't matter to him. The fans that booed him didn't matter to him either. Jealous of his reputation, Medwick knew how good he was and expected everyone else to know that, too.

And Joe was still the complete hitter. Playing left field in game two on the twenty-seventh, "Muscles Medwick delivered the big blow, a two-run double to left center." He also bunted for a hit in the ninth (against his old Cardinal teammate, Si Johnson) and then scored.

Though close to the Cardinals in the pennant race, the Dodgers apparently didn't believe in themselves. And they didn't believe in Leo, particularly because Durocher still expected to be fired any minute. His gambling and womanizing, his palling with celebrities, did not win him the admiration of the efficient and sanctimonious Rickey. There was lots of talk that Rickey simply had expected Durocher to be drafted and did not want to fire him before he went off to serve his country.

But two and a half months of the 1943 season had passed, the trading deadline of June 15 was two weeks past, and the team stayed pretty much as it was. Still, a big deadline was coming up. In about three weeks, Bobo Newsom's salary was about to go up by $3,000 for staying with the team until after the All-Star break.

Medwick, more intense than ever about his hitting, was working hard at getting back into the lineup. But his age began to betray him and he knew it. He tried, as ballplayers will, to find a way to stay with the team and with his pal Durocher, even if their friendship had cooled in direct proportion to Joe's RBI output.

Joe knew he had not played all that well so far this season. Against Cincinnati, he not only went hitless, he also made a bad throw. Though he had brought his average up to .264, he was benched for two games, then went 3-8 in a doubleheader taken from the Cardinals. Then he was sat down; the team lost and they were four games behind on July 6, a date many players remembered for having been booed in Ebbets and deserted by half of the fans. Leo announced that his outfield was now "Waner-Galan-Walker . . . from now on regardless of whether the enemy uses fork flippers or human beings." Conveniently forgetting Medwick had 2,100 hits, Durocher commented, "Waner had three thousand hits in the National League . . . and I guess he must have got some off left-handers."

Ballplayers were asked to travel overseas to the Pacific to be part of a USO show tour. Commissioner Landis suggested "eighteen players on each team as a good figure to conjecture with," to go overseas after the 1943 World Series. Medwick was one of the thirty-five who volunteered to go.

When Fitzsimmons lost on the eighth, the team was five games back. Back in May, Leo told Joe to replace Dixie Walker in right field. Dixie Walker was the most likable man on the team—indeed, he seemed to be the most likable man in the borough of Brooklyn. In one pre-game show, Walker sang "Mexicali Rose" and "My Buddy" while Gladys Gooding played the organ for him. Medwick had not worked hard at being likable; he had worked hard at being a better player. Some of the players who liked Walker were resentful of this move by Durocher, seeing it as favoritism. Players hoped to be judged on their merits; any worker does.

Any worker also likes to think that he knows how to do the best job. Durocher wanted Newsom to pitch to Vince DiMaggio one way and Newsom wanted to pitch to the Pirate outfielder another. DiMaggio hit a home run Newsom's way. According to catcher Bobby Bragan, near the end of that game, which was won by the Dodgers, Newsom was pitching to Elbie Fletche. With the count 3-2, Bragan called for a fastball, but Bobo threw a spitter and the pitch got past Bragan to the backstop. Newsom put hands on his hips as if to say to everyone that he was exasperated—it's the catcher's fault.

After the game, Durocher was quoted as saying, "I'm not gonna stand for it when a pitcher shows my catcher up," and he told Newsom that he was suspended indefinitely. Holmes quoted Durocher as saying, "I'm not going to stand for that big show boat showing up Bragan." The full story was written up by Tom Meany of the *Telegram*, but when it came out, Durocher claimed it wasn't true, insisting he suspended Newsom for not following his orders on how to pitch to Vince DiMaggio. Leo had told Newsom "high and inside." Durocher yelled it wasn't inside enough. Newsom called Durocher a liar.

And that next day, many of the players were furious at Durocher. If Durocher could get away, they thought, with suspending a player—that is, deprive him of his pay—for something so inconsequential as what Newsom did, then maybe all of their paychecks were in trouble. Arky Vaughan came to Durocher's office on July 10 and told Durocher, "Here's another uniform" you can have. "If that's the way you feel about it, you're suspended too," yelled

Durocher. "You can't suspend me," Vaughan replied, "I quit." Vaughan was famous for his hard work on the team, his seriousness about the sport, and people listened to him. Dixie Walker also quit, supporting Vaughan and Newsom. Leo then tried to change his story; now, Leo said, he was suspending Newsom for insubordination in how to pitch to DiMaggio. But everyone knew it was a lie.

Murray Polner told what happened next at a meeting before game time with reporters present, including Tim Cohane, who had been present for the initial conversation between Durocher and Newsom: "The next day, a few hours before a Sunday game, Rickey perched on a large trunk, the players at the edge of the room, listening to Cohane speak. Frank Graham of the *Sun* was also there and he observed Durocher 'white with rage and shaken by the hostility of his players, who glared at him from every corner of the clubhouse,' all the time saying he had been misquoted. As Cohane talked, Rickey held a cigar tightly in his right hand, whispering from time to time to Branch, Jr., seated alongside him."

"Throughout the stormy sessions in the Dodger clubhouse," Holmes wrote later, "Medwick was an innocent bystander or sitter. He just lounged around, sucking a curve-stemmed pipe and doubtless wondering why Newsom was in the doghouse."

Polner continued, "Cohane resembled a district attorney. Repeatedly he destroyed Durocher's credibility until, finally, his case was set down—the manager had lied. All eyes spontaneously turned to Rickey: What was he going to do now with his troublemaker?"

Polner finished this story by saying, "Privately, Rickey met with Durocher and warned him—as he would do often in the years ahead—that his uncontrolled temper and would-be friends would surely lead him into trouble, trouble even he, Rickey, would not be able to rescue him from. 'Act like a leader of men, Leo,' he advised."

And Rickey? Rickey could dump Bobo and achieve three things: first, he could show Leo that he supported the manager. This was simple administrative sense: you must support your supervisory staff. From his rumpled bed in his suite, as he ate, Rickey held forth, saying "While he's my manager, he's entitled to my undivided loyalty and support and that's what he'll get." Second, he could erase Bobo's salary and upcoming raise. Last, he could get some new players for Bobo, who was almost at his thirty-sixth birthday. In exchange for Newsom, who was the best pitcher on the Dodgers, he received, from the St. Louis Browns, Fred Ostermueller, a pitcher who was the same age as Bobo, but was 0-2 with an ERA of 5.02, and Archie McCain, who would never pitch another major league game. Both pitchers, in fact, were sent to the minors to bring up Luis Olmo, an outfielder. Would Newsom now learn not to catch his manager in a lie?

Newsom's being traded to the St. Louis Browns was, to Parrott, Rickey's way of "tying the can to Newsom . . . essential to the retention of Durocher as manager of the Dodgers." The addition of Ostermueller and McCain meant someone had to go, the club being over the player limit.

Would it be one of the rebels—Vaughan? Walker? No, it was Joe. Joe knew it when Durocher told him that he didn't have to go to all that bother of packing to go to Boston on the sixteenth, the day after Bobo was exiled to the Browns. Joe waited in his room at the Hotel New Yorker.

Joe was a problem for both Durocher and Rickey. For Durocher, Joe's rare lazy play should have resulted in a fine, and Durocher threatened Joe with just such a fine. But the manager didn't carry it out. Rickey wanted Medwick off the team for many reasons. For Rickey, the first reason was always money—Joe's salary. The speeches Rickey had been making about "anesthetics" and "veteranized" players now sounded particularly loud.

Holmes commented, "If the current Dodgers couldn't win this year with guys like Newsom and Medwick, then they can't win without them." Arthur Patterson of the *Herald-Tribune* stated that "in the waning hours before the trading deadline of June 15, Rickey made feverish attempts to get rid of Medwick but none of the other teams wanted him."

Waivers were asked for Medwick. Just after the All-Star break, the Giants claimed him for $7,500. Much was made of the disparity between the large number of dollars Medwick cost the Dodgers and the amount that Rickey was paid for him. But few knew about the Reiser part of the 1940 trade from the Cardinals.

In dollars, Rickey paid Joe half a year, or $6,000, and got from the Giants $7,500. Rickey himself made $150 from the deal, enough to buy many shirts he could throw away. Rickey now had to negotiate a salary with Olmo, coming up from the minors for half a year. Olmo would probably sign for $2,000 or less for the rest of 1943. The meant that another $4,000 was saved. Did Rickey pay himself $400?

As Joe got ready to join his new team, the Giants, in Philadelphia, many sportswriters reflected on Medwick and wrote about events that did not receive comment at the time they happened. Some talked only about 1943, when Joe had played in just forty-eight of the seventy-nine games. Tommy Holmes let his readers know a number of things, including the following: "In his last six months of service with the Dodgers, Joe had been chained to the kennel so often . . . and nobody got very indignant about it. . . . But the Dodgers won the pennant in '41 and they wouldn't have done it if Joe hadn't hit .318 with 18 homers and 88 runs batted in. That was much more than the margin the team won by even if Joe's personal record did not call to mind a banner season by Babe Ruth." Parrott thought about Joe's beaning and wrote, "Although most baseball men think the Bob Bowman beaning in 1940 ruined Ducky as a hitter by making him plate shy, there were many who think that fast pitch really shook Medwick's seeing apparatus out of kilter. It wasn't until the next year that the story came out. Durocher blamed himself for putting Joe back into the game too soon. Medwick had headaches and double vision. . . . But he took the boos and criticism in tight-lipped silence. That's Medwick all right."

At least for Medwick, these were not strangers that he was going to. Joe had played against Ott for his whole career. He had played against pitcher Van Mungo since 1933, and briefly in Brooklyn; Joe Orengo was his Cardinal teammate in 1939 and early 1940; Mancuso had been a Cardinal teammate in Joe's first time in the majors.

By 11 A.M. on June 16, Joe's new job with the Giants was definite. When writers at Joe's "open house" at the Hotel New Yorker asked Medwick about his leaving the Dodgers, "his first remark was 'I am going to prove to Mr. Stoneham [Giants' president] that he didn't make a bad deal.'" Joe sat on a sofa sucking on his pipe. Asked about the Bobo trouble, "Medwick refused to discuss" the brouhaha saying simply, "I didn't have anything to do with the Bobo Newsom incident, but there's more stuff coming out of the Brooklyn club than a German propaganda office." Some writers were trying to tie Medwick to what they were calling "the mutiny," but Joe did not have any part of the rebellion.

With his luggage, glove, bats, and spikes, Medwick traveled to Philadelphia and arrived in time for the doubleheader on July 17, entering the Giants clubhouse and finding Ott. As Ott welcomed Medwick and went over the signs, Joe dressed in the uniform with "New York" in black and orange on the front of a zippered jersey with white undersleeves. Wearing number 3, Mize's old number, Joe became the full-time left fielder: except for sitting out the first game of a doubleheader, Joe would play every inning the rest of the season on a team that was, at the time, 30-47, a winning percentage below .400.

In St. Louis, Joe went 3-4 and 2-5 in the doubleheader, but the Cardinals scored seventeen runs to the New Yorkers' six. Drebinger wrote: "That the Giants lost the first game could scarcely be laid to the doorstep of our muscular Mr. Medwick. Joe, variously cheered and jeered by the crowd in his first appearance in St. Louis in a New York uniform, delivered two singles and a double in a desperate effort to rouse his new-found colleagues." His colleagues had seen him get eleven hits in twenty-seven at bats. The next day Joe was hitting third as the team lost again, and then sixth in the fourth loss against old teammate, Spud Krist. Joe threw out a runner at the plate. He was showing his team what he had left.

But what about his team? Harry Cross, for the *Herald-Tribune* claimed that "the New York players . . . are in a low, defeatist state of mind . . . the club continues to play the type of baseball which was unquestionably below its capabilities." What does a player do under these circumstances? Play well, but not hard? What if you played hard and still lost? Do you get so discouraged that you no longer play hard? And if you still play hard, how was that interpreted? In Norman Macht's book *Rowdy Richard* (1987), Dick Bartell commented: "Although some players disagreed with me, I thought Joe was always for himself first. He was concerned with his own stats and records. Maybe that was the way it seemed to me because the only year I played with him we were on a last place club and that was not an uncommon attitude among cellar dwellers." Joe still wanted to achieve, still wanted to win as fiercely as ever, and still wanted self-respect, but how could he win with a loser club? Joe was still sliding hard, still throwing out runners, still trying. Quitters love company. If Joe refused to join their company, what was he, then, to them? No one else made Bartell's claim about Joe's self-interest and Bartell himself said, "some players disagreed with me."

The month ended with a loss in Cincinnati for the Giants, and with Freddie Fitzsimmons traded from the Dodgers to replace Bucky Walters as manager of the Phillies. From the Giants, the Dodgers got two pitchers, Bill Lohrman and Bill Sayles, plus first baseman Joe Orengo. In return, they got pitcher Johnny Allen and first baseman Dolph Camilli, but Camilli wouldn't report.

Many Dodger fans were furious at Rickey, failing to understand the hardened businessman aspect of Rickey, an aspect described in the following two sentences: "he played baseball's cozy gentleman's agreements to the limits in waiving players, he diddled his minor league rosters, and double-talked his players into contracts for stingy salaries. In this, of course, he was not unique, just more sanctimonious." Dan Daniel wrote in his column "with the departure of Newsom, Medwick, Fitzsimmons, Camilli and Allen . . . a total of $63,500 was dropped off the pay roll (and replaced by three players whose pay was $15,000) . . . [and] the defeat of the Brooklyn mutineers was complete . . . in making his stand for constituted authority, even if that authority be somewhat less than satisfactory by Rickey standards." Less satisfactory, perhaps, because, though no one seemed to notice, the two loudest mutineers, Vaughan and Walker, had not been dealt away. Less satisfactory because Dodger attendance for the year was sharply declining. More satisfactory because Rickey had saved the team $48,500.

Carl Hubbell, veteran of 3,500 innings, won a 3-2 game against the second-place Pirates in late August with the help of Joe, who "led off with a double to right field, advanced to third on a wild pitch and scored on Sid Gordon's fly to right," and then, later, "Medwick blasted his second straight extra base hit, a triple to left center, sending Witek home. . . . Gordon batted in his second run, laying down a bunt as Medwick slid home." Of the three runs in the game, then, Joe scored two and drove in the other. (Could this be characterized as "playing for himself"?) A loss the next day led to a sweep of a doubleheader on the twentieth when Joe raised his average to .304, fifty-four points higher than his team. Since being traded, Medwick played in all of the twenty-nine full games his team had played. Was he really playing all these games for himself? The team was short of outfielders; he was doing his job.

By September 26, the Giants dropped to forty-three games back and to their ninety-first loss of the year. It was the worst losing record in the history of the club, worse even than the 1892 team, before Muggsy McGraw took over.

By season's end, Joe hit two points above the league average of .276. But making just 27 hits in his last 126 at bats (.185) kept him from his first .300 year in the majors. It was Joe's first year playing fewer than 130 games, coming to bat fewer than 500 times, and his first year with fewer than 86 RBIs. For the first time, Joe was not in the top five in the league in any category; his highest mark was eleventh in RBIs.

As Naples fell to the Allies, the Commissioner's Office made plans to send two squads of volunteers to the Pacific Theater. In addition to Joe, by now the volunteers included pitcher Bucky Walters, and other National leaguers, such as Stan Musial, Dixie Walker, Vince DiMaggio, Dick Bartell, Walker Cooper, and Augie Galan. But it was not long before the players were told that the need for military use of transport canceled the trip. A few players made a trip to the Aleutians instead.

18

The Best Right-Handed Hitter in Baseball, 1944

The *Herald-Tribune*'s Rud Rennie tried to sum up, as the 1944 season was about to begin: "Going into the third year of war-time baseball, the major league teams were not so good as they were. But, like all war-time products, they were the best available. . . . Continually uncertain of what fate and selective service may do to them, the managers believe they can put on a good show if they can just keep what they have. In any event, they believe they will play the full schedule of 154 games. . . . Mistakes will increase the uncertainty of play and make it more exciting."

The Cultural Encyclopedia of Baseball cited Bill James, "[who] estimated that 40 percent of the major leaguers during the war years were qualified to be at that level of play. He bases the statistics on an analysis of how many wartime players lasted beyond the end of the war as compared to a later, nonwar year."

From Medwick's Sappington home, Joe had been "employed as personnel counselor at the Curtiss-Wright St. Louis plant on the 1 to 8 A.M. shift . . . classified 2-b in the draft [he] said he liked his war plant job but that he might make up his mind at any time to join the New York Giants." He began to eat carrots for his night vision, since his job was at night and the probability increased that he may play in more night games than the previous years as wartime restrictions loosened. He told John Drebinger that his goal was to "climb back into the .300 circle."

The Giants training camp was in Lakewood, New Jersey, on the South Branch of the Metedeconk River, thirty miles east of Trenton. Lakewood, known as a health resort, received many of the Giants, who were bussed there from the Hotel New Yorker. Medwick was not with the team yet, and in fact, for a while there was some doubt whether Joe would show up at Lakewood for the training season since he had "an industrial job."

Joe apparently arrived in New York by plane but did not hurry out to Lakewood. He may have seen himself on the big screen as a Dodger in the Red Skelton movie *Whistling in Brooklyn*, the movie that was just opening at Loew's State. Then Joe arrived at camp in a snowstorm, reporting to the Monterey Hotel.

Drebinger described Joe's first practice: "Joe Medwick . . . was among the first on the field and refused to believe his senses when he felt the unusual heat. 'It's a plot to get me to take off in a hurry those extra five pounds I'm carrying,' he said as he plunged into the drill."

On March 22, Cross told his readers "every evening in the Monterey lobby Joe Medwick and Danny Gardella were in earnest conversation. Muscles was giving the Bronx pepper box some advice on outfielding and batting. . . . Medwick had a bat in his hand today for the first time." Gardella told me that he thought of Joe as "cordial and unaffected . . . his strong personality showed itself in how Medwick would overexert himself" on the ball field.

From this we can see that Medwick continued to have the respect of other players who sought him out for advice. There was plenty of time for that advice with the rain arriving and the cold continuing.

A few days later, Joe King led off his column in the *World-Telegram* with the headline "Medwick Seen as Cleanup King of the Senior Circuit." King reported:

> There was a hunch in the Giants camp that Joe Medwick once again will be the cleanup terror of the league. The thought was based on Ducky's timing and power in hitting drills, his eagerness to grind off the suet, and his obvious pleasure to be here. . . . "Ball playing's my trade. I'm at the disposal of the draft board, same as anyone else, and I'm ready when they are."
>
> Ernie [Lombardi] was deeply interested in Ducky Medwick who in turn seems deeply engrossed in pulverizing the pill. "Hey, meathead," Schnozz called Joe the other day. "Mize used to be meathead, but since he left we call Medwick that." Lombardi explained. "Meathead, I hear

you were going for .350 this season," Ernie continued. "That was what they tell you," countered Ducky, "but I do say that it will be over .300." . . . Lombardi commented when Ducky strolled on, "He wouldn't be kidding a bit if he got hot. He was absolutely the toughest hitter I ever worked against."

Lombardi had caught almost 1,200 National League games since 1931.

The Giants traveled to Bader Field in Atlantic City to play the Yankees on April 9 and 10, and after winning one of the games, they traveled back to New York with the season due to open in a week. They worked out in the morning at the Polo Grounds on April 11, and then were driven by Navy bus to play at Floyd Bennett Field that same Tuesday afternoon, where the temperature gauge read forty degrees. The Wednesday game at the army base at the Newark airport was rained out.

The Giants finished their training season not having played very much at all. They played eight exhibitions, three of them major league games; in those games, four starters pitched a total of forty-six innings. As the season began on April 18, Medwick may have noticed that he hit twenty-eight points lower in 1940, the beaning year, than in 1939, and that in 1943 he hit twenty-eight points lower than in 1942.

In Brooklyn, Ace Adams won 3-2 as the Giants moved one half-game game into the lead. As the game began, Dodger "relief hurlers marched to the bullpen adorned in gaudy knee-length coats that looked like blue silk shower curtains trimmed with fur collars." After the game, Cross of the *Herald-Tribune* said,

> it was Joe (Hot-Shot) Medwick . . . who made the masses moan. . . .
> "Medwick beat us all alone . . . ," chanted the ancient newsboy . . . near
> Ebbets Field yesterday. . . . A Dodger castoff . . . was the despair of the
> 12,343 loyalists who breasted a wintry wind. . . . The scoffers say that
> Ducky will cool off as soon as he ducks a few beanballs. The other side
> maintains . . . that he was happier under Mel Ott and had more incen-
> tive under Mel Ott than he had with Rickey, Durocher and Rickey
> again . . . when he stepped into the batter's box a fifth time there was
> not a boo but the scattered cheers with which knowing but reluctant
> Flatbush acknowledges a gallant enemy.

With the Giants a game ahead of the Cardinals, Joe was 9-19 with five RBIs in the first five games of 1944. Rain caused game three at

Ebbets to end a tie. Then it was time to board a train for Philadelphia, where Joe made two more hits in the team's first loss of 1944. Medwick told Jim McCulley of the *News* that he thought the carrots that he'd been eating a lot more of (for night vision) had helped his eyes.

Then, because of wartime housing problems, there was no hotel space for the team, and they boarded the train back to New York for an open day; they then returned to Shibe Park on April 27, but the rain there forced a return to the home-field Polo Grounds to play Brooklyn.

With all this time passing and no game to report on, Stanley Woodward's column, "Views of Sport," commented on "The Saga of Medwick's Revenge." Woodward quoted a letter concerning Medwick's two games at Ebbets and the unsettling effect that performance had on Rickey. And, seeing Joe's place in history, he described Medwick as a "stationary outfielder, inventor and perfector of the sitting down catch."

> When historians get around to summarizing the 1944 debacle, it may well be that Medwick's two-day rampage in Brooklyn will be cited as the most memorable contribution to an outlay season. When the Carteret vendettist ambushed the Dodgers he paid off a lot of old scores, scores climaxed with his release on waivers to the Giants last summer. Medwick's notions about his worth always has a curdling effect on the Swami's [Rickey's] sense of economy. Many hold that it was Joe's sulking resentment of Rickey's devotion to the coolie minimum that led to the slump in his play at St. Louis, his trade to the Dodgers. . . . Fierce in his pursuit of the loot which he denied Medwick, Rickey found himself in Brooklyn. And who was that smoldering in left field? . . . It was Medwick! . . . In this crisis, he [Rickey] reverted to his old formula . . . even though the Cardinals had just disappeared up the road in a cloud of dust . . . Branch . . . committed assault and battery . . . on the pay roll.

The deletion of Newsom, Camilli, and Medwick made Rickey think that "there seemed slight prospect that any of the victims of his strategies would bob up to haunt him on the playing field. . . . But hell hath no fury like a Medwick scorned. All last winter he lay in the weeds whetting his dirk. That he should elect the first week of the season to plunge it into the gizzard of his ancient foe would seem to be the epitome of poetic justice."

Sunday April 30 was doubleheader day, as most Sundays were, and "the opener was by far and away one of the most bizarre exhibitions seen under the lee of Coogan's Bluff," Harry Cross wrote. "The Giant players, before a crowd of 56,068, were walked seventeen times to tie a forty-one-year-old record and were even walked six times in a row. The final score of 26-8 was one that the winner Harry Feldman didn't have to worry about, particularly when one player, first baseman Phil Weintraub, drove in eleven runs by himself." The attempt to pin on Feldman the nickname "Phalin' Phil" might not work anymore.

Joe had two hits but scored five times in four at bats. The hits were enough to bring his average up to .378, fifth in the league. After game one, as usual in the Polo Grounds, all the players walked to the clubhouses in center field, visitors climbing the left stairs, and the home team climbing the right. Then "a firebrand threw a pop bottle at the Giants players [and] it hit Joe Medwick in the groin." Joe did not play in game two. Charley Mead was played left field for one of his thirty-nine appearances in 1944, but the next day was open and Joe could play on May 2 against the Blue Jays (a name that the Philadelphia team tried out for a while). Joe drove in all of his team's runs with a homer—it broke up a seven-inning 1-0 no hitter by Charley Schanz—but also lost a ball in the sun, and Bill Voiselle took his first loss, 5-2. When Ace Adams lost the next day, suddenly the Giants had three teams in front of them. The trip to Boston resulted in four losses in five games. Joe was 8-19 in the series, .421, raising his average to .381, second in the National League and one hundred points above his average with the Giants in 1943.

Two open dates ended with a game at Crosley Field in Cincinnati. The 4-3 game on May 11 was lost by right-hander Rube Fischer. Medwick, hitting .366, was benched the next day and Ott put himself into the lineup. Why? "The Giants' skipper," Drebinger explained, "gave the impression that he was more than a little dissatisfied with Muscle Joe's recent fielding lapses. Most surprising of all, Ott seemed to consider Medwick largely at fault for the two eighth inning doubles that dropped in left center to wreck yesterday's game, although according to observations from the park's lofty press coop, it appeared that [center fielder] Rucker was largely, if not wholly, responsible." Could it be that Ott was tired of being outshone by Joe? Was there anger on the part of manager Ott since player Ott was hitting a mere .144? (And Ott was just a year and a half older than Medwick.)

Then, in the game on May 17, "Joe Medwick snapped out of his recent slump" with four hits, a run scored, and four RBIs. Then he was 2-4 in the last game to bring his average to .371. (This was a slump?)

The team stayed overnight in Chicago and took a morning train to St. Louis for a night game that would begin the series. Just before the start of this game, "the fellow workers of Joe Medwick last winter in the Curtiss-Wright plant . . . gave him a scroll before the game."

Next, in Ebbets Field for a night game (the first in two years in Ebbets), Durocher decided to walk Ott, loading the bases with one out, to get at Joe. "The crowd didn't like it when Ott was purposely passed and they liked it less when Medwick promptly smacked one to left field to drive in two. Medwick the old Dodger, was not popular at Ebbets Field." The Giants' lead of 2-1 was lost in the ninth when the center fielder and right fielder collided. The New York team moved into a tie at eight games behind the leading Cardinals—tied, that is, with Boston and Brooklyn for fifth. A record of 13-17 would not get a team into the first division.

Then it was time for a three-way game for the Fifth War Loan Drive at the Polo Grounds, the three teams being the New York area clubs. Before the game, Cal McLish won the fungo-hitting hitting contest, Bobby Bragan won the closest-to-the-barrel-with-a-throw-for-catchers contest; then there was "a series of musical numbers that were boisterously ushered in by Milton Berle." The game ended with the scores being 5 for the Dodgers, 1 for the Yankees, and 0 for the host Giants. For the War Loan, the fifty thousand fans bought $56,500,000 in bonds.

Joe was picked for the 1944 All-Star game. Only Ott had played in more—ten to Joe's nine.

At 9 P.M., Eastern War Time, the second night-time All-Star game began. Though the American League scored first, the National Leaguers scored four in the fifth, two in the eighth, and one in the ninth to win, 7-1. Marion, Musial, and Medwick sacrificed in the game as Joe hit for Sewell in the eighth. After the 1944 game, Ott was given a "magnificent silver cigarette case with a diamond in the center of it. All the players received mementos, ranging from plaques for newcomers to Master Melvin's cigarette case." Net receipts went to the Bat and Ball Fund for soldiers and sailors.

At the end of July, the Giants were keeping a seat in the first division by a half-game, and Joe was 34-126 in July, .270.

August 1944 ended with idle days. Joe was 11-25 in the third ten days of the month and for the month he hit .474: 47-99. At .343, Joe had raised his average thirty-five points and netted a gain of forty-four points on Stanley Musial and on 33-year-old ex-teammate Dixie Walker.

Arthur Daley began his column of September 3 with the headline "A Man Who Collects Hairpins":

Maybe it was just coincidence but you never could convince Joe Medwick that that's all it was. In Pittsburgh, he picked up twelve hairpins in the hotel lobby, and during the series with the Pirates, he slashed out twelve hits. Mrs. Medwick probably had the largest collection in the country—in spite of their scarcity on the open market—because her devoted spouse was an avid picker-upper of any hairpins he can find.

This was not a new superstition with the Muscle Man. He's always done it in the fond belief that each hairpin means a base hit. Stories [about grabbing hairpins meant for other players] . . . have led to the belief that Joe plays strictly for Medwick. In fact, he never had had too favorable a press, an item he never had fully been able to understand, although he always had tried to be cooperative.

"I've always hustled for the good of the team," he declared in his blunt outspoken fashion. "But I always felt that the best way I could do it was by having the best batting average I could get. There's no sentiment in this game and by helping myself I'm best helping the team. The thing that hurt me most this year was when Mel Ott fined me $100 in Cincinnati. I admit that I pulled a boner and deserved the fine but the story came out that I'd been fined for not hustling instead of for pulling a stupid play. That's what hurt. . . ."

Joe's decline in popularity at St. Louis he lays firmly at the door of Branch Rickey, a man he'd never vote for as president—or even a dog catcher.

"In 1937," he said, a trace of bitterness in his voice, "I led the league in everything. . . . . I was living in St. Louis that winter and never a word did I hear about a contract from Rickey until about twenty-four hours before the deadline. Then it came with—get a load of this, brother!—a $5,000 cut in salary. Naturally, I wouldn't sign and the papers were given the story that Medwick was a holdout. Instantly I was in bad with the fans and I never recovered the popularity I'd always enjoyed there. . . ."

Medwick can't quite explain his hitting renaissance. Finding hairpins wasn't entirely responsible for it. . . .

"Sometimes I think that it's because I know more about it," he mused. "But then I wonder if all this scientific study and analysis was the bunk because you tend to outsmart yourself. In the old days, I just used to step up there and take my cut. As long as you're swinging, you're dangerous.

"Another thing was that I was a long time in recovering from the beaning. . . . I've always felt that I've never had as much power since then. Maybe I was a little gun-shy at the plate, too. That would be natural, but the thing that helped me most was when MacPhail ordered helmets for all batters. . . . I've worn one ever since."

The superstitious Medwick paused for a moment and added brightly, "Maybe I can give you an even better reason on why I'm hitting this season. When Charley Mead was with the club he was using one of Dick Bartell's old bats. The day he left the team, I broke my bat and picked up the Bartell model. All I did was bang out six hits and I've adopted Dick's old war clubs ever since."

Joe had mellowed and softened considerably since the days he was a member of the flamboyant Gas House Gang of a decade ago. But he still swings a potent mace at the plate even though he probably had walloped more bad pitches for solid hits than any man ever to swing a bat. And he'll undoubtedly continue to do so unless the Government clamps down completely on the manufacture of hairpins. As long as he can find them, the Muscle Man will produce at the plate.

But not after he was again hit by a pitch. "Medwick's left elbow was so bruised and numbed by the Art Herring pitch which removed him from the Ebbets Field series that he hasn't been able to swing a bat and he didn't make the Philadelphia trip. . . . Ducky was on one of the most productive splurges of his career and the layoff might disturb his swatting focus." But the report on the x-rays was slow in being read, so Medwick rested his left arm for about nine days and missed seven games. At least he was able to work out before the Boston game on September 7, and then he was back in the lineup on September 9. He was determined to catch both Dixie Walker and Stan Musial in the batting race.

September 21 was marked by two more losses to visiting Chicago and by the Cardinals winning the pennant. The Giants, on the other hand, were five and a half games out of fourth place but had twelve games left.

No hits were left for Joe that year. Against the Cubs, he did contribute "three spectacular catches to keep down the hit total," but on the last of these catches, he injured his back. He could not play; he could not gain on the leaders. In the last eleven games of the year, Joe had one at bat, and so had to settle for 165 hits in 1944. His team won one-third of their games in September, so there would not be any cut of the series money.

In July 1943, the *Herald-Tribune* characterized Medwick being waived to the Giants as a "bargain-counter deal . . . the drabbest chapter in Medwick's glamorous career as a major leaguer."

Joe Medwick in 1944 was the top right-handed hitter in the majors and third overall.

But—there always seemed to be a "but" during wartime—Musial, at age twenty-four, didn't hit .500, or even .400, against the presumably weaker pitching. Other players whose careers lasted well beyond the war years—competent players like Vern Stephens (twenty-three), Johnny Hopp, Whitey Kurowski, Wes Ferrell, Wally Moses, Tommy Holmes (all at age twenty-seven), and Frank McCormick—did not have their highest years during this period. Stan Hack did not hit as well as Joe, nor did Andy Pafko (twenty-five), Marty Marion (twenty-six), Bill Nicholson (thirty), Mickey Owen, Babe Dahlgren (thirty-two), Phil Cavaretta (twenty-eight), Lou Boudreau (twenty-seven), or Stirnweiss (twenty-five). Of all these players, only two hit above .300. Why weren't they inflating their averages if the pitching was so easy?

Dan Daniel put Medwick on his All-Star team at left field. (Could the Dodgers have used him?)

For his team, Medwick was one of two .300 hitters; he was first in RBIs and fewest strikeouts; he produced 21 percent of the Giants' runs, and made 12 percent of the team's hits. He had the highest fielding percentage on the team at .993. His batting average was seventy-four points higher than the team's. (Could the Dodgers have used him?)

In the National League, with fewer than five hundred at bats, Joe finished third in average, fourteenth in hits, ninth in on-base percentage, eleventh in RBIs, and fifteenth in slugging average. He was the fifth best clutch hitter in the league. He was second in fielding percentage among outfielders. (Could the Dodgers have used him?)

Joe Medwick was twentieth in Most Valuable Player voting.

In early summer of 1943, Commissioner Landis's office in Chicago had asked for volunteers from baseball to travel to the Pacific theater after the World Series. The idea was that eighteen players—two teams—would conduct clinics, play games, show movies, and in general help to raise the morale of the servicemen and women serving in the Pacific. At the time, "U.S. forces advanced through the Central Pacific, continuing the offensive thrust aimed ultimately at the Japanese home islands. The plan of attack called for them to take the Gilbert Islands, then the Marshalls and the Marianas." Tarawa, for instance, was taken in November 1943.

Joe Medwick was one of the few who volunteered for that trip. But the trip was canceled, the rule in effect being the answer to the wartime question, Is this trip necessary? The decision was that it was not. Transport would be used for battle.

Again in 1944, Commissioner Landis asked for volunteers for USO (United Service Organizations) work. Medwick once again signed on. "'Rounding up a group of volunteers was no easy feat,' [Cardinals outfielder Danny] Litwhiler recalled. 'Ford Frick said to me, I've asked a lot of guys to go but they refused and you'd be doing me and baseball a personal favor.'"

The trips would not begin leaving until the season was over, and meanwhile, Frick's office worked on rounding up more volunteers. Umpires, sportswriters, and managers were approached, and soon a group of twenty-three men agreed to go, with a departure date penciled in for about a month after the 1944 World Series.

Receiving orders on October 25 to gather in New York, Medwick was told in his papers to go to the TWA ticket office in St. Louis to pick up tickets reserved by the Army Office of Special Services. Medwick was ordered to fly to New York City for processing and assignment.

Once in New York, Medwick was instructed to check into the Hotel New Yorker and there he palled around with the twenty-two other baseball men who would be put into five groups. Joe, of course, after being in baseball for fifteen years, knew just about everyone there very well: Carl Hubbell and Mel Ott from the Giants; Freddie Fitzsimmons and Frankie Frisch, teammates before, and managers now; Paul Waner and Dixie Walker, old Dodger friends; a sportswriter from New York's newspaper *pm*, Tom Meany; and the St. Louis writer, Roy Stockton. And Leo Durocher. As Daniel told it: "It developed today that Medwick had asked to accompany his erstwhile pal, Durocher. And it was an open secret that Leo was opposed to having Joe with his unit. Once close friends, they parted when Durocher sent Medwick to the Giants, and Leo wonders why Ducky Wucky is so eager to accompany him. Said Durocher to a friend, 'I hope Medwick goes with some other unit. The boys are sure to ask why I traded him to Ott, and I am sure not to gloss things over. I will tell them I had to get rid of Medwick because he was not playing ball for the Brooklyn club. I am not going to lie.'" Joe and Leo did get along, however.

The five groups were processed, getting inoculations for small-
pox, cholera, yellow fever, typhus, and tetanus, and then the men
were told to make out emergency wills and send them home. (USO
work resulted in twenty-eight deaths during World War II.) Next,
each man was given an identification card and the back of each card
said that in case a person was captured he was to be given the same
privileges as a captain in the Army of the United States. The twenty-
three volunteers were then measured for officers' uniforms at one of
Manhattan's toniest stores.

With the majority of the processing in Manhattan now finished,
from their hotel on Fifty-fifth Street the men were put on a bus for
Fort Totten, located at the confluence of the East River and Long Island Sound in Queens. At Totten, more processing was completed
and more equipment was handed out. Then they were told to wait;
their travel did not have priority.

As the five groups waited for air transport, Special Services suggested some rehearsing in this country, so Medwick and the others
practiced their shows at Fort Totten and at nearby camps, and got
used to army food.

For more than nine days, as departure became more likely, every
morning at a ten o'clock formation, some groups were alerted to the
possibility of leaving soon; those groups were confined to the barracks area. But the odds were that they would stand down at the five
o'clock gathering in the afternoon. The groups, going different
places, would all be leaving at different times on different transport.

The different units were now clear, but their assignments, as was
usual, were kept vague so as to remain, in effect, secret. In the unit
heading for the Pacific were players Johnny Lindell of the Yankees
and his teammate Tuck Stainback; from Detroit, 53-year-old manager Steve O'Neill and the umpire Beans Reardon; and Frank Lewis,
a Cleveland sportswriter.

The Near East unit featured Carl Hubbell, who was now director
of the Giants' farm system, Fat Freddie Fitzsimmons, who was no
longer a player, and Harry Heilmann of the Tigers, who no longer
played either. They were joined by Umpire Bill Summers and
Chicago sportswriter John Carmichael.

Going to India, Burma, and China were players Dixie Walker,
Luke Sewell, and Paul Waner, along with *New York Herald-Tribune*
writer Arthur Patterson.

Heading for France, Belgium, Luxembourg, Holland, and Ger-
many were manager Frankie Frisch and players Bucky Walters of

Cincinnati, Dutch Leonard of Washington, and part-time player Mel Ott, joined by *St. Louis Post-Dispatch* writer J. Roy Stockton.

Joe Medwick's group was bound for Italy. Along with manger Durocher of the Dodgers was Tom Meany, writer for the short-lived New York newspaper *pm*, and Yankee outfielder Nick Etten, an Illinois-born left fielder who was two years younger than Ducky but only got to the majors in 1941. Joe knew Etten as a good hitter but an erratic fielder. Thus Medwick was one of just seven full-time major league players to go on the USO tours. At the time, there were four hundred major league players (plus sixteen managers and about twenty-five umpires), many of whom, of course, had off-season jobs.

The days passed well into November. The group of twenty-three decided that the only way to handle being on and off alert so many times was to joke about it, or in this case, sing a song about it; the song was a new version of "Shuffle Off to Buffalo." In his best Flatbush/Alabama tenor, Dixie Walker took the lead on the song with the rest joining in and contributing verses. Singing was heard, too, as Medwick's thirty-third birthday was celebrated in the barracks on November 11.

After three weeks of waiting, the volunteers were ready to get on any plane at any time. Four of the units had left; only Medwick's waited to go.

When a sergeant came up the stairs and called the names very early on Thanksgiving Day, Joe's group dressed in their uniforms and excitedly finished packing their bags.

Once the men were driven to headquarters, the bags were weighed and Joe, Leo, Nick Etten, and Tom Meany were shown to the bus that took their unit the seven miles to LaGuardia Airport. As soon as they passed through customs, Medwick's group moved quickly to a final briefing room, for the instructions on water landings, the use of Mae Wests, and the use of a raft and a signal generator. A giant airplane awaited them.

Getting into the plane, they made sure to have aboard with them two hundred dozen autographed baseballs and the twenty-two-minute movie of the 1944 World Series. The USO unit called "Here's the Pitch" was airborne. Stockton's column later said that "Flying the ocean in years to come may be a commonplace weekend lark. It was a thrill to us."

Once out over the ocean, the plane ride was spent napping, going to the cockpit for a smoke, signing the crew's taped-together collection of currency from countries visited, the sort of autograph pads that air crews favored so much (called "short snorters"). They quickly realized that the uniforms that looked so good in Manhattan might not be all that comfortable (or serviceable or warm). They ate their Thanksgiving meal—baloney sadwiches. They worried, as Tom Meany wrote, "how able-bodied men such as themselves would be welcomed—or vice versa—by a bunch of guys fighting for their lives," particularly since both Etten and Medwick were under thirty-five. Joe told no one about his punctured eardrum (although Durocher did know about it).

Roy Stockton remembered the particular frustration of the newspapermen: "We were told we couldn't keep diaries or any record showing places we had visited, army units or individuals. We couldn't carry cameras. We couldn't carry written messages."

But these men were doing what they considered to be their patriotic duty and accepted the hardships as they knew all the service men and women must accept their hardships.

As the plane droned on through the November skies, Medwick might have thought about the family war map. Like many Americans, a map cut from a newspaper was pinned up in his home. It was a practice among many to keep track of the war on the maps as the news arrived. In this way, Medwick would know that in Italy "Axis forces tenaciously defended every mountaintop and valley amid deteriorating winter weather from behind a series of fortified lines that stretched across Italy from the Tyrrhenian Sea to the Adriatic." Yet, moving through German defensive lines, the Allies

> liberated Rome in June. Then, in a two-month long summer campaign that was very uncharacteristic [for its speed] of Italian operations until that time, Allied forces pushed the enemy 150 miles north to the Arno River by mid-August [1944]. Axis forces, however, began new preparations to frustrate any continuation of the Allied drive by building another belt of fortifications, the Gothic Line. The new line generally consisted of a series of fortified passes and mountaintops, some fifteen to thirty miles in depth north of the Arno River and stretched east from the Ligurian Sea through Pisa, Florence, and beyond. Farther east, along the Adriatic coast where the northern Apennines sloped down onto a broad coastal plain, Gothic Line defenses were generally anchored on the numerous rivers, streams, and other waterways flowing from the mountains to the sea. One key to the line appeared to be the central Italian city of Bologna, . . . only a few miles north of the defensive belt.

Joe knew about the bloody landings in Salerno, with 9,000 Allied casualities, as well as the murderous fire at Anzio and Monte Cassino. He also knew that the most newspaper-worthy battles were being fought in France. The soldiers in Italy were told that veteran units were to be pulled out of Italy and put into France. Lady Astor (stupidly even for her) called the British Eighth Army, which was carrying much of the burden in the Italian campaign, "D-Day Dodgers." It was unlikely that the American Fifth Army in Italy liked the label either. The fighting had been muddy and murderous, with the Nazis often having the high ground.

In 1944, "Between 10 September and 26 October . . . there were 29,000 Allied casualties," and "Losses were so severe that on 10 October, Prime Minister Churchill asked the United States to send at least two additional divisions to the Italian front. His request was turned down by U.S. Army Chief of Staff General George C. Marshall, who preferred to send new U.S. units to France where significant progress was being made rather than to Italy for an increasingly bloody and stalemated campaign in a secondary theater."

Then, as the baseball season wound down in America,

> The U.S. 34th and 91st Divisions, with support from corps artillery, assaulted the Gothic Line on 12 September [1944]. The fighting was typical of the Italian campaign. The terrain facing Fifth Army units consisted of numerous mountain peaks, streams, deep valleys, broken ridges, and rugged spurs, all offering excellent defensive positions to the enemy. Although significant numbers of troops were involved on both sides, small unit actions predominated and rarely were units larger than a battalion engaged at any one time. The compartmented terrain tended to erode the Allies' three-to-one advantage in manpower, and whatever successes were gained were due largely to the individual soldiers' valor, resilience, and determination.

As Frank Coffey's book, *Always Home: Fifty Years of the USO* pointed out, in World War II there were four USO circuits. The first was called the "Victory Circuit," which was comprised of big movie and radio stars who appeared far from the front and performed in front of larger audiences that came to see the show. The second circuit was labeled "Blue," and was for vaudevillians and other lesser-known performers who performed in smaller shows closer to the front. The third was called the "Hospital Circuit." The fourth kind of USO tour, the kind Joe Medwick was on, was known as the "Foxhole Circuit," the battlefront circuit.

At the end of a twenty-four-hour flight, the four-man group landed, probably in Naples.

Once off the runway, the mud on their dress shoes made Joe and the rest of the volunteers find out quickly about the need for field footgear and canvas leggings, items they quickly purchased at the Post Exchange. After that shopping, their Special Services officer introduced them to their driver, who showed them to their vehicle, a converted weapons carrier towing a trailer. As they loaded the trailer with the baseballs and film canisters, the driver sternly reminded them, yet again, about wearing their steel helmets. They were now on the foxhole circuit, in what the Army called the MTOUSA, for Mediterranean Theater of Operations United States Army.

Soon they learned how taxing this trip would be. They learned that they would pretty much live in the clothes that they had on, and they began to learn the new slang—especially the phrase "sweating it out." In Italy (called the "Forgotten Front" since D-Day) the phrase still meant that "Jerry is always looking down your throat." Baseball chats with GIs were called "Walkie-Talkie Fanning Bees." The servicemen had only been alerted that some players might come to Europe; as was usual, the various papers—*Yank* and *Army Talks,* as well as local unit papers and the daily *Stars and Stripes*—kept silent about exactly where the shows would be. (Twice in December in the Naples edition of *Stars and Stripes* there were interviews with Durocher. But the questions were very vague.)

For the USO troupe traveling first up Amalfi Coast, the show really started as soon as the weapons carrier pulled into a unit area. Soldiers swarmed around the truck, tossing questions at each member of the group. Leo was the best known, having been on radio shows and having had some dialogue in the Red Skelton movie *Whistling in Brooklyn.* Joe was as well known and questions were asked of him in the friendliest way possible.

For Medwick's group, the rehearsals proved that the show ought to work like this: Tom Meany served as the master of ceremonies, first introducing the ballplayers. Next, the World Series film of twenty-two minutes was shown and then each player would talk for a while and answer questions. (Sometimes the audiences were ill suited for the movie. British soldiers, for example, hearing that an

American movie was about to be shown, would arrive, and then quickly groan and leave after learning that the movie was not a cowboys and Indians show.) A ten-minute quiz program would be the end of the show. Ten or twelve GIs would be asked up to the front of the building (or tent or barn) and Meany would ask true or false questions until there were three winners left, each of whom would be given autographed baseballs. That would have been the end of the show for Medwick and the others except that afterwards, many soldiers, hungry for baseball news—hungry for life back home— would come up to the stage and ask for autographs and ask about their favorite players and how their favorite teams might do in 1945. In this way, the group might do about four shows a day, traveling some distances over rough terrain between shows, terrain strewn with destroyed German armor. The shows, Tom Meany wrote in *pm*, were "most unusual. Any time four guys with a twenty-five-minute film can hold a soldier audience for two hours just by talking, it is a defiance of all theatrical theories and the law of gravity. Neither Etten, Medwick nor I hold any illusion about our talent . . . but the stories of Medwick and Etten always were well-received and in the bull sessions afterward they were quite as well received as Leo," who often spoke for forty-five minutes of the two hours.

Traveling north from Naples, one of the places the troupe performed was the Aldorado Playhouse in Caserta; they also appeared on a radio show, with Joe acting as an umpire. *Yank* magazine reported that "Lippy Leo Durocher carried his grudge against umpires all the way to Italy with him. 'My only regret,' he told GIs, 'is that I can't see how Beans Reardon is taking it on his trip to the Pacific. No self-respecting foxhole would take *him!*'"

It was around this time that Medwick, along with many others in uniform, were given a meeting with the Pope. The story goes that the Pope asked about Joe's occupation and Joe answered, "Your Holiness, I'm Joseph Medwick. I, too, used to be a Cardinal."

By Christmas, the troupe "entertained on a hill north of Rome and fell to, with all the others, on a real turkey dinner with all the trimmings." The troupe also filled the Red Cross theater in Rome, the Barbarini, which no other entertaining group could do. (The Rome USO Canteen was the first overseas canteen.)

Traveling to other outfits, the group certainly saw plenty of blown-out buildings, wrecked railroad yards, and bomb craters. They learned there were three signs you needed to pay close attention to: "Road and ditches cleared of mines." Then "Road *to* ditches cleared of mines." Lastly, "This road not swept for mines." They learned to remember and give passwords, and did not hesitate to show their dog tags to sentries. They learned to eat and like powdered eggs and grapefruit juice, a GI staple, as well as lots of Spam and canned chocolate pudding. They learned to live by candlelight, to not break down at the sight of terribly wounded soldiers in hospitals, but to try to cheer them up. As the draft regulations were changing, Medwick learned to talk to GIs interested in the "work or fight" policy. That is, if you weren't in uniform, then you had to be in defense work.

Before long, as they traveled, they let Special Services and their driver watch out; they were too tired. The days of their shows lasted from 5 A.M. to 11 P.M. since they talked as soon as they were dressed. They sometimes performed more than those four shows a day and often to small groups because the majority of their shows were so close to the front lines that their audiences were limited to small groups, the officers not wanting to risk larger units within range of enemy artillery.

One time they set up for a show, but the audience was mudbound so there was no show—not with a crowd of zero. At the end of the day's work, "Here's the Pitch" was billeted with a unit and was expected to talk to all hours there as well. They were glad to do so, seeing how happy everyone was to see them there. Since eleven of the sixteen major league teams were in five cities, and since only radio was the same-time mass medium, few soldiers had ever seen the players this close: this was exciting for the soldiers because Joe's group had players and managers from the Giants, the Phillies, the Yankees, the Pirates, and the Dodgers.

Tom Meany tells the story of being asked by one soldier, "'How's Smitty,'" referring to a fanatical Brooklyn fan, an undertaker who closed down his shop so he could travel on the road trips. Joe had solved the question he and Durocher knew they would be asked. Tom Meany wrote about it this way: "One of the questions invariably asked of Joe Medwick was why he was traded from Brooklyn to the Giants . . . it was really an attempt to embarrass Leo Durocher. Joe finally came up with an answer that pleased everybody, 'Rickey came and I went.'"

The worry about how they, as healthy men not in service, might be treated was dispelled early in their tour, once Durocher spotted Mule Haas, now a $60-a-month corporal. Haas told Meany that "'morale was an overworked word. Every civilian enterprise from manufacturers to night clubs professes to be maintained for the purpose of the serviceman's morale [but] I know that the kids tonight got a kick out of the show. They were talking about it for days in advance. . . .' I asked Haas how he felt about ball players who were not in the Army. 'Being in the Army or being in baseball is a matter of luck. There is nothing more democratic than the draft. When your number is called you go.'"

While the armies of Patton and others rapidly advanced through central Europe, the Fifth Army was still slowly slugging it out and frequently under attack. But, as Meany pointed out, war doesn't have to be spectacular to be dangerous. So "Here's the Pitch" was greatly appreciated simply because the soldiers in the Mediterranean theater knew what they were doing wasn't glamorous. A future Congressional Medal of Honor recipient named Red Shea, nominated for the award for his capture of three German machine-gun emplacements in one battle, was riding in the weapons carrier with the troupe and asked Meany "if I could spare one of the autographed baseballs signed by Durocher, Etten and Medwick. When I gave him the ball, Red thanks me profusely and said, 'This is the biggest thrill I ever had—getting a baseball and riding in the same vehicle with Durocher, Etten and Medwick.' There was nothing for us to do but look out the window and pretend we hadn't heard." Meany claimed that "Shea's reactions were like those of practically all the soldiers. . . . The war went out the window when they had a chance to talk about home life. It wasn't just baseball, although that was the principal medium in our case. It was anything about home."

Home and baseball evoked images of bright colors; in the war everything seemed to be either white or brown. Brown was the mud that everyone in Italy dealt with—mud on the lines before the mess tents and barracks; mud in waves as you traveled, or mud frozen into hard ruts and frozen into waves; mud caught up in the wheels of trucks and the treads of tanks; mud to yank each foot out of. Brown was the color of everyone's clothing as well. Medwick, like the others in "Here's the Pitch," wore a brown top thigh coat over a brown vest, over a brown shirt and light brown tie, the whole uniform being splattered and caked over with brown mud. You might see white in some of the hospitals, white in the starched outfits of nurses away from the front; white on the bed sheets and bandages and casts. White and red for the wounded. The white, too, of the snow in Italy during winter as the troupe moved up the Italian peninsula.

Once the troupe was told there would be no film because the Germans had recently captured the Special Services projector and generator. Once they did a show for an audience of 9,500 at a Naples race track. Along the way they met Phils pitcher Herman Besse among the wounded in Italy, and Shirley Cobb (daughter of Ty Cobb), who was working as a nurse in Italy. They kept moving north toward the Gothic Line, a line at which the Allied offensive had stalled due to the rain and even more mud.

By New Year's Day 1945, after being in Italy a month, the troupe moved south again, and then from Naples, Medwick's unit flew to Peretola airfield in Florence and then were billeted in the Hotel Excelsior on the Arno River, which had been liberated four months earlier. "The Excelsior has been taken over by the British but it was also used by war correspondents, visiting USO Camp Shows units and ENSA troupes . . . the British equivalent of USO. The resulting welter of uniforms in the lobby gives it the appearance of a cafeteria on an MGM lot during the filming of a war picture—Scotsmen in plaids and kilts, British officers with swagger sticks and monocles, turbaned and bearded Sikhs from India and Americans." Nick Etten, making history he said, lobbed a baseball from the fourth balcony to a military policeman below.

Medwick ate in the opulent dining room, which was included as part of the 25-lira-a-day charge. While a string ensemble played to the diners, consommé was served on fine linen and eaten with fine silver. The main course was served on a covered dish, and after the cover was removed with flourishes by one of the many waiters, what Medwick saw was Spam.

Up in his room, Joe could listen to Armed Forces Radio as well as hear Berlin Sally spew her propaganda. In Florence, the unit played the Apollo and saw the Spaghetti Bowl, a football game in the Stadio Communale between teams from the Fifth Army and the Twelfth Air Force, before twenty-five thousand, along with WAC (Women's Army Corps) cheerleaders and seven generals.

As the troupe visited soldiers in Empoli and Sesto, Meany reported that "We were up and down [Route 65] every day . . . and in the general direction of Bologna but not quite to Bologna because there was a guy named Von Kesserling and some of his associates between us and Bologna." It was in Sesto that someone not only slept, but also snored, through Medwick's talk. "Backstage, Joe complained about the visitor's manners" until he was told that the snorer was "an Eyetie who is supposed to be working for Capt. Tracy."

Many of the troupe's performances were, in fact, north of Florence, in places very close to the Gothic line. They were now doing many of the shows in tents, in the cold rains of January. Even when "Here's the Pitch" played to combat units like Fano to the east or Via Reggio to the west, everyone carried a rifle since Nazi soldiers from the Russian front were reinforcing the German side of the Gothic line. In Gagliano and Monghidora and Loiano, all north of the Hotel Excelsior, everyone was well armed. Medwick's USO unit went to Porretta, inside the province of Bolgna, where they were told that they were "within seven hundred yards of the front."

One of the last places the troupe did a show was Pistoia, at an evacuation hospital twenty-two miles northwest of Florence. And then they left from that airfield. After forty-two days in the Mediterranean, after playing to seventy thousand men, after twenty thousand miles, Joe arrived back in the United States on January 15.

Once the men were back, many of them received requests from the War Department to talk to defense-plant employees about the conditions on the battle front. The War Department had found that workers' absenteeism dropped dramatically after speeches by the USO baseball men. Unlike men in the service, the workers knew that the players were not under orders to deliver a government-written speech. It was unlikely that the baseball men would gloss over, lie, or exaggerate. For some of the men, therefore, even though they were back from overseas, their war work would not be done until it was time to report for the 1945 season.

19

New York and Boston, 1945

Now back from the Mediterranean, Joe watched with the rest of the country as the war neared its end, though there were still rumors of a "work or fight" edict being put into place for everyone. Medwick probably returned to the Curtiss-Wright plant until he had to report to the Giants' 1945 training season in what Doc Weaver, the Cardinals' trainer, called "the Long Underwear League." In the meantime, insurance man Ray Hunsacker in St. Louis talked to Joe about joining the firm when his playing days were done. Those days might, indeed, be done because the treatments for his back, which was injured on September 22 in a game against the Cubs, were not restorative.

The back trouble was clearly inconstant so manager Mel Ott was careful with Joe, not letting him play too many innings early on in 1945.

By April 5, Medwick was getting angry and impatient. "Joe Medwick, suffering from a dislocated sacroiliac [for two weeks] . . . visited a NY specialist yesterday," the *World-Telegram* reported. "Medwick was confined to bed with the painful injury until a local osteopath succeeded in snapping the bone into place," said the *Herald Tribune.*

When Joe returned to the team, his back was strapped into a corset and even then he was not put into the lineup. The Giants didn't seem to need his bat because by May 4, they were 9-4 and leading the league. "Medwick's ailing back had improved and he had been working out every day. Steve Filipowicz had been doing so well in left field that Ott will not break up a winning combination at the present time." Filipowicz would make twenty-three hits in thirty-five games in 1945.

After V-E Day had been celebrated, the games resumed following three days of rain and a game at Camp Upton. Medwick got into his second game, 0-1, but he didn't play a full game until May 14, a month into the 1945 season. Then he hit only 1-12, though during the 6-0 game on May 16 Joe King related, "Medwick certainly saved the shutout and may have insured the victory with a galloping, tumbling one-hand grab of Roy Hughes' liner to left center in the fifth with one aboard, two out. . . . Medwick held the ball, although he stepped on Johnny Rucker's foot as he made the play. Voiselle thought so much of the catch that he shook Ducky's hand as he came off the field." Medwick's willingness to go all out probably meant he felt cured, and on May 17, he homered into the right field seats off right-hander Rip Sewell; he also doubled, driving in his first run of the year. Joe homered again on the May 19, and went 1-3 against Preacher Roe.

Through May 26, the Giants kept winning, but Joe was not contributing very much, going 3-21. Though still batting cleanup, he was called upon to sacrifice ("obediently," as John Drebinger described it), but he warmed up a little on May 27 as he made two hits against right-hander Rip Sewell. But the performance was not enough for Mel Ott, and on May 28 Joe King wrote that "Medwick had had a fair trial in his accustomed clean-up berth during the last thirteen games and he had failed to step into the ball, to hit it solidly and he had not knocked in runs . . . batting in five markers only three of them with hits." Medwick's cleanup spot was taken by Napoleon Reyes, the Cuban third baseman. At 13-56 (.232) Joe was not bringing enough power to the RBI slot. Red Treadway moved into left field.

Through June 4, Joe pinch-hit and filled in at St. Louis. But when the team returned home to play Brooklyn, Joe was in the lineup. "Joe Medwick at the moment was the unmistakable hero of the occasion," Drebinger reported. "In an astounding comeback, Muscles Joe had blasted four hits, including a homer and a double to bat in all the Giant runs . . . [and] made a nifty one-hand catch of Basinski's drive in the seventh. . . . The return of Medwick came as a complete surprise as Ott had intimated out West that he had given up on the veteran slugger."

After being benched for the June 15 game, "Secretary Eddie Brannick of the Giants announced . . . that Joe Medwick, the Ottmen's veteran outfielder . . . had been traded." Joe missed seventeen games (about a third) and the Giants wanted to trade him before the June 15 deadline. Joe and Lefty Pyle were swapped to the Braves for backup catcher Clyde Kluttz. Joe was hitting a mere .304 and eleven RBIs in ninety-two at bats, which projected to about sixty-five in a full season. Medwick's trade was a very small item in the *Herald-Tribune*. Mel Ott's daughter asked her father about the trade: "Why did you trade him, Daddy?" As far as Medwick understood, Ott didn't like him.

Roger Birtwell wrote in the *Boston Globe*, "In acquiring Medwick, the Braves were gambling on a guy with a tricky back. His sacro-iliac . . . had kept him out of the Giants' lineup a good part of the season . . . and it must be remembered that Medwick—slowly recovering from his 1940 beaning—finished third in the NL batting derby with a mark of .337. But if Mel Ott thought Ducky would do it again, would he have sent him away?"

Manager Coleman immediately placed Joe as the Braves' cleanup hitter and put him in left field, forcing the move to right field by Tommy Holmes, who had a batting streak going since June 6. Under the heading "Smoke Signals," Harold Kaese's report on Joe's first game read, "Joe Medwick broke in with the Braves by being hit his first time up [Pitcher Art Herring apparently wanted to send Joe a message] walking his second trip, driving in a run with his third try and then going out his last three times at bat."

Whitey Witelmann pitched an exhibition game against a service team on June 18 and the team went on to the Commodore Hotel in New York. The next day, after General Eisenhower rode in a ticker-tape parade through Manhattan, "his automobile enter[ed] the center-field gateway under the clubhouse" at the Polo Grounds. Eisenhower got out of his car at first base and sat in a box, keeping score until rain forced him to the office of Horace Stoneham. The general got to see "three rousing singles by Joe Medwick, whom the Giants . . . had shipped to Boston on the theory that Muscles Joe had outlived his usefulness," the New York paper said. Melville Webb, for Boston, said "the Wigwam tourists beat the New York Giants . . . for Jim Tobin, the flutter-ball boy."

Even being at home didn't seem to help Joe. The Braves dropped a doubleheader to the Reds, won on June 28 and then lost again on June 29, even though there was a "great peg by Medwick to nip Eric Tipton at second base." Though the team was losing—now at 30-31—Tommy Holmes, Joe's outfield partner, had now hit in twenty-five straight games and had made over one hundred hits. When the Cardinals won on June 30, Joe had made 4-21 in the last five games, lowering his average to .293. And when Adams in the sixth made a fine running catch of one of Joe's fly balls, "Joe went to his position," the cartoon caption the next day read, "kicking his glove all the way." He still loved base hits; he still loved his own excellence. He was still serious.

July began with a doubleheader against second-place St. Louis. Joe contributed one hit and one RBI to the two wins with his bat and his arm, too: "Verban was thrown out at the plate by Joe Medwick as he tried to score from third with the tying run on Debs Garms' pinch hit fly to left." Game two also marked the twenty-eighth straight game with a hit for Tommy Holmes, tying him with Joe for one of the longer streaks in National League history.

Holmes had to wait a day to continue his streak, which he did on July 3 against the Cubs. During that game (and after a 5-32, .156 streak in the last seven games), Medwick was replaced by "Square Jaw" Ramsey. Joe had a good seat to watch a mob of three hundred come after Umpire George Barr to celebrate the Fourth of July. Both Barr and Charlie Grimm had to be rescued. Medwick was used as a pinch hitter in the next three games and went hitless in them, although he did watch Holmes pass Hornsby by hitting in his 34th straight game, while taking the RBI lead at the same time. Butch Nieman, known for his skill as a pinch-hit home-run man, played for Medwick in most of the games: Joe's average was stalled at .265.

What must he be thinking? He knew his speed had been severely slowed, and yet his fielding still remained good. His arm had not given out on him the way his legs had. He had played in forty-five this year out of seventy and not always full-time; of the eighty-four games that remained, how many would he play in? How many would he start?

Joe didn't play on July 7 or 8, and July 9 was an off-day. Normally the time of year for the 1945 All-Star game, the Office of Defense Transportation had so limited travel that "War Fund Ball Games Replace All-Star Tilt," as the *Globe* headlined. For the Braves, a July 10 game at Fenway against the Red Sox took the place of the All-Star game.

The next day, the team boarded *The Minute Man*, a Boston & Maine Railroad train, for Chicago. There, on July 12 Joe sat in game one while Tommy Holmes's streak ended at thirty-seven games, seven short of Willie Keeler's record in the National League, and sixth all-time. But Medwick played in the second game, placed in the fifth spot, and he started the next six games, both in Chicago and St. Louis. Though hitting .375 in the games, he only drove in one run while scoring two. These performances seemed to make him a full-time player again, at least until the last eight games of the season. Now fourth on the team in hits, fifth in average, and sixth in RBIs, his team still was stalled at or below .500. Pitcher Mort Cooper's sore elbow kept him out of many games so that he could only throw just over one hundred innings in 1945. The 1945 race seemed to be coming down to Chicago, St. Louis, and Brooklyn.

Boston started August at 42-52, in seventh place, nineteen games behind the leading Chicago Cubs. "Bob Coleman, the manager who was so deeply hurt at two weeks of bad baseball by his players that he gave up his job," was replaced by Del Bissonette for the last sixty games of the season. In a column by Roger Birtwell, Medwick said of Coleman: "He's the best manager I ever had." Del Bissonette said that one of the few things he knew for sure about the team was that Joe Medwick would play first base. Bissonette also knew he would play without pitcher Mort Cooper, whose performance showed an "utter collapse" in his ability to throw strikes. As a team, twenty-two names would appear as Braves pitchers that year.

By mid August, there was a pattern to Medwick's assignments for Boston. Joe was being run for and hit for against right-handers, which made him yet again a victim of traditional baseball thinking. Eventually, of course, all hitters stop producing, and it is management's job to decide when the lack of production is hurting the team. Certainly, by now, neither Joe nor anyone else had any illusions about him being the Medwick of 1937. He most certainly couldn't get down to first base fast enough. His fielding remained competent, and his throwing was still to be feared by base runners. But the choice for interim manager Bissonette seemed to be between Butch Nieman or Joe at bat.

And Roger Birtwell had this non sequitur to offer: "Butch Nieman will be in left in place of Medwick. Butch usually hits well in Cincinnati." Joe, in fact, played game one of a doubleheader and pinch-hit in game two. Mort Cooper's arm hurt too badly for him to continue pitching his game in Cincinnati. Then, fearing the loss of the only sleeping cars available when the team was scheduled to travel to Pittsburgh, the Crosley Field series was stopped early.

Joe started four of six games—the team lost five—and got six hits in seventeen at bats. Joe's abilities had been doubted and he had been replaced; yet he had hit .348 on the western road trip, to join Wietelmann and Gillenwater as the Braves' hitters over .300 for the sixteen games.

In Brooklyn, Joe pinch-hit in the first game, lost by Bill Lee, Joe's old Cub rival and another Scottdale player. After Medwick doubled in the second game off of right-hander Hal Gregg to drive in the only Boston run, Bissonette sent in Bill Ramsey to play left field. In the July 29 doubleheader, Medwick was 3-4 and 2-4. Ebbets was a friendly place: 6-12 with two RBIs. He had now made 65 hits in 220 at bats for the year and had raised his average to .295.

In the Polo Grounds, "Medwick, filling in for the injured Vincent Shupe, covered first base for the Braves," Drebinger of the *Times* wrote. "He did not perform badly either and enlivened the show with a bit of byplay whenever Gardella happened to be there." Joe went 3-12 while playing first base in the Polo Grounds as he struggled to go above .300 for the year. For now, the best he could do was .295.

With the Dodgers in town for seven games with three consecutive doubleheaders, Joe must have been eager to play. In many of the games he was the major offensive force: in the August 3 game, the first of the series, "Muscles Joe Medwick . . . closed the portals of baseball's hall of fame in Hal [Gregg's] face." Gregg had a no-hitter until "Medwick, first up in the eighth went back to his old-time Gashouse Gang habit of swinging at bad balls by whacking a line single to left on a high, fast ball that was about level with his eyebrows."

After a travel day, he was in the lineup again with a left-hander pitching, this time as a cleanup hitter against the second-place Cardinals' Harry Brecheen. Brecheen allowed six hits and three of them were Joe's, who also threw out a runner at second base. Bob Coleman sat Medwick with Red Barrett pitching and Joe only pinch-hit in game two on September 6. Against George Dockins on September 8 Joe got his 85th hit in a 4-0 loss.

Medwick played in two of the four games in Chicago and got just one hit as he was playing first base again. Still in the infield, Medwick made two doubles and two singles against Pittsburgh, but the team lost two and dropped twenty-one games under .500.

Though he had two more at bats, he made no more hits all year. He was unwell, and on September 19 the newspapers were calling what he had the grippe. By September 25, when only four regular season games were left on the schedule, a number of Boston players left the team for the year, including Bill Lee and Joe Medwick.

Eleven million men would be getting out of military service very soon and Medwick knew he had not impressed anyone this year, even with five steals. (His teammate on the Braves, Dick Culler, tied for twenty-first in the league in steals with seven.) Medwick's pinch-hitting numbers were 3-17. If the Braves weren't going to use him in 1946, then would he be released so that he could look for other work? Surely, a .284 hitter could find work.

20

\

The First Play-Offs, 1946

Joe took his family to Florida again, near St. Petersburg, at the beginning of the year. And on February 8, the AP reported from Boston that "Joe (Ducky) Medwick, one of the greatest right-handed hitters in National League history, today was unconditionally released by the Boston Braves. . . . Despite his comparative youth, Medwick's legs had slowed up so much that he now appears 'all washed up' as a major leaguer after fourteen years of brilliant campaigning."

On March 3, the AP reported: "Mexico Seeks Medwick. Star Outfielder also had Two U.S. Major League Offers. Joe Medwick . . . disclosed today that he had three baseball offers under consideration. One of the bids was from the Mexico City club of the Mexican National League, Medwick said. 'It was most tempting,' he declared, 'but I wouldn't want to leave this country to play ball unless I had to. The game had been very good to me and I'd feel like a heel if I jumped it.' Medwick said he had two major league offers, one from each circuit."

One of Joe's contacts was Bill DeWitt, who had been treasurer of the Cardinals until 1936, when he moved next door at Sportsman's Park to take the position as the St. Louis Browns' general manager. Medwick told the executive that he had worked hard in a gymnasium all winter and had brought his weight down to about 7 pounds below his normal game weight of 179 pounds. Questioned later about his situation, Medwick said, "Gosh I'm only 34 and I can still play in the big leagues. They have been saying a lot about my legs betraying me. I never was one of those speed merchants, as they say. But I can still hit if they give me a chance to stay in there."

Medwick signed that day with the Browns and soon Browns manager Sewell said, "there must be good reasoning by eight National League managers who have been seeing Joe to let him depart." Still, Medwick packed his bags for Anaheim, California, to report for spring training with determination "to show the National League its folly in turning him adrift." When a game with the White Sox at Pasadena was canceled, Joe, as he had done in Scottdale seventeen years before, ate a sandwich and drank a bottle of milk as he rode the bus with twenty-four teammates. Joe Schultz, Jr., who was Joe's batboy in Houston in 1931, was now his teammate on the bus.

Medwick did not make it to the Browns' opening day. He didn't play against Pittsburgh on March 7 or against Hollywood on March 9. Through the end of the month, as the team moved south and east, Medwick was never in the lineup against Phoenix, El Paso, Del Rio, or San Antonio.

On April 5, 1946, in Houston, Medwick was unconditionally released by the Browns. "He had no chance to beat out any of the more youthful St. Louis outfielders," the *St. Louis Post-Dispatch* said: "His career probably came to an end here today."

Joe's son and daughter got to see a lot more of their father at an odd time for him—during the baseball season. Medwick had not given up hope that he could still be in the majors; he didn't look for other work just yet.

April and May passed for Joe in St. Louis—nine weeks passed.

With the trade deadline set at June 15, the Dodgers came to town to play the Cardinals on June 10. Joe still felt he could play and could be useful.

Joe visited the Dodger dugout in St. Louis, looking, some said, surprisingly trim. The first-place Dodgers lost that game to "Harry the Cat" Brecheen, a left-hander, on June 10, and the second-place Cardinals were just two games behind the Dodgers. The next day, Joe and Leo met to play golf, and in addition to a newspaperman, playing in the foursome was Jack Benny, who had been traveling with the Brooklyn team. As they played, it seemed as if either Joe was selling himself to Leo or Leo was more carefully considering hiring Joe. It was likely that Leo wanted to see if Joe was ready to be a part-time player. Many believed it was this golf outing (Joe being the winner) that brought Medwick back to the Dodgers.

That night, the Dodgers lost to still another left-hander while they felt the absence of starting right-handed outfielder Luis Olmo, who had jumped to the Mexican League. Olmo, once touted as "the Spanish Joe Medwick," hit .313 in 1945, driving in 110 runs. As the Dodgers left town "according to Leo, several Brooklyn players formed a Medwick lobby, and talked Joe up in the clubhouse." The players all knew "Eddie Dyer's well-grooved practice of using left-handed starting pitchers exclusively against the Dodgers" and that was a problem the team had to solve if they were to win the pennant in 1946.

Rickey had many problems in Brooklyn. One was that, like many men as they age, Rickey was thinking about his legacy. Considered by many a genius—a pioneer—he knew there was a nine-year gap between the winning of pennants in St. Louis, just as he knew he had not won a pennant in Brooklyn in his time there.

Medwick was a changed man, too. A milder man by now, he could watch as his contemporaries faded, were traded, moved out of baseball. From his 1934 Gashouse Gang days, only infielder Burgess Whitehead remained, a part-time player with Frankie Frisch at Pittsburgh.

Then Daniel's report read: "'It was Durocher's idea to spot the old slugger in the pinches against left-hand pitching . . . his bat might win two or three games for us . . . and I have an idea he still hits left-handers pretty good. As good as any spare we have now, that's a cinch. . . .' Leo said he took the hint and signed Ducky as a free agent." Medwick, in fact, hit .392 in twenty-four games against Brooklyn in 1945; he made thirty-one hits and drove in eighteen runs. At this point, Durocher was willing to say he'd win the pennant if the team got to be eighteen games over .500. Leo would be half right.

Medwick may or may not have been good luck to his team, but it was ahead by five and a half games by the end of June. But the next night, just before game time, Joe signed his Brooklyn Dodger contract for 1946 and then he was put into the starting lineup against the seventh-place Phillies and their left-hander, Art Lopatka, when Reiser's throwing arm was too sore to play left field. Before a crowd only one hundred short of capacity, Joe, hitting third, doubled to right-center to score Reese with the tying run, the first of six that inning. When right-hander Tommy Hughes replaced Lopatka in that inning, Durocher replaced his right-handed hitters with his strong left-handed hitting lineup—but not Joe. In the fourth inning, Medwick singled behind Eddie Stanky's walk and then both scored on Cookie Lavagetto's double. He was replaced late in the game by Gene Hermanski. So in his first game back in the majors after nine months, Joe had two hits, scored two runs, and drove in one.

After the game, Tommy Holmes's headline read, "A Marked Down Medwick May Be Bargain-Basement Special for Our Dodgers." After describing Medwick as "the old muscle man [who] had been . . . a bit of driftwood on the baseball beach," Holmes noted that "Joe was likely to see quite a bit of action . . . as long as Reiser's throwing arm suffers its periodic aches and squeaks." Soon it became clear that many times against starting left-handed pitching, Furillo would be in right, Dixie Walker in center, and Joe in left. Galan was used for his switch-hitting but Leo no longer seemed to favor Hermanski. Joe, in effect, became the number two right-handed outfielder, behind Furillo. But that move would take a while.

But between July 2 and July 14, Joe was only at bat two more times with one hit as a pinch hitter. On July 15, "Durocher, angered by yesterday's double defeat, came up with the odd remedy of starting Hugh Casey, his relief pitcher, for the first time and putting Muscles Joe Medwick, recently acquired solely for pinch hitting purposes, at first base." Medwick's two hits in three at bats didn't produce any runs and his two errors, in front of 26,877, led to Cardinal scoring. Joe's play at first base "was a surprise to no one, since that was never his trade." By the end of July, the lead was still three and a half games over the Cardinals.

After a three-game series with the Cardinals, the lead was one and a half and Pete Reiser was out again. His wall-head concussion in the fifth inning on August 1 caused him to be carried off the field on a stretcher. Medwick, playing now for Reiser, sent a ball "whistling out toward the left field stand on a flight that might have carried it into home-run territory on a less windy day. But [Four Sack] Dusak . . . made a near duplicate catch of the one that brought Reiser to grief." With just nine at bats, Joe had five hits and a walk in July of 1946. Joe would be used much more frequently as a pinch in the next two weeks and he would play an even more important role in September.

When the Reds came to town, Joe started in left and batted fifth against lefty Johnny Vander Meer. With the Dodgers down 2-1 in the sixth inning, pitcher Rube Melton guessed he had a loss coming. Melton had been hit for in the inning by Stan Rojek, who tripled; after Stanky's single and Reese's fly ball, Rojek scored. After Furillo made out, Walker singled. Harold C. Burr of the *Eagle* told what happened next: "'I'll get you off the hook,' Joe told the crestfallen Melton as he picked up his bat. . . . 'I'm going to sock Johnny Vander Meer for a home run.' [Melton] stood to be the losing pitcher. It was pleasant for him to listen to Medwick's prediction, but it all sliced up like baloney to the Rube."

When Medwick homered, "Melton didn't sit quietly on the bench. He bounded up the dugout steps and was a one-man welcoming committee after Stanky and Walker . . . had pounded the self-appointed hero on the back and shaken his horny hand. 'What were you going to do with a guy like that calling his shots?' the Rube asked the rest of the Brooklyn bench when the roar had subsided and the boys stopped throwing towels." The home run was memorable as well for Joe since it was his 200th home run in the majors. This would not be Medwick's last called shot in the majors.

Those three runs were what Brooklyn needed, not just for the lead, but to stay in the game, as the Reds scored twice in the eighth to force extra innings. After the replacement of "Fireman" Beggs, Galan went into left and Reese's squeeze bunt in the fourteenth scored "Stretch" Schultz to win the game 5-4.

Joe continued to pinch-hit in the next eight games and drove in two runs on sacrifice flys.

Medwick made out for Behrman on the fifteenth and then he was put into the game on the eighteenth against the Phillies and pitcher Lefty Hoerst. It was a game the Dodgers won 3-2, but "none of the Dodgers was as jubilant as he might have been," Louis Effrat reported, "because Joe Medwick . . . was beaned, removed on a stretcher [by four teammates], and taken to Peck Memorial Hospital. Medwick, unable to get away from a wild curve, was hit [behind the ear] . . . [and] fell to the ground but retained consciousness until he was brought to the clubhouse where he passed out for a short time. . . . Medwick did not wear a protective helmet." As for Medwick's concussion, "the Brooklyn ball team [was] heartened that the beanball injury suffered by Joe Medwick . . . was not serious." Joseph C. Nichols told his *Times* readers, as the Brooklyns headed west to finish out the month. Joe's stats appeared in the *Times*: 9-29 with nine RBIs.

At Pittsburgh and Cincinnati, the Dodgers won four, but the Cardinals were winning even more. Joe rejoined the team for a split with the Cardinals at Sportsman's on the twenty-fifth and a loss the next day, putting the St. Louis team ahead by one game. But the race was tied the next day with a 7-3 Dodger win. With two losses at Chicago, the Dodgers ended August two and a half games behind. The early April prediction about the Cardinals running away with the pennant now seemed about to happen.

On September 1, the Dodgers won game one with the Giants, and then Joe kept his team in game two by tying the score at one in the seventh, the Dodgers going on to win 2-1. On September 2, Joe was 2-7 with a walk, a run, and an RBI. The RBI tied game two. Medwick waited on the third but on the fourth, with Warren Spahn pitching, "the Dodgers tied it in the third . . . carrying the tally across on Muscles Medwick's rifle shot single to left." His fly drove in what would be the winning run in a 3-1 game.

When Reiser came back, mostly recovered from his pleurisy, Joe sat for a while and only got up to give Reiser some relief in a runaway Dodger win on September 8. By September 10, Brooklyn was still two games back of St. Louis, though they had won ten of eleven.

On September 14, the Dodgers split with Chicago, and on September 16, "Joe Medwick, whose absence was felt so much on Sunday, had got over his stomach trouble and had himself quite an afternoon. He got a double and two singles and drove in two runs . . . with the left-handed Bob Chipman replacing starter Hank Wyse in the first inning, Leo rushed in his right-handed batting reinforcements, shifting Galan to first base . . . and placing Carl Furillo and Medwick on the picket line."

After the game, Roscoe McGowen relayed team secretary Harold Parrott's surprise announcement that "the Brooklyn management would present an automobile to every Dodger who was voted a full share in the World Series spoils."

The Dodgers lost to Chicago 10-7, though Joe went 3-5 with a run and an RBI, but they won the next day to be two back with twelve to play. Medwick played both games of a Pittsburgh doubleheader, and after being 0-4 in game one, he drove in the second run and scored the third in a 3-0 win for Ralph Branca.

Wednesday, September 25 started with ceremonies. Before the game, the Reverend Benson prayed, "We ask You not to give the Anheusers out there in St. Louis any better break than You give us." Murray Polner wrote about a gift presented to Branch Rickey at the ballpark: "the 1946 Dodgers spontaneously presented him . . . with a Chris-Craft boat they named 'Dodger,' each player paying about $300 toward the gift." There were three games left; Brooklyn was behind by one game.

After Reiser broke his fibula four days before season's close, Higbe won 8-2, and Medwick, Reiser's replacement, was 2-3 with a single, a home run and three RBIs. St. Louis, idle, now led by one half-game. Friday, the Cardinals lost and the teams were tied with two games to play.

On Saturday, a day was given for Higgleby, Kirby Higbe's clubhouse name. The seventeen-game winner was presented with a set of golf clubs and two $500 bonds. September 28 was also the day when, for the thirty-six men who had been voted full shares of the team's World Series money, "Ten Studebaker cars—the brand Branch Rickey was presenting to the players—were driven onto the field and the players, one by one," McGowen reported, "were called to the field microphone to pick publicly the models wanted. Several of the boys, notably Walker, Reese and Higbe, called on their wives to make the choice." In the game, Joe didn't start against Boston Braves right-hander Johnny Sain. The 7-4 win gave the Dodgers a temporary half-game lead and Durocher was exuberant. "We've caught 'em—in fact, now we've passed 'em. Let 'em catch us tonight if they can."

When the Cardinals beat the Cubs that night, the teams were tied on the last day of the season, September 29, a Sunday. Durocher's column in the *Eagle*, ghosted by Parrott, said, "If it's any news to you, I'm bringing no suitcase to the game today. . . . I'm not planning any trip to St. Loo."

President Truman, a Missouri man, understood that "the Cardinals still just have to win tonight" if the Dodgers lost. In Brooklyn "despite objections from members of the Marble Collegiate Church Men's League," who were making a short excursion over the city on an American Airlines plane, when the plane "circled over Ebbets Field, Dr. Benson, pastor, remarked 'God bless everyone on that field' and later 'Pray thy protection, oh Lord, on this plane . . . and we ask for the success of the Dodgers.'"

But the season-ending Sunday resulted in a Dodger 4-0 loss. After the game, many fans stayed on the field in front of the right field scoreboard to see how the Cardinal game ended. "Not all the Dodgers waited in the clubhouse," Arthur Daley reported, "for the definite news that the Cubs had officially won from the Cardinals. . . . The real diehards who waited [in the trainer's room where a radio was positioned] until the final flash were Bruce Edwards, Joe Medwick, Ed Head and Danny Kaye." Joe was still serious. Once the 8-3 Cub win was final, the Dodgers started to pack to travel to St. Louis.

After his game, Cardinal manager Eddie Dyer told reporters: "There was something I want you all to know. It was Branch Rickey who assembled this team. He got these ballplayers while he was still running this ball club before the war. And he was responsible for what I know about this game."

In July, Durocher said that he would win the pennant if the team got to be eighteen games over .500. The regular season ended with the Dodgers 96-58.

The Dodgers caught a train to St. Louis that night to begin the two-wins play-off, the first-ever major league play-off.

October 1 was the date of game one, and after Durocher was visited by Al Simmons and Ray Blades, among others, he announced that Medwick would start, partly because Reiser was finished for the year, and partly because of a pitching surprise. Murry Dickson, the Cardinal right-hander who was everyone's guess as the starter, was replaced by Howie Pollett, the left-handed twenty-game winner, who was supposedly too sore with a pulled muscle in his left side. Durocher had to change his lineup with the appearance of Pollet, and so Galan came out and "Muscles Medwick, still an eyesore to St. Louis, replaced Augie Galan in left while Schultz took over first in place of Ed Stevens," John Drebinger related.

His team down 2-0, Medwick came up in the eighth and singled Reese to second. It was one of just eight hits against Pollett, and after Tepsic ran for Joe, Walker forced him and shortstop Marty Marion made his "miraculous catch." Harry Walker, Dixie's brother, made a fine catch of Reese's drive in the ninth, and after Schultz was struck out, the game ended.

The team's baggage had been brought from the Chase Hotel (where Branca had left his wallet and glove back in the room) and they met at Union Station for the ride back to Brooklyn on the train called "the Dodger Special." It arrived at Penn Station at 4:45 P.M. on October 2. The game was due to start in twenty-one hours.

In that game, when Joe batted for the fifth Dodger pitcher in the eighth inning, his team was behind 8-1. The three runs the Dodgers scored in the ninth were not enough, and left-hander Brecheen, in relief, struck out two with the bases loaded.

After the 8-4 win, Dyer "was almost sentimental in his remarks about the courage of the Dodgers, so much so that there actually were tears in his eyes when he had concluded."

Before the World Series was over, Joe was released by the Dodgers. Branch Rickey had gotten rid of Medwick for the third time, and once again he claimed it was for a good reason. Rickey explained to the *Times:* "Joe was released at this time because our roster was crowded with younger players for whom we must make room. The early release may give Medwick a chance to find a place somewhere. Medwick was signed last June at the behest of manager Leo Durocher for the express purpose of acting as a pinch hitter against left-handed pitching."

Before the play-offs began, the *Eagle* wrote that "Joe Medwick continued to earn his keep."

Here was how Joe earned that keep:

1. In the field, he made no errors.
2. When Reiser was hurt in early September, Joe hit 15-47, that was .319, with ten RBIs and four runs scored.
3. His 1946 on-base percentage was .369.
4. In a year that started for Joe on July 1, Medwick hit for a .312 average.

Joe was voted a full share of the second-place money.

Referring to year's end, Medwick said years later, "When I first entered baseball, I figured about fifteen years for my top earning power in the game and planned accordingly."

But there was still work for him in the game. There was some talk that he might be offered the job of manager at Niagara Falls, New York, in the Eastern League. But then, on December 10, 1946, the AP reported the following: "The New York Yankees announced the signing of outfielder Joe Medwick . . . as a pinch hitter." Joe was on his third New York team.

21

Yogi in the Spring and
Sportsman's Again, 1947

If Larry MacPhail was running the Yankees and Charley Dressen
signed as a Yankee coach, those two things may or may not have
had something to do with signing Medwick. Who can say? But it
seemed clear that, in addition to his undiminished skills with a bat,
Joe's reputation as a teacher was becoming well known in baseball.

As Joe thought about his career, he knew how lucky he was to
have a job in baseball, particularly as a hitter. With only seventy-
seven at bats in 1946, and only that many because Reiser was injured, he knew it was no longer his base running or fielding that was
keeping him employed.

As Medwick worked out on the beaches near St. Petersburg in
February, he may have thought about his 1929 Newark Bears tryout.
The Bears were then a farm team of the Yankees—the Yankees,
which could have been his team. But now Joe was on his third New
York City team, and he left Florida on February 14 to check into the
team hotel, the Normandie, in San Juan, Puerto Rico.

Medwick was being well covered by the New York newspapers.
On February 16, John Drebinger of the *Times* reminded readers that
Babe Ruth's uniform number 3 had been worn after Ruth by "Twinkletoes Selkirk [and had fallen] into a state of neglect. However, the
fellow now wearing it appears determined to bring it back to its
former high rank and he was not lacking in confidence or self as-
surance. . . . Still down in weight to the trim lines that startled the

natives in Flatbush when he came to Brooklyn to help the Dodgers in their flag fight last summer, Medwick was determined to make a go of his present bid to hang on with the Yankees."

After five games against the local All-Stars, the team flew three hours to Caracas, Venezuela, on February 28. (The Yankees were guaranteed $6,200 per game in Venezuela.) Joe DiMaggio flew north, to Baltimore and Johns Hopkins, for his second heel operation. There was also some talk that the Yankee center fielder was finished as a player, having hit but .290 in 1946, and the rumor was that the Yankees were looking for a trade for DiMaggio. His medical problem and the possible trade forced Bucky Harris to look for another outfielder and decided on a rookie catcher, 20-year-old Yogi Berra.

In *It Ain't Over* (1989), Berra talked about his "good things" list. Here was something from that list: "My childhood hero, Joe Medwick, was picked up by the Yankees after he had been released by the Dodgers. He did not stay with the Yankees long, but he did help me a lot in spring training. He was more like me, so he could help me, and Bucky Harris made me his job." Medwick's expertise in the field, his invention of the sliding, sit-down catch, for instance, and the respect he would get from any ballplayer, but especially young Berra, age twenty, made Harris's decision a smart one. We can imagine Medwick and Berra—Dressen hitting flies to right field— working together in the sun in Venezuela. The South American country is two thousand miles from Grand Boulevard in St. Louis, on a corner from which Yogi, ten years before, sold newspapers to Joe, who was on his way home from the ballpark.

After a game on February 28 in Cervesa Stadium, when Joe doubled against Dan Bankhead who was pitching for Caracas (a team made up of Negro National League stars), Harris put Berra, wearing number 47, in right field, where he played acceptably well and continued to be a successful all-ball/bad-ball hitter, like Medwick. The Yankees recognized Joe's teaching ability, and this seemed to be something that he was comfortable with. Did Medwick think that he may be training his own replacement in the outfield?

The Dodgers arrived on March 4 for the three-game Venezuela Cup series against the Yankees. Berra was in the outfield and "it was Harris' intention to keep him on the picket line for an indefinite period." Berra and many others "will wear batting helmets this season. . . . There was . . . a special type for Joe Medwick who prefers the heavily padded Hank Lieber model." After the beaning without his helmet back on August 18, Medwick was taking even more protection with him up to the plate. And with Durocher managing the Dodgers, protection was needed.

Before 9,000, spectators, the Yankees won both the game, 4-0, and the Venezuela Cup, two games to one. Then the team was up at dawn and, at 7 A.M., began the eighteen-mile climb over the mountains to be at the plane by 8:30, which was the departure time for the flight to Havana.

The Dodgers arrived hours after the Yankees touched down in Cuba and it may have been on this travel day that Berra and Medwick got together. In a *Parade* magazine story in 1960, Yogi said, "I didn't get to know Joe really well till 1947 . . . he said he remembered me and we laughed about when I sold newspapers to him. One day I just couldn't help but blurt it out. 'You know. Joe,' I said, 'you were my boyhood idol.' I was sorry the minute I said it. When you were a kid in a big league camp, you're always the butt of jokes. If Joe had repeated what I had said, the bench jockeys would have made my ears burn. . . . But Joe just smiled and slapped me on the back. He never mentioned what I had told him."

On March 11, the Yankees flew to St. Petersburg on Pan American, carrying the huge Venezuela Cup. After medical checks by the customs doctors, packages began to be searched and "Joe Medwick grew quite annoyed because he had to open a pink cellophane-sealed package, tied daintily with a white ribbon. It was an orchid he purchased for his wife in Caracas, left undisturbed the entire time he was in Havana and then had to rip the attractive wrappings apart."

Also under scrutiny was the Durocher situation in Brooklyn. Charges and countercharges circulated from Durocher to Yankees owner MacPhail, and from MacPhail to Durocher, about Leo's gambling and about his marrying a movie star when forbidden by a judge. Defamation of character threats and boycotts by the Brooklyn Catholic Youth Organization were seen almost daily in the press. Meanwhile, Jack Robinson was playing with Montreal in many games against the Dodgers. In one of them, "Jackie Robinson . . . was knocked out when Bruce Edwards slid hard back to the bag as Robinson was reaching for a high throw from Jack [Spider] Jorgenson."

But Joe was far from all that now, busy working with Berra. Berra was thrilled. "Joe Medwick was my idol and my favorite player, too.

You could tell by the way he moved he was good." Yet Medwick had all the problems and worries of an aging player. Berra commented: "I would like to say that my boyhood hero and newspaper customer and I became buddies. I can't, and I think it was because he was with the Yankees only a short while. It was not the best time for him. It never was in the last days of a baseball career. Baseball players get old twice." All through March, in games against big-league pitching, Joe had hit 2-21.

After two days of rain in New York City, new baseball commissioner Happy Chandler, "irked [to] no end by steady criticism that inferred he was a lightweight in a heavyweight's job, decided to flex his muscles" and suspended Durocher for the whole year.

The contract of Jackie Robinson was purchased by the Dodgers from the Montreal team on April 10.

Rickey knew exactly what he was doing. Parrot quoted Rickey this way: "The Negroes will make us winners for years to come. I will happily bear being called a bleeding heart and a do-gooder, and all that humanitarian rot." (Bob Broeg later wrote: "No matter how cynically or how sincerely the Mahatma's motives might be evaluated, he will be remembered by the Negro for having opened up a new vista for the race.")

Robinson, who came out to play first base against the Yankees in the Ebbets Field exhibition game on April 11, found "a pleasant reception from the fans" for the "first Negro with a major league club since 1884." Keller was in left for the game and Berra was in right.

Joe was now traveling with a team that was picked to win the pennant in 1947, but he had no at bats.

April 27 was a Sunday, and it was a day when, as the headline on page one of the *New York Times* said, "58,339 Acclaim Babe Ruth in Rare Tribute at Stadium." Medwick played against Ruth in New Jersey when he was a high-school boy in Carteret, almost twenty years previously. Now Medwick, wearing Ruth's number 3, was in the same dugout with him. Joe knew it might be the last time he would ever be in a dugout in uniform as part of a team. If so, it was most memorable, as two number 3's in Yankee pinstripes stood next to each other.

A road trip to St. Louis was scheduled for Monday, April 28, and it was then that Joe was given the news that no one had claimed him from waivers and he was being unconditionally released. Dan Daniel summed up Joe's time with the Yankees: "Medwick played some for the Yankees during the training season, but in their eleven American League games he was a mere bench warmer, without even one time at bat. Joe had hoped to stay on as a right-handed pinch hitter, but Bucky Harris finally voted against that luxury at the expense of a young pitcher." The pitcher was probably either Spec Shea or Vic Raschi.

No doubt Joe flew with the team on United Airlines to St. Louis— to his home—on April 28. Berra remembered, "As I was saying goodbye to him, I thought this to myself: 'I'm just a rookie. But if a kid someday ever idolizes Berra as a kid idolized Medwick, I hope I never disappoint that kid—because Joe never disappointed me."

Once at home at 9616 Geyer Drive, Joe must have wondered if he would ever work in baseball again. It was too late into the season to find a job in the minors, the majors had two managers who had traded him already and one team administrator, Branch Rickey, who had, in effect, fired him in 1940, 1943, and 1946. By now he had been traded or released in his career by the Cardinals, Dodgers, Giants, Braves, Browns, and the Yankees—six of the sixteen major league teams. About the Cardinals owner, Hall of Fame sportswriter Bob Broeg reminded me that "Medwick left Breadon with insults and all that crap so Breadon was much aloof toward him." Still, Hornsby had been hired back seven years after having been swapped for Frisch and after Hornsby had insulted Breadon. Was there hope? Maybe—not much, though. Joe took his glove and his spikes, trudged up to the attic stairs and set down his tools among the dust and boxes.

Joe's life now would be with his children, now ages nine and seven. Playing baseball meant that he had never spent the Fourth of July with his family. Now he would think more about his future and theirs. Medwick had met Ray Hunsacker, an insurance salesman, a few years ago, when it was time to let Hunsacker handle his insurance. That, at least, would be taken care of. He would settle into his off-season life—he would play golf, hunt, and fish with his friends in St. Louis. He would go to the St. Louis Arena for boxing matches.

And he would wait for the phone to ring to call him back to play baseball again. There were still hits in his bats.

And there was always the *Sporting News* to read thoroughly.

Eddie Dyer was managing the Cardinals in 1947. Joe had known Eddie since June of 1930 when Medwick reported to the Scottdale, Pennsylvania, club, of which Dyer was both manager and secretary.

Explaining Dyer's background, Bob Broeg told me, "Eddie, desperate for a right-handed pinch-hitter, just someone to hit a fly ball when you need it," recommended Joe to Breadon, and Dyer "was a persuasive guy." Bing Devine told me that "Eddie Dyer was not just the manager—he had great influence on the organization. If you're looking for a ballplayer, you don't want to deal in memories or former adversaries. Things change . . . and you have to roll with it, and I think Medwick was smart enough to do that, and the club was smart enough to do that."

Sam Breadon thought about his team, which was six games back with an awful record of 11-19. Sitting in his office on May 25, a sunny Sunday morning, Breadon asked his secretary to find Joe Medwick. Medwick's home was called and Mrs. Medwick told the secretary that Joe had a golf date right across the street from his house at Sunset Country Club. There the phone rang and Joe was paged.

When Joe said hello, Breadon went right to his point:

"We feel you can help us. Do you want to play for us again?"

"Yes, Mr. Breadon, I do."

"Can you start today?"

"I'll be there in an hour, Mr. Breadon."

Can we imagine Medwick's excitement? To be a player again. To be a hitter again. To be in the game again.

Medwick canceled his golf game and drove quickly across the street to his home. There he climbed the attic stairs and retrieved his glove and spikes. Perhaps he drove the usual forty-five minutes to the ballpark a little faster than he might ordinarily.

Entering the Cardinal offices at 3623 Dodier, Joe found a contract prepared for him, and for only the second time in his life, he did not argue salary with Sam Breadon.

Then he went to the locker room, where the familiar Butch Yatkeman gave him a locker and uniforms with number 21 on them, Paul Dean's old number. Medwick quickly dressed in his blue undershirt and ran the black belt though the red-trimmed belt loops. On his head, he adjusted a blue cap that had a red bill and a red "ST.L."

By now it was a little past noon and Joe went into the dugout, checking in with Eddie Dyer. He said hello to coach Buzzy Wares, who was a coach from Joe's first days in the majors. Joe went into the outfield then and did some stretching. Early fans had no notation in their scorecards for any number 21, and Joe hadn't had run in four weeks—hadn't hit in four weeks; he thought he would have some time to get into playing condition. "Those who noticed him in uniform figured an old-timer was just getting a workout in his old pasture," Stockton wrote. Medwick knew just about everybody in the club. The infield of Musial and Marion and Schoendienst and Kurowsi, certainly; the outfield had Terry Moore and Enos Slaughter, both of whom were Joe's teammates from many years ago.

The home team lost the first game of the doubleheader against the visiting Pirates. Medwick remembered this well—ten years later he told the *Post-Dispatch* it was his best moment in baseball. "I was just sitting on the bench. It was a beautiful day. Sunny . . . in the fifth we were losing and Dyer looked at me and said, 'you're the hitter.' I think this was the first time in my life I was scared. I broke out in perspiration. I didn't even have a bat in the rack. I reached out and grabbed one." As he went up to the plate, he was swinging two bats to hit for pitcher Jim Hearn against lefty Fritz Ostermueller

Erv Fischer recalled, "I had tears in my eyes when public address announcer Charlie Jones identified the pinch hitter." Bob Broeg described the reaction of the 26,817 spectators when they realized who the batter was: "there was a prolonged roar."

Joe saw the count go to 2-1. "I was just trying to hit anything that looked good. And then he gave me one high and outside and I hit the '5' in the 354 foot sign in right center . . . and I missed a home run by a foot and a half. But I hadn't run in four weeks—and I stretched a triple into a double. . . . Dyer put a pinch runner in for me and I had tears in my eyes running across to the dugout with everybody applauding. On the way back to the dugout I can remember seeing Mr. Breadon in his box. In all the years I knew him, that was only the second time I can remember him smiling. . . . He used to sit there like Ned Sparks, you know what I mean? I tipped my hat to him to say 'Thank you' and he smiled and stood up like the rest and applauded. In the dugout, everybody slapped me on the back and shook my hand."

Broeg told me, "Sitting in the press box was a salty, sarcastic, intellectual basketball coach, Ken Loeffler of the St. Louis Bombers and he turned to a reporter and said, 'My god, that's one of the most dramatic things I've ever seen in my life.'"

"He became the dimpled darling of the fans," after that, Broeg said.

Joe had come home, but not to star—not to have his way anymore. He just wanted to play baseball. He sat on the bench, content. He had a job—it was in baseball, and he knew he had made his money from the sport. No one was expecting him to carry the team, only to contribute when he could. Musial was the star of this team. Joe was working in familiar surroundings and in less than an hour he could be home.

Medwick could read his declining stats; he could feel his declining speed. Certainly, he was very much aware of the judgments of his abilities and fitness that had been made since 1945. But by then he was a respected player among his teammates and in the league, a major leaguer since 1932, a star for almost all this time. Though his speed was gone and his stamina diminished, many players had asked for his help in hitting many times. No doubt Joe had learned proportion, too. In the war years, everyone understood the relative importance of baseball and that position was stated very clearly.

Joe was still ferocious in wanting his due, but now he was getting his due from almost everyone. He knew his greatness as one of the stars of the national game was dimming. Old guys like Greenberg and Medwick did not have that much time left in the league and the spotlight shone elsewhere.

With his hunger for greatness and respect mostly sated, Medwick begin to have a different effect on people. Slaughter wrote about it this way: "Joe was a lot nicer guy when he was on his way down than he had been in my early days with the Cardinals." But in a relentless chase for excellence, there was little time for amenities. Yeats said the choice is always between perfection of the life or perfection of the art.

On June 11, in the first inning, Medwick produced three RBIs with a homer off Ken Roffenberger. It was Joe's home-run number 202, but the Cardinals lost, 5-4.

When the Dodgers came to St. Louis for a day and night doubleheader with Ralph Branca and Rex Barney doing the pitching, Joe's team had moved up to sixth place with a record of 23-28, at six and a half back. And although there were stories of strikes against Jack Robinson, one of his biographies claimed that in St. Louis, "the Cardinals seemed friendlier—or so Jack carefully chose to describe them. In the *Courier*, he saluted Joe Medwick, Stan Musial, Joe Garagiola, and the manager Eddie Dyer 'as a swell bunch of fellows. . . . They treated me so nice I was actually surprised."

On June 23, Joe doubled in the eighth inning against Hardrock Shoun, who was a Cardinal teammate in 1938 and was now a reliever for the Braves. With Joe starting in right field, the strongest pitcher for the Braves—Warren Spahn—was not too strong for Joe, who homered in the sixth with Musial on. Though the Cardinals lost, they lately had a record of 10-2. Using Dusak as the third baseman limited Dyer's choices but increased his wins. The team was now 30-30—one game out of the first division.

On June 26, Dyer sent Medwick to bat for pitcher Ken Burkhart. This was a curious choice for two reasons: first, the pitcher, Ewell Blackwell, was a right-hander; second, Blackwell was at his peak. Blackwell had just pitched a no-hitter against the Braves; in 1947, he would win 22 (16 in a row) and strike out 193, And he was a side-arm thrower. Joe was not supposed to be able to hit right-handers, and certainly not side-armers, but he singled for his 11th hit. Medwick also had 11 RBIs and was hitting .323.

With center fielder Terry Moore suffering an injured left leg, Joe got more playing time. On July 6, he played in both games of the doubleheader and even drove in the game-winning run in game two with a sacrifice fly.

After the National League loss in the All-Star game, Dyer continued to use Joe and Dierring, and Dusak and Northey very flexibly, so that often two would start and then be removed, depending on pitching changes for the opposition. At the Polo Grounds, when the Giants scored eleven runs in the first two innings, Medwick was gone before he ever came to bat, because in one of Medwick's rare major league ejections, Umpire Al Barlick threw him out when he insisted that a fan in the stands had touched the ball, causing it to drop onto the playing field. But the fire remained. He played the next day's doubleheader as well, and so in four games in New York he was 3-10.

At Braves Field, Warren Spahn threw a six-hitter, as Joe got one of the hits, bringing his average to .299. Again there were three right fielders in a 5-2 win on July 17, but Brecheen was hurt on July 18 at Ebbets Field.

The Dodgers, under 62-year-old Burt Shotton, had played well all season; their relief pitching was particularly strong. With the influence of Jackie Robinson, the Dodgers would steal a lot more bases and take a lot more walks. Medwick, who took walks infrequently, always preferring to put the ball in play, had only had fourteen at bats so far in August. His speed, which allowed him to lead the league in triples in 1933 had clearly deserted him. That lack of speed frustrated Joe, for like Frisch, he wanted to make things happen: to make a fielder try to throw him out when he was stretching a hit; to hit the ball hard and have the fielder try to handle it while he was heading for first. Medwick knew, too, that a measure of a player's age was how often he hit into double plays, something that he was accused of when he was traded in 1940. Yet in his last two years of full-time play, he hit into only twelve and ten double plays.

Joe walked in the first game of the series in a 12-3 loss. And something else happened: the following appeared in the *New York Daily News* at the end of the "Diamond Dust" section: "Medwick, bearing down on first base to prevent a seventh-inning double play in his role as pinch-hitter, came down on Robby's left foot, and both toppled to the ground. Robinson continued in action, but Joe limped off the field for a sub runner." In Broeg's play-by-play, the same action reads, "In a play at first, too late to get Medwick, the batter tripped over Robinson's right foot and fell to the ground. Robinson was spiked slightly on the right instep and Medwick limped off. Diering ran for Medwick." *Baseball's Great Experiment* records the incident as "Joe Medwick spiked Robinson on the left foot, leaving a bloody gash." Running to first to prevent a double play was a complicated act.

Another Robinson story appeared in *The Cultural Encyclopedia of Baseball:* "Jackie Robinson once roll-blocked Yankee shortstop Phil Rizzuto on a double play. Later in the game, Robinson took a throw at first base on a ground ball hit by Joe DiMaggio. Robinson put his foot awkwardly on the bag and DiMaggio had to make an off-balance step on the bag to avoid spiking Robinson. Asked later by a reporter why he did not retaliate against Robinson by spiking him, DiMaggio said, 'I thought about it running to first. But Rizzuto and I were Italian, and I didn't want them to think it was the guineas against the niggers. If Phil was black and Robinson white, I guess I would have done the spiking.'"

After a collision with substitute shortstop Bernie Creger, Enos Slaughter was taken to Temple Hospital in Philadelphia with a cerebral concussion. Slaughter would only be gone for four days, but Joe was written into the lineup, playing right field. The AP led its story on the game in Philadelphia on the twenty-third with "Those never say die St. Louis Cardinals found a winning homer in venerable Joe Medwick's bat today. . . . Medwick's sixth inning homer with Stan Musial and Whitey Kurowsi aboard was a called shot. Just before the pitch he stepped from the batter's box and, as though speaking to someone [Ben Chapman] in the Phillies dugout, pointed first to his bat and then the left field bleachers. ["You son of a bitch. I'll hit the next one upstairs," Broeg wrote that Medwick said.] Then he stepped back to the plate and slammed a line drive into the second deck 385 feet away." Joe drove in four of the five Cardinal runs against left-hander Kenny Heintzelman, enough to beat the Phillies, limited to three runs by three Cardinal pitchers. Joe even made the last put out of the game.

As for his home run, had it been hit in different circumstances, who knows how famous it might be. It was home run 205. It was his last home run in the big leagues. It was another called shot. "These things enhanced him," according to Bob Broeg.

The next day "Ducky Medwick . . . greeted Walt Lanfranconi, the last of the Boston chuckers by driving in the last two St. Louis runs with a two bagger to deep center while batting for Ron Northey in the eighth." The next day Joe got two hits, both against Warren Spahn in another Cardinal win. By now Spahn must have hated to see Medwick with a bat in his hands.

In seventeen games in August, Joe went 7-24 or .291.

While the Cardinals played their last game at Cincinnati for 1947, the Giants had set a new home run record for the league at 183. (In Joe's first full year, the Giants won the pennant with 82 homers.)

With seventeen games left, Joe, playing right field against left-hander Lombardi, sent Dodger Gene Hermanski playing left to the wall and then singled in the third but vainly tried to make it a double and was thrown out by a long space. This space did not prevent Joe from arguing with Umpire Beans Reardon either out of vanity or because he thought a tag was missed. The fire was there. Joe was 2-4 with an RBI. "In one of those Brooklyn games and again against the Giants, Dyer had Joe Medwick batting cleanup. Medwick will hit when he is 90 years old as Leo Durocher used to say, but Ducky can't play every day and he is no longer a first division outfielder," Bill Roeder wrote. (Joe knew it, too.)

Winning five of six in Pittsburgh, St. Louis also won their first two in Chicago. These wins moved Boston further behind them and assured the Cardinals of second-place money. In the last game of the year, Joe played the whole game in right field, partly to give the regulars a rest or an early trip home. Since Joe lived in St. Louis, he stayed with the team and had a hit in three at bats.

Over the whole season, St. Louis scored only six fewer runs than the first-place Dodgers.

Medwick was still dangerous at bat and he played in 75 of the 126 games that remained on the schedule after he joined the team, averaging two at bats per game. Though not a star anymore, Medwick made significant contributions to the team:

1. Twenty-eight RBIs in 150 at bats—the same RBI number as Dusak, who was in 111 games with 328 at bats.
2. Forty-six hits, with 16 of them long hits.
3. One of three men on the team with a batting average over .300.
4. Most pinch-hit at bats on the team, and most pinch hits.
5. Joe was 8-28 in September, .285.

Still, on October 19, 1947, Medwick was released yet again, Sam Breadon saying: "We appreciate the fine effort Medwick made in 1947 and should Joe not make a connection to his satisfaction, he will be welcome in the Cardinals' training camp in 1948." This generous offer by Breadon allowed Joe to try to sign with some other team and yet have the opportunity to rejoin the Cardinals.

22

Up and Down, 1948

For Medwick, the most unsettling thing that happened during the winter of 1947–1948, though Sam Breadon made certain promises to him, was that real estate operator Fred Saigh and U.S. Postmaster General Robert Hannegan bought the Cardinals for three million dollars. Joe did not have any background experience with these two men as he had with Breadon, and, again, he had to begin to think of his future outside of the Cardinals and the major leagues. In 1948, many players Joe knew were working as managers in the minors. The idea of having coaches for these teams was far away; traveling instructors were few. But there were fifty-eight leagues—the Cardinals alone had twenty-one teams—and the men who were working in the minors were good, capable baseball men.

Not long after Joe and his family again returned to Florida in early January, the Hall of Fame announced that the Baseball Writers of America had voted in pitcher Herb Pennock and third baseman Pie Traynor. Medwick's numbers, except for triples, were much higher than Traynor's. And before the five-year-wait rule was implemented, Joe, in 1948, got one Hall of Fame vote.

Joe knew he was just about done in the majors as a player. Yet he would probably sign with the Cardinals and they were picked 8-5 to win the pennant. Though he could work out with the team, he was not yet on the roster as spring training ended.

That year—1948—was to be Musial's great year. One day after the season opened in Chicago, Stan got hit number 1,000 in game number 762. (Joe did it in 702 games.) But then Musial was discovered to have an inflamed appendix and Medwick re-signed with the Cardinals and Dyer on April 29, 1948, to help fill in.

And it was truly a fill-in position, with just two at bats and no hits in April and May. His first hit for the 1948 season came on June 4 as Dodger right-hander Branca was pitching a nine-hit shutout.

The Braves came to Sportsman's and swept the Cardinals. After two fly-outs and a strikeout so far in June, Medwick singled for pitcher Harry Brecheen on June 17, with Dusak running for him. Musial tripled in Dusak, making Joe's run the game winner.

On July 8, after two more fly-outs, Joe singled again in the second inning against the Pirates to drive in a run. The next day, July 9, the Reds had come to town. Joe's single this time drove in the tying run. It was his last big-league hit and his last RBI.

All throughout the first half of the season, Musial had been the big news. Joe was very protective of his excellence and wanted to be recognized for it. But here Musial, playing left field, Joe's spot for so long on the Cardinals, was having his best year among many very good years in the majors. Bob Broeg related conversations he had with Joe about Musial (once Medwick had learned to feel comfortable enough with the sportswriter to talk about such things): "Joe and I would talk on the train occasionally about Musial's year and I could see him battling . . . his own ego and the judgment he was starting to get about human relationships. Here he had this great opportunity—he was back in good graces . . . he would analyze fair enough, but I think it hurt him like hell to acknowledge that Musial had little edges in there, which he did. . . . I could see he was learning a little bit more about the give and take of a writer." In Broeg's view, over the years Joe had learned to act in a "reserved, pretty polite way for a guy that was pretty goddamm jealous."

If you take Medwick's best year, 1937, and Musial's best year, 1948, and Joe Dimaggio's best two years, 1941 and 1937, how does Joe fare? He leads the others in games played, at bats, doubles, RBIs, and hits (see table).

Joe still had the reputation of being the greatest right-handed hitter in the game, after Hornsby. Musial, of course, was left-handed.

At the 1948 All-Star game break at Sportsman's Park, St. Louis, the Cardinals were seven games back.

	G	AB	R	H	2B	3B	HR	RBI	BB	SO	AVG	slg	obp
Medwick													
1937	156	633	111	237	56	10	31	154	41	50	.374	.641	.414
Musial													
1948	155	611	135	230	46	18	39	131	79	34	.376	.702	.450
DiMaggio													
1941	139	541	122	193	43	11	30	125	76	13	.357	.440	.643
1937	151	621	151	215	35	15	46	167	64	37	.346	.412	.673

After two more unsuccessful at bats in July, Joe was sent up to bat on July 25. He worked out a walk from pitcher Gerry Staley in the second. The next day, July 26, 1948, Joe was sent to Houston as the Cardinals were leaving to go East to play the Dodgers. "Being a ten-year man, Medwick did not have to go to Texas. He made the shift as a favor to Bob Hannegan [St. Louis club president]." The AP reported: "Cards Drop Medwick and Burkhart, Get Babe Young. Norman 'Babe' Young first baseman—outfielder of the Reds—was acquired by the Cardinals via waivers today and two veteran Redbirds—Medwick and Burkhart—were dropped from the squad, the Cardinal office announced. For Medwick it was a return to the club from which he sprang . . . Houston of the Texas League. Inasmuch as the 36-year-old Medwick was a ten-year man in the majors, his transfer to Houston was with his consent."

Medwick's consent came because he believed that going to Houston was "another potential career for him." Bob Broeg recalled, "Dyer wouldn't promise Joe any managerial jobs because Dyer was looking to hold onto his job." Dyer, however, certainly had considerable influence on the club. Medwick remembered it this way: "When Mr. Hannegan called me into his office in St. Louis and told me that he'd like to send me to Houston, that the Houston club had asked for me, I told him I was ready. I joined the club as quickly as I could." "I was on my way out in 1948," Medwick told Robert E. Hood, "And they said I was going to get the Houston ball club to manage. So I went down there."

The Houston Press covered Medwick's return in four different articles over three days. George Wright's piece said that he was "pleased to see Ducky Medwick coming home," and happy, too, because the many left-handed pitchers the Buffaloes had been facing would now have to deal with right-hand hitting Joe. Lack of right-hand hitting had dropped the Houston team five games behind Fort Worth. The Houston team had Solly Hemus, the 25-year-old shortstop, who would, in eleven years, become the manager of the St. Louis Cardinals; now he was Joe's roommate. The Buffs manager was old Cardinal hand Johnny Keane, who was the same age as Medwick almost to the day in November. In thirteen years, Keane would manage the Cardinals. Medwick was moved to where he would play most of his games—right field—and the series at Fort Worth ended with Joe 2-12 with three RBIs.

Joe played half of a doubleheader at the Tulsa Oilers, and then to start August, was moved to first base, from where he singled and scored a run. But then he was put in the lineup for only one of five games at the home park of the Oklahoma City Indians and one of three at the San Antonio Missions.

In those days, only the most useless player would be the first-base coach—an injured man or last night's pitcher—but when Medwick wasn't playing, he eagerly volunteered to coach first base.

August 8 was a Sunday, a doubleheader, and Joe's first game at Buff Stadium. In Robert E. Hood's account:

> Joe Medwick led off the second inning, his first time at bat since leaving sixteen years before. The fans began shrieking, "Hit it over the wall, Joe. Hit it over the wall." Ken Sterling, the opposing pitcher, ran the count on Medwick to three balls and one strike. Then Medwick lashed the ball high and far toward left field. "It's a home run," the crowd yelled. The ball was hit in the same spot as the one he hit in his last at bat in 1932.

The *Houston Press*'s coverage remarked that

> up and down Main Street and wherever baseball fans gather, the talk today was about Joe Medwick, even at the expense of the fact that Houston won two games Sunday, pulled to within a game of second place Tulsa and to within six and half tilts of league-leading Fort Worth. Many of the 6889 paying fans had not been in Buff Stadium since 1932 but they were back Sunday to see Medwick keep the faith. It was on August 29, 1932 that Medwick last swung his big black bat for the Buffs. He was swinging a new white one Sunday.

Joe also hit two singles and "fielded that right field job like a spring chicken."

The next day, in his column "Press Time," *Press* sports editor Clark Nealon reported on a Medwick that might surprise people in Houston. Under the headline "Medwick Still Gashouser, Working Hard as Any Buff," Nealson commented:

> Joe Medwick, old Ducky Wucky himself, draws our honor as the big leaguer who came back to the Texas League with the most hustle, the most earnest desire to do everything he can do for his club. . . . For more than 20 years now, we've been watching the big timers return to the Texas League, nearing the end of the baseball trail. Generally it's been pretty sad, because most of them had not become accustomed to the drop. They groaned about conditions not being just so, groaned when asked to coach, play out of position or pinch-hit. But not Ducky, the picturesque right-handed hitter who first banged Texas League fences 18 years ago and whose bat still whistles when he took that pinwheel cut at high pitching.
>
> We watched Medwick in a series at San Antonio. He had the energy of the rawest rookie on the club, the know-how of a guy with the years behind him. Joe was the first to take over the duties of hitting to Bud Hardin, the injured Buff shortstop. . . . Between hitting practice turns, Joe was fungoing grounders to Hardin and Sam DiBasi. He took a turn in the outfield in pre-game drills, came in to handle a few at first base. . . . He's just plain frisky. "That's the way I always played it," smiles Joe when you ask him about it, and he said it with a forthright frankness. . . . "You know I've always been an active player. I didn't get to play much with the Cardinals this season so it'll take me a few days to get my eye on the ball, but I think I can help this ball club. Above all I want it understood that Johnny Keane is my manager, that I'm an active player, ready to play and that I'm ready to help the ball club any way I can. I'm just a ball player. And I'm glad to be back in Houston . . . where people were fine to me and I look forward to playing here again." Doesn't sound like a guy with a "big league" complex, does it? And Joe acts just like that on the field.

On a Tuesday night, to end the series with Beaumont "about 100 Houston boys were made very happy when a 'friend' donated 100 Joe Medwick baseball gloves . . . distributed among members of the Knothole Gang by members of the Junior Chamber of Commerce. Joe was there, too," giving out the gloves. By the time the three-game series was done, Joe was 6-11, with seven RBIs.

From then to the month's end, Joe came to bat just a few times. Also during this time, the president of the Cardinals, Bob Hannegan, came to Houston for a visit and Clark Nealon interviewed him. "Hannegan indicated that Medwick would wind up somewhere in the Cardinal chain next season, although he didn't precisely say so. At the same time the prexy said that assignment of Ducky Wucky, if there was to be one, would have to wait until the spring, when all Cardinal assignments to farm chains were made. . . . However, our guess was that Keane was going to be promoted next season, perhaps to Rochester, and that Medwick was a good bet to manage the Buffs then."

By September 7, the Buffs had guaranteed possession of third place, with Joe getting four hits in fifteen at bats to begin the month. Joe had been recalled to the Cardinals but he was not scheduled to go back to the big club until next year.

Joe got five more at bats and no hits to season's end on the twelfth. While the Fort Worth Panthers were playing the fourth-place Missions of San Antonio, the next day the team left on the 560-mile trip to Tulsa for a best-of-seven series against the Oilers in the league play-offs.

There the Buffaloes lost two to Tulsa with Joe singling and stealing a base in game one and pinch hitting a single in game two. Medwick did not play in the two wins at home or in the 2-0 loss at home and he was safe on an error, putting the ball in play, in the last game won by Tulsa by 7-1. His season was done.

And though his option was picked up by the Cardinals, Joe was unconditionally released on October 1, 1948.

23

Miami Manager
Medwick, 1949

At the end of the 1948 season, Medwick went looking for a job. Thinking of all of his contacts in the game, he may have felt certain that there would be a job for him somewhere in the 108 minor league teams affiliated with the National League. Joe understood that asking to manage one of the 20 Cardinal teams might be asking too much. Up until the baseball winter meetings, whatever he was offered as a managing job, if any were offered, was not suitable for him (the job may not have been in a high enough minor classification, meaning that the salary would not be high enough, nor the status, in a "C" league or lower).

Some men will not settle. Babe Ruth, for instance, was offered the job of managing the top Yankee farm team but he would not go to the minors to work. Did it hurt Medwick to know that his batboy in 1932 in Houston, Joe Schultz, Jr., who had just turned thirty, was given a coaching job with the Browns?

Medwick found a job in a league, the Florida International League (FIL), where most teams did not have a working agreement with a major league team, and on December 18, 1948, he signed for $10,000 to be player-manager for the Miami Beach Flamingos.

In early February, J. G. Taylor Spink, publisher of the *Sporting News*, speaking at a Miami Beach luncheon said, "Joe Medwick would do a capable job as pilot of the Miami Beach Flamingos. . . . Medwick . . . had visited the offices of The Sporting News getting detailed information on Miami Beach players. 'Medwick was a changed man,' said Spink. 'He no longer was as short-tempered as he was in the early days as a player.'"

Travis Jackson, interviewed before the season, commented on baseball in the Miami area and the excitement likely to be caused by two old Gashousers in the same league. "Medwick won't go after Martin, but Pepper will go after Joe. Don't think he won't. He loves a scrap," said the former Giants infielder. Martin had managed in many places when he moved to the FIL, his last year in the majors being in 1940 before a wartime appearance in 1944. He was still a Gashouse Gangster.

The Florida International League was called "international" simply because one of the eight teams was in Havana—the Cubanos, or "Cubans." In 1948 it had been a C league, but in 1949 its rating was raised to B. This was a nonrookie league, so generally the players were older. These men played for teams that had a $4,000-a-month total salary cap for players, which was calculated on teams drawing 90,000 fans for the seventy-seven home dates—about 1,180 fans per game. The salary cap for each umpire was $375 per month, while the fans paid from 85¢ to $1.50 for seats at the parks.

On March 3, the *Sporting News* covered Medwick. "Joe Medwick, former big league star, had arrived to perform his duties as player-manager. . . . 'This was the realization of a dream, getting a job as manager,' Joe declared. 'Every ball player wants to become a manager. Maybe this will lead to something bigger.'"

If Medwick needed a reminder that he was working in the minors, the game of April 16 at Miami brought it to mind. In the game against Johnny Martin's Miami Sun Sox team, a base umpire called a Sun Sox runner out even though the ball slapped off the Flamingos' first baseman's glove and rolled ten feet away. The two runners for the Sox therefore did not score. When the first-base coach "picked up the ball and shoved it in the face" of the umpire, the home-plate umpire reversed the decision, which "sent Medwick into a near-frenzy," Luther Evans wrote. The umpires reversed and altered their decisions twice more before the game resumed. There were also nineteen walks in the game.

Joe was also coming to a number of realizations about his job as a manager and his job in the minors. "Joe Medwick was concentrating so intensely that he isn't keeping up with the big league races." "You may not believe me but I've been so busy," he told Jimmy Burns, of the *Miami Herald*, "I've been so busy that I haven't kept up with the National scramble. When you [are] away from the league, it doesn't seem so important." Joe also thought that his Flamingos were "set to make a real bid for the F-I pennant and [he] said that he does not contemplate any changes in the roster." Joe was, of course, dependent on the team president and the business manager to make most of those kinds of decisions. The owner at least must have been pleased with the increase of almost fourteen thousand in attendance over the last year.

The Flamingos' win against Lakeland on Sunday, June 19, raised the team's record to 40-32, a .555 winning percentage that would not get them to a pennant. That win was followed by a loss and then a win. Again, winning one game in an at-home series against the last-place team couldn't help the team enough. Joe was getting angrier as well, and the "Beach skipper made a vehement protest . . . storm[ing] out, and after several minutes of heated discussion, departed to the showers—a victim of the heave-ho." It is impossible to measure the effect of Medwick's intensity on the team.

At a traditional halfway point, the 1949 All-Star Game break, team defense had become a little stronger and the hitting was a little more potent. Being in second place, it made sense that they were second in runs scored and second in total bases, but the team average was .246. The manager, still a great hitter, was at .355, but after Ed Lewinski, the team RBI leader with sixty-one, there was a sharp drop-off, so much so that only two other players from Miami Beach were even listed in the weekly statistics for hitting. About ten players were hitting below .250. Only six pitchers' records were listed.

In the All-Star Game played at Tampa, the two opposing teams were the league all-stars and ex-big leaguers. It was a time when, together, Joe could play left and Johnnie Martin could play right, as they had done seventeen years before. Martin, in fact, drove in the only run for his team, although Medwick, playing to the moment once more, "hit two doubles, cut down a runner at the plate and made a sparkling catch of a long drive near the fence."

After sweeping a doubleheader against Lakeland, the next night, July 27, "the story was that Medwick and his catcher had exchanged words all evening," and in the fourth inning, there was an "impromptu scuffle started when Cabrera, who'd just scored . . . returned to the dugout and . . . a mysterious flurry of fisticuffing in the Flamingo dugout. Fiery Cabby Cabrera, the Beach catcher, was the only pugilist visible to the 861 fans, but it was established that the other puncher was manager Joe Medwick. The altercation raged until umpire Willie Williams rushed over and assumed command. Peace was restored and both batters remained in the game. Club officials were not available for comment as to whether all would be forgotten and forgiven in view of the ultimate victory."

The victory was ensured by Joe's home run in the fifth inning of the game, his double, and two runs scored. The next few days were filled with news of club officials deciding to suspend Cabrera, and with Medwick "willing to forget the difficulty," particularly since Cabby was Joe's best catcher (though a weak hitter). The solution seemed to be to suspend Cabrera, but only for a few days. The rest of July was typical enough: Joe went 5-14, the team split the four games, and the month ended with a team record of 14-13 for July and Joe 25-81, with sixteen RBIs.

Medwick kept looking for any way to help the team improve. He took out a pitcher, for instance, even though a new one had not yet warmed up. These managerial moves made no impression. Approaching season's end, Whitey Kelly's *Herald* column stated that "without reservation, it can be stated that Joe Medwick will not return as the Flamingos' skipper. The reasons were twofold. First, Medwick had aspirations of ascending the baseball ladder. Secondly, the three [owners] have a policy of seeking a new manager each season and . . . their record of four different skippers in as many years indicates as much." Under Joe, though, the team was playing well enough to draw as many fans by August 1, 1949, as it did in all of 1948. Medwick's ambition was for some dramatic climb out of the lower minors: Billy Southworth, who quit the Boston Braves due to poor health around this time was making $50,000 a year compared to Joe's $10,000.

Miami Beach split with Tampa and they were followed into Flamingo Park by the league-leading Havana Cubans. On August 19, "Manager Joe Medwick's three-run homer in the fourth inning provided the only plate-punch of the victory-starved birds." Joe also made two of the runs the next day in the 7-6 win for his team. He played most of game one against Fort Lauderdale, getting two hits, and walked and scored late in the 6-1 win in game two. But just as the team started producing, they stopped: they only got ten hits in the next day's doubleheader. After those wearisome losses, they got on a plane and flew to Havana for their third and fourth consecutive doubleheaders. They lost all four games, scoring just five runs.

If there was any good news in all of this for Joe, it was in the comments of Andy High, Dodger scout and former Dodger and Cardinal infielder, who had been watching the Florida International
League for a week. "'Joe Medwick was working harder than he ever
had in baseball . . . now Medwick had to see to it that the players
don't leave their hats on home plate, or forget to bring their gloves
off the field. He had to look after 'em, teach 'em, and from what I've
seen he hasn't done too badly.' High left the impression that he
thinks that if and when Joe pulls up stakes at the Beach, he'll have
no difficulty landing another managerial contract."

At one game back of Tampa for third place, all the Flamingos
could play for in the remaining seven games was third place. The
pitching came through. By halving a doubleheader on September 1,
the win being a shutout, they moved into a tie for third. When two
shutouts followed, third place was theirs. The complete game
shutout on September 3 was pitched by outfielder Roy Lindbladh.
Two more wins and a loss in game two of the season-ending doubleheader against Miami meant that first-place Havana would be
the play-off opponent. Whoever won the championship of the
Florida International League would play the champion of the South-
eastern League, which would probably be Pensacola.

Flying to Havana to start the best-of-five series, Medwick knew it
was going to be tough to beat the Cubans. Yet with only thirteen
runs scored by both teams in the split four games, Medwick had his
team in position to win the series against the most dominant team in
the league. But in a close copy of game four of the 1941 World Series,
"Rookie catcher Leo Marrero lost a baseball . . . so Miami Beach lost
a game to Havana and the right to perform in the F-I playoff finals.
. . . Chino Hidlago raced all the way from second base with the winning run of the deciding fifth game in its seventh inning as Marrero
permitted a third strike to get away from him and then couldn't find
the ball."

Manager Medwick was unconditionally released on September
16. In sportswriter J. Roy Stockton's column "Extra Innings" in the
St. Louis Post-Dispatch two days later, there was a report on how the
last game was lost on a wild pitch. Stockton commented that "second was about the best any club can hope for in the league, except
for the Havana club, which was too strong for the league. That Joe
was able to give the Cubans such a close tussle indicates that he
must have handled the .200 hitters fairly well." The team also drew

thirty thousand more spectators than the year before. In his talk with Stockton, Medwick tried to "'clear up a few things. No, I wasn't fired as manager at Miami Beach. . . . It was understood that I was to be released after one year. That protected me from the draft too. And I left the club with everything on a friendly basis. And now that I've served my year in class B, I'd like to take a shot at a club in a higher classification.'"

How well did Medwick do as manager to earn his right to be in a higher minor league? He had seen thirty-five players come and go and he had to devise a team of six pitchers and twelve position players throughout a season of 151 games; only three of his players had more than 500 at bats. He had to deal with at least one problem player and a schedule that was unremitting. Although he was blessed with two All-Star outfielders, Conroy and Rocky Rotzell, only first baseman Ed Lewinski hit near 300 (.295) and the rest of the infield hit at .248 or below; three regulars hit below .205. His Flamingos were last of eight in hits and batting average, sixth in total bases and runs scored. The team fielding was third in most errors made, with over 240. The four pitchers with the most wins had a combined record of 58-49, for a percentage of .597.

Joe kept hitting: with just 375 at bats, he climbed to eleventh in the league for batting average, with .323, fourth in total bases, and seventh in runs batted in, with 72. He even made 3 double plays and 8 assists from the outfield.

But now that league was done. It was time to look for a job managing in "A" ball or higher.

24

Insurance Man, 1950

In 1950 there was no job in baseball for Joe—no job he would take, at any rate.

The lack of baseball job prospects for Joe may have been payback for years of aggressive play and aggressive behavior on the field. It is difficult to get into the minds of owners and general mangers. There were some who were only interested in having their employees kowtow. Medwick—with men, at least—did not do that, except in those circumstances where a man had earned that level of respect. Most men Joe knew were baseball players, not baseball team owners, who seemed to know very little about baseball. There were some who were only interested in having their employees be a kind of trophy for them. Joe could not do that, except very grudgingly.

That Joe knew baseball was undeniable. That no owner wanted to work with Medwick in 1950 at a level at which Medwick was willing to work, was also undeniable.

But Joe still needed a paycheck. At his birthday on November 24, 1948, Joe turned thirty-seven. A small pension from the deal worked out with Major League Baseball, at this date, would provide cash at age fifty. But that was some years away.

What did Medwick know, outside of the world of baseball, that he could sell to an employer? He could offer his celebrity and try to sell himself on his contacts in baseball and those he had made through baseball. He could offer his knowledge of the St. Louis area, since he was now a fourteen-year resident homeowner. And through the years, he had been called on to accept awards and speak at dinners, to talk to reporters and with fans, so he could converse with people, particularly if he was starting from the point that he was the star. He had spoken to many people at once, as in the USO tour in 1944–1945.

Joe had done business with Braun-Hunsaker and Associates, Insurance; it was that firm that offered him a job. "I felt that insurance offered the best possibility for a good income, and I also like to get around and meet people," Medwick said later in the pages of the *St. Louis Commerce*. "When I first entered baseball I figured about 15 years for my top earning power in the game and planned accordingly. The baseball player was often through at 35, an age when others were nearing their top earning power."

So Medwick took up being an insurance salesman in 1950. People in St. Louis certainly remembered him as a ballplayer and he could use that high profile to do his new work. He stayed involved with his old work—his love—at events like the annual Writers Dinner in St. Louis at the end of January. There were enough ballplayers who lived in the area that he could socialize with; it was with them that he was most comfortable.

In July, Medwick was invited to an old-timers game between ex-Giants and ex-Gashousers at the Polo Grounds. He accepted the invitation and flew to New York on July 29 for the July 30 game. In fact, the outfield for the three-inning game, for a while, was Rothrock in right, Orsatti, and then Terry Moore, in center, and Joe in left. Medwick could once again look in on Johnnie Martin at third and Leo at shortstop. And he could face Hubbell again—and bat cleanup again, even if Fitzsimmons struck him out. Joe would remember his batting performance in these games; his pride was undiminished.

Then it was back to St. Louis and his family, and insurance.

25

Raleigh, 1951

The winter meetings in 1950 at St. Petersburg marked the second year that Joe couldn't find a managing job. Through the holidays and the new year, Medwick was still without a job in league baseball. (There was no job he would take, at any rate.) For a while, he served as an instructor at the baseball school in Hollywood, Florida, where, in addition to Yogi Berra and Paul Waner, Medwick worked with his old pal Pepper Martin.

Then a manager who had been hired for the Carolina League at the winter meetings decided his business needed all of his attention. Rudy Knipe, the team president of the Raleigh (North Carolina) Capitals, contacted Medwick, and after meeting with Knipe, Joe signed a contract to manage on February 9, 1951.

Once again, Joe turned to the offices of the *Sporting News* to gather information on the Raleigh team in the six-year-old Carolina League. The owner of the team, a dry cleaner, saw his Raleigh team finish seventh of eight teams in 1950 in the B-level league. Part of the success of the league was due to the limited miles traveled. With Raleigh being one of the three teams in the league without any major league affiliation, Joe and the management would have to search for older players to fill out the roster. Some men from 1950 would be sure to return.

In mid March, as Medwick drove his car from Raleigh down to spring training, the *Raleigh Observer* noted, "a goodly portion of the players . . . will go by a 37-passenger bus acquired special for the spring training trek and use in Florida. . . . In all about 50 players, plus officials and followers will move in on Titusville," which is forty miles southeast of Orlando.

Claude Voiselle—called Diz—a pitcher who would later join the club, said that Medwick was "right demanding" and "started out rough" with his players, making sure these veterans understood who was in charge. Subtlety was not Medwick's style. If necessary, he would "challenge them to fight" to determine his priority on the team; in Medwick's view, this was how a man did things.

As the Capitals played exhibition home games against Greensboro, Lakeland, Scranton, and Deland at Titusville, Medwick saw that his youngest outfielder was twenty-eight and four were over thirty. In the away games at Cocoa, Ocala, and Lakeland, Medwick learned that his pitching was very uncertain.

After twenty-seven days in Florida and Georgia, the Capitals were down to eight pitchers. The season preview noted that there was much good pitching in the league, but pitching for Raleigh "was the club's biggest question mark." Most writers picked the team to finish sixth.

After two exhibition games in Raleigh on April 14 and 15 against Hagerstown, and after Joe scored from second on an infield hit, Raleigh fans read: "The players show a deep respect for Medwick's ability and knowledge. Local fans can expect one of the most colorful teams in Raleigh's seven-year history. Veteran observers figure this club had more spirit at this stage then any ever fielded here. Medwick's inspiring chatter was responsible for this." For example, "Skipper Joe Medwick did a good job of building up [Felix] Frasier's self-confidence. Realizing the boy was a good prospect, who needed seasoning badly, Medwick used him at every opportunity. Frasier responded by showing marked improvement before camp broke up." Club president Knipe was heard to say, "Medwick puts a lot of fire in the boys. I guess one reason was because he has so much in himself."

As for the players, most lived in apartments that would allow cooking. At $250 per month as an average salary, the men had to look for ways to economize. In the clubhouse, the team sold them jockstraps and sweatshirts; the pitchers got no bats to use of their own, so they had to negotiate with other players to use theirs. When team members asked for game tickets, they were told tickets were saved for special occasions. These shared experiences led to a certain camaraderie. There was a close kinship, too, with the fans, who would pass the hat for extra money for the players; after the game, the money would be evenly split up. For meal money on trips, the club would hand out cash as the players were boarding the bus for the trip.

Yet they all traveled in the inconstant bus so much and they all had the feeling they were part of the brotherhood of baseball, so they were "like a family and treated each other like family." By then, "Joe was family, too" and "got along with most everybody."

In the beginning of June, the team purchased the contract of Bob Pearson, who was a fine shortstop and an infielder they needed badly because at 23-21, they were tied for third with Danville, a Giants farm team, at two and a half games back. Reidsville was second and Durham first until the Capitals' first doubleheader sweep on June 4 against those league leaders. The addition of Pearson as a double-play partner to Crash Davis aided the team immeasurably, and the two men, in fact, would set a league record. The other addition was pitcher Claude "Diz" Voiselle, brother of Joe's Giants teammate, Bill "96" Voiselle. Diz had played in the Coastal Plains League and became the Capitals' top pitcher.

Ben Templeton, the Raleigh *Times* sports editor, had a column that appeared under the headline "Medwick, Fired By Writers' Fuel, Fans Flames with Willow. Look out, Carolina League." The column began with the following: "The Hungarian Rhapsody was in tune again and ready to strike a resounding chord that'll carry his Caps to the top. . . . Certain parties around the Class B circuit were waxing the tempers of the fiery ex-Gas Houser . . . no matter what [his] enemies may do to discredit or try to stop him or his Caps." Templeton went on to quote other newspapers in their descriptions of Joe's argument with the umpire, one of which said that Joe "mauled" the umpire. "Actually, Medwick bumped shoulders with Vanderhoff, after being ejected and after Vanderhoff had backed into Medwick as the argument began." After mentioning that a newspaperman had talked to many players in the league, he said that "few have any kind words for Medwick . . . they would rather beat Raleigh than most any other club in the circuit." Joe said, "I play to win. Off the field I try to be nice to everyone but once that bell sounds, I'm out there to beat 'em." That was what he was paid for.

When Joe tripled in three runs as part of a game that had to be replayed (it was one of three hits in the game), he was 17-60, or .283, causing him to be picked to be "Cap of the Week" by the *Raleigh Observer*.

Medwick was working hard to have his team succeed. He had very weak pitching and the team played the whole season without a left-handed batter. But when he protested a strike call by Umpire Art Talley on June 21, again he was asked to leave. "Fireworks erupted frequently when the Raleigh Capitals played," Jim Sumner wrote in his fine history of the Carolina league, *Separating the Men from the Boys: The First Half-Century of the Carolina League* (1994). "Joe Medwick . . . was hot tempered and verbally abusive. He won few friends around the league, particularly among umpiring crews . . . and [was] in constant hot water with the league office." Joe remained fiery on the field, intolerant of what he understood as incompetence or indifference; he saw no need to try to bridle that fury. Joe knew that his paychecks, as usual, depended on how well he and the team played. And he believed there was only one way to play baseball: wholeheartedly.

Of course there were laughs, too, often from on-the-field contests for the enjoyment of the fans. Most of these contests—cow milking, for example—were done by the players "not for money, just for fun . . . or a prize, like a shirt."

The games scheduled for the Capitals from June 28–30 were rained out, and with half the season over as June ended, Medwick's team was 36-34. The rainouts provided time for many men to go home and bring back their families. Isabelle Medwick and the children came to Raleigh and rented a house. They stayed for two months until school was to start up again; Joe, Jr., was the team's batboy for a while.

July started out with far too many losses—six consecutively. "I guess if Reidsville and Raleigh had the pitching, they would be the best teams in the league," said Durham Bulls manager Ace Parker. But Parker was sent some good pitchers from his affiliate, the Detroit Tigers. Medwick, without an affiliate, had to rely on President Knipe to buy him some arms, particularly a fourth starter to go along with Voiselle, Foxworth, and Hennecheck. On a roster hitting .254 and fielding .958, there were only six pitchers. Diz Voiselle recalled that this deprivation caused the team to pull together and feel a strong sense of unity.

On a short hop to Burlington, North Carolina, Nick Panella missed the bus and Joe fined him an exorbitant $500. Seeing the size of the fine, Diz Voiselle went to Joe and said with a smile, "I want $500 for *making* the trip." In front of 210 fans in Burlington, Medwick's six-inning homer scored the third run against the Burlington Bees in a 3-2 Diz Voiselle win to begin the month of July. Joe was coming to bat about 70 percent fewer times than his everyday players. On the second day of the month, again in Burlington, Crash Davis's single in the tenth inning yielded a win that took the team into first place by .001. Joe was hitting .305.

A rainout at home was followed by a split with the Cardinals at Southside Park. In his "The Sports Observer" column, Dick Herbert reminded his readers that "Four weeks from tonight the Carolina League season will come to the end of its 140-game season . . . in the tightest race in the league's history." He told them that the double-play combination for Raleigh was excellent, but with "the present pitching sensation of the league" with Winston-Salem and "the best hitter in the league in Ray Jablonski . . . if there must be a favorite . . . it would have to be Winston Salem. . . . Pitching will hold the key to the pennant race." For the Capitals, "The loss of Dick Baxter, the league's best relief pitcher, was a crippling blow. . . . With him available, the Capitals could have a rested starter ready for every game. Now every man on the staff had to be ready to start and to relieve. . . . Ordinarily the Capitals would go with seven pitchers, but now they have only five." It was going to be very difficult for Joe's team to win in this situation. That he had finessed his team into the lead said a lot for his managerial ability. This was a team of veterans, mostly playing against some of the top prospects that five other teams had to supply. Raleigh was second in home runs and steals in the league and third in fielding average.

Scheduled next were seven games against seventh-place Fayetteville at home over a four-day time span. This would be a pitching staff ordeal in any circumstance, but in the last days of the pennant, and with five pitchers, Medwick had to be thinking of trying to make the play-off group of four. Indeed, he had to be watching the four-game lead over fourth-place Reidsville.

Medwick also had to be alert to the condition of the team bus. Unlike the team Studebakers in Scottdale, this vehicle was untrustworthy and it was on the eighty-mile trip to Danville, Virginia, on August 22 that the "drive shaft fell off of the bus and we [players] had to jump out hoping the brakes held on a hill." Nevertheless, that problem got solved; it was just the pitching problem now.

It was the Cardinals who let the Capitals know about their pitching. Manager Medwick went hitless at home in a 14-4 loss, and then his team lost again, 12-0, on August 27. After a laugher like that one, the team got together to enjoy themselves, going to the beach down below Cherry Point as a group, perhaps even on the team bus.

A win by Diz Voiselle in game two of August 28 stopped a four-game losing streak. With sixty runs scored in the seven games with Fayetteville, the Capitals won those games in which they scored many runs, losing those games that ended 3-2 and 2-0. Medwick walked twice in these games, three of which saw him as a pinch hitter.

September began with three days and four games left, and Raleigh was four back. But they owned third place. A crowd of 3,728 in Devereaux Meadows greeted the Capitals in their last two games against the Bulls, which they split. But in those games, the team set a league record for double plays at 177, mostly the work of shortstop Bob Pearson and second baseman Crash Davis. Joe kept a commemorative ball of that record.

The play-offs ended quickly. Raleigh was swept by Winston-Salem by a combined score of 30-9. *Separating the Men from the Boys* recounts the Winston-Salem story: "The champion Cardinals produced . . . first-rate future major leaguers. . . . Stu Miller (13-10, 2.88) became one of baseball's best relievers, pitching in 704 big-league games . . . and 1951 Carolina League Player of the Year Ray Jablonski, Winston-Salem's standout third baseman." This team won the championship in just five games against Reidsville. It was judged to be the 62nd greatest team in minor league history.

Dick Herbert, in "The Sports Observer," admitted "Third place was the best the Raleigh Capitals could do . . . not one Raleigh player was on the first [All-Star team]. It was felt all along that the Raleigh pitching staff wasn't good enough to land the club in first place. . . . Voiselle was the only steady winner in the stretch drive. . . . When the Capitals reported for a month of spring training in Florida . . . of the ten chunkers who showed up at camp, only one was with the team [at the end]. . . . But after a seventh-place finish in 1950, third place was a big advance this season for Raleigh." By finishing six games back, Medwick did a fine job with awful pitching and without a left-handed batter. Finishing in third place and having the team rank third in attendance with 80,976 spectators meant almost 13,000 more paid than was the case for the fourth-place team.

Joe tied for second in the voting for the Manager of the Year. (Some people seemed to understand what a good job he was doing as a manager.)

But it was clear that independent teams such as Medwick's were in serious trouble in the minors. The teams with affiliations could supply not just young players but quality young players to their teams, and the number and quality of the unsigned older players had to be distributed over many teams and leagues. Besides, what pay could be offered to the veteran players was modest since those teams were not particularly successful, and therefore, like Raleigh, often finished in the red.

The Coastal Plain League, the Tri-State League, the Western Carolina League, the Piedmont League, and the Virginia League—all alive in 1951—would not live much longer. Consequently, the jobs managing these teams also diminished.

Joe Medwick, at the least, did not have the reputation of being a flatterer, so many owners would be reluctant to hire him, no matter how productive a team might become under his management. Joe was running on his reputation as a player of quality. Anything else he might have to offer an owner was generally not well known. His excellence clearly resided in his dedication to performance, and he certainly had demonstrated his ability to handle men and to get them to play together harmoniously and produce.

26

Tampa and Out, 1952

There were 16 fewer minor leagues in 1952 than in 1949, and 137 fewer minor league teams, as the lower minor leagues began to disappear. Medwick returned to the class B Florida International League (F.I.L.). There were changes. Havana, the biggest city in class B baseball, sold off most of its stars in 1951. The Tampa team, the Smokers, won the pennant in 1951 under Ben Chapman, and when Chapman went on to a job as a Cincinnati coach, Joe was hired for Tampa.

The league opener on April 8 was announced as a "clash at Al Lang Field in the Sunshine City at 8:30. . . . The first Negro player in the history of the Florida International League will start for the Smokers in right field. He was big Claro Duany, giant outfielder." In the ninth, the team down, Joe sent himself to bat, the third pinch hitter, and "blasted out a triple," which scored a run. But the next hitter was out at first and the Smokers lost by 3-2.

The home opener was Wednesday, April 9, sponsored by Egypt Temple Shrine, where tickets could be bought, as well as at Walgreen's drugstore. Joe had a pinch-hit double in this game and was given an intentional walk the next day, both wins for Tampa.

At the St. Petersburg Saints, the Smokers won again and were now 4-1. On April 13, the team went to Miami Beach to oppose the Flamingos, managed by Pepper Martin. Johnnie was now forty-eight to Medwick's forty-one. Against Martin's team, Joe pitched Jose Nakamura, who was known as the "young Japanese-Cuban southpaw." Medwick helped his pitcher by pinch-hitting an RBI on a fly, still not counted as a sacrifice. At the end of the series with Miami Beach, the Smokers were in first place.

But by May 12, Tampa had lost six in a row and occupied third place, though they were 21 and 14. On May 14, Joe was tossed out of the game after quarreling about a decision at third base. Coach Oscar Rodriguez managed in his place. At game's end, and after a week since Medwick took himself off the active roster, the team was scoring four runs on average, while the opponents were scoring nine in each game. Another loss followed on May 15, prompting Pete Norton to write, "there was nothing wrong with this year's Tampa club that a little better pitching and a few timely base hits wouldn't cure." But a crowd of 902 on May 16 saw a Tampa pitching collapse in the ninth and the 5-2 loss resulted in the Smokers dropping into the second division, four and a half games back. With its win, Pepper Martin's Flamingos stayed in front by two and a half games. Being 1-8 in the last nine games had dropped the team into the second division after forty games. That Tampa was out of the first division for the first time since 1950 didn't help Joe or the team.

By May 19 the team was back in fourth place. A game was stopped by rain in the third inning on May 20 and the team traveled 280 miles for a three-game series with Miami Beach. A win on May 21 kept them in fourth, as did a loss the next day.

The next day, May 23, "owner Tom Spicola [had] a lengthy conference with [Medwick] and members of the Tampa club," Tampa *Tribune* sports editor Byron Hollingsworth reported. Spicola said, "I like Joe very much and have high respect for him. But I feel that change was necessary for the best interest of all concerned." The same writer the next day in his column wrote, "Joe Medwick lost his job. . . . Whether this will solve the problems only time will tell. . . . Early in the season, Medwick said his club was winning without capable pitching. When the team hit the skids, Medwick said the pitching had caught up with them." As of May 20, the team was first in batting average and fourth in fielding average. But the team won in 1951 and the owner was impatient for another championship, so he chose to have running his team a proven success in the league, Oscar Rodriguez, the former manager of the four-time champion

Havana Cubans. (Tampa finished in third in 1952, 19 games back. Half of the F.I.L. teams changed managers.)

In nine at bats, Medwick hit .333, all extra-base hits: this was his farewell to baseball as a player.

There were those who thought that Joe believed it wasn't fair to be away so much when his children were in high school; others speculated that this was a cover. When Joe flew the one thousand miles back home to Geyser Drive and St. Louis, he had been in baseball for ten months of the preceding thirty-six, and he knew it was time to be out of baseball. From now on, he would have to earn his living by selling insurance.

Within a few months, Joe was invited to the second annual reunion of Houston Buffaloes and Texas League Old Timers, a game that would serve as a model for others that followed. Once it was time to go to Buff Stadium for a five-inning game, Joe signed a lot of autographs and hit the fence with a double in batting practice. Under a photo caption that said "Ol' Diz got aid and comfort after galloping three bases" was a picture of Joe fanning Dean with a large white towel. Clearly this was a time to have some fun, to recall memories—to let fans see your age. Then it would be time to go home and disappear.

Still, Medwick did not altogether disappear from the newspapers. An AP article with Joe Reichler's byline tried to select "the top sluggers of all time" and listed "the top 25 run producers based upon their five best consecutive seasons." Joe, one of fourteen with more than 600 RBIs in a five-year span, is ranked tenth with an average of 131.4 RBIs per season from 1935–1939.

By the end of August, Arky Vaughan, Joe's Dodger teammate who was four months younger than Joe, was dead.

As Joe left baseball, the game was changing. For the first time, four umpires were required at all games. In the next three years, three teams would move from their homes of fifty years or more to the strong minor league towns of Milwaukee, Baltimore, and Kansas City.

Medwick would never stop believing he was a baseball star, but it was not Joe's game anymore.

27

Amadee and the Billikins
Until . . . , 1953–1967

As 1953 began, Medwick had turned forty-one and his children were both in high school. His decision was firm to stay in St. Louis and to stop going to the winter meetings looking for a job in baseball. At odd times, he still tried to get down to Florida at the beginning of the year and work out in uniform at the Cardinals camp. Back home, he began to follow a mostly new routine, one that did not have him in his Cardinals uniform. What he wore to work now was what he used to wear after work when he was a professional ballplayer.

When he was a ballplayer, he was a celebrity among celebrities. Benny Goodman, for instance, who worked nights, came to the day ball games and he and Medwick traded tickets to each other's events.

Medwick was a different person out of uniform, as had always been the case. Ballplayers are frequently different people "when the bell rings" or "between the lines," and this was true in Joe's case. But Joe was not a ballplayer anymore, and although he would have liked to be in uniform, he was not.

Clearly, Joe was unhappy about his inability to find a job in baseball, particularly since, as in this year, so many others he had played with did have jobs in the game. Dizzy Dean and Al Simmons were elected to the National Baseball Hall of Fame, so now Frisch and Dean, two teammates, were in the Hall.

Bill Terry, age fifty-six, was also due for enshrinement, but failed to be elected by seven votes. There was much for Joe to learn here about what Bill James calls "the politics of glory." Dizzy Dean, a broadcaster for years now, was elected with 150 wins, while Terry, with a .341 lifetime average, was not. Except for lifetime average, Medwick's statistics were superior to Terry's. But Terry was "disliked by the media for his coldness and impatience." *Total Baseball* pointed out what Joe knew: "Some oldtime sportswriters were kind of happy to see Terry low-rated. He was the kind of player who, if he thought you were a jerk, said so. Some call that 'refreshing honesty'; others call it 'arrogance.' Once the reputation was set, he couldn't say anything to please some writers." It was those writers who had the power to elect or not elect to the Hall of Fame. This description fit Joe as well as Terry.

Still, Joe felt that his achievements alone would get him elected; he was still learning.

While he waited, he had to learn the insurance business, so he took "courses with the Aetna Company and spent hours with the top men in the business to learn the fundamentals."

Joe followed the changes in the Cardinals when August Busch, Jr., bought the team from Fred Saigh, who was about to go to prison for tax evasion. And then Busch bought Sportsman's Park when the Browns moved to Baltimore, just as the Braves had moved to Milwaukee.

In the next year, along with Bill Dickey, Terry was elected to the Hall of Fame, twenty-seven years after his career ended. Medwick led Dickey in every single offensive category. The other big baseball news was Joe DiMaggio, idol of New York, missing election by 14 votes. Many people have pointed out DiMaggio's statistics showing that he had as many strikeouts (369) as home runs (361). Medwick had as many strikeouts (551) as doubles (540), but it appeared that voters didn't think doubles were important enough to get Joe 1 vote. DiMaggio had one season of 200 hits; Medwick four. This year fifty-three players got votes. Elected also was Rabbit Maranville, whose lifetime average of .254 was 70 points lower than Medwick's. Could Joe learn from this?

The Athletics moved to Kansas City, leaving Shibe Park for the Phillies, just as the Browns/Orioles left Sportsman's for the Cardinals.

The next year, 1955, DiMaggio, playing in the same era as Medwick, was elected three years after his career ended with the same
lifetime batting average (.324) as Medwick. This was also the year
that photographers were banished from the field forever.

This year Medwick was in the newspapers again, this time because he was

> now a Vice-President with Braun-Hunsaker and Associates, Insurance. In
> the insurance business three years, he was now "batting" around .250
> and, according to Hunsaker, he was improving his average rapidly after
> clinching one sale in ten during his "rookie" year. The transition from
> baseball to insurance was not an easy one for Medwick. He said, "In base-
> ball you have yourself to sell, but in insurance, you have an intangible
> item to sell." He adds that his baseball background was a wonderful
> "door opener." People who know him or had heard of him call for insur-
> ance advice. . . . Fortunately, during his baseball career, Medwick had
> made many personal appearances before large groups and had met and
> talked to many people during his travels with the team. This gave him
> the poise and confidence so necessary to an insurance salesman.
>
> In summing up his reasons for turning to insurance as a career, Med-
> wick said, "Although I had many opportunities to go into other fields
> of activity, I felt that insurance offered the best possibility for a good in-
> come, and I also like to get around and meet people."

How he must have missed baseball.

Luckily for Joe, around this time he met sports cartoonist Amadee
Wohlschlaeger and made a friend for life. Two people called Amadee
"Am": his wife, Vi, and his friend Joe. To everyone else he was "Dee."
Just as Joe had not been given artistic talent, Amadee had been denied
athletic ability. Amadee and Joe fished together. Amadee recalled that
"Joe tried to teach me to play golf at a nine-hole course. I had so much
bad luck hitting the ball in the wrong place that Medwick would say,
'If I spit on the ground you'd be in the water.'" But Amadee could talk
to Joe about the sorts of things that an artist who was alert to people
was attuned to.

The *Sporting News* at that time picked its all-time All-Star team
and placed Joe as a utility outfielder for the National League team,
with Frisch listed as the utility infielder. The amazing moves of the
Dodgers and the Giants (two of Medwick's former teams) from New
York to the West Coast dominated the baseball news during this
time. This was also the era when the Cardinals signed their first
black player.

Joe was in the news a little more, too, appearing at Tulsa's Diamond Dinner, a favorite among Texas League players. Joe and Cardinal shortstop Marty Marion ran the Marty Marion Camp for Boys at Sherwood School, a fourteen-acre space with a swimming pool, mess hall, and ball fields. Nine others were on the staff for basketball, swimming, and archery. Joe was described as "the bronze mellow gentleman working so hard and patiently to teach these youngsters how to swing a bat."

Medwick made the newspapers now when he won golf championships at Sunset Hills, wearing Bermuda shorts, shooting a two-handicap. His reputation was recalled: "He was a bad-ball hitter," Jack Rice wrote on July 7. "That means that the pitcher thought it was a bad ball. Medwick and the few blessed batters like him were realists. If it's a hit, it's a good pitch."

This was also the period when Joe's father, John, died. He was buried in St. James Cemetery in Woodbridge, New Jersey.

By 1959, it seemed clear that Joe had become more comfortable as a former ballplayer. He even filed for election for the post of collector of the City of Sunset Hills, a vacancy that opened when Collector Joseph Redel moved up to alderman. Less than two weeks later, Medwick beat Orval Waterhout, a former Sunset Hills alderman, in the election by 87-74.

The year 1959 was also the twenty-fifth anniversary of the Gashouse Gang team and the World Series games of 1934. Before a dinner for the Capuchin Charity Guild of Detroit to mark the event, Bob Broeg wrote, "Medwick had always contended he was wronged. We've always nodded politely . . . because he's a gentlemanly insurance salesman now and a member of the country club set [but then] Joe was tough as a kid. Mean and hungry, hungry for base hits and buckerinos, a slashing symbol of the Gashouse Gang and not nearly so lighthearted as more carefree comrades. Now the way Marvin Owen, Tiger third baseman and party of the second part that day, told the story recently to Lyall Smith, sports editor of the Detroit Free Press, we—like Detroit—owe Joe an apology."

At the dinner, Joe remembered 1934. "We weren't leaving until the next morning and they sent three cops to my hotel room," Medwick said. "When I got off the plane in Detroit for that celebration . . . 25 years later, there was three cops to meet me. I said, 'Jeez, are you guys still here?'" Owen who now scouted for the Orioles, spoke at the dinner on April 30 and "by loudspeaker hookup, Owens admitted, 'It was my fault. I was on the bag faking as if the throw was coming to me and Joe did what any good runner would do.'"

This public acknowledgment of Joe's uprightness in events from so many years ago may have had a soothing effect on him. He always wanted to have what he considered his due, and he felt, it seemed, contented by Owen's confession. This confession, in combination with Medwick's adjustment to life after baseball, may have made him into a different man, like a soldier adjusting to peacetime and civilian life. Not that Medwick was no longer eager to be respected and appreciated, and not that his anger at the failure to be esteemed was missing, but he was more accepting of what his life had to offer him now.

No one was given a place in the Hall of Fame election of 1960; Ed Roush, the highest vote-getter, was sixty-six votes short. Joe was lacking too, in seventeenth position, and worse, he received fewer votes than he did in the previous election. Roush, with only 4 percent fewer at bats than Joe, led Medwick only in career steals and triples. Medwick, for example, had 400 more RBIs and 200 more doubles than the former Reds outfielder. And as Bob Broeg pointed out in *Baseball from a Different Angle*, Roush's "outfielding never came within spittin' distance of his charm or his bat." Joe was quietly furious about being denied what he knew belonged to him—what he had earned: election to the Hall of Fame.

By the time Medwick would be playing golf again in Florida most other years, he was now staying in St. Louis, partly because he had a radio show on KMOX. His name, at least, was there for the public to see. *Post-Dispatch* reporter Harold Tuthill allowed us a look at what Medwick kept as mementos of his career:

In the Medwick manor on Geyer Road were baseballs, bats, gloves, plaques, good luck charms . . . he treasures his two World Series gloves which have been done in bronze. . . . All-Star game bats . . . a good luck bronze elephant given to him by Mrs. Charles C. Spink . . . mother of the editor of *The Sporting News*. . . . "After I hit a home run . . . I carried another baseball in my pocket to trade with the fan who got the ball. After I brought the ball in, Doc Weaver would mark it with India ink, the date, the circumstances under which it was hit, the batteries and the final score . . . one autographed by Harry Truman . . . Babe Ruth . . . a ball from Houston . . . this one I got in Raleigh in 1951 when our club set a double play record of 163 . . . this was from the 1937 All-Star game in Washington . . . ." On the west walls in his den there were framed scrolls of the years he was elected to Christy Walsh's All-American team 1935-39 . . . photographs and caricatures of him . . . on a ball was written "2,000."

The wonderful things that Yogi Berra said about Medwick in the March 20, 1960, *Parade* were well appreciated. The 35-year-old Berra regarded Joe with affection.

But something was happening at St. Louis University, a Catholic university. The story seems to be that Head Coach Jerry DelGaudio was losing favor with the administration. As the school hoped to be more competitive in intercollegiate baseball, Medwick was offered the job of associate baseball coach. That he was offered the job had something to do with his being Catholic, but because he was not a high-school graduate, much less a college graduate, he could not be offered the job of assistant coach, according to university regulations. Medwick signed to coach with athletic director Bob Stewart on July 24, 1960, saying, "I'm proud to be associated with St. Louis University in a baseball capacity. . . . We hope to bring the sport to the same level as soccer and basketball at the school. We hope in the future we'll be able to attract more of the top young players in the local area to come to the university. That will be one of my concerns, along with helping DelGaudio." He was back in baseball; he was back in uniform.

It was probably true that Medwick's experience working at Marty Marion's Camp and at Mickey Owen's Baseball School for Boys did him some good at the university. But when Joe went to work with the team, DelGaudio was no longer with St. Louis University and the *University News* told how the team would play five games in the fall against McKendree and Concordia, among others, coached by Medwick, until a head coach was hired by the school.

An honor came Joe's way on June 20, 1962, when he was given a certificate and a plaque for 200 homers, received as a member of the newly formed "200 Home Run Club." The plaque was signed by Warren Giles, National League president, and Joe Cronin, American League president. Only fifty-four players had hit 200 or more home runs at this point in baseball history. And when Joe retired he was in the top twenty of all home run hitters. (He is in the top fifty of Hall of Fame players now.)

Another good thing happened to Joe earlier in the year when Roy Lee took the place of Head Coach Jerry DelGaudio for St. Louis

University. Having played a few games in the majors, Lee was one of a number of men who made up the baseball group in St. Louis. Mrs. Margaret Lee and her son, Bill, and Mrs. Isabelle Medwick and her children had visited each other in their homes before Joe and Roy worked together. Medwick signed to work with the team from January to mid June.

With Roy and Joe doing their jobs well, the team had a winning season, though just barely, with a 13-12 record. The team made it into the College World Series tournament for the first time in the school's history.

Yet what Joe considered to be the slighting by the Baseball Writers of America still burned in him. The year 1963 was a time for the veterans committee to vote and they could only elect players whose careers ended at least fifteen years before Joe's did.

One way or another, Medwick kept busy in baseball. The Art Gaines Baseball Camp, which was held at Hunnewell, Missouri, for boys ages 9–22, hired Joe as part of the instructional staff, as did the Hall of Fame camp at the St. Thomas More school in Colchester, Connecticut.

During this period, Medwick's grandson, John, was born. Medwick was showing his signs of aging. His hip was so painful by now that he stopped playing golf. But he and Amadee still went to many athletic events in the area and at one of them, as Amadee related, Joe exploded:

> Joe was struggling to get in the Hall of Fame and was pretty disappointed with all of that neglect and failure. He knew that in three years his eligibility would be gone. We were out at a basketball game and . . . Jack Herman, a local sportswriter, asked him about that and Medwick replied, "if the young writers would read my records, I would have been in ten years ago." The next day, St. Louis headlines read, "Medwick Feels Blackballed by Writers."
>
> The headline pissed off [Bob] Broeg and [Bob] Burns, who then wrote columns with negative stories, and Joe became very upset.

This was what Broeg wrote on February 24, 1963:

> Instead of sulking in Sunset Hills, Ducky Wucky, the old muscle man of the Cardinals, might consider a few facts of baseball life. . . . Since Muscles retired . . . just three younger men—Joe DiMaggio, Bob Feller and Jackie Robinson—have been elected to the Hall of Fame. They had

more impressive credentials. So, too, will the next crop of outstanding players . . . Ted Williams, Stan Musial and Warren Spahn . . . Yogi Berra . . . and certainly Willie Mays. Most of the good ones, though, including the Medwicks, must wait and hope. . . . Medwick will have to make it on merit alone because, to be frank, old Jersey Joe at his peak wasn't worried nearly as much about making friends as he was in influencing opposing pitchers. Sentiment won't carry the day for Medwick as it did for lovable little Rabbit Maranville. . . . The Hungarian Rhapsody and Muscular Magyar . . . was not likely to be able to politic as skillfully as Ray Schalk . . . who slipped into Cooperstown with a .253 average.

But how it must have exasperated Joe, with his lifetime average of .324, the same as DiMaggio's, almost 40 points higher than Berra's and with 220 more doubles than his old pupil had.

Medwick, still the master batsman, had been sought out for batting tips by Bill White, Julian Javier, and Carl Warwick. "Medwick, careful not to step on any toes, has made it a point to help the Redbird players only if they seek him out. 'When Johnny Keane was manager [1961–1964], he suggested that I go ahead and volunteer to help anyone, but I told him, no, that the players would have to come to me.'"

Now Medwick's friendship with Amadee was most important to Joe because it was Wohlschlaeger's advice to "Be more diplomatic." Medwick finally learned his lesson and "went to sportswriters Bob Burns and Broeg and apologized."

But Medwick was also smart enough to begin serious campaigning for election to the Hall of Fame, and from 1963 on, Medwick devoted a lot of time and energy to the work. Joe re-signed a contract with radio station KMOX in St. Louis to conduct a weekly hitting-lesson show, which helped keep him in front of the public.

On February 2, 1963, Medwick said to Morris Siegel of the *Sporting News*:

"I don't want to be remembered as the guy who got thrown out of a World's Series game," Medwick complained. "I don't want to be remembered as some kind of freak, like Wrong Way Corrigan or that guy who ran the wrong way in the Rose Bowl game. I want to be remembered," he said bitterly, "as Joe Medwick, ball player. Am I wrong?"

"Jackie Robinson?" Medwick asked. "Good player, but how many second basemen do you suppose rate Cooperstown over him? He made it the first year he was eligible and he made it principally because he was the first Negro player." Medwick, a boyish 51 now in the insurance business in St. Louis, thought baseball had blacklisted him. "How many jobs have I been offered?" he asked. "My pals? Leo Durocher, did he ever do anything for me when he had the Dodgers and the Giants? And I could add many more names, but what's the use?"

Jack Herman, writing on February 20, 1963, recorded Joe:

"Roush," he said, "at an old timers reunion last year in New York needled writers there, 'How can you vote me in and leave Medwick out?'" Blunt spoken as always. Medwick reeled off several instances when baseball officials reneged on promises to him. "Whenever I negotiated my contracts," he recalled, "Mr. Breadon and Mr. Rickey said, 'We'll take care of you, Joe, and keep you in the organization later on.' . . . And Leo Durocher . . . turned out to be something less than his best friend. "I know I could have helped him as a coach," Medwick insists, "He knows I wanted to get back into baseball, too."

"If players were going to be judged by what they did on the field, I should be in."

Medwick was only one of many players who turned angry at being denied a place in the Hall of Fame. For example, "Mize . . . was a cranky, drawling master of disgust over the years when the Hall of Fame was denied him," as Bob Broeg wrote in 1981.

Medwick softened his approach. Broeg wrote on March 26, 1963, finding Medwick "sunning himself in the bullpen at Al Lang Field. . . . 'Too many of the writers who knew me were gone and the new cities means that new men who never saw me soon will be voting as ten-year members of the baseball writers' association. . . . There were others who belong . . . Arky Vaughan . . . Lloyd Waner . . . Frank McCormick . . . Billy Herman . . . Ernie Lombardi . . . Chick Hafey. . . . But if those men aren't interested in speaking up for themselves, I'm not going to sit silent.'"

In an interview, Bob Broeg recalled that it was at this time that Medwick, clearly, "was pretty blatant about [campaigning for the Hall]—he kinda nailed me one day in St. Pete.

"'After Chick Hafey' I said. Joe said, 'But that's Hafey. What about yourself?' He tried not to get too mad at me that time."

Mr. Broeg preferred that Hafey be elected before Joe, since Hafey's career ended eleven years earlier than Joe's. That Hafey did not lead Joe on a per-season basis in games, at bats, runs, doubles, triples, or RBIs didn't matter. That Joe led Hafey by an average of sixteen more hits per average season didn't matter. Broeg thought that Hafey was the better fielder. Yet the statistics don't say so, particularly fielding runs in *Total Baseball*, in which Joe had a ranking of 52 and Hafey 0, but the players of one's youth are, after all, more significant than any that follow.

Impediments such as these slowed Medwick's progress into the Hall of Fame, but meanwhile, the St. Louis University team, the Billikens, became stronger, at 18-12-1, and went to the College World Series tournament again in 1963.

For the year 1964, there was a runoff election for the Hall of Fame; Joe wasn't in it, but he did receive more votes in the runoff than he did in the original election. This is the way *Total Baseball* describes the system:

> A nominating system was installed after the 1945 election, providing for the top twenty vote-getters in a preliminary balloting to be listed alphabetically on a second and final ballot. The preliminary election's vote totals were not to be divulged until after the final balloting (so as not to influence voters), nor would they assure anyone of automatic election. However, this system proved an utter failure in 1946 and was amended in December of that year. Thereafter, anyone receiving 75 percent of the votes on the nominating ballot would be automatically elected, eliminating the runoff election. No runoff was required until 1949, when Charlie Gehringer was elected on the second ballot. The nominating system was discontinued after that year but revived from 1960 to 1968 (providing for reconsideration of the top thirty vote-getters), being put into practice in 1964 and 1967.

Take a look at 1964:

Needed to Elect: 151
Luke Appling: 142
Red Ruffing: 141
(Medwick was given 108 votes.)
1964 Runoff
Needed to Elect: 170 (One-Player Maximum)
 Luke Appling: 189
 (Medwick was given 130 votes.)

By now many were speaking up for Joe's election, including former opponents who recognized Medwick's greatness as a player, even as Joe continued to work for election.

"I always hit fourth but I don't like it at the present time. . . ." The former Cardinal slugger . . . suggested that the rules of admission may be too stringent. "I don't know how they can be relaxed. . . . Under the original voting plan, those who received the most votes came in. The writers have seen fit to change the rules. I have no complaints with them," Medwick continued, "whatever the sports writers want is fine with me. They elected a tremendous player. I feel sorry for Ruffing, who came so close and yet was so far away. I'd rather miss by 30 or 40, I think, than just a few." Medwick will be eligible two years hence.

"Getting into the Hall of Fame was every player's dream. I happen to feel that I deserve the honor. I've been criticized for expressing that feeling," he told Rich Koster. "But I don't see anything wrong with voicing my belief. . . ." Frisch . . . calls him "the best bad-ball hitter in baseball history. He was also a pretty fair good-ball hitter. . . . When I was managing, I used to think he'd have been the greatest hitter in baseball if he laid off bad pitches. But now that I'm older, I'm not so sure. . . . He was a vicious hitter, the hardest I ever saw next to Babe Ruth." To this Hank Greenberg added, "I don't see how they can keep him out." And Carl Hubbell pays him this tribute: "He was the toughest hitter for me to get out." Medwick feels that his chances for election have lessened as the years have passed. He first became eligible in 1953 and received a number of votes in the years immediately following. . . . "Now I'm campaigning for myself to get into the Hall of Fame. It would make my dream come true. It would round out my life in baseball; everything else had happened. . . ." During the twenty-seven years since that awesome [1937] season no National Leaguer had yet matched his totals for hits, doubles, runs batted in or total bases and only Stan Musial had bettered his .374 mark.

Describing Medwick's play, Arthur Daley of the *New York Times* remembered "the chunky outfielder with the built-in swagger [who] was a ferocious hitter. . . . He was an excellent fielder too and he hustled like all getout. He . . . fought the enemy with grim intensity," recognizing that it may have been that "grim intensity" that made Joe so different from players like Dizzy Dean, who got votes for charm and cooperation with the press. In Daley's view, "Medwick was not at all presumptuous in thinking he rates a place in the Hall. He has it coming to him."

And in October in Jack Mann's column in the *New York Herald-Tribune,* Medwick lashed out, his bitterness evident. Mann supported Medwick and mostly let him talk:

> "What do they want me to do?" he asked. "Die a natural death in a small town?" . . . Medwick still burned about 1934, mostly because no one will let him forget it. "Mr. Landis said he was sorry," Medwick said, "but he had to get the game finished. I told him I had a right to slide hard. How the hell do you play baseball? . . . Marvin Owen did a bush thing, he faked a tag. . . . No. I didn't spike him. He stepped on me—by accident. I met him 25 years later and we got along okay, but I told him it was still bush."

Here we see an important element in Joe's attitudes. To a player, "bush" means both being nasty in a small-minded way and being unprofessional. Jack Mann quoted someone else: "'There was a time,' said Biggie, 'when he was a louse.' Biggie is Julius Garagnani, who minds the store at Musial's restaurant when The Man isn't there, which is often. 'And now,' Biggie said, 'he's crying to get in the Hall of Fame. When he was going good he didn't give a damn about anybody and now he knows you need friends.'"

Joe, the "solitary one," did have friends, even if Biggie wasn't one of them. But he needed votes.

Biggie understood: "'But that don't matter,' Biggie said, 'That ain't what you're voting for. He belongs in that thing because he was a great ball player. They voted for Hornsby didn't they?'"

Rogers Hornsby was not a friend of Biggie's either. But Biggie obviously had no need to excel, so he was not liable to understand that need so powerful in Hornsby and in Medwick. Perhaps Biggie could only understand and appreciate the sweetness of Musial. Being a great ballplayer sometimes means *not* being something else. It was a matter of what a player wanted, what drives him. If he wanted to be liked, he tended to work at that and develop the ability to charm.

But charm was only one quality. If Joe didn't value charm, then he did value courage, toughness; those were men's qualities. Playing silently under criticism while suffering double vision—and hitting .302—in 1940 perhaps should be a quality that merits as much admiration as charm does. Should charm get you into the Hall of Fame? Should grace? Should the lack of charm or grace keep you out?

Joe clearly didn't think of himself as a louse. (In fact, the only other person who reportedly didn't like Joe was Pete Coscarart, who was still angry that Joe, in Havana in 1941, would not give Coscarart a ride in his car.) There were people like Bob Broeg who thought Medwick was crude, but then again the desire among athletes and sportswriters—and gangsters—for what they called "class" was painfully clear, even if what passed for "class" might also be called "style." During his playing days, Medwick was stylish, but not elegant, except on the ball field. Medwick thought the ball yard was the place to be who you were. And perhaps character—honesty being an important part of that trait— was more important than what was called "class."

Mann continued to let Medwick talk: "'I wanted a baseball job,' he said. 'I wrote letters to everybody. Gabe Paul wrote me back and it was a nice letter. But I didn't hear from anybody else.'"

Joe still didn't really understand the complicated politics of baseball; he didn't have to—he was a player. But not understanding the politics had hurt him, and would continue to hurt him until he was elected.

Mann said, "It was only now occurring to Joe Medwick that in its silence, baseball was trying to tell him something. He was just beginning to get the message, but he's not giving it his undivided attention. He's too busy watching time pass by.

"Joe Medwick hit .374 in 1937 and nobody has hit that since, except Stan Musial and Ted Williams (twice). He was .324 lifetime, and nobody playing baseball today can make that statement. Joe Medwick knows that some day he'll be voted into the Baseball Hall of Fame. He knows that some day he [is] going to die.

"What he doesn't know is which of those eventualities is going to come first. It bugs him. It has become an obsession."

It was what he wanted because it was what was due to him. It was not an obsession; it was a desire for justice.

Medwick continued his work with Roy Lee at St. Louis University in 1965. In uniform again, though now wearing black horn-rimmed glasses, Medwick didn't mind screaming at opposing players to incite his own to greater achievement. This was not fashionable—Joe's intensity was not fashionable. To his players, he was "The Duck"—an odd duck, too.

To Bill Lee, the batboy and son of the coach (and now son of the president of the Frontier League as well), Joe was, of course, a grown-up—a grown-up who chewed him out for eating peanuts in the dugout (bad luck), and for letting bat handles stay crossed (also bad luck). But one day in Des Moines, Joe called young Bill Lee in his hotel room and said, "C'mon and take a walk with me." They walked together out of the hotel and down the street to a sporting goods store where Joe had Bill sit down and told the salesman to bring over his best baseball spikes, the kangaroo leather kind. "You're old enough now," Joe told Lee, "to have real spikes, the kind professional players wear." The salesman brought over many boxes for Lee to try on, and Joe made Bill put many different shoes on and walk around in them until the absolutely best pair was chosen.

One of Joe's players still talks about him with awe. At practice at Forest Park—still an "incredible hitter"—he hit "a frozen rope" during practice at age sixty.

Medwick practically incited a riot in Peoria during a game with Bradley. There was a "tall black fella pitching against us. Medwick called him a 'nigger' to ignite something—and he started throwing at us and we had to get Joe out of the park." Roy Lee sending him to the clubhouse to protect the players didn't affect the way Joe thought about the game and the winning. Insulting the opposition in every way was a managerial technique Joe learned at a young age, and continued with Frisch and with Durocher. In Joe's view, there was a connection between winning and manhood—and selfhood. He had "very little need and appreciation if you didn't want to play the game—if you didn't have the balls that The Duck thought you should, he let you know that."

Whether that intensity—that insistence on success from a 60-year-old man in black horn-rimmed glasses—helped the team or not, no one can say.

What *can* be said was that St. Louis University, the Missouri Conference champion, beat the University of Missouri, the Big Eight Conference champions, in the regional play-offs at Sportsman's Park, and were ranked sixth in the nation. The win gave them entry to Omaha's Rosenblatt Stadium for the College World Series. They had been involved in the tournament since the first year Joe and Roy Lee began coaching. But now they were in the final group of teams to play for the national championship.

In Omaha, Medwick insisted that the players eat steak for all their meals, no matter what else they ate (for the protein and energy, he said).

On June 7 at 8:30 St. Louis beat the University of Connecticut 2-1. The next night they lost to Arizona State, 13-3. Then the next day, their third game, they beat Florida State, eliminating that team from the series. But game four was against Arizona State again, when that team beat Ohio State, 9-4. Arizona State was now 52-7, using the abilities of Rick Monday and Sal Bando. Lee and Medwick's team lost 6-2 on June 10. But their 25-9 record and play in the College World Series earned them third place in the country.

The next year, 1966, the Hall of Fame elections were changed so that the voting would now occur every year. Ted Williams was elected that year, and Joe, in fourth with 61 percent of the vote, finished twenty-one votes behind Yankee pitcher Red Ruffing in second, and ten votes behind Roy Campanella in third.

Early in the winter of 1965–1966, as Red Schoendienst (then the St. Louis Cardinals manager) related, he was at a gathering with Amadee and when they talked, Dee told Red that Joe wanted to get back into baseball. While Schoendienst would not allow Medwick a seat with the big club, he did recommend a place in the minors. Amadee said that was fine; Joe just wanted to get back into baseball. Red asked Amadee if Joe would be interested in being the batting coach for the minor league teams and Amadee said yes.

In the next series of steps, Joe approached Bob Howsam, the Cardinal general manager:

> "I told Mr. Howsam I had an idea that I had been interested in for four or five years," Joe related. "I told him, "Gee whiz, when was the last time the Cardinal organization came up with their own good hitters?" In fact, the Cardinals had dropped from first to seventh in the league in 1965.
>
> "Mr. Howsam said he had an idea along the same lines and, finally, he and [Sheldon] Chief Bender [director of Minor League clubs] called me in" [in late January 1966].
>
> Result: Medwick finally will have a shot at working for a major league club. He will serve as special hitting instructor for Cardinal farmhands at St. Petersburg, starting March 17 and continuing through April 17. Medwick's last season as a player in the majors was 1948, with the Cardinals, his original club. He managed three years in the low minors.
>
> "I'm very thankful to Bob Howsam for the opportunity to get back into Organized Ball," Medwick said, "Baseball's been my life and I feel I can help some young hitters."

Joe said the opportunity to work for the Cardinals couldn't have come at a better time. "I was really down in the mouth about the Hall of Fame (he finished fourth in the balloting) and this thing really picked me up," Medwick said. "So I was 1-for-2—that's batting .500 and that's not bad." As Medwick noted, home-grown hitting standouts have been indeed rare among the Cardinals since Ken Boyer came up in 1955, six years after he was signed. Ken put in two years in the service. Tim McCarver was the only Cardinal farm product on the current varsity who had proved himself with a bat over an extended period. Medwick helped coach the St. Louis University teams in recent years. "I enjoyed that very much, but this should be even more exciting." Medwick will take over his new duties March 5 and remain on duty for at least a month.

When Joe went downtown to 3625 Dodier St. to sign his contract, it was one of the last things he did in the ball yard that had been called Sportsman's Park for so long; now it was called Busch Stadium.

Three days later, on February 5, 1966, datelined Matecumbe, Florida, Ted Williams said about Medwick, "I rate him the N.L.'s number two hitter, right behind Hornsby. When Joe was in his prime, he absolutely owned the National League."

The teams Medwick worked with were the Tulsa Oilers of the Pacific Coast League; the Arkansas Travelers; St. Petersburg, managed by Sparky Anderson; the Cedar Rapids Cardinals of the Midwest League; the Eugene Emeralds of the Northwest League; the Rock Hill Cardinals of the Western Carolina League; and the Gulf Coast Cardinals.

In Florida, Joe worked with Stan Musial, now a Cardinals vice president. Butch Yatkeman was still the clubhouse man.

On April 17, Neal Russo published an article on Joe, who was now finishing up his month-long duties.

128 Cardinal farmhands have been entrusted to hitting professor Medwick . . . and Joe, happy to be back in professional baseball, knows all 128 by name. "It took me two weeks to learn them all."

While his friends surrendered to the sun and surf, Medwick was up at 7 A.M. each day. He was at Busch Field, the minors camp, for 9:30 meetings. Calisthenics came at 10. Then work in batting cages, individual instruction periods and squad games. The only breaks were brief ones for a cup of soup. . . . "A lot of them come up to me for advice in private. They're young and they don't like to ask certain questions in front of a group because they'd feel embarrassed." As a

reminder, the former Cardinal great keeps a roster of all 128 farm players and on it he made notations of things the players should work on.
The other day his roster had these things penciled in: Ed Spezio, feet
. . . Burroughs, stride. Even on the soup breaks, Medwick volunteers
advice to the players. When squad games are in progress he sits in the
stands near the bench and talks to players as they come by. . . . Medwick, who was hired to try to speed the flow of better hitters to the majors, had done an excellent job, Sheldon Chief Bender said. . . . Of
course he likes to grab a bat and take a few swings himself.

That month's work done, Joe went back to St. Louis to work with the
university's team again. The team would make it to the college
World Series tournament for the fourth consecutive, and last, year
St. Louis University would ever make it to the College World Series.

As the college season was about a month from its end, and since
May 8, 1966, would be the end of Sportsman's Park as a major
league ball yard, Medwick was called to Busch Stadium to be honored as one of the Cardinals' eleven living Stadium immortals.

Then Joe was given coins struck in his honor with his likeness on
one side and his achievements in baseball on the other. A university
player coached by Joe told me that he was "the most humane individual to me" and "Ducky was a goofy guy." "One of my cherished
moments in my life was when he handed out to us a gold coin in a
little blue velvet pouch. He only gave them to a few people." Medwick was shy about the honor but clearly very proud to be one of
eleven.

Then on November 12, 1966, baseball honored Medwick for his
1937 Most Valuable Player award, an award marked, before the
Judge Landis Trophy started in 1944, "with a suitable emblem," such
as a wristwatch or a shotgun. Now Joe, along with nine others, was
presented with an engraved cigarette box as evidence of winning the
MVP award.

"In his later years, Joe got to be really nice," Terry Moore, Joe's
former roommate, was often quoted as saying. It may be that this
recognition of his excellence was causing the change.

A typical social outing for Joe now took place on December 4: he
rose at 4 A.M. and met his pals at 5, then traveled east for forty-three
miles near Breese in Illinois. There, at the East Fork Hunting Club,
members of the St. Louis East Side and West Side Pheasant and Bud-
weiser Society hunted for pheasants with 12- and 16-gauge shot-
guns. Amadee, Joe, and Red Schoendienst hunted together.

But later that month, Joe's "Moms" became very ill, and at age eighty-eight, died in Linden, New Jersey. She was buried in St. James Cemetery in Woodbridge. Joe's New Jersey friends saw him walking awkwardly at the funeral, his arthritic hip slowing him and taking his athlete's grace.

The next month, in the Hall of Fame voting, there was a required first ballot, and then in case of a tie, a runoff, which provided for reconsideration of the top thirty vote-getters. This system was used for most of the 1960s.

In 1967, the voting looked like this:

Nominating Ballot
Needed to Elect: 219 (292 cast)
Ducky Medwick: 212 (73 percent)
Red Ruffing: 212

Because both Ruffing and Medwick had 212 votes, there was a runoff of the top thirty. Jack Lang wrote, "It was still possible for Medwick or Ruffing or Campanella to gain 99 percent of the vote and still fail to gain election."

The writers saw the flaws in this system; it was, in fact, the end of this system. "Much of the difficulty and embarrassment surrounding writers' elections for MVP, Hall of Fame, etc. traces to carelessness or warped humor on the part of the elector. To cure this, Bob Addie, president of the BBWAA, proposes to set up a policing committee on elections. The committee will investigate and possibly disenfranchise voters of proven frivolity."

Jack Herman explained more, writing on January 26, 1967:

Now Medwick, Ruffing and 29 top vote-getters in the just-finished election will get another chance in the runoff. Under rules of the run-off, the only way Medwick and Ruffing both could step into the Hall of Fame would be to wind up tied in the voting. Only the No. 1 player named on 75 percent of the ballots will be elected in the run-off. "I'm pleased with the progress I've made so far," Medwick said Wednesday. A call from an unidentified source in New York the night before, however, upset him. "I was told I had been elected but I tried not to get my hopes up too much."

So another ballot went out with 31 names on it, two tied for spot 30; 306 people voted and the rules said only one could be elected. This was Ruffing's last year of eligibility for the writers.

1967 Runoff
Needed to Elect: 230 (304 cast; One-Player Maximum)
Red Ruffing: 266 (87.5 percent)
Ducky Medwick: 248 (82 percent)

Joe's reaction, after receiving that high of a percentage of the runoff vote was reported by UPI (United Press International) to say, "Each year I have been advancing nicely in the voting and this was the first year I have been on top. Naturally it made me proud. Let's be honest about it. This was every baseball player's dream. Little did I know when I broke into baseball in 1930 that I would even be mentioned for the Hall of Fame. I hate to see Campanella knocked out of the box but he is still a young man and his name will come up again. Maybe he'll have better luck next time."

How sweet it would have been to go into the Hall the same year as Branch Rickey, elected by the Veteran's Committee. Lloyd Waner, a .316 lifetime hitter, was also elected with 598 RBIs, though with almost 2,500 hits. Joe, on the other hand, drove in 1,383 runs and made 12 more hits than Waner.

How wonderful, though, that Joe could keep working in baseball, even if not in the big leagues. It was probably impossible to imagine how much baseball was doing for him now (his hip was giving him even more pain).

After calling the new telephone number for the Cardinals, Garfield 1-3060, Joe went down to the new address for the Cardinals, 250 Stadium Plaza, and signed his 1967 contract. On March 3, Joe signed to work both spring training and the minor league regular season.

Thus, in mid March, Joe flew down to Florida and checked in at the team hotel, the Sheraton Inn, in St. Petersburg. Once again he worked with Stan Musial, the general manager; he also met with Sheldon Bender and his assistant, Arthur Fetzner. Joe's teammate from Scottdale days, Mike Ryba, was still working with the team as a scout from Brookline Station, Missouri. Listed as instructors were Barney Schultz and Ray Hathaway (for the pitchers) and George Kissell and Joe Medwick (general instructors). At the minor league complex where Medwick worked were four fields, with three for drills and one for game play. The new teams this year for the Cardinals were the Modesto, California, club managed by Sparky Anderson and a team at Lewiston, Idaho. Tulsa was managed by Warren Spahn.

But even with the pain from his hip, as the *St. Louis Post-Dispatch* wrote on April 8,

> While his pals snooze, Joe was up at 7 A.M. He got to Busch Field, the minor league headquarters long before the 9:30 meetings. Calisthenics come at 10, followed by work in the batting cages, individual instruction and squad games. . . . As he strolls by the batting cages, he yells, "Line up your hands properly. Make your hands firm. Look straight at the pitching machine. Stay in short stride, front foot first, then hit with your arms." Medwick said many of the kids come to him for private instruction. "They're young and they don't like to ask questions in front of a group . . . ," the swatting professor said. . . . The Cardinal varsity, though heavy on pitching talent from the farms, had been short on swatters. Hence, the presence of Medwick, considered by many second only to Rogers Hornsby among right-handed hitters in the National League. So, Ducky glowed deservedly as he reeled off the name of the nine .300 hitters last year at Tulsa. . . . Medwick worked a lot with Alex Johnson, Ed Spiezio, Bobby Tolan and Ted Savage.

Joe's life in the minor leagues often was spent with Barney Schultz. In those years, there were only two minor league traveling instructors for most teams. Schultz was the pitching coach and Joe served as both hitting and fielding coach. Each team had only a manager, so a player was responsible for the first-base coaching.

During spring training, a schedule for the year would be made out with the advice of farm director, George Silvey. "Joe was kinda friendly with everyone," Barney Schultz told me, "and we became pretty close. . . . We became quite close. So he came to me and said let's arrange our schedules so we're in the same town on the same date."

There were seven teams that had to be coached—teams in the southeast, the Midwest, the southwest and the far west—"and we worked closely with each manager." Special trips might be made "if a player needed help or if the major league team was thinking of bringing a player up. Otherwise, Joe and I would meet and work with players together. Then we'd talk to each other, compare information, and write our reports." Schultz pointed out something often forgotten about Medwick. "He was devoted to his work, serious in his work. Joe was a very active hitting instructor and he knew what he was talking about with hitting."

There was fun for the two as well on the trips. "There were days when we'd have an off-day. Like in Tulsa, the club owner introduced us to a member of a rich country club and we'd play there. He liked to joke around a lot you know. Anything for a little laugh." This included Joe stepping deliberately on Schultz's ball on the green; Barney would play dumb and try to putt it.

The new election rules for the Hall of Fame for 1968 said that anyone who was named on 75 percent of the ballots was elected. In their last year of eligibility for election by the writers were Joe, Terry Moore, Frank Crosetti, Frank McCormick, and Arky Vaughan. Once again, Joe campaigned.

In December, more than 400 ballots were put in the mail to ten-year members of the BBWAA as well as to retired writers who had actively covered baseball for ten years. More than 280 of the ballots were returned.

28

A Godlet, 1968

Thirty-eight years before, as Medwick started playing professional baseball, the country tried to find a way to deal with poverty, joblessness, and dust storms, while veterans fought with their own army. The year 1968 was a terrible year in American history as the country tried to deal with a war, poverty, and civil rights simultaneously, while two of the country's best men were murdered. But the country survived; its institutions, though weakened, survived, and people went to work every day.

For Medwick it was a year of honors from many parts of the country. The Halls of Fame in Texas, Pennsylvania, and New Jersey brought Joe in. On January 12, 1968, Carl Yastrzemski and Joe were given Babe Ruth crowns at the Tops in Sports banquet in Baltimore. "The award [the Babe Ruth crown] for Medwick was retroactive for his feats as a National League slugger."

On January 19, 1968, Medwick was hired back as full-time batting instructor for Cardinal farm teams, a full-time baseball man even beyond the fall Instructional League.

There was a list of qualified men "currently being considered by the members of the Baseball Writers' Association of America for election to the Hall of Fame"; in addition to Joe, there were ten on the list who would eventually be elected. Joe had played with, against, or for almost everyone on this list.

On January 21, 1968, Arthur Daley's column titled "The Last Time Around" spoke up.

> It is my fervent hope that a long-standing injustice [will be corrected] by electing Joe Medwick to the Hall of Fame. . . . From an artistic standpoint he was easily number one [on the alphabetical listing submitted by the BBWAA]. . . . No one was more deserving of enshrinement than he. None of the other 50 come close to matching his impeccable credentials. . . . He hustled in the outfield, was a good ball hawk and had a strong arm. Superimposed on his physical assets was his flaming spirit. . . . He deserves the honor.

On the morning of January 23, 1968, with Medwick "Fearing the worst," New York City called at 10:47 and Joe got the call that for him was "the thrill of all thrills." On the other end of the phone was the head of the Baseball Writers of America, who had spent the day before counting ballots on the floor of his home near Huntington on Long Island. The ballots had squares on them that had to be checked. The writer's name was Jack Lang, and back in October 1934 he was the boy who begged Medwick for his autograph in Dexter Park.

Lang told Joe that he needed 212 votes and was given 240 of the 283 cast.

> The graying insurance executive considered Tuesday's honor his No. 1 baseball thrill—"the climax of everything," but the memories of the 1934 Series, the '37 All-Star game, the whole season of 1937 and coming back to the Cards in the '40s would be close behind.
>
> Medwick had two sleepless nights. "It's a good thing I have a good heart," said Joe, who keeps trim with golf and hunting. "The waiting was worse than waiting for the birth of my son." Medwick, neatly dressed in a gray plaid suit, said, "For the first time in my life I'm speechless. I'm all hopped up, like a June bride." Later he said, "That was the longest slump I ever had. I'd gone 0 for 20 before but not 0 for 20 years."

And then:

> I was sorry to see that Campy didn't make it. It would have been nice to have someone go in with me.

On January 24, 1968, Robert L. Burnes wrote in the St. Louis *Globe-Democrat*:

It was a tough struggle for Joe and the problem of entry was created more by the complexity of the rules than any shortcomings on Joe's part. Medwick belongs in the Hall of Fame. Let it be said that simply. He was one of the great right-handed hitters of modern times. . . . His credentials . . . were superior to those of a Jackie Robinson who was elected six years ago. . . . Baseball had been Medwick's whole life. . . . He constantly talks hitting with any major league player who seeks him out.

On the same day, Dan Daniel of the *World-Telegram* remembered that "Medwick . . . had the temperament of a barracuda as a ball player. . . . He was flamboyant and tough." Red Smith of the *Times*, remembered Joe well:

Medwick . . . was 85 percent immortal, having been certified as a godlet . . . in baseball's annual plebiscite of deities. . . . There was little resemblance between the self-assured insurance man of today with the callow 18-year-old who came out of Carteret High. . . . He wasn't the sort of rookie who was dubbed Sunny Joe. He was a pretty brash kid [and] as a rookie he was "all wood" as the ball players say. He had the complete ball player's equipment but in his youth the only position that interested him was batter. If his hitting fell off, he would brood and his defensive play suffered. By the time he was old enough to vote, however, he was also old enough to realize that the way to compensate for a slump was to step up his value on defense. He became a fine outfielder, with sure hands and a strong arm. As a competitor, he fitted comfortably into the mold of St. Louis's truculent, swashbuckling Gas House Gang of 1934. Indeed, writers describing that team today usually mention Medwick first, though he was no more warlike than his colleagues, none of whom backed away from a fight. The first pitcher in the Middle Atlantic League who tried to throw a fastball past him must have realized that here was a crasher who couldn't be kept out of the Hall of Fame at gunpoint.

Joe's hometown of Carteret passed a resolution stating, "whereas he had made us proud . . . be it resolved that . . . Joseph Michael Medwick be and was hereby recognized as a favorite son," proclaimed Mayor Thomas E. Deverin.

All of these wonderful things being said were followed by Joe receiving the Brian P. Burnes Nostalgia Award at the St. Louis Baseball Writers' Dinner on Thursday, January 25 at the Sheraton-Jefferson Hotel's Gold Room, a dinner that was carried over KMOX. He had plastic fruit and vegetables tossed at him as he moved to the podium. "'You people made me feel right at home,' Ducky told the crowd."

As Joe flew down to spring training, it seemed as if all of the injustices that had been done to him had finally been redressed. Others had better jobs—say, in the major leagues—but Medwick knew that for all time he was a member of that 1 percent of players who were elected to the Hall of Fame; no one and nothing could take that away from him. His intensity, determination, and devotion to baseball had given him what he wanted.

In Florida, the coaching work was good and clearly baseball people and fans treated him with much more respect than they ever did.

Medwick's hometown also honored his accomplishments. On May 22, Joe went back to Carteret for a weekend of honors, and he and his family stayed at the familiar home of his sister Bennie and her husband, Bill Beisel. The next day was a Saturday parade, with players from the Babe Ruth League and the Joe Medwick Youth League, and Medwick was seated in a red Cadillac convertible with Bennie and Bill in the back. On Sunday, Joe attended a testimonial dinner for six hundred held in the St. Demetrius Community Center in the St. Elias Church, which Medwick's parents had helped to build. Two tables in front seated his classmates from 1930 and players from the Young Yanks. John Medwick, Joe's brother, of 177 Carteret Avenue gave his testimony about the greatness of his brother. Then Joe "gave a speech that touched all hearts." Joe himself was touched and was teary in the beginning of his speech.

"Baseball was, and always will be, my first love and it has given me some of the greatest thrills of my life."

Those honors over, it was time to pick up a bat again and go back to work in the minors until the month of July. On July 9, in Houston, Medwick tossed out the first ball at the 1968 All-Star Game, the first All-Star Game played indoors. Joe Schultz, Jr., the Houston Buffaloes batboy in 1931, was now a coach of the Cardinals. Carey Selph, an old teammate from 1931, talked to Wells Trombley of the Houston *Chronicle* after Joe was elected. Trombley reported that Selph "noticed the sacred flame flickering deep in the pupils of Medwick's eyes. He had come cheek-to-jowl with a genius, and he knew it."

Joe loved Houston, and when he was interviewed on July 13 he said, "Baseball's been wonderful to me. Seventeen years. All-Star Games, two World Series, a chance to work with kids, election to the

Hall of Fame and then this honor of throwing out the first ball at the All-Star Game."

Bob Broeg attempted to sum up Joe by saying, "No one ever exposed to Medwick will forget him. . . . Talking now to the gray, dapper, articulate, amusing, smiling, and yes, charming Medwick, it's hard to reconcile this mild pleasant personality with the cantankerous cuss who was aggressive, truculent, even mean at times."

Other men commented on Medwick, too. In *Voices from Cooperstown*, Ralph Kiner remembered: "I think there's a lot of personality in [getting into the Hall of Fame.] Look at Ducky Medwick. A great player and he went in on the last ballot, but he was antagonistic and difficult with the reporters and that hurt his chances of getting in. It shouldn't have anything to do with it, but it does."

Pie Traynor, who played in the majors beginning in 1920 and managed the Pirates for six years said, "I'd rate him among the great right-handed hitters in the game. I always regarded Rogers Hornsby as the number one right-handed batter and I'll put Medwick number two."

Joe DiMaggio said, "What I don't understand was how the writers could keep Medwick out this long. He was a great hitter—one of the greatest. It just makes a man wonder what goes through the minds of the writers."

And Joe's boss, Stan Musial commented: "Joe Medwick distinguished himself as one of the finest players ever to wear the Cardinal uniform and his .324 career batting average was an indication of the tremendous ability the man had. He was a great leader of the Cardinal teams of the '30s and his terrific spirit was contagious. He was great for the Cardinals, great for baseball. And no one was more deserving of being elected to the Hall of Fame."

Before flying to the Hall of Fame induction ceremonies in Cooperstown, Joe returned to St. Louis to gather his family and Amadee. On the plane to New York Joe told Amadee he was going to say that Amadee was very helpful, and Amadee said, "You give me credit, you Hungarian bastard, I'll shoot you on the spot."

This kind of kidding continued at the Otesaga Hotel, the place where baseball people stay on Hall of Fame weekend. While Joe sat with his old manager, Frankie Frisch, and Commissioner Bowie Kuhn, Frisch jokingly yelled in his nasal tone at Amadee, "Dutchman come here." Frankie asked Amadee, "What did you do, swing the bat for Joey? Were you gonna accept the award for Joey? You made him throughout his career." Amadee said he heard that for years afterwards.

As for Joe, he said nothing but nice things: "I've waited a long time for this. It's my happiest day." Medwick said to Ed Rumill of the *Christian Science Monitor:*

> "Baseball had been very kind to me. . . . This Hall of Fame thing rounds out my career. I won batting championships, the MVP award, played in the World Series with the Cardinals and the Dodgers, and in ten All-Star games. This makes it complete. I'm very grateful." This sounded like mighty sweet talk coming from one of the swaggering, swash-buckling ballplayers of his time. Obviously he had mellowed with the passing years. "Well I'll tell you," he said, looking at me in a way that made me think he wanted to argue about it, "it was a rough game the way we played it. . . . We were always getting knocked down. It was part of the game. We dished it out and we expected the same in return. But there's a different approach to the game now. You don't bear down on these kids the way they did in my day. You speak nice and polite to them. Maybe that's why I've mellowed a bit. . . . I'll admit I was dis-appointed when I just missed being elected the time before. But I guess it can be sweeter when you have to wait a while."

The 10 A.M. Cooperstown ceremonies were moved for the first time in 1968 from the front steps on Main Street to the steps of the new National Baseball Research Library. So for the first time, Cooper Park was used for the ceremony, during which the library was ded-icated. Seated on the steps of the new library were Hall of Famers Max Carey, Joe Cronin, Heinie Manush, Sam Rice, Edd Roush, Red Ruffing, Ray Schalk, and Lloyd Waner. Old Dodger outfielder Zack Wheat was seated there, too, Medwick playing his "Wheatfield" when he went to Brooklyn in 1940. Opponents in the 1934 World Se-ries were there, too: Charlie Gehringer and Goose Goslin. Lefty Grove, the pitcher off whom Medwick hit an All-Star home run, was there, as were men who managed against Joe, Casey Stengel and Pie Traynor. Frankie Frisch, who had so loved the way Medwick played baseball, was there, too.

When it was Joe's turn, he spoke for less than two minutes. He thanked his family, his in-laws, and New Jersey fans from Carteret and New Brunswick who had traveled to the small upstate New York town by bus. Joe thanked Amadee for his help. He said he was proud of having "worked hard" to get here, and said: "Anything in

baseball that could have happened *had* happened to me." He reminded everyone that the induction was "a long time coming. . . .
This was the longest slump of my career. I had gone 0 for 20 before,
but never 0 for 20 years."

Joe was one of seven men elected to the Baseball Hall of Fame by
the writers in the 1960s.

After lunch at the Otesaga, it was time for Joe to go to Doubleday
Field, a park he helped to open in 1939, to be introduced and to
watch an exhibition game between Pittsburgh and Detroit.

Afterwards, sitting in a rocker on the porch of the Otesaga House,
Medwick told stories. "The Cardinals had a pitcher named Ed
Heusser. One day he popped me on the chin, in the dugout, right in
the middle of a game. I'd been playing over in left-center for a left-
handed hitter and he sliced one inside the foul line in deep left.
Heusser didn't think I hustled enough chasing it, and told me so.
One word led to another between innings and finally he hit me on
the chin. I told him I took a riding from the manager and no one
else."

Then it was back to work. By the time the minor league season
was over, Joe could point to Boots Day, an All-Star from the
Arkansas Travelers, who finished first under Spahn. For the fourth-
place Modesto Reds, the league MVP was Ted Simmons, who was
first in batting average, while the team was first in hits and runs.

The year wound down with the death of Ernie Orsatti, the
Gashouse Gang outfielder. But there was some good news also. Curt
Flood was commissioned by the Cardinals to do a present-day por-
trait of Medwick. Jim Toomey, at Busch Stadium on September 29,
presented it. Joe said, "Looks just like me."

At year's end, with the Cardinals in the World Series (fittingly, as
in Joe's year they played against Detroit), Joe was hired as a com-
mentator for St. Louis television.

And then on October 19, 1968, Joe threw out the first ball in game
two of the series. "I guess this was what they call progress. In 1934 I
got thrown out and thirty-four years later, I throw something out—
the first ball."

29

Batting Teacher, 1969–1974

Now time began to play its tricks on Joe. As the 1969 St. Louis team payroll reached $1 million, Bing Devine returned from the Mets front office to again take the job as vice president and general manager of the Cardinals. As a young office boy thirty years before, Devine had volunteered to pitch batting practice. Devine rose through the ranks of the Cardinals, only to leave on August 18, 1964, for a number of reasons, one of them being his clash with "senior consultant" Branch Rickey. Now that former office boy was with the Cardinals again, and now he was Medwick's boss.

Bob Kennedy, forty-eight, an American League player for three decades, served as the director of player personnel and was someone with whom Joe often conferred.

Time had given Joe an arthritic condition of the right hip and knee, which caused him more than a little pain, and he showed the damage done to his right side when he walked. After Medwick went to an early season Mets-Cards night game in 1969, he entered the Deaconess Hospital in St. Louis for an operation. The surgery on his hip, which caused him severe pain and cut down on his activity, involved shearing off the hip socket and then placing an aluminum ball in its place. A day later Medwick said, "I'm getting along all right now. But imagine I've got to take therapy and learn how to walk all over again with my new socket." Joe's eighteen-day stay in the hospital caused him to miss some road trips with his pal Barney

Schultz, the pitchers' coach for all the minor league teams during the season.

After a while, Joe, while proud still to be a Hall of Fame member, was still a working man, and a happy working man, listed in the Cardinal media guide as a general instructor. Even with his not-quite-perfect hip, he helped the Tulsa Oilers under Jack Krol to finish second and also helped Ted Simmons to be a league All-Star. The five other teams in the system were not particularly successful.

Joe didn't seem to mind the traveling that his job required—travel to Iowa, Oklahoma, Arkansas, California, and then to two teams in Florida. Occasionally, he traveled as well to old-timers' games; the supposedly placid Medwick had not lost his pride in his own hitting, telling an interviewer that he was eleven for thirteen in all of those games.

His pride in his work, so typical of Joe, was never gone. As he told Robert Hood, "When I joined the Cardinals, he [Street] said, 'You're my left fielder,' and that was it. Nobody said nothing. They didn't have coaches like they do now. They didn't have hitting instructors. I'm one of the first to start hitting instruction. There aren't too many major league hitting instructors. They don't want someone making $15,000 telling someone making $65,000 how to hit. But they listen to me."

Medwick was also one of the few invited to be celebrated at the All-Star banquet at professional baseball's centennial on July 21 in Washington, D.C. The next week he returned to Cooperstown to see inducted teammate Stan Musial, Dodger catcher Roy Campanella, and American League pitchers Stan Coveleski and Waite Hoyt. Medwick spent time at the Otesaga Hotel with men he knew as a player: Bill Terry, Lloyd Waner, and Charlie Gehringer. Hood wrote, "Medwick's memories of a period and the men with whom he associated don't seem to be fogged by the romantic ideals of the good old days. He speaks in terms of their just being men, playing the game of baseball, in a most realistic sense."

Medwick could not attend the Hall of Fame ceremony when his old teammate Pop Haines was given his place of honor there. But Joe did get to see Haines in the 1971 gathering, the year Joe's predecessor in left field at Sportsman's, Chick Hafey, was inducted.

By year's end another change came. The Cardinals, like other teams, were working more and more at their farm systems, with more coaches. So Joe, at sixty-one, once spring training and extended training finished, was asked to travel only to Arkansas and Modesto during the season and to continue with the instructional league in the fall.

And for 1972, the Cardinals added more coaches, now listing four: Vern Benson, Ken Boyer, George Kissell, and Barney Schultz. Likewise, now there were, for the minors, two pitching instructors. For the first time, Medwick was given the title of hitting instructor, although that was what he had been doing all along in the Florida heat at Busch Field in St. Petersburg. Inducted into the Hall of Fame was Joe's newspaper boy and former outfielding student, Yogi Berra; Joe went to Cooperstown for that ceremony. He also witnessed the election of Josh Gibson, Buck Leonard, and pitchers Gomez, Koufax, and Wynn.

But 1973 was marked by pain for Medwick. Early in the year, Joe's old manager, Frankie Frisch, died from a car crash in Delaware. Medwick said, speaking of himself as well as Frisch: "he was a fighter from the old school and hated to lose. He inspired me as a young player." Joe still suffered pain in his right hip, which had not yet repaired properly. Because of this condition, he couldn't play golf, the game he loved so much, although he did go to another old-timers' game in New York and attended the induction once again. He knew he belonged there and loved to visit.

Yet Joe's hip pain and the immobility that resulted from the condition were too much. Robert Hood recounted: "He would require a second operation. It took place in October 1973 at Barnes Hospital, St. Louis, and was performed by Dr. Fred C. Reynolds, a distinguished orthopedic surgeon." Medwick had a complete artificial hip implanted.

"If it weren't for this operation, Medwick could have wound up in a wheelchair and from there, when pain intensified, to a bed flat on his back, a vegetable waiting for the end. A great athlete was spared a hellish ordeal. Of course, instead of par golf he would have to settle for a bogey game, which was a level of golf most people never reach on two healthy legs. To shoot 90 playing on an artificial hip was a splendid achievement, one only a great and stubborn athlete could reach . . . a 5 handicap."

Thus, when 1974 began, Joe was feeling very good. His old coach from Carteret, Frank McCarthy, had dinner with him in Florida. Joe threw himself into his work in spring training. The minors, once extensive, were now five teams per big league team, so Joe had fewer men to work with.

Again, in 1974, he went to Cooperstown and sat on the steps of the library, where players first sat the year he was inducted, with players from all the leagues, from all the decades he knew, even with those players he knew as a very young man. "Joe loved to come back to the Hall of Fame weekends and frolic in the pool when he did," Bob Broeg, a Hall of Fame writer, recalled.

But there was bad news, too. Joe's 1931 roommate in Houston, Tom Carey, died in Rochester. When Dizzy Dean died in July of 1974, the Cardinals asked Medwick to go to the funeral in Bond, Mississippi, to represent the team. He did, saying at the end of the service, "Well, that is the ball game." Ripper Collins was dead, and so were Flint Rhem and Jim Winford.

Even when Joe was hit by a batting doughnut, Hood, from a 1974 interview with Medwick (an interview for which Medwick demanded $250), remarked: "never once did he mention any suffering involved in his experiences, and he never discussed the pain connected with his bearings. In fact, he never spoke of any physical pain. Were pain and suffering beneath contempt? Unworthy of a star's acknowledgment? An indication of imperfection? Of human vulnerability?"

Medwick concentrated on what he loved: hitting and the game of baseball. Barney Schultz told me, "He'd come by and sit in the dugout with me during a game" at Busch Stadium; the ballpark, though Astroturf, was Joe's Eden.

30

Muscles, 1975

Early in January of 1975, the Medwicks flew down to Florida again. Cardinal outfielder Lou Brock signed for $185,000 in the year before free agency began, an amount that was about the equivalent of what Joe made from 1932 to 1948. Joe was being paid about $12,000 in 1975.

The Medwicks checked in at the Edgewater Beach motel in St. Petersburg. Again Joe was working with Bob Kennedy.

Joe reported for work at the Farm System Complex at Busch Field, and worked hard and conscientiously with batters, as he had always done; it was hitting and it was baseball.

On March 19, Medwick once again attended the dinner of the Florida governor with other Hall of Famers in Bradenton, the town in which the Cardinals had trained in Joe's first big-league year.

There was a baseball dinner back in St. Louis the next night, with Mickey Owen as the chief speaker to a crowd honoring the new members of the St. Louis Amateur Hall of Fame. Owen said, "If there's one thing I've learned as a ballplayer, it's that you've got to be a bragger. That's what makes a ballplayer."

That same night in St. Petersburg, Bob Kennedy got a call from Isabelle Medwick, about ten o'clock. She asked Bob to take Joe to the hospital. She was worried about his chest pains. Kennedy came up to the Medwick's room. Then, with Joe in his pajamas, he and Kennedy rode the elevator down to the lobby. Once in Kennedy's car, the trip to the hospital took no more than ten minutes and Joe was able to get out of the front seat and walk into the hospital, where he was instructed to lay down on a gurney.

Soon the emergency-room doctor appeared and took a stethoscope from around his neck to listen to Joe's chest. From what the doctor heard, he ordered Joe to be admitted. Kennedy heard the doctor say that "he's got massive fluid on the lungs—it's not pneumonia. He's not gonna be here very long."

The doctor was right. Officially, a massive heart attack killed Joe Medwick at 2:37 A.M., March 21, 1975, before Medwick's wife Isabelle could get to the hospital. Dr. Stan London, Cardinal team physician and Dr. Joseph Levitt attended, to no purpose.

But Isabelle saw to it that Medwick was "fortified with the Sacraments of Holy Mother Church" before the body was transferred to the Wilhelm-Thurston Funeral Home in St. Petersburg for shipment to St. Louis.

Hitting coach Harry Walker commented the next day: "It's a helluva shame because the guy had just gotten back to enjoy the game again. You know, for a while there, he was kinda bitter and I don't think he ever thought he could love baseball again as he did with this job. . . . All the time he was a player he was a push-push-push guy. He was one of the greatest right-handed hitters the game ever saw and an aggressive guy who really liked to hit. Now when he was finally able to relax, it seems a shame the lights had to go out." Marty Marion was quoted as saying, "Later in life Joe mellowed. Everybody loved Joe then, after he came over from the Dodgers. He was practically a has-been then. He was on the way down. Joe got to be a real nice guy. He died too soon."

The morning of Joe's death, the *St. Louis Post-Dispatch* featured a cartoon of a weeping Redbird. A letter to the editor appeared that day from a fan, Stephen Thomas, who understood Medwick well: "He . . . hated the taste of defeat and mediocrity." As far as Bob Broeg was concerned, "he died a happy man."

The ceremonies were observed. "Funeral services will be Tuesday (the twenty-fifth) at 10 A.M. at the Michael Fitzgerald Mortuary at 4580 South Lindbergh. Visitation will be after 2 P.M. Monday. The family had asked that in lieu of flowers donations be made to the Herbert Hoover Boys Club, 2901 North Grand Avenue, built on the site of the old Sportsman's Park."

Medwick's body was buried in St. Lucas United Church of Christ cemetery at South Lindbergh Road and Denny Road in Sappington. The Cardinals were matched with the Dodgers that day.

31

Since Medwick

Since Medwick's death, his name appears every so often, more in the last years of the twentieth century than in the years right after his death.

A true fan named Ed Marcou, after moving from Wisconsin to St. Louis in 1983, visited Medwick's grave and was appalled to discover that Medwick's achievements were unmentioned there. Marcou wanted to correct that error, so after a few years (and with the help of the local Bob Broeg chapter of the Society for American Baseball Research), a Joe Medwick Memorial Committee was formed, with Marcou as the chairman.

May 19, 1990, was the date for the dedication ceremony of the Medwick gravesite memorial marker with "an inscription noting Medwick's National League Most Valuable Player award and triple-crown achievement in the 1937 season, his .324 lifetime batting average and election to the Hall of Fame in 1968. He was the only member of baseball's Hall of Fame interred in the St. Louis area. . . . More than 100 persons, including such notables as Stan Musial and former general manager Bing Devine, were in attendance." On hand, too, were Mrs. Medwick, her son, and three grandchildren. Mr. Marcou keeps the gravesite clean every two weeks.

32

Medwick's Legacy

Here are just some of the many accomplishments Joe Medwick made over the course of his illustrious career:

- Medwick was the "inventor and perfector of the sitting-down catch."
- He was perhaps the first National League player to adopt a batting helmet.
- Medwick was the only National Leaguer to have made four hits in an All-Star game.
- He was the only right-handed hitter to have made four hits in an All-Star game.
- No National Leaguer has ever topped Medwick for number of doubles hit in a season.
- No right-handed hitter has ever topped Medwick for number of doubles hit in a season.
- Medwick led the league in extra-base hits for three consecutive years. Only Honus Wagner had done that before him; only Mize and Musial have done it since.
- Medwick is 20th lifetime in most doubles in a career.
- On the Cardinals, a team whose history features Hornsby, Musial, and McGuire, Joe Medwick still holds the record for both doubles and RBIs.

- He holds the Cardinals rookie record in both doubles and total bases.
- His name appeared in the top five in the league in twelve offensive categories seventy-seven times.
- He made more than 222 hits three years in a row.
- Medwick's single-season doubles placed him at second, eleventh, fifty-ninth, and seventy-second in two-base hits all time.
- He is one of twenty-eight players to have enjoyed at least three streaks of twenty or more games in their careers.
- Since Joe, no National League hitter has made more hits in a season.
- Since Joe, no right-handed hitter has made more hits in a season, either.
- Since Joe, only three National League hitters have accumulated more than 400 total bases in a season.
- Since Joe, only Sammy Sosa made more RBIs in a season, and Sosa need sixty-six home runs to do it.
- Since Joe, only two hitters have led the league in doubles three years consecutively.
- Since Joe, only two other National League players have ever led the league for three consecutive years in RBIs.
- Since Medwick, only two National League players have topped his .374 average in 1937.
- From 1901–2000, Medwick is one of eight players with at least seven seasons of double-digits in doubles, triples, and home runs.
- Only four other players have had five or six doubles in a doubleheader.
- Medwick was voted the high-school athlete of the century in New Jersey.
- Medwick is 79th all-time in career hits and in career slugging average.
- Joe's lifetime batting average places him 40th all-time.
- His RBIs in his career place him 58th of all players.
- Medwick's 154 RBIs in 1937 tie him with Babe Ruth for 32nd place all-time.
- In January 1999, when the top 100 players of the century were being chosen, 15,001 men had played major league baseball. Of those 15,001, Joe was one of the 100 chosen. He was one of the

100 on the list compiled by major league baseball and by S.A.B.R. This means that Medwick was in the top .006 of every major leaguer. That is, he was evaluated as better than 99.004 of all major league players.

In 1976, a park in Carteret, New Jersey, was named in Joe's honor, a place where, fifty years earlier, his sister had picked apples. Then, forty acres owned by the borough were donated to the county, which expanded the park by another forty-two acres. Underdeveloped, work began on the park in 1990, and by the dedication date of October 22, 1991, eighty years after Medwick's birth, parkgoers could use an exercise trail, three picnic groves, street-hockey rinks, soccer fields, and a baseball field.

The park was not located down Chrome, but there is a ball yard down Chrome. Where Joe's house used to be on Union Street down Chrome, there is now a ballpark's left field.

The park, however, is in West Carteret on the Rahway River.

There in the park, one can remember that Joe was called the best diver off the Central Railroad of New Jersey trestle into that Rahway River in West Carteret. You can see that trestle from Joe's park. And if you look hard, you can still see him making a big splash in the water, his muscular body smashing against the hard water and passing through it.

Bibliography

Author's note: This book was largely written by reading microfilm of newspapers. I read one newspaper for each day Medwick spent in the minors. For Medwick's time in the majors, I read two newspapers for every day: I read the *New York Times* at Valerie Prescott's library for at least every day of the season. For his St. Louis years, I read the *Post-Dispatch* at Colgate University; for Brooklyn, I read the *Eagle;* for New York, the *Herald Tribune;* for Boston, the *Globe.*

Alexander, Charles C. *John McGraw.* New York: Viking, 1988.
———. *Our Game: An American Baseball History.* New York: Henry Holt, 1991.
———. *Rogers Hornsby: A Biography.* New York: Henry Holt, 1995.
Allen, Frederick Lewis. *Only Yesterday.* New York: Harper, 1931.
———. *Big Change.* New York: Harper, 1952.
Allen, Lee. *One Hundred Years of Baseball.* New York: Bartholomew House, 1950.
———. *The Hot Stove League.* New York: A.S. Barnes, 1955. Reprint, Mattituck, N.Y.: Amereon House, 1993.
———. *The Giants and the Dodgers.* New York: Putnam, 1964.
Allen, Maury. *Baseball's One Hundred.* New York: Galahad Books, 1982.
Andersen, Donald Ray. "Branch Rickey and the St. Louis Cardinal Farm System: The Growth of an Idea." Master's thesis, University of Wisconsin, 1975.
Barber, Red. *1947: When All Hell Broke Loose in Baseball.* Garden City, N.Y.: Doubleday, 1982. Reprint, Mattituck, N.Y.: Amereon House, 1993.

Barber, Red, and Robert Creamer. *Rhubarb in the Catbird Seat.* 1968. Reprint, Mattituck, N.Y.: Amereon House, 1993.

Bartell, Dick, and Norman Macht. *Rowdy Richard.* Berkeley, Calif.: North Atlantic Books, 1987.

Bell, Joseph. *World Series Thrills.* New York: J. Messner, 1962.

Berra, Yogi, and Ed Fitzgerald. *Yogi: The Autobiography of a Professional Baseball Player.* Garden City, N.Y.: Doubleday, 1961.

Berra, Yogi, and Tom Horton. *Yogi: It Ain't Over.* New York: McGraw-Hill, 1989.

Berrett, Jesse. "Diamonds for Sale." In *Baseball History.* Vol. 4. 1991. Westport, Conn.: Meckler Publishing, 1991.

Bevis, Charlie. *Mickey Cochrane: The Life of a Baseball Hall of Fame Catcher.* Jefferson, N.C.: McFarland Publishers, 1998.

Billet, Bret L., and Lance J. Formwalt. *America's National Pastime: A Study of Race and Merit in Professional Baseball.* Westport, Conn.: Praeger, 1995.

Blake, Mike. *Baseball Chronicles: An Oral History of Baseball through the Decades: September 17, 1911 to October 24, 1992.* Cincinnati: Betterway Books, 1994.

Boston, Talmage. *1939, Baseball's Pivotal Year: From the Golden Age to the Modern Era.* Fort Worth, Tex.: Summit Group, 1994.

Bragan, Bobby, as told to Jeff Guinn. *You Can't Hit the Ball with the Bat on Your Shoulder: The Baseball Life and Times of Bobby Bragan.* New York: The Summit Group, 1992.

Broeg, Bob, and William J. Miller, Jr. *The Pilot Light and the Gas House Gang.* St. Louis: Bethany Press, 1980.

———. *Bob Broeg's Redbirds: A Century of Cardinals' Baseball.* St. Louis: River City Publishers, 1981.

———. *Baseball from a Different Angle.* South Bend, Ind.: Diamond Communications, 1988.

Broeg, Bob, and Jerry Vickery. *The St. Louis Cardinals Encyclopedia.* Indianapolis: Masters Press, 1998.

Carmichael, John P., ed. *My Greatest Day in Baseball.* New York: A.S. Barnes: 1945.

Chadwick, Bruce, and David M. Spindel. *The St. Louis Cardinals: Memories and Memorabilia from a Century of Baseball.* New York: Abbeville Press, 1995.

Charlton, James, ed. *The Baseball Chronology: The Complete History of the Most Important Events in the Game of Baseball.* New York: Macmillan, 1991.

Cochrane, Gordon S. *Baseball: The Fan's Game.* New York: Funk and Wagnalls, 1939.

Coffey, Frank. *Always Home: Fifty Years of the USO.* Washington, D.C.: Brassey's, 1991.

Coffin, Tristram Potter. *The Old Ball Game: Baseball in Folklore and Fiction.* New York: Herder and Herder, 1971.

Connor, Anthony J. *Voices from Cooperstown: Baseball Hall of Famers Tell It Like It Was*. New York: Collier Books, 1984.

Craft, David, and Tom Owens. *Redbirds Revisited: Great Memories and Stories from the St. Louis Cardinals*. Chicago: Bonus Books, 1990.

Creamer, Robert W. *Stengel: His Life and Times*. New York: Simon and Schuster, 1984.

———. *Baseball in '41*. New York: Viking, 1991.

Crissey, Harrington E., Jr., comp. *Teenagers, Graybeards, and 4-F's: An Informal History of Major League Baseball during the Second World War, as Told by the Participants*. Philadelphia: H.E. Crissey, 1982.

Daley, Arthur. *Times at Bat*. New York: Random House, 1950.

Dean, Jerome. *Dizzy Baseball: A Gay and Amusing Glossary of Baseball Terms Used by Radio Broadcasters, with Explanations to Aid the Uninitiated*. With cartoons by Hugh Devine. New York: Greenberg, 1952.

Devaney, John. *Greatest Cardinals of Them All*. New York: Putnam, 1968.

Devaney, John, and Burt Goldblatt. *The World Series: A Complete Pictorial History*. Chicago: Rand McNally, 1976.

Dewey, Donald, and Bart Acocella. *Biographical History of Baseball*. New York: Carroll and Graf, 1995.

Dickson, Paul, ed. *The Dickson Baseball Dictionary*. New York: Facts on File, c1989.

DiClerico, James M., and Barry J. Pavelec. *The Jersey Game: The History of Modern Baseball from Its Birth to the Big Leagues in the Garden State*. New Brunswick, N.J.: Rutgers University Press, 1991.

DiMaggio, Dom, with Bill Gilbert. *Real Grass, Real Heroes: Baseball's Historic 1941 Season*. New York: Zebra Books, 1990.

Durocher, Leo. *Nice Guys Finish Last*. New York: Simon and Schuster, 1975.

Enright, Jim, ed. *Trade Him! One Hundred Years of Baseball's Deals*. Chicago: Follett, 1976.

Eskenazi, Gerald. *The Lip*. New York: Morrow, 1993.

Faber, Charles F. *Baseball Ratings*. Jefferson, N.C.: McFarland, 1985.

Falkner, David. *Great Time Coming*. New York: Simon and Schuster, 1995.

Fields, Wilmer. *My Life in the Negro Leagues: An Autobiography*. Baseball and American Society, no. 23. Westport, Conn.: Meckler, 1992.

Fleming, G. H. *The Unforgettable Season*. Austin, Tex.: Holt, Rinehart and Winston, 1981.

Frisch, Frank. *Frank Frisch: The Fordham Flash*, as told to J. Roy Stockton. Garden City, N.Y.: Doubleday, 1962.

Gallico, Paul. *Farewell to Sport*. New York: Knopf, 1938.

Gerlach, Larry. *Men in Blue*. New York: Viking, 1980.

Gilbert, Bill. *They Also Served: Baseball and the Home Front, 1941–1945*. New York: Crown, 1992.

Gilbert, Thomas. *The Good Old Days: Baseball in the 1930s*. New York: F. Watts, 1996.

Goldstein, Richard. *Spartan Seasons: How Baseball Survived the Second World War*. New York: Macmillan, 1980.

———. *Superstars and Screwballs: One Hundred Years of Brooklyn Baseball*. New York: Penguin, 1992.

Golenbock, Peter. *Bums: An Oral History of the Brooklyn Dodgers*. New York: Putnam, 1984.

———. *Spirit of St. Louis*. New York: Spike, 2000.

Graham, Frank. *The Brooklyn Dodgers: An Informal History*. New York: Putnam, 1947.

———. *The New York Giants: An Informal History*. New York: Putnam, 1952.

Gregory, Robert. *Diz*. New York: Viking, 1992.

Gutkind, Lee. *The Best Seat in Baseball, but You Have to Stand: The Game as Umpires See It*. New York: Dial, 1975.

Higbe, Kirby, with Martin Quigley. *High Hard One*. New York: Viking, 1967. .

Holmes, Tommy. *The Dodgers*. New York: Collier, 1975.

Holway, John. *Voices from the Great Negro Baseball Leagues*. New York: Dodd, Mead, 1975. Revised ed., Mattituck, N.Y.: Amereon House, 1993.

Honig, Donald. *Baseball between the Lines*. New York: Coward, McCann, and Geoghegan, 1976.

———. *October Heroes*. New York: Simon and Schuster, 1979.

———. *Baseball America*. New York: Macmillan, 1985.

———. *The St. Louis Cardinals: An Illustrated History*. New York: Prentice-Hall, 1991.

———. *Baseball When the Grass Was Real*. Lincoln: University of Nebraska Press, 1993.

———. *The Man in the Dugout: Fifteen Big League Managers Speak Their Minds*. Lincoln: University of Nebraska Press, 1995.

Hood, Robert E. *The Gashouse Gang*. New York: Morrow, 1976.

Hornsby, Rogers. *Secrets of Baseball Told by Big League Players*. Bedford, Mass.: Applewood Books, 1927.

Hornsby, Rogers, with Bill Surface. *My War with Baseball*. New York: Coward-McCann, 1962.

James, Bill. *The Bill James Historical Baseball Abstract*. New York: Villard Books, 1986.

———. *Politics of Glory*. New York: Macmillan, 1994.

———. *The Bill James Guide to Baseball Managers from 1870 to Today*. New York: Scribner, 1997.

Johnson, Lloyd, Miles Wolff, and Steve McDonald. *The Encyclopedia of Minor League Baseball*. Durham, N.C.: Baseball America, 1997.

Kaese, Harold. *Boston Braves*. New York: Putnam, 1948.

Kahn, Roger. *The Era 1947–1957: When the Yankees, the Giants and the Dodgers Ruled the World*. New York: Ticknor and Fields, 1993.

———. *Memories of Summer*. New York: Hyperion, 1997.

Karst, Gene, and Martin J. Jones, Jr. *Who's Who in Professional Baseball*. New Rochelle, N.Y.: Arlington House, 1973.

Kashatus, William C. *One-Armed Wonder: Pete Gray, Wartime Baseball, and the American Dream.* Jefferson, N.C.: McFarland, 1995.

Katz, Lawrence. *Baseball in 1939.* Jefferson, N.C.: McFarland, 1995.

Kiersh, Ed. *Where Have You Gone, Vince DiMaggio?* New York: Bantam, 1983.

Koppett, Leonard. *The New Thinking Fan's Guide to Baseball.* New York: Fireside, 1991.

Laird, A. W. *Ranking Baseball's Elite: An Analysis Derived from Player Statistics, 1893–1987.* Jefferson, N.C.: McFarland, 1990.

Langford, Walter M. *Legends of Baseball.* South Bend, Ind.: Diamond Communications, 1987.

Lieb, Fred. *St. Louis Cardinals: The Story of a Great Baseball Club.* New York: Putnam, 1944.

———. *The Baseball Story.* New York: Putnam, 1950.

———. *Baseball as I Have Known It.* New York: Coward McCann, 1977. Reprint, Mattituck, N.Y.: Amereon House, 1993.

Light, Johnathan Fraser. *Cultural Encyclopedia of Baseball.* Jefferson, N.C.: McFarland, 1997.

Lowry, Philip J. *Green Cathedrals.* Cooperstown, N.Y.: Society for American Baseball Research (S.A.B.R.), 1986.

Macht, Norman L. *Rowdy Richard.* Ukiah, Calif.: North Atlantic Books, 1987.

Macht, Norman L., and Rex Barney. *Rex Barney's Thank Youuuu for Fifty Years in Baseball from Brooklyn to Baltimore.* Centreville, Md.: Tidewater, 1993.

Mann, Arthur. "Baseball Reconverts." *Baseball Magazine,* June 1, 1946.

———. *Branch Rickey.* Boston: Houghton Mifflin, 1957.

McBride, Joseph. *High and Inside: The Complete Guide to Baseball Slang.* New York: Warner, 1980.

McCullough, Bob. *My Greatest Day in Baseball.* Dallas: Taylor, 1998.

Mead, William B. *Baseball Goes to War.* Washington, D.C.: Farragut, 1985.

Meany, Tom. *Baseball's Greatest Teams.* New York: A.S. Barnes, 1949.

———. *Baseball's Greatest Players.* New York: Dell, 1955.

Murdock, Eugene. *Baseball Players and Their Times: A History of the Major Leagues, 1920–1940 .* Westport, Conn.: Meckler, 1991.

———. *Baseball between the Wars.* Westport, Conn.: Meckler, 1992.

Nash, Bruce, and Allen Zullo. *Baseball Confidential.* New York: Pocket Books, 1988.

Neft, David S., and Richard M. Cohen. *The World Series.* 5th ed. New York: St. Martin's Press, 1992.

Obojski, Robert. *All-Star Baseball since 1933.* New York: Stein and Day, 1980.

Okkonen, Marc. *Baseball Uniforms of the Twentieth Century: The Official Major League Guide.* New York: Sterling, 1991.

———. *Baseball Memories 1900–1909: An Illustrated Chronicle of the Big Leagues' First Decade: All the Players, Managers, Cities, and Ballparks.* New York: Sterling, 1992.

———. *Baseball Memories, 1950–1959*. New York: Sterling, 1993.

———. *Memories, 1930–1939: A Complete Pictorial History of the "Hall of Fame" Decade*. New York: Sterling, 1994.

Okrent, Daniel, and Harris Lewine. *Ultimate Baseball Book*. New York: Houghton Mifflin, 1979.

O'Neal, Bill. *The Texas League, 1888–1987: A Century of Baseball*. Austin, Tex.: Eakin Press, 1987.

Owen, V. *The Adventures of a Quiet Soul: A Scrapbook of Memories*. San Jose, Calif.: V. Owen, 1996.

Paige, Satchel. *Maybe I'll Pitch Forever*. Garden City, N.Y.: Doubleday, 1962.

Parrot, Harold. *The Lords of Baseball*. New York: Praeger, 1976.

Peary, Danny. *We Played the Game*. New York: Hyperion, 1994.

Philips, Cabell. *From the Crash to the Blitz*. New York: Macmillan, 1969.

Polner, Murray. *Branch Rickey*. New York: Atheneum, 1982.

Rains, Rob. *The St. Louis Cardinals: The Official 100th Anniversary History*. With a foreword by Jack Buck. New York: St. Martin's Press, 1992.

Rains, Rob, and Bob Rains. *The Cardinals Fan's Little Book of Wisdom*. South Bend, Ind.: Diamond Communications, 1994.

Rampersad, Arnold. *Jackie Robinson*. New York: Knopf, 1997.

Reichler, Joseph L. *The Great All-Time Baseball Record Book*. Revised and updated by Ken Samuelson. New York: Macmillan, 1992.

Reidenbaugh, Lowell. *Cooperstown: Where Baseball's Legends Live Forever*. Edited by Joe Hoppel. St. Louis: Sporting News Publishing, 1983.

———. *Take Me Out to the Ballpark*. Illustrations by Amadee Wohlschlaeger. St. Louis: Sporting News Publishing, 1983.

———. *The Sporting News Selects Baseball's Twenty-five Greatest Pennant Races*. St. Louis: Sporting News Publishing, 1987.

Rice, Grantland. *The Tumult and the Shouting*. New York: Barnes, 1954.

Ritter, Lawrence S. *One Hundred Greatest Baseball Players*. New York: Crown, 1981.

———. *The Glory of Their Times*. New York: Macmillan, 1966; expanded edition from William Morrow, 1984.

———. *Lost Ballparks: A Celebration of Baseball's Legendary Fields*. New York: Viking, 1992.

Robinson, Jackie, and Al Duckett. *I Never Had It Made*. New York: Putnam, 1972.

Robinson, Ray. *Greatest World Series Thrillers*. New York: Random House, 1965.

Rogers, Will. *Sanity Is Where You Find It*. New York: Houghton Mifflin, 1985.

Rosenburg, John. *They Gave Us Baseball: The Twelve Extraordinary Men Who Shaped the Major Leagues*. Harrisburg, Pa.: Stackpole Books, 1989.

Rowan, Carl T. *Wait Till Next Year: The Life Story of Jackie Robinson*. New York: Random House, 1960.

Scheinin, Richard. *Field of Screams*. New York: Norton, 1994.

Sehnert, Chris W. *St. Louis Cardinals*. Edina, Minn.: Abdo and Daughters, 1997.

Seidel, Michael. *Ted Williams*. Chicago: Contemporary Books, 1991.

Seymour, Harold. *Baseball: The Early Years*. New York: Oxford University Press, 1960.

———. *Baseball: The Golden Age*. New York: Oxford University Press, 1989.

Shannon, Mike. *Baseball: The Writer's Game*. South Bend, Ind.: Diamond Communications, 1992.

Shoemaker, Robert H. *The Best in Baseball*. New York: Crowell, 1974.

Shouler, Ken. *The Real 100 Best Baseball Players of All Time . . . and Why*. Lenexa, Kans.: Addax Publishing Group, 1998.

Skipper, John C. *Umpires: Classic Baseball Stories from the Men Who Made the Calls*. Jefferson, N.C.: McFarland, 1997.

Slaughter, Enos, with Kevin Reid. *Country Hardball: The Autobiography of Enos "Country" Slaughter*. New York: Tudor, 1991.

Smith, Curt. *America's Dizzy Dean*. St. Louis: Bethany, 1978.

Smith, Ira Lepounce. *Baseball's Famous Outfielders*. New York: Barnes, 1954.

Smith, Ira L., and Harvey Allen. *Low and Inside: A Book of Baseball Anecdotes, Oddities and Curiosities*. Garden City, N.Y.: Doubleday, 1949.

———. *Three Men on Third: A Second Book of Baseball Anecdotes, Oddities and Curiosities*. Garden City, N.Y.: Doubleday, 1951.

Smith, Robert. *World Series: The Games and the Players*. Garden City, N.Y.: Doubleday, 1967.

Spalding, A. G., and Bros. *Spalding's Official Baseball Guide*. New York: American Sports Publishing, 1907–1941.

Stang, Mark, et al. *Baseball by the Numbers: A Guide to the Uniform Numbers of Major League Teams*. American Sports History Series, no. 4. Lanham, Md.: Scarecrow Press, 1997.

Staten, Vince. *Ol' Diz*. New York: HarperCollins, 1992.

Stockton, J. Roy. *Gashouse Gang and Other Guys*. New York: Bantam, 1945.

Sullivan, Neil J. *The Minors: The Struggles and the Triumph of Baseball's Poor Relation from 1876 to the Present*. New York: St. Martin's, 1990.

Sumner, Jim. *Separating the Men from the Boys: The First Half-Century of the Carolina League*. Winston-Salem, N.C. : John F. Blair, 1994.

Taylor, Robert Lewis. "Borough Defender." *New Yorker*, July 12 and 19, 1941.

Trager, James. *The People's Chronology: A Year-by-Year Record of Human Events from Prehistory to the Present*. New York: Holt, Rinehart and Winston, 1979.

Turner, Fredrick. *When the Boys Come Back*. New York: Henry Holt, 1996.

Tygiel, Jules. *Baseball's Great Experiment: Jackie Robinson and His Legacy*. New York: Oxford University Press, 1983.

U.S. House of Representatives. *Organized Baseball* (no. 2002).

Van Blair, Rick. *Dugout to Foxhole: Interviews with Baseball Players Whose Careers Were Affected by World War II*. Jefferson, N.C.: McFarland, 1994.

Van Overloop, Mark E. *Baseball's Greatest Total Hitters*. Washingtonville, N.Y: On The Mark Publications, 1990.

Voight, David Quentin. *American Baseball*. University Park: Pennsylvania State University Press, 1983.

Vricella, Mario T. *The St. Louis Cardinals—The First Century: A Short History of the National League's Greatest Team*. New York: Vantage Press, 1992.

Wallechinsky, David. *The People's Almanac*. New York: Bantam, 1981.

Warfield, Don. *The Roaring Redhead: Larry MacPhail*. South Bend, Ind.: Diamond Communications, 1987.

Williams, Peter. *When the Giants Were Giants: Bill Terry and the Golden Age of New York Baseball*. Chapel Hill, N.C.: Algonquin Books, 1994.

Williams, Ted. "Hitting Was My Life." *Sports Illustrated,* June 24, 1968.

Wireless Age. August 1921.

Other Sources

Collier's Encyclopedia, CD-ROM unabridged text version. New York: Collier's, 1996.

Robert E. Hood's tapes in the National Baseball Hall of Fame Research Library.

Microsoft Complete Baseball: The Ultimate Multimedia Reference for Every Baseball Fan. Redmond, Wash.: Microsoft Corp., 1994.

Thorn, John, and Pete Palmer. *Total Baseball*. Portland, Ore.: Creative Multimedia Corporation, 1994.

Websites

baseball1.com
baseball-almanac.com
baseballstuff.com
Skilton (www.baseball-links.com)
stathead.com

Periodicals

Anscott News (Carteret, New Jersey, high-school newspaper)
Baseball Digest
Baseball Magazine
Boston Globe
Collier's
Connellsville Daily Courier (Pennsylvania)
Danville Commercial-News (Illinois)
Houston Post-Dispatch

Houston Press
Life
Literary Digest
Miami Herald
Newark Evening News
Newark News
Newark Star-Ledger
New Brunswick Daily Home News
New York Daily News
New York Herald-Tribune
New York Journal (American)
New York Mirror
New York PM
New York Times
New York World-Telegram
Parade
Raleigh Observer
St. Louis Commerce
St. Louis Globe-Democrat
St. Louis Post-Dispatch
St. Louis Star-Times
St. Louis University News
Saturday Evening Post
Scottdale Independent Observer (Pennsylvania*)*
The Sporting News
The Stars and Stripes (Mediterranean Edition)
Tampa Tribune
Trenton Evening Times
Yank

Index

A. Schrader's Sons, 222
Adams, Ace, 238, 240
Adams, Sparky, 57, 75
Addie, Bob, 325
Aetna Co., 309
Alexander, Grover Cleveland, 47
Ali Baba, 107
All-American Team. *See* "Babe Ruth's All-American Team"
Allen, Johnny, 225, 233, 234
All-Star Game, 58, 70, 95, 108, 125, 140, 152, 171, 172, 184, 185, 204, 241, 259, 260, 312, 330, 332, 334, 343
Alston, Walter, 114
Always Home: Fifty Years at the USO, 249
Andersen, Donald and Ray, 136
Anderson, Andy, 25, 34, 35
Anderson, Sparky, 323, 326
Ankenman, Mr. and Mrs. Fred, 29, 35
Appling, Luke, 112, 317
Arizona State University, 322
Arkansas Travelers, 323, 335
Art Gaines Baseball Camp, 314
Associated Press (AP), 77, 114, 127–28, 131, 132, 134, 145, 263, 271, 281, 286, 307
Athletic Park, Scottdale, 14, 19
Averill, Earl, 112, 125

"Babe Ruth's All-American Team," 101, 112, 130, 143, 150, 157, 313
Bader Field, 238
Baker Bowl, 114, 121, 122, 140
Ballafant, Lee, 28
Bando, Sal, 322
Bankhead, Dan, 273
Barber, Red, 191, 201–2
Barlick, Al, 188, 280
Barney, Rex, 224, 279
Barr, George, 259
Barrett, Red, 261
Barrymore, Ethel, 187
Bartell, Dick, 131, 201, 214, 223, 235
Baseball Chronicles, 193
Baseball Hall of Fame, 70, 143, 150, 284, 308, 309, 312, 313, 314, 315, 316, 317, 318, 319, 322, 323, 325, 326, 328, 329, 330, 333, 335, 337
Baseball War Bond League, 227
Baseball Writers of America Association (BBWAA), 131, 132, 134, 284, 314, 325, 328, 329, 330
Baseball's Great Experiment, 281
Batista, Col. Fulgencio, 117, 180
Battling Beavers, 222–23
Baxter, Dick, 302
Bear Mountain Inn, 221

Bear Mountain, New York, 220, 221
Beazley, Johnny, 224
Beisel, Bill, 5, 9, 12, 14, 31, 78, 89, 116, 332
Bellevue-Stratford Hotel, 139
Bendel, Fred J., 131
Bender, Chief, 322, 324, 326
Benge, Ray, 99
Benny, Jack, 189, 264
Benson, Rev., 269
Benson, Vern, 338
Berger, Wally, 24, 105, 121
Berle, Milton, 241
Bernardino, Johnny, 159
Berra, Yogi, 120, 273, 274, 275, 276, 298, 313, 315, 338
Besse, Herman, 254
Birmingham Police Band, 30
Birtwell, Roger, 258, 260
Bishop, Max, 104
Bissonette, Del, 260
Bittan, Eddie, 189
Blackwell, Ewell, 280
Blades, Ray, 47, 145, 148, 150, 151, 152–53, 154, 155, 159, 161, 164
Bodner, Jackie, 185
Boggs, Wade, 131, 156
Bonham, "Troy," 197
Bookwalter, Robert R., 21
Bordagaray, "Frenchy," 99, 119, 120, 129, 200, 222, 226
Boston Globe, 258, 259
Boston Braves/Bees, 91, 100, 101, 105, 106, 107, 110, 112, 123, 126, 128, 139, 151, 155, 176, 190, 207, 258, 259, 261, 262, 263, 269, 276, 280, 285, 293
Boston Red Sox, 7, 98, 151, 205, 222, 260
Bottomley, Jim, 48, 133
Boudreau, Lou, 185, 244
Bowman, Bob, 153, 155, 166, 167, 168, 169, 170–71, 172, 173, 178, 181, 215, 232
Bowman, Joe, 121
Boyer, Ken, 323, 338
Boyle, Buzz, 71, 73
Brack, Gibby, 121
Bragan, Bobby, 221, 222, 226, 229, 241
Branca, Ralph, 268, 270, 279, 285
Brands, Edgar, 142

Brannick, Eddie, 183, 201, 258
Braun-Hunsaker and Associates, 297, 310
Braves Field, 108, 280
Breadon, Sam, xiii, 12, 49, 53, 56, 58, 85, 98, 129, 135, 136, 138, 146, 148, 149–50, 158, 159, 160, 161, 170, 216, 218, 220, 276, 277, 278, 283, 284, 316
Breechen, Harry, 261, 264, 271, 280
Brian P. Burnes Nostalgia Award, 331
Bridges, Tommy, 78
Broeg, Bob, 60, 91, 111, 134, 152, 161, 275, 276, 277, 278, 281, 282, 285, 286, 311, 312, 314, 315, 316, 317, 320, 333, 339, 341
Brooklyn Catholic Youth Organization, 274
Brooklyn Dodger Victory Committee, 189
Brooklyn Dodgers, 7, 45, 58, 71, 74, 92, 99, 109, 112, 121, 124, 126, 130, 136, 140, 145, 149, 153, 157, 159, 160, 161, 162, 163, 164, 165, 167, 168, 171, 172, 173, 174, 175, 176, 179, 180, 182, 183, 184, 185, 186, 187, 188, 189, 190, 191, 192, 194, 195, 196, 197, 199, 200, 201, 202, 203, 204, 205, 206, 207, 208, 209, 210, 211, 212, 213, 214, 215, 216, 218, 220, 221, 222, 224, 225, 226, 227, 228, 230, 231, 232, 233, 239, 241, 244, 260, 261, 264 265, 266, 267, 268, 269, 270, 271, 273, 274, 275, 276, 279, 280, 283, 286, 310, 334
Brooklyn *Eagle*, 71, 80, 87, 88, 163, 164, 186, 188, 193, 195, 197, 203, 220
Brooklyn Navy Yard, 199
Brooklyn Red Cross, 222
Brooklyn Trust Co., 216
Brooklyn Union Gas Co., 222
Browder, Dr. Jeff, 169
Brown, Jake, 2
Brown, Jimmie, 122, 123, 188
Brown, Mace, 183
Brown, Max, 4
Budge, Donald, 132
Buffalo Stadium, 23, 32, 35, 287, 307
Burke, Kitty, 98
Burnes, Robert L., 330
Burns, Bob, 314, 315

Burns, Jimmy, 291
Burns, Mayor Cornelius F., 88
Burr, Harold C., 267
Busch, August, Jr., 309
Busch Field, 323, 327, 338, 340
Busch Stadium, 324, 335, 339
Bushwicks, 86
Byrd, Sammy, 98

Cabrera, Cabby, 292–93
Camilli, Dolph, 141, 147, 165, 172, 181, 182, 184, 186, 189, 190, 191, 194, 195, 200, 202, 207, 211, 216, 222, 226, 233, 234, 239
Campanella, Roy, 16, 322, 325, 326, 337
Campbell, Gillie, 129
Capuchin Charity Guild of Detroit, 311
Cardinal Boys' Band, 98, 139
Caren, Max, 133
Carew, Rod, 131
Carey, Max, 334
Carey, Tom, 24, 339
Carleton, Fannie, 75
Carleton, Tex, 24, 26, 28, 29, 38, 39, 46, 55, 56, 57, 64, 66, 73, 75, 94, 162, 165
Carmichael, John, 246
Carolina League, 298
Carson, George, 106
Carteret, New Jersey, 19, 21, 39, 50, 57, 73, 86, 89, 139, 275, 331, 332, 345
Casaleggi, Beaner, 3, 5, 12, 49, 50, 51, 88, 224
Casaleggi, Peanuts, 3, 49
Casey, Hugh, 170, 183, 189, 196, 197, 205, 207, 266
Castelman, Foster "Slick," 99, 102, 117
Cavaretta, Phil, 244
Cedar Rapids Cardinals, 323
Cervesa Stadium, 273
Chandler, Happy, 275
Chapman, Ben, 282, 305
Charleroi Governors, 17
Chester, Hilda, 188
Chicago Cubs, 32, 42, 73, 94, 95, 96, 98, 100, 101, 102, 103, 108, 111, 114, 115, 119, 124, 126, 131, 132, 136, 138, 140, 142, 143, 151, 184, 217, 243
Chicago White Sox, 264

Chiozza, Lou, 101, 121
Chipman, Bob, 192, 268
Christy Walsh's All-American Team. *See* "Babe Ruth's All-American Team"
Christian Science Monitor, 334
Chrome, 1, 2, 3, 11, 90
Chrome Steel Works, 1
Churchill, Winston, 249
Cincinnati Reds, 46, 47, 70, 92, 98, 112, 114, 117, 128, 129, 130, 155, 156, 161, 164, 175, 182, 185, 203, 204, 210, 211, 227, 228, 240, 259, 267, 268, 282
City Series, St. Louis, 54, 64, 136
Civilian Defense Volunteer Office, 222
Claasen, Dr. Henry, 167
Cleveland Indians, 181
Coastal Plain League, 304
Cobb, Shirley, 254
Cobb, Ty, 38, 52, 76, 85, 101, 131
Cochrane, Mickey, 70, 76, 78, 79, 82, 84, 86, 120
Coffey, Frank, 249
Cohan, George M., 119
Cohane, Tim, 200, 201, 223, 230
Cole, Ed, 159
Coleman, Bob, 258, 260, 261
College World Series, 314, 317, 321–22, 324
Collins, Eddie, 150
Collins, Ripper, 32, 48, 63, 64, 72, 73, 75, 77, 80. 89, 93, 94, 95, 96, 98, 101, 103, 107, 108, 339
Collins, Phil, 99, 100, 102
Comerford, Dan, 199
Conlan, Jocko, 7
Conrad, Harold, 195
Coogan's Bluff, 240
Cooney, Johnny, 221
Cooper, Morton, 154, 209, 211, 260
Cooper, Walker, 202, 203, 209, 235
Coronado Hotel, 64, 204
Coscarart, Pete, 189, 191, 320
Country Hardball, 166
Coveleski, Stan, 337
Crabtree, "Crabby," 188, 189
Craft, Harry, 203
Crawford, Pat, 53, 86
Creamer, H. E., 12, 13, 21

Creamer, Robert, 171, 182
Creger, Bernie, 281
Crespi, Frank, 202
Critz, Hughie, 102
Cronin, Joe, 140, 313, 334
Crosetti, Frank, 328
Crosley Field, 91, 95, 97, 108, 119, 130, 143, 149
Cross, Harry, 233, 237, 238, 240
Crowder, Alvin, 76
Cuban Winter League, 105
Culler, Dick, 262
Cultural Encyclopedia of Baseball, 165, 236
Curtiss-Wright, 236, 241, 256

Dahlgren, Babe, 186, 244
Daily, Elmer M., 12, 13
Daley, Arthur, 181, 221, 223, 225, 227, 242, 270, 318, 330
Dallas Steers, 142
Daniel, Dan, 153, 154, 173, 176, 205, 208, 213, 217, 226, 234, 244, 245, 265, 275, 331
Danning, Harry, 131, 152, 183
Danville, Illinois, 16, 21
Danville Veterans, 21, 22
Davis, Crash, 300, 302, 303
Davis, Curt, 136, 139, 152, 155, 161, 162, 165, 173, 185, 187, 207, 209
Davis, Justice Lee Parson, 190
Davis, L. C., 90, 117, 127, 155
Davis, "Peaches," 119, 130
Davis, Spud, 64, 102, 111
Davis, Virgil, 97
Day, Boots, 335
Dean, Dizzy, 24, 26, 29, 34, 38, 39, 55, 56, 57, 60, 61, 64, 69, 70, 73, 74, 75, 76, 77, 79, 81, 84, 86, 90, 92, 93, 94, 96, 97, 100, 101, 102, 103, 105, 107, 112, 113–14, 115, 117, 119, 121, 122, 123, 124, 125, 126, 135, 136, 137–38, 148, 151, 163, 223, 307, 308, 309, 318, 339
Dean, Patricia, 117–18
Dean, Paul, 64, 65, 72, 73, 74, 78, 86, 90, 91, 93, 96, 97, 98, 101, 107, 128, 142, 143, 150, 277
Death on the Diamond, 69, 74
Del Prado Hotel, 40

DeLancey, Dee, 64, 74, 78, 80, 97
Delio, Jo-Jo, 189
DelGaudio, Jerry, 313
Demaree, Al, 33
Demaree, Frank, 62, 112
Dempsey, Jack, 44
DeOro, Alfred, 87
Derringer, Paul, 56, 57, 74, 100, 143, 149, 156
Detroit Free Press, 311
Detroit Tigers, 20, 70, 76, 79, 84, 105, 150, 151
Deverin, Mayor Thomas E., 331
Devine, Bing, 52, 151–52
DeWitt, Bill, 263
Dexter Park, 330
Diamond Dinner (Tulsa), 311
DiBasi, Sam, 288
Dickey, Bill, 70, 112, 140, 197, 227, 309
Dickman, Mayor Bernard F., 85
Dickson, Murry, 270
DiMaggio, Joe, 7, 105, 112, 117, 129, 130, 133, 134, 135, 143, 152, 162, 194, 195, 197, 208, 273, 281, 309, 310, 313, 315, 333
DiMaggio, Vince, 212, 229, 230, 235
Dixie Grande Hotel (Tampa), 51, 64
Dixie Series, 29, 30
Dockens, George, 261
"Dodger Spring Offensive," 222
Dodgers Rooters Band, 192
Doubleday Field, 335
Douglas, Casey, 18
Douthit, Taylor, 32, 47
Doyle, Carl, 161
Doyle, Jack, 119
Drebinger, John, 127, 193, 194, 197, 233, 236, 240, 257, 261, 270, 272
Dressen, Charley, 148, 165, 166, 168, 272, 273
Driscoll, Dave, 6
Duany, Claro, 305
Duffy, Hugh, 131
Dunn, Tom, 187
Durocher, Grace, 167, 169
Durocher, Leo, 56, 57, 61, 64, 65, 66, 79, 81, 84, 91, 93, 102, 105, 108, 109, 111, 119, 122, 128–29, 133, 139, 145, 148,

153, 157, 160, 162, 163, 165, 166, 167,
    168, 170, 171, 173, 174, 175, 176, 177,
    178, 179, 180, 182, 183, 184, 186, 187,
    191, 192, 193, 197, 200, 201, 207, 208,
    210, 212, 213, 214, 219, 220, 221, 222,
    223, 225, 226, 227, 228, 229–30, 231,
    232, 238, 241, 245, 247, 248, 250, 251,
    252, 253, 264, 265, 266, 268, 269, 270,
    271, 274, 275, 297, 316, 321
Durocher, Nellie, 169
Dusak, "Four Sack," 266, 280, 283, 285
Dyer, Eddie, xiv, 13, 15, 16, 17, 19, 265,
    270, 271, 276–77, 278, 279, 280, 282,
    285, 286

East Fork Hunting Club, 324
Ebbets Field, 44, 56, 72, 109, 126, 141,
    170, 171, 176, 182, 185, 188, 195, 197,
    201, 203, 205, 208, 214, 215, 221, 222,
    228, 238, 239, 241, 243, 269, 275, 280
Edwards, Bruce, 274
Edwards, Henry P., 131
Effrat, Louis, 195, 267
Eisenhower, Dwight, 258
Elias, Al Munro, 123
Etten, Nick, 247, 248, 251, 253, 254
Eugene Emeralds, 323
Evans, Luther, 291
Evansville (Indiana) Hubs, 21
Evers, Johnny, 88

Fairground Hotel, 46
Falzer, G. A., 7
Feder, Sid, 131
Feldman, Harry, 240
Feller, Bob, 314
Fenway Park, 260
Ferrell, Wes, 244
Fetzner, Arthur, 326
Filipowicz, Steve, 257
Fischer, Carl, 7, 85
Fischer, Erv, 46, 278
Fischer, Rube, 240
Fitzsimmons, Freddie, 57, 58, 74, 117,
    121, 165, 167, 180, 185, 188, 196, 222,
    229, 233, 234, 245, 246, 297
Fitzsimmons, Mrs. Freddie, 185
Fleischer, Bill, 189

Fletcher, Elbie, 229
Flood, Curt, 335
Florida International League, 290, 291,
    294, 305
Flowers, Jake, 48
Floyd Bennett Field, 238
Forbes Field, 43, 121, 129, 190, 210
Forest City Manufacturing Co., 91
Forest Park Hotel, 46, 48
Foxx, Jimmie, 56, 65, 99, 104, 106, 121, 146
Frank, Stanley, 219
Franks, Herman, 180, 189
Frasier, Felix, 299
French, Larry, 197, 199, 201, 204, 207
French, Oliver, 160
Frey, Bennie, 46
Frey, Lonnie, 112
Frick, Ford, 133, 170, 189, 245
Frisch, Frankie, 8, 44, 45, 51, 57, 58–59,
    60, 61, 63, 64, 65, 69, 70, 73, 74, 78,
    79, 80, 81, 82, 83, 84, 85, 87, 91, 92,
    93, 95, 96, 98, 99, 101, 103, 105, 107,
    111, 120, 121, 123, 128–29, 142, 143,
    145, 171, 211, 245, 265, 276, 281, 308,
    310, 318, 321, 333, 334, 338
Frontier League, 320
Fullis, Chuck, 65, 76
Furillo, Carl, 266, 267, 268

Galan, Augie, 108, 192, 200, 202, 203,
    206, 210, 211, 213, 214, 220, 222, 225,
    226, 228, 235, 266, 268, 270
Gallagher, Joe, 167
Gallico, Paul, 81
Garagiola, Joe, 279
Garagnani, Julius "Biggie," 319
Gardella, Danny, 237, 261
Garms, Debs, 25, 28, 259
The Gashouse Gang, 7, 36, 53, 55
Gashouse Gang, 65, 77, 85, 91, 96, 107,
    119, 120, 126, 132, 137, 138, 139, 190,
    243, 261, 265, 291, 297, 311, 331, 335
Gehrig, Lou, 6, 70, 112, 114, 125
Gehringer, Charlie, 70, 112, 151, 317,
    334, 337
Geisel, Harry, 76, 82
Gelbert, Charlie, 56, 111, 112
Giles, Warren, 313

Gillenwater, Carden, 261
Gillespie, Ray, 139–40
Golenbeck, Peter, 138, 151, 158, 161
Goodman, Benny, 308
Gomez, Chile, 106, 107
Gomez, Lefty, 70, 197
Gonzalez, Mike, 40, 55, 60, 64, 75, 79, 111, 118, 139, 141, 143, 145
Gooding, Gladys, 229
Goodman, Ival "Goodie," 98, 156
Gordon, Joe, 197
Gordon, Sid, 234
Goslin, "Goose," 77, 78, 79, 101, 334
Grable, Betty, 189
Grace, Bob, 59–60
Grace, Earl, 122
Graham, Frank, 230
Great Depression, 31
Greenberg, Henry "Hank," 32, 45, 76, 82, 84, 150, 279, 318
Gregg, Hal, 261
Gregory, John Lloyd, 23, 26, 28, 32, 33, 35, 36
Griffin, Johnny, 199
Grimes, Burleigh, 41, 44, 65, 133, 145
Grimm, Charley, 44, 11, 133, 259
Grissom, Lee, 128, 174
Grove, Lefty, 151, 334
Gulf Coast Cardinals, 323
Gumbert, 117
Gutteridge, Don, 46, 113, 207

Haas, Bert, 161
Haas, "Mule," 252
Hack, Stan, 244
Hafey, Chick, 10, 23, 28, 31, 32, 34, 38, 40, 47, 50, 65, 316, 317, 337
Haines, Jesse "Pop," 45, 48, 57, 75, 91, 92, 111, 122, 123, 126, 128, 146–47, 337
Hale, "Bad News," 188
Haley, Mike, 173
Hall of Fame Camp (at St. Thomas More School), 314
Hallahan, "Wild Bill," 46, 61, 64, 72, 75, 78, 84, 92, 97, 99, 101, 112, 139
Hamlin, Luke "Hot Potato," 45, 165
Hammer, Jerry, 189
Hannegan, Robert, 284, 286, 289

Hardin, Bud, 288
Harris, Bucky, 273, 276
Hartnett, Leo "Gabby," 108, 131, 132
Hassett, Buddy, 191
Hathaway, Ray, 326
Hayworth, Ray, 223
Head, Ed, 201, 270
Hearn, Jim, 278
Heilmann, Harry, 246
Hemus, Solly, 287
Hendrick, Gink, 46
Henrich, Tommy, 193, 196–97
Herbert, Dick, 302, 303
Herbert, Preacher, 226
Herman, Babe, 97, 98
Herman, Billy, 115, 125, 149, 151, 185, 187, 191, 196, 204, 211, 216, 316
Herman, Jack, 314, 316, 325
Herman, Joe, 88
Herman, Mayor Joseph A., 86
Hermanski, Gene, 266, 282
Herring, Art, 243, 258
Heusser, Ed, 32, 91, 99, 111, 112–13, 335
Heutel, Mr. and Mrs. Joseph H., 111
Hidlago, Chino, 294
Higbe, Kirby, 131, 175, 182, 185, 186, 187, 190, 210, 222, 269
High, Andy, 294
Hock, Eddie, 26
Hoerst, "Lefty," 267
Hollingsworth, Bryan, 306
Hollywood, Florida, 298
Holmes, Tommy, 80, 83, 151, 165, 170, 172, 173, 174, 181, 182, 183, 184, 186, 188, 189, 200, 201, 203, 204, 206, 208, 210, 213, 217, 222, 223, 225, 227, 231, 232, 266
Holmes, Tommy (player), 218, 244, 258, 259, 260
Hood, Robert E., 7, 9, 36, 53, 55, 57, 59, 64, 66, 91, 93, 286, 287, 337
Hopp, Johnny, 188, 244
Hornsby, Rogers, 8, 12, 132, 135, 181, 203, 259, 276, 285, 319, 323, 327, 333
Hotel Commodore, 70
Hotel Nacional, 180, 200
Hotel New Yorker, 162, 164, 166, 171, 192, 231, 232, 237, 245

House of David, 47, 190
Houston Buffaloes, 22, 34, 287, 307
Houston Chronicle, 332
Houston Post-Dispatch, 23, 26, 32, 34, 36
Houston Press, 25, 286, 287, 288
Howsam, Bob, 322
Hoyt, Waite, 72, 180, 337
Hubbell, Carl, 7, 69, 70, 73, 99, 101, 102,
    108, 109, 110, 112, 114, 115, 117, 125,
    127, 131, 234, 245, 246, 297, 318
Huggins, Miller, 76
Hughes, Roy, 257
Hughes, Tommy, 266
Hungling, Bud, 32
Hunsacker, Ray, 256, 276
Hurst, Don, 43
Hutchings, Johnny, 185
Hyland, Dr., 126

Island Heights, New Jersey, 11

Jablonski, Ray, 302, 303
Jackson, Travis, 69
James, Bill, 177, 215, 236, 309
Javier, Julian, 315
Johnson, Alex, 327
Johnson, Lyndon, 135
Johnson, Roy, 123
Johnson, Syl "Si," 61, 111, 122, 130, 228
Jones, Charlie, 278
Joost, Eddie, 185
Jorgensen, Jack "Spider," 274
Jurges, Billy, 174, 183, 207

Kaczmarek, Buck, 16
Kaese, Harold, 258
Kaye, Danny, 270
Keane, Johnny, 287, 288, 289, 315
Keeler, Willie, 203
Kelchner, C. S. "Pop," 11, 12
Keller, Charlie, 197
Kellogg's All-American Baseball Poll, 142
Kelly, Jim, 65
Kelly, Whitey, 293
Kennedy, Bob, 85, 336, 340–41
Kiernan, John, 85, 96, 125, 137, 139, 183,
    194, 215
Kiner, Ralph, 333

King, Joe, 237, 257
King, Lynn, 107, 152–53
Kissell, George, 326, 338
Klein, Chuck, 48, 69, 114
Klem, Bill, 76, 80, 81, 82, 112, 122–23
Kluttz, Clyde, 258
KMOX, 312, 315, 331
Knipe, Rudy, 298, 299, 301
Knothole Club, Scottdale, 16
Knothole Club, St. Louis, 55
Knothole Gang, Houston, 288
Kolibas, Mrs., 90
Koster, Rich, 318
Koy, Ernie, 161, 167
Krist, "Spud," 233
Krol, Jack, 337
Kuhn, Bowie, 333
Kupcinet, Irv, 117–19, 137–38
Kurowski, Whitey, 202, 244, 278, 281

La Tropical Stadium, 180, 200
Labredo, Dr., 190
LaGuardia, Mayor Fiorello, 150
Lakewood, New Jersey, 237
Landis, Kenesaw Mountain, 76, 82, 83,
    84, 96, 98, 100, 136, 160, 228, 245, 319
Lanfranconi, Walt, 282
Lang, Jack, 86, 325, 330
Lanier, Max, 135, 138–39, 168–69, 189,
    202, 211
Lavagetto, "Cookie," 130, 167, 173, 180,
    183, 189, 191, 192, 195, 201, 266
Launce, Jack, 189
Law, Jack, 9
Lee, Bill, 103, 172, 261, 262, 320, 321
Lee, Cliff, 121
Lee, Roy, 313, 320, 321
Leiber, Hank, 129
Lennox Hotel (St. Louis), 74
Leonard, Dutch, 71
Leslie, "Sambo," 74
Lewinski, Ed, 192, 295
Lewis, Frank, 246
Lindblath, Roy, 294
Lindell, Johnny, 246
Lindstrom, Freddy, 90
Litwhiler, Danny, 206, 218, 245
Loetfler, Ken, 278

Lohrman, Bill, 233
Lombardi, Ernie "Schnozz," 140, 141, 143, 144, 237–38, 316
Lopatka, Art, 265–66
The Lords of Baseball, 161, 214

MacFayden, Danny, 110, 151
Macht, Norman, 233
Mack, Connie, 6, 140
Macon, Max, 142, 204, 207, 215, 223
MacPhail, Larry, 140, 145, 148, 153, 159–60, 161, 167, 168, 169, 170, 171, 172, 176, 180, 184, 192, 206–7, 212, 213, 214, 216, 243, 272, 274
Magerkurth, George, 54, 60, 189
Mahem, Sam, 161
Mancuso, Gus, 58, 232
Manion, Johnny, 116
Manion, Pete, 75
Mann, Jack, 319, 320
Manush, Heinie, 82, 334
Maranville, Rabbit, 309, 315
Marcov, Ed, 342
Marion, Marty, 202, 208, 209, 241, 244, 270, 278, 311
Marrero, Leo, 294
Marshall, George C., 249
Martin, Johnnie "Pepper," 28, 31, 32, 55, 60, 61, 64, 70, 72, 73, 75, 76, 77, 79, 80, 81, 85, 92, 93, 94, 95, 96, 107, 108, 113, 116, 119, 122, 129, 136, 137, 139, 140, 149, 150, 167, 170, 224, 291, 292, 297, 298, 306
Martin, Stu, 107, 119, 120, 149
Martin, Tony, 190
Marty Marion Camp for Boys, 311, 313
Mattingly, Don, 131
May, Pinky, 225
Mays, Willie, 315
Mayo Clinic, 177–78
Mcateer, Dr. Daniel A., 169
McCain, Archie, 231
McCarthy, Frank, 5, 8, 12, 338
McCarthy, Joe, 175, 193
McCarver, Tim, 323
McCormick, Frank, 141, 184, 244
McCullough, Bill, 72
McCully, Jim, 239

McDonald, John, 176, 214
McDonough, Pat, 174, 186
McGee, Bill, 114, 133, 155–56, 187
McGowen, Roscoe, 180, 181, 182–83, 184, 185, 188, 192, 202, 206, 268, 269
McGraw, John, 7, 8, 59, 87, 96
McGraw, Ted, 153
McKechnie, Bill, 12, 126, 128, 148, 211
Mead, Charley, 240, 243
Meany, Tom, 91, 120, 180, 222, 245, 247, 248, 250, 251, 252, 253, 254
Medwick, Anna (Bennie), 1, 5, 9, 12, 31, 78, 116, 332
Medwick, Helen, 1
Medwick, Mrs. Isabelle Heutel, 95, 96, 105, 109, 111, 116, 123, 142, 154, 158, 167, 169, 186, 192, 194, 277, 301, 313, 340, 342
Medwick, Joe "Ducky": 1932 with Scottdale, 20; 1932 with Houston, 36–37; 1933 season, 62; 1934 season, 88; 1934 world series, 77–84; 1935 season, 103; 1936 season, 114–15; 1937 season, 132–33; 1938 season, 144; 1939 season, 156; 1941 season, 198; 1942 season, 215; 1943 season, 234–35; altercation with Dizzy Dean, 93–94; American Legion Baseball, 6; bats used, 56, 65, 196, 203; batting stance, 16, 33, 42; beanings, 166–71, 267–68; birth of second child, 158; draft status, 199; "Duckie-Wuckie Bar," 33, 36; elected county collector, 311; fight with Carleton, 66–67; golf, 116; high school basketball, 9; high school football, 8; hits for cycle, 95; joins New York Giants, 231–32; Lackawanna League, 6, 10; lumbago, 137; major league debut, 41–42; marries, 111; named "Cap of the Week," 361; Newark Bears tryout, 7–8; origin of nickname, 26–27, 28; professional debut, 17; radio show, 312; recruited by Notre Dame, 9–10; relationship with press, 227; released by Brooklyn Dodgers, 271; released by Houston Buffaloes, 289; selected MVP, 131; suffers double vision, 178;

superstition, 55; ten consecutive hits, 109–10; wears head protection (helmet), 181; World War II tour, 244–55

Medwick, Joe, Jr. (son), 136, 301
Medwick, John (brother), 1, 5, 9, 332
Medwick, John (father), 1, 311
Medwick, John (grandson), 314
Medwick, Lizzie (Erzebiet), 1, 2, 139
Melton, Cliff "Mountain Music," 152, 175, 187
Melton, Rube, 267
Mertikas, Jim, 75
Metcalfe, Harry, 190
Mexican National League, 263
Miami Beach Flamingos, 290, 291, 292, 293, 305–6
Miami Herald, 292, 293
Miami Sun Sox, 291
Mickey Owen's Baseball School for Boys, 313
Middle Atlantic League, 12, 14, 18, 331
Midwest League, 323
Miley, Jack, 117–18
Miller, Bing, 195
Miller, Eddie, 185, 227
Mills, Howard, 180–81
Mississippi Mudcats, 116
Mitchel Field, 227
Mitchell, Jerry, 88
Mize, Johnny, 106, 107, 111, 119, 123, 128, 130, 131, 135, 141, 143, 144, 152, 154, 156, 167, 170, 188, 189, 218, 316
Mize, Mrs. Johnny, 154
Modesto Reds, 335
Monchey, 190
Monessen, Pennsylvania, 123
Montay, Rick, 322
Mooney, Jim, 68
Moore, Dee, 222
Moore, Gene, 191
Moore, Joe "Jo-Jo," 102, 125
Moore, Terry, 61, 89, 97, 98, 100, 101, 109, 111, 119, 131, 133, 150, 156, 159, 167, 168, 190, 224, 278, 280, 297, 324, 328
Moran, Charley, 82
Moser, Bryon, 143
Moses, Wally, 244

Mueller, Heine, 133
Mulchay, Hugh "Losing Pitcher," 122
Mullin, Willard, 95
Mulver, Jim, 216
Mulvey, Dearie, 216
Murdock, Eugene, 58
Murphy, Bob, 6
Murphy, Johnny "Grandma," 195
Musial, Stan, 114, 132, 204, 212, 235, 241, 242, 243, 244, 278, 279, 281, 285, 315, 318, 319, 323, 326, 333, 337, 342
Musicians Post Band, 119

Nakamura, Jose, 306
Navin Field (Detroit), 76
Navin, Frank, 86
Nealon, Clark, 288, 289
New York City Crescent Club, 86
New York Daily News, 81, 118, 163, 164, 239, 281
New York Giants, 32, 44, 56, 59, 64, 69, 71, 73, 75, 91, 95, 96, 98, 99, 100, 101, 102, 106, 115, 117, 119, 120, 121, 124, 125, 127, 129, 130, 138, 140, 151, 152, 153, 155, 162, 174, 175, 182, 183, 187, 206, 210, 213, 222, 231, 232, 233, 234, 237, 238, 239, 240, 241, 243, 244, 252, 256, 257, 258, 268, 280, 282, 310
New York Herald Tribune, 200, 201, 231, 233, 236, 238, 244, 256, 319
New York Mets, 336
New York Sun, 230
New York Times, 56, 77, 99, 119, 125, 137, 146, 163, 170, 181, 186, 193, 194, 196, 205, 261, 267, 271, 272, 275, 318, 331
New York World Telegram, 78, 91, 99, 103, 172, 176, 178, 195, 205, 217, 237, 256, 331
New York World's Fair, 150, 165
New York Yankees, xiv, 7, 10, 12, 20, 44, 57, 70, 71, 133, 193, 194, 195, 196, 197, 216, 238, 241, 252, 271, 272, 273, 274, 275, 276
Newark Athletic Club, 140
Newark Bears, 7, 8, 85, 163
Newark Evening News, 131
Newark Kennel Club, 90

Newark News, 86
Newsom, Bobo, 210, 226, 228, 229, 230, 231, 232, 234, 239
Nice Guys Finish Last, 166
Nichols, Joseph C., 267
Nicholson, Bill, 104, 244
Nieman, Butch, 260
Norris, Leo, 122
Northey, Ron, 282
Northwest League, 323
Norton, Pete, 306

O'Dwyer, William, 169
Ogrodowski, Brusie, 119
Olmo, Luis, 231, 265
O'Malley, Walter, 216
O'Neill, Steve, 246
Onslow, Jack, 20
Orengo, Joe, 232, 233
Orsatti, Ernie, 54, 55, 61, 65, 69, 76, 79, 80, 85, 95, 297, 335
Ostermueller, Fritz, xiv, 230–31, 278
Otesaga Hotel, 333, 335, 337
Ott, Mel, 16, 33, 57, 74, 99, 101, 102, 125, 129, 130, 140, 143, 151, 164, 204, 218, 232, 238, 240, 241, 242, 245, 247, 256, 257, 258
Owen, Marv, 78, 79, 80, 82, 83, 84, 88, 105, 311, 319
Owen, Mickey, 138, 180–81, 186, 188, 189, 191, 193, 195 196, 197, 204, 207, 209, 216, 222, 244, 340
Owens, Brick, 76, 79, 81

Pacific Coast League, 323
Padgett, Don, 123, 137, 139, 143, 154, 166, 168, 170, 188
Pafko, Andy, 244
Paine, "Cornbread," 88
Panella, Nick, 302
Parker, Ace, 301
Parker, Dan, 158
Parmalee, Roy, 74, 111
Parrott, Harold, 161, 169, 186, 189, 190, 195, 200, 204, 210, 212, 214, 216–17, 220, 222, 231, 232, 268, 269, 275
Patterson, Arthur, 222, 231, 246

Paul, Gabe, 320
Payne, George, 25
Pearson, Bob, 303
Pearson, Ike, 182
Peck Memorial Hospital, 267
Peel, Homer, 23, 32
Pegler, Wesbrook, 148
Pennock, Herb, 284
Pennsylvania State League, 123
Perkins, Johnny, 148
Perry, Charles, 149
Perth Amboy General Hospital, 90
Perth Amboy, New Jersey, 6, 108–9
Pesky, Johnny, 205
Petosky, Ted, 75
Phelps, Babe, 167
Philadelphia Athletics (A's), 10, 31, 104, 211, 309
Philadelphia Phillies, 43, 95, 101, 121, 122, 123, 128, 139, 140, 151, 155, 175, 182, 203, 207, 213, 220, 252, 265, 267, 282, 309
Philips Delicious Tomato Packing Co., 104
Piedmont League, 120, 304
Pierce, Jack, 192
Pipp, Wally, 7
Pippen, Cotton, 76
Pittsburgh Pirates, xiv, 43, 48, 61, 93, 96, 100, 102, 106, 119, 120, 121, 123, 128, 137, 140, 143, 151, 171, 191, 201, 209, 210, 225, 234, 242, 252, 262, 264, 268, 278, 285
Polish American Club (Jersey City, N.J.), 6
The Politics of Glory, 177
Pollett, Howie, 270
Polner, Murray, 136, 149, 230, 269
Polo Grounds, 44, 57, 58, 70, 73, 95, 99, 108, 112, 129, 140, 150, 152, 182, 183, 202, 205, 225, 238, 239, 240, 258, 261, 280, 297
Port Reading Railroad, 1
Porter, Dick, 104
Potter, Harry, 16
Powers, Jimmy, 163
Professional Baseball Players Association, 70

Prothro, Doc, 182
Puccinelli, George "Pooch," 23, 24, 46–47, 51
Pule, Lefty, 258

Quigley, Ernie, 60

Raft, George, 189
Rahway AA, 6
Raleigh Capitals, 298, 301, 302, 303
Raleigh Observer, 298, 230
Raleigh Times, 300
Ramsey, Bill "Square Jaw," 259, 261
Raschi, Vic, 276
Reardon, Beans, 76, 79, 83, 246, 251
Red Star Billiard Academy, 3, 49, 51, 88
Redel, Joseph, 311
Reese, Pee Wee, 164, 171, 172, 17 180, 181, 183, 185, 188, 191, 194, 195, 196, 204, 205, 207, 211, 214, 216, 224, 267
Reichler, Joe, 307
Reiser, Pete, 136, 149, 159, 161, 176, 177, 178, 185–86, 187, 188, 189, 190, 191, 200, 201, 202, 203, 204, 205, 206, 207, 208, 213, 216, 217, 218, 224, 265, 266, 268, 269, 270
Rennie, Rud, 236
Reyes, Napoleon, 257
Reynolds, Dr. Fred C., 338
Rice, Grantland, 85
Rice, Jack, 311
Rice, Sam, 334
Rickey, Branch, 11, 12, 19–20, 22, 25, 32, 49–50, 51, 52, 53, 56, 63, 85, 98, 105, 117, 129, 134–35, 136, 139, 143, 145, 146, 148, 149–50, 158, 159–60, 161, 162, 165, 211, 216, 217, 218, 219, 220, 223, 224, 228, 230, 231, 234, 238, 239, 242, 252, 265, 269, 270, 271, 275, 276, 316, 326, 336
Rickey, Branch, Jr., 230
Rickwood Field, 29
Riggs, Lew, 200, 209, 213, 215
Rigler, Charley, 54, 98
Rizzo, Johnny, 143, 200
Rizzuto, Phil, 194, 195, 197
Robinson, Frank, 164

Robinson, Jackie, 52, 274, 275, 280, 281, 314, 315, 331
Rock Hill Cardinals, 323
Rockne, Knute, 22
Rodriguez, Oscar, 305, 306
Roeder, Bill, 282
Roetger, Wally, 104
Roffenberger, Ken, 279
Rogell, Billy, 79
Rogers, Will, 76, 83
Rojek, Stan, 267
Roknek, Meir, 1
Rolfe, Red, 125, 143
Roosevelt, Franklin D., 125
Rosenblatt Stadium, 321
Roth, David, 2
Roth, Paul, 9
Rothrock, Jack, 65, 78, 79, 92, 99, 103, 297
Rotzell, Rocky, 295
Rousch, Ed, 312, 316, 334
Rowdy Richard, 233
Rowe, Schoolboy, 45, 76, 86, 108
Rowell, "Bama," 191
Rucker, Johnny, 176, 240, 257
Ruffing, Red, 143, 219, 317, 318, 322, 325, 326, 334
Rumill, Ed, 334
Russell, Jack, 162
Russo, Marius, 193, 196
Russo, Neal, 323
Ruth, Babe, 6, 16–17, 33, 70, 91, 119, 140, 141, 151, 155, 186, 272, 275, 290, 312, 318
Ryan, Blondy, 73
Ryba, Mike, 15, 76, 106, 113, 114, 118, 123, 124, 139

Saigh, Fred, 284, 309
Sain, Johnny, 269
Saint Louis Bombers, 278
Saint Louis Browns, 54, 106, 159, 230, 231, 263, 264, 276, 309
Saint Louis Cardinals, xiv, 11, 12, 16, 31, 34, 38, 39, 40, 41, 42, 43, 44, 45, 46, 47, 48, 49, 51, 54, 55, 56, 57, 58, 59, 60, 61, 62, 63, 64, 65, 67, 69, 70, 71, 72, 73, 74, 75, 76, 77, 78, 79, 83, 84,

85, 87, 88, 89, 91, 92, 93, 94, 95, 96,
97, 98, 99, 100, 101, 102, 103, 104, 105,
106, 108, 111, 112, 114, 116, 117, 119,
120, 121, 122, 123, 124, 126, 129, 132,
133, 134, 135, 136, 137, 138, 139, 140,
141, 143, 145, 146, 147, 149, 150, 151,
152, 153, 155, 156, 159, 160, 161, 162,
163, 167, 181, 182, 183, 186, 187, 188,
189, 190, 191, 192, 202, 203, 204, 206,
208, 209, 210, 211, 212, 213, 214, 215,
217, 228, 231, 233, 238, 243, 252, 259,
260, 263, 264, 266, 268, 269, 270, 276,
278, 279, 280, 281, 282, 283, 284, 285,
286, 288, 289, 308, 309, 310, 322–23,
326, 334, 335, 336, 337, 341
Saint Louis Commerce, 297
Saint Louis Globe-Democrat, 330
Saint Louis Post-Dispatch, 38, 42, 44, 54,
67, 90, 101, 107, 117, 120, 141, 147,
154, 264, 278, 294, 312
Saint Louis Star-Times, 65, 139
Saint Louis University, 313–14, 317, 320,
321, 323, 324
Saint Lucas United Church of Christ
Cemetery, 341
Sanders, Jimmy, 23
Sappington, Mo, xiii, 236
Savage, Ted, 327
Sayles, Bill, 233
Schalk, Ray, 334
Schanz, Charley, 240
Schenley Hotel, 43
Schoendienst, Red, 278, 322, 324
Schultz, Barney, 326, 327, 336–37, 338, 339
Schultz, Joe, Jr., 23, 264, 290, 332
Schultz, Joe, Sr., 23, 24, 25, 26, 34, 133
Schumacher, Hal, 102, 108, 117, 130
Sears, "Ziggy," 126, 129
Selkirk, George "Twinkletoes," 272
Selph, Carey, 28, 332
Sewell, Luke, 246, 257, 264
Shaw, Bob, 205
Shea, Merv, 141
Shea, Red, 253
Shea, Spec, 276
Shibe Park, 189, 239, 309
Shorr, Toots, 162
Shotton, Burt, 145, 280

Shoun, Clyde "Hardrock," 136, 155, 203,
279
Shupe, Vincent, 261
Siegel, Morris, 315
Siekierka, Frank, 2
Siekierka, Pinkie, 4
Silvey, George, 327
Simmons, Al, 16, 33, 35, 38, 42, 101, 117,
177, 270, 308, 337
Simmons, Ted, 335
Sisti, Sibby, 185, 207
Skelton, Red, 222, 237, 250
Slade, Oskie, 54
Slaughter, Enos, 138, 154, 155, 159, 166,
167, 170, 204, 205, 209, 224, 278, 279,
281
Smith, Al (P), 127
Smith, Curt, 117
Smith, John L., 216
Smith, Lyall, 311
Smith, Mike, 190
Smith, Red, 162, 331
Society for American Baseball Research
(SABR), 152, 342, 345
Sorrentino, Stonewall, 189
Southern League, 294
Southworth, Billy, 160, 162, 170, 171,
189, 206, 293
Spahn, Warren, 268, 280, 282, 315, 326,
335
Sparks, Ned, 278
Speaker, Tris, 7, 8, 110
Spence, Stan, 205
Spezio, Ed, 324, 327
Spicola, Tom, 306
Spink, J. G. Taylor, 142, 290, 291
Spink, Marie Taylor, 142
Spink, Mrs. Charles C., 312
The Sporting News, 34, 45, 81, 88, 90, 100,
107, 114, 133, 142, 143, 155, 276, 290,
291, 298, 310, 312, 315
"Sports Salad," 38, 90, 117, 129, 133, 154,
155
Sportsman's Park, xiv, 46, 55, 71, 74, 96,
102, 111, 128, 138, 149–50, 154, 159,
170, 172, 188, 200, 205, 208, 109, 211,
215, 220, 268, 285, 309, 321, 323, 324
Stainback, Tuck, 136, 246

Staley, Gerry, 286
Stanky, Eddie, 266, 267
Stark, Dolly, 98
Starr, Ray, 45
Stengel, Casey, 77
Stephens, Vern, 244
Sterling, Ken, 287
Stewart, Bill, 98
Stewart, Bob, 313
Stockton, J. Roy, 42, 44, 54, 67, 72, 74, 97, 108, 118, 122, 127, 130, 141, 147–48, 153, 154, 157, 158, 177, 247, 248, 278, 294–95
Stoneham, Horace, 220, 232, 258
Stout, Fish Hook, 57, 75
Street, Gabby, 10, 40, 43, 53, 54, 58, 337
Stripp, Joe, 146
Suhr, Gus, 143
Summers, Bill, 246
Sumner, Jim, 301
Sunset Auto Co. (Ford), 96
Suzuki, Ichiro, 131
Swift, Bill, 180
Szelag, John, 5, 49

Talley, Art, 301
Tampa Smokers, 305, 306
Tampa Tribune, 306
Tamulis, Vito, 185
Templeton, Ben, 300
Terry, Bill, 64, 69, 70, 72, 74, 97, 108, 125, 164, 309, 337
Texas League, 23, 26, 34, 35, 45, 286, 288, 307
Thomas, Bud, 104
Thomas, Ira, 6
Tiant, Luis Sr, 105
Tips, Kerrn, 28
Tipton, Eric, 259
Tobin, Jim, 258
Tolan, Bobby, 327
Toomey, Jim, 335
Total Baseball, 61–62, 216, 309, 317
Traynor, Pie, 44, 69, 70, 284, 333, 334
Treadway, Red, 257
Trench, Dr., 190
Tresh, Tom, 224
Tri-State League, 304

Trombley, Wells, 332
Troy, New York, 88
Truman, Harry, 159, 269
"Tuberculosis Day," 69
Tulsa Oilers, 323, 337
Turkin, Hy, 164, 166, 167, 222
Turkus, Burton, 169
Tuthill, Harold, 312
Tyson, Ty, 81

Union Station (Houston), 38
United Press International (UPI), 326
University of Missouri, 321
Urbanski, Bill, 88, 126
Urbanski, Joe, 88
USO, 228, 245, 246, 247, 249, 250, 251, 254, 255

Van Mungo, Lingle, 71, 74, 112, 136, 167, 232
Vance, Dazzy, 44, 75–76, 87, 132
VanderMeer, Johnnie, 182, 267
Vaughan, Arky, 60, 92, 94, 97, 98, 99, 100, 151, 199, 201, 204, 211, 216, 222, 226, 227, 229–30, 234, 307, 316, 328
V-E Day, 257
Veteran's Committee (Hall of Fame), 326
Virginia League, 304
Voiselle, Bill, 240, 257
Voiselle, Claude, 299, 300, 301, 302, 303
Vosmik, Joe, 98
Vulcan Proofing, 222

Wagner, Honus, 150, 343
Walker, Bill, 60, 64, 72, 73, 75, 95, 96, 100, 102, 103, 133
Walker, Dixie, 168, 172, 176, 186, 188, 189, 191, 195, 199, 200, 202, 206, 213, 215, 216, 221, 222, 225, 226, 227, 228, 229, 230, 234, 235, 242, 243, 245, 246, 247, 266, 267
Walker, Gee, 77
Walker, Harry, 270, 341
Walters, Bucky, 185, 204, 233, 235, 247
Waner, Lloyd, 334, 337
Waner, Paul, 43, 48, 60, 110, 114, 117, 125, 130, 137, 143, 151, 221, 222, 225, 228, 245, 246, 298, 316, 326

Wares, Buzzy, 60, 64, 75, 109, 111
Warneke, Lon, 114, 117, 120, 122, 124, 137, 149, 15, 173, 205
Warwick, Carl, 315
Washington, George, 35
Wastell, Jimmy, 185
Waterhout, Orval, 311
Watkins, George, 10, 32, 54, 61, 64
Weaver, "Bucko" or "Doc," 60, 68, 84, 95, 250, 312
Webb, Melville, 258
Weil, Sid, 56
Weiland, "Lefty," 121, 137, 141, 142, 143
Weinrig, Benny, 214
Weintraub, Phil, 240
Werber, Billy, 104, 149, 156, 184, 185, 207
West, Max, 191
Western Carolina League, 304, 323
Wheat, Zack, 334
Wheaties, 140
Whistling in Brooklyn, 222, 237, 250
White, Bill, 315
White, Jo-Jo, 78, 83
Whitehead, Burgess "Whitey," 52, 91, 95, 108, 265
Williams, Joe, 78, 96, 117, 119, 172
Williams, Ted, 17, 125, 132, 315, 320, 322, 323
Williams, Willie, 293
Wilson, Ace, 43, 44
Wilson, Hack, 24, 25, 81

Wilson, Jimmie, 122
Winford, Jim, 129, 339
Witek, Mickey, 207
Witelmann, Whitey, 258, 261
Wittig, Johnny, 183
Wohlschlaeger, Amatee, 310, 314, 315, 322, 324, 333, 334
Woodward, Stanley, 239
World Series, 31, 53, 57, 59, 61, 68, 76, 81, 82, 84, 85, 87, 90, 96, 190, 193, 194, 195, 196, 216, 247, 294, 311, 315, 330, 334, 335
World War II, 179, 199, 219, 246, 249
Wray, L.G., 120, 125, 154
Wright, George, 286
Wrigley Field, 41, 171
Wyatt, Whitlow, 165, 168–69, 174, 182, 189, 191, 197, 204, 205, 207, 209, 211, 222
Wyse, Hank, 268

Yank magazine, 250, 251
Yankee Stadium, 5, 194, 222
Yastrzemski, Carl, 329
Yatkeman, Butch, xiv, 277, 323
York, Frank, 6, 7
Young, Babe, 206, 207, 208, 286

Zemanski, Happy, 16
Zussman, Benny, 2, 5, 7, 49

About the Author

Thomas Barthel is a past contributing editor of *Diehard*, the official monthly newsletter of the Boston Red Sox. He has published three essays in *The Dictionary of American Biography*, two essays in *The Scribner Encyclopedia of American Lives*, and five essays in the *Biographical Dictionary of American Sport: Baseball*. He was team photographer for the Utica Blue Sox and has contributed team histories of the Blue Sox, which are included in the research library at the National Baseball Hall of Fame.

Tom was born ten blocks from Ebbets Field, the lights of which he could see from his bedroom. He misses greatly his beloved, defunct Utica Blue Sox, as extinct as the Dodgers. He lives in Clinton, New York, and is currently at work on four new books about baseball before 1962.